THE ARCHITECTURAL PATTERN BOOK

THE ARCHITECTURAL PATTERN BOOK

URBAN DESIGN ASSOCIATES

AUTHORS

Ray Gindroz and Rob Robinson
principal authors

Donald K. Carter
Barry J. Long, Jr.
Paul Ostergaard

with contributions by
David R. Csont
Donald Kaliszewski
James H. Morgan
Donald G. Zeilman

PREFACE BY

David Lewis

EDITOR AND
CONTRIBUTING WRITER

Karen Levine

W. W. Norton & Company
New York • London

Printed in the United States of America
First Edition

Book design by WOLFE | DESIGN

Manufacturing by Courier Kendallville, Inc.
Production manager: Leeann Graham

Library of Congress Cataloging-in-Publication Data

The architectural pattern book / Urban Design Associates ; authors, Ray Gindroz ... [et al.] ; with contributions by David R. Csont ... [et al.] ; preface by David Lewis ; editor and contributing writer, Karen Levine.
p. cm.
Includes bibliographical references and index.
ISBN 0-393-73134-0 (pbk.)
1. Architecture, Domestic—United States—Designs and plans.
2. City planning—United States—Handbooks, manuals, etc.
3. Pattern books—United States. I. Gindroz, Ray. II. Csont, David R. III. Levine, Karen, 1950– IV. Urban Design Associates.

NA7205.A74 2004
728'.37'0973—dc22 2004046083

ISBN 0-393-73134-0 (pbk.)

W. W. Norton & Company, Inc., 500 Fifth Avenue,
New York, NY 10110
www.wwnorton.com

W. W. Norton & Company Ltd., Castle House,
75/76 Wells Street, London W1T 3QT

0 9 8 7 6 5 4 3 2 1

CONTENTS

ACKNOWLEDGMENTS

Urban Design Associates would like to acknowledge the clients whose projects appear in this book:

BAXTER, FORT MILL,
SOUTH CAROLINA
Baxter Clear Springs, Inc., and
Celebration Associates

CRAWFORD SQUARE
PITTSBURGH, PENNSYLVANIA
McCormack Baron Salazar

DIGGS TOWN
Norfolk Redevelopment and Housing
Authority and the City of Norfolk, Virginia

DUCKER MOUNTAIN
BILTMORE, NORTH CAROLINA
Biltmore Farm, Inc.,

EAGLE PARK
BELMONT, NORTH CAROLINA
Graham Development

EAST BEACH
Norfolk Redevelopment and Housing
Authority in association with
East Beach Company, LLC

EAST GARRISON
MONTEREY COUNTY, CALIFORNIA
East Garrison Partners I, LLC
Urban Community Partners
Woodman Development Company, Inc.
William Lyon Homes

GÉNITOY EST
BUSSY SAINT GEORGES, FRANCE
Establissements Publics d'Amenagement
Marne-La-Vallee and
E.R.A.S.M.E. Etudes Urbaines

LIBERTY PATTERN BOOK
LAKE ELSINORE, CALIFORNIA
The Town Group

MASON RUN
Crosswinds Community and
the City of Monroe, Michigan

MIDDLETOWN ARCH
Norfolk Redevelopment and Housing
Authority and the City of Norfolk, Virginia

NORFOLK PATTERN BOOK
City of Norfolk, Virginia

PARK DUVALLE
The City of Louisville,
Housing Authority of Louisville and
The Community Builders

PINEWELL-BY-THE-BAY
Norfolk Redevelopment and Housing
Authority and the City of Norfolk, Virginia

THE LEDGES OF
HUNTSVILLE MOUNTAIN
AMERECO Real Estate Services, Inc.
The Ledges Village Builders
John Blue

WATERCOLOR
WALTON COUNTY, FLORIDA
ARVIDA, a St. Joe Company

As urban designers, our focus is the design of the public realm. Our goal is to create beautiful and congenial streets, parks, and squares in which the character of individual buildings is in harmony with other buildings, with the treatment of the ground plane, and with the scale of the space.

Urban designers often produce perspective drawings of a proposed space that we hope embody the qualities that are important to the citizens of the town. Those drawings illustrate not only the buildings that define the space but also the landscaping, paving, and other elements between the buildings. Unfortunately, in current practice, the built results frequently fail to fulfill the goals set by the drawings because the quality of the architecture produced falls short of the vision for the space.

In the design of neighborhoods, a number of different builder/developers may be involved in the process, each with a different idea about the best way to build and market a house. All too often, they deal only with the interior of the house, with very little regard given to the impact the exterior has on public space. This has become especially true since the advent of front-loaded garages that take up much of the street facade of houses. As a result, the most important qualities of traditional neighborhood streets—the complex ways in which houses relate to the street—have been compromised.

In addition, standardization and industrialization of building components have tended to diminish the influence of local traditions. The schism between the architecture profession (with its insistence on modernism) and the building industry (which knows that customers want "traditional" architecture) has resulted in a watered-down version of traditional building forms.

Therefore, beginning in the mid-1970s, UDA began to search for ways of working with the homebuilding industry to find effective ways of implementing urban designs.

It was not necessary to go very far to find keys to a solution. All around us, in every American town and city, we have traditional neighborhoods in which collections of interesting and diverse houses and sequences of small shops join together to create beautiful streets and public spaces. Mostly, they were built between 1880 and 1930, often rapidly, as part of a building boom that resulted from the great urban expansions that followed the industrial revolution.

Even more striking than the visual richness of these neighborhoods is the way in which the work of so many different builders was woven together into a consistent series of public spaces without limiting the individual creativity of each builder or homeowner.

To our eyes, there are three aspects of these traditional neighborhoods that can inform current practice:

First, each neighborhood has its own unique qualities that distinguish it from other neighborhoods in the same city—qualities that are different from neighborhoods in other cities and regions.

Second, each individual house has a clear relationship to the street or public space and makes its most generous gestures to the public realm.

Third, there are no discordant or ill-proportioned houses. Although they display a variety of architectural styles including hybrids, the houses and the sequencing of small shops are true to the qualities of their particular style and to the scale of the street.

So we ask, "How did this happen? And why can we not do it today?"

Clearly, the answer to the first question is that these houses were the product of both a well-established local building tradition and the limits of available technology at the time of their construction. Second, the houses were the result of a cultural consensus on the nature of the street. And third, we suggest, they came about in part as a result of architectural pattern books developed by architects and used by builders as guides to good design.

We became convinced that the tradition of pattern books could be revived to provide an effective means of communication between architects and builders. To be effective, however, the traditional form of pattern books needed to be modified to suit today's needs. These needs include:

→ Creating a shared vision among all those involved in building neighborhoods
→ Providing clear definition of the character and form of the public spaces on which houses are located
→ Providing a primer on well-proportioned, correctly styled architecture

For this reason, UDA Pattern Books have three sections:

- → The Overview describes the vision for the particular development and includes documentation of the local traditions for public spaces and architecture.
- → The Community Patterns section provides guidance for the relationship between houses and public spaces.
- → The Architectural Patterns section provides the elements appropriate to each of several architectural styles for houses in the neighborhood.

To put the contemporary usage of pattern books into its proper context, Part 1 of this book first surveys the development and use of pattern books from their beginnings with Vitruvius in Rome in the first century A.D. to their application today. Then we provide a discussion of the method UDA has developed for creating a pattern book responsive to twenty-first century needs. Part 2 of this book offers a representative collection of pages from UDA's Pattern Books, demonstrating the broad-reaching applicability of this approach, regardless of project scope or geographic location, in helping to inform and shape the desired form and character of urban communities, their streetscapes, and their houses. The collection of pattern book pages is organized into three chapters that parallel the three sections of a typical UDA Pattern Book: Overview, Community Patterns, and Architectural Patterns. Within each chapter, you will find reproductions of selected pages from several UDA Pattern Books, illustrating how our approach translates into finished pattern books for our clients.

It is our hope that this publication will help advance the process of bringing architects, developers, planners, and builders closer together in working collaborations in order to re-establish the consensus that once existed among all those involved in building and rebuilding our towns and cities.

RAY GINDROZ AND ROB ROBINSON, *Principals*
Urban Design Associates

Three decades ago, UDA was working in York, Pennsylvania. In collaboration with Jules Gregory of Princeton and John Schein of Historic York, our task was to catalog York's National Register District. It was, at the time, one of the largest historic districts in the nation.

A little known (and perhaps inconsequential) fact is that, for a brief moment in 1777, York was the capital of the thirteen States before the Continental Congress moved to Philadelphia. Of greater consequence, a railroad connection between Baltimore and York was completed in the 1840s; following that, York grew rapidly and with astonishing consistency.

Indeed, we quickly realized that we had a National Register District in the center of York, built over a span of about thirty years, that was "all of a piece."

At first we were awed by the variety of detail in the facades — the brickwork, lintels, bay windows, brackets, dormers, doors, steps, and ironwork. When we looked more closely, we realized that the blocks were a repetitive grid. The sequences of townhouses and main street shops had been laid out with repetitive lot sizes within the blocks. And, in consequence, the visual richness of these streets was held together by an underlying mathematical discipline of repetitive floor plans and sections.

Inside the townhouses, we once again found rich varieties of details — hardwood floors, fireplace mantels, paneled staircases, pocket doors, and cut glass windows. As with the facades, in every house these details were different, but always in unity of scale. Then we discovered that the builders and their clients had chosen their details from the catalogs of suppliers who manufactured their products to obey common modules. Hence the richness and the unity of street after street in this beautiful town.

Traveling around the region, we found similar buildings and details in Reading, Harrisburg, Baltimore, Philadelphia, and other towns, indicating that, during the building boom that came with the industrial revolution, builders were using pattern books and suppliers' catalogs in a wide market area. But what surprised us most was how the basic language and vocabulary of these buildings had entered into the minds of ordinary people.

As architects, we had read James Marston Fitch, Vincent Scully, and John Summerson, and had experienced precedents like Georgian London. But we began to realize that these precedents were also embedded unconsciously in the language of the builders of these streets and therefore had laid the basis for urban community building.

Parallel with our work in York, we were working as urban designers in communities and neighborhoods in other towns and cities. We would hold public meetings and workshops to find out what the citizens felt to be important to them and to their futures. At these meetings, we were continually struck by how non-architects in the older communities could address the basic language of their own urban streets. They talked not just about their buildings as objects, but about how children and parents would use porches, sidewalks, street widths, and the amenities of their neighborhoods — and how everyone else in the meeting would understand in detail that exactly what their neighbor was striving to describe was also important to them.

In those days, we were seldom asked to work in urban communities in which all was well. The urban communities we were invited into were old, inner-city neighborhoods that had suffered the turmoil of civil rights, the downturn of industrial economies, and the drainage created by suburbanization. Invariably, these neighborhoods resembled a worn and torn patchwork quilt.

Because part of our work had to be restitching, we would sometimes ask people in public meetings to make a "map of memories." It was then that we would learn what these ravaged streets were like three or four generations ago, when they were whole. We would see and hear architectural and urban design echoes of how immigrants transplanted old and far-off cultures, whether from Europe or from the Deep South, not just into pattern book houses and streets, but into churches and shops, customs and foods — simply because the language of those original patterns was something that people living in these communities today also recognized and could merge into.

We were able to understand that the language of neighborhoods is both collective memory and collective aspiration, and that, while history concerns the past, tradition concerns the thresholds from heritage into the future. As urban designers, this notion of tradition, of urban evolution, of creating and recreating wholeness, became our primary focus.

How often we have found that, when we ask in public meetings for descriptions of a commercial main street or a residential street, we don't hear about shopping centers or one-acre suburban lots. We hear about sequences of owner-occupied shops with awnings and apartments on the upper floors, and we hear about tree-shaded neighborhood streets lined with houses and porches.

This book, like our *Urban Design Handbook*, is about re-establishing this heritage of language, so that planners, architects, and citizens alike can continue the American tradition of beautiful streets and livable urban neighborhoods.

DAVID LEWIS, *Founder*
Urban Design Associates

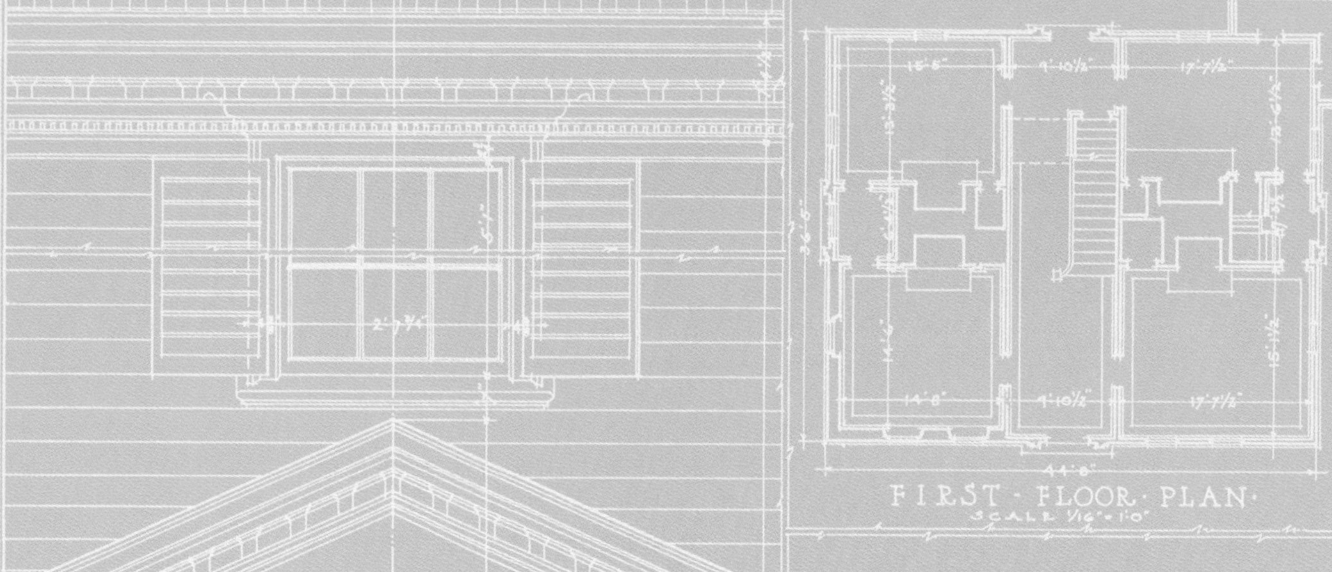

PART 1:
PATTERN BOOKS: PAST AND PRESENT

This section provides a general overview of the development of architectural treatises, pattern books, and builder's guides beginning with the Greek and Roman precedents. The discussion focuses on the intended use, the structure of the information, the techniques, organization, and presentation of the material. These precedents served as models for the development of new pattern books for current building types, techniques, and methods that are also illustrated and described in this section.

CHAPTER

I

Precedents for Pattern Books Today

OVERVIEW

The current revival of pattern books as a tool to assist in the building of towns and cities is only the most recent instance in the long history of architects attempting to communicate with those who build. Historically, each period produced manuals, handbooks, or pattern books that served to coordinate the building process by providing designs that were particularly suited to both the technology of the time and the objectives of those engaged in the process. In thinking about the factors that contributed to the broad acceptance, use, and success of historic pattern books—and their applicability today—three aspects of these books have been particularly interesting for our purposes:

1. The formats and structures of the books and the sequence in which material is presented provided models.
2. Each of these books describes some aspects of the building process in great detail, but is silent on other key factors. This provides a clue to understanding those parts of building practice that were well understood and with which the authors agreed. The topics on which they lavished the most attention are those that were new at the time, or that they felt needed to be taught.
3. The relationship between the ideas in the book and then-current building practices is also instructive regarding which ideas the authors thought were key concepts to communicate.

In studying historic pattern books, we have identified five separate types:

1. *Treatises* present a theory of building or building design. Many of these describe and illustrate the elements of classical architecture which, of all the approaches to architectural style, seems to be the most susceptible to objective and mathematical description.
2. *Precedent Books* provide plans, elevations, and details of historic buildings intended to be used as models for projects that follow.
3. *Plan Books* provide plans, elevations, and three-dimensional representations of exemplary buildings that the authors encourage readers to emulate or use directly.
4. *Construction Manuals* provide practical information on how to design and construct buildings.
5. *Catalogs* describe standard parts and illustrate how to use them in a number of designs. Typically, catalogs were created to sell building materials but, in some cases, companies (e.g., Sears and Roebuck) sold the whole house in a kit.

Most of the historic examples discussed in this book combine one or more of these qualities into one volume. Palladio's book, for example, opens with a treatise, provides precedents, includes construction advice, and presents a series of plans.

Both historically and contemporarily, the audience for pattern books has been quite diverse. Pattern books have proved to be of value to architects, sovereigns and other rulers, politicians, developers, builders, and customers for a variety of reasons that will become clear from the discussion that follows.

When did the use of pattern books begin? To answer that question, we must go back to ancient Rome.

VITRUVIUS

Vitruvius, generally thought to have been an architect under the reign of Augustus in the first century, documented Roman building practices of his time. In the preface to the first book of his *Ten Books on Architecture*, Vitruvius addresses himself directly to the Emperor regarding the intentions for the treatise. The book served the Empire well, standardizing the planning and construction of military camps and towns throughout the Roman world.

In the *Ten Books*, Vitruvius provides practical advice on how to build properly, including prescriptions for the correct use of architectural orders—that is, the style of column and entablature to be selected. The sequence of the ten books is especially interesting for the thought process it sets forth regarding the steps entailed in the process of designing cities and the systematic role of architecture within that process.

In the first book, after describing the architect's education as both general and technical and listing fundamental principles of architecture, Vitruvius describes the process for designing cities. He admonishes readers to find a "healthy site" with a temperate climate and one closely related to food production. After a discourse on walls, Vitruvius provides instruction on how to orient the pattern of streets and alleys to shelter the city from strong cold winds and to ventilate it in the hot seasons, as a way of building a healthy city. Once the framework of streets and alleys is established, the next step, he writes, is to locate the principal monuments and public buildings of the city. Vitruvius makes no mention of the building fabric, but it is clear that he intends readers to understand that the fabric is to be created by standard urban residential and commercial building types that were the norm throughout the Empire.

In the second book, after discussing the origins of the dwelling place, Vitruvius describes the materials and techniques of building as the basis for all architecture. It is not until the third and fourth books, which deal with the architecture of temples, that Vitruvius addresses the three orders—Doric, Ionic, and Corinthian—and the rules for their correct use. These rules include the system of proportions for each order and details for their construction. It is this manual of design for correct architectural elements that has inspired so many generations of designers as well as subsequent treatises.

After describing the orders, the fifth book moves on to set out principles for the design of other public buildings in cities. In the sixth book, Vitruvius tackles the design of houses, urging that these buildings be designed appropriately for the climate of the region and the geometry of the site. He then describes the design of rooms—the atrium first, followed by the various types of rooms in the house.

Except for a statement in Book One that explains the meaning of the word "propriety" by saying that the entrance to a house should be in keeping with the scale and elegance of the interior, nothing is said about the exterior of the houses. This is reasonable since houses were mostly within the framework of streets of the town and were "fabric" buildings rather than monuments. The facades were usually shops or storerooms with only an entrance to the atrium on the street.

The remaining four books, seven through ten, deal with materials and methods of construction, technical matters such as the control of water, and the design of various machines.

The *Ten Books of Architecture* provides a comprehensive view of building. Individual works are seen in the context of the whole town of which they are a part. Even though much is not described, we have a sense of a total process and the means by which the details of individual buildings fit within the overall image of the town and, indeed, the society. Vitruvius articulated a clear plan for building new towns throughout the Empire and, in so doing, established the basic framework for many of the great cities we know today. We can assume that those items he did not cover were well-established practices of the time and that Vitruvius was focusing on those aspects that were likely to be overlooked or that he believed had not been dealt with properly.

ALBERTI AND PIENZA

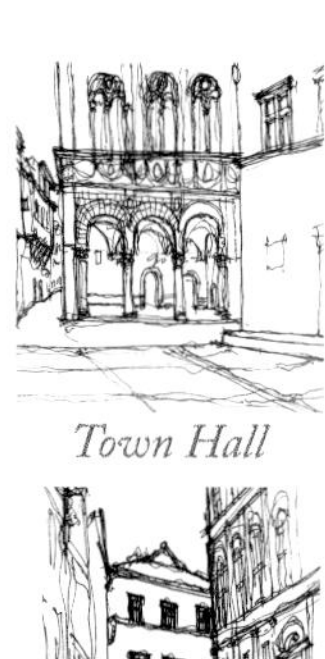

Town Hall

Bishop's Palace

Cathedral

Palazzo Piccolomini

Vitruvius's *Ten Books of Architecture* were lost at the end of the Roman Empire and not rediscovered until the early fifteenth century. The Florentine architect and theorist Leon Battista Alberti used them as the basis for his own ten books, entitled *On the Art of Building in Ten Books*. Alberti's education and training would have pleased Vitruvius since they combined broad cultural training with detailed technical knowledge. Indeed, Alberti is often referred to as a "universal man of the Renaissance."

Although a bit grumpy about the condition of Vitruvius's document and even its grammar, Alberti nevertheless used it as the basis for what was the most influential treatise of the early Renaissance. In his work, Alberti greatly expanded the theories of harmony and further refined the formulas for the architectural orders. Again, the organization of the book is useful to consider today.

Alberti begins, as Vitruvius did, with the building in relationship to its site. Next, he discusses the way the elements of each building relate to each other and to the whole, then the relationships within each unit, and he ends with the classical orders. More clearly than Vitruvius, Alberti demonstrated great concern that a harmonious relationship exist among the parts and the whole that they create. This is further extended to "harmonic" relationships among the parts of buildings, both in their proportion and in their composition. He believed that the harmonic systems in music were directly applicable and governed the proportion of rooms as well as the architectural elements.

Piazza Pio (looking south)

By applying principles of harmony to the facades of buildings, Alberti changed the nature of urban space. For example, the facade of the Palazzo Rucellai in Florence is elegant and in scale with humans, a condition that is dramatically different from the much more monumental forms of typical Florentine palazzos with their heavily rusticated first floors. In these, the facades imply the street to be a somewhat forbidding place that calls for a defensive face. The street is simply the way between buildings. With Alberti's harmonious facade, the street is transformed into an urban room, a civilized and comfortable place.

We see this especially clearly in the Piazza Pio II in Pienza, which is attributed to Rossellino, Alberti's protégé, but which actually may be the master's concept. Four new buildings define the piazza. Each building has a facade in keeping with its status: the most elaborate is the cathedral, followed by the pope's palace, then the bishop's palace, and finally the town hall. The orders are different on these facades, but within each facade the proportions and uses of the orders are correct. The horizontal surface of the piazza is patterned to organize all of the elements—it is a true urban room, located along the main street of a town that clearly follows Vitruvian principles for organizing streets. The streets are shielded from the north winds and open to the south. The architectural elements can be seen as a kind of kit of parts, many of which were used by other builders on subsequent buildings throughout the town, giving a further sense of harmony to the fabric of the entire town.

Alberti's work was extremely influential. From it, we can track the emergence of other such books and the astonishingly rich architecture of the early Renaissance. A key issue for Alberti and the others was how to apply the "knowledge of the ancients" to the current building technologies of the fifteenth century. Part of the beauty of the buildings that resulted is the way in which the classical formulas have been interpreted and adapted to the local sensibilities and traditions. For example, in Pienza, the architectural detailing is clearly less Roman than Tuscan, and the work of Donato Bramante in Lombardy takes its architectural vocabularies from those local traditions.

Sebastiano Serlio on Architecture
(top) Precedent: Coliseum
(middle) Architectural patterns
(bottom and right) Architectural possibilities

SERLIO AND THE PICTURE BOOK

One hundred years later, Sebastiano Serlio began publishing his five books on architecture. In Serlio's work (see the English translation by Vaughan Hart and Peter Hicks, *Sebastiano Serlio on Architecture*), we see the format of the pattern book emerging. The five books begin with general principles of design and composition. Serlio transforms Alberti's theories of harmony and proportion from philosophical language into a series of diagrams and charts.

The second book provides instruction on perspective drawing (with several different types of three-dimensional projection) and concludes with the three famous stage sets, two showing three-dimensional representations of a city street and one a rural wooded scene. The streets include a variety of buildings, mostly humble in character for comedies (i.e., expressions of everyday human life) and monumental in character for tragedies (which typically convey the more dramatic, more exalted struggles of humanity). Buildings are combined to create the image of an urban space, and we begin to see how the details of architecture contribute to a space.

Serlio's third and fifth books document precedents in the form of public buildings built by "the ancients," but in a manner that combines architectural details with full or partial building elevations. Architecture is seen as a kit of parts to be assembled in a variety of ways.

Most powerfully, in the fourth book, we see the orders described in detail followed by drawings of building elevations that demonstrate how these elements can be used to create a wide variety of building types. This approach has enabled builders, literate or not, to learn how to build correct classical-style buildings. Of course, builders have interpreted the rules according to local materials and methods, but the forms, proportions, and details remained correct. This, then, is the root from which the modern pattern book grew.

Of Perspectiue

HOuses for Tragedies, must bee made for great personages, for that actions of loue, strange aduentures, and cruell murthers, (as you reade in ancient and moderne Tragedies) happen alwayes in the houses of great Lords, Dukes, Princes, and Kings. Therefore in such cases you must make none but stately houses, as you see it here in this Figure; wherein (for that it is so smal) I could make no Princely Pallaces: but it is sufficient for the workeman to see the manner thereof, whereby he may helpe himselfe as time and place serueth: and (as I sayde in the Comicall) hee must alwayes study to please the eyes of the beholders, and forget not himselfe so much as to set a small building in stead of a great, for the reasons aforesayd. And for that I haue made all my Scenes of laths, couered with linnen, yet sometime it is necessary to make some things rising or bossing out; which are to bee made of wood, like the houses on the left side, whereof the Pillars, although they shorten, stand all vpon one Base, with some stayres, all couered ouer with cloth, the Cornices bearing out, which you must obserue to the middle part: But to giue place to the Galleries, you must set the other shortening Cloth somewhat backwards, and make a cornice aboue it, as you see: and that which I speake of these Buildings, you must vnderstand of all the rest, but in the Buildings which stand far backward the Painting worke, must supplie the place by shadowes without any bearing out: touching the artificiall lights, I haue spoken thereof in the Comicall workes. All that you make aboue the Roofe sticking out, as Chimneyes, Towers, Piramides, Oblisces, and other such like things or Images; you must make them all of thin bords, cut out round, and well coloured: But if you make any flat Buildings, they must stand somewhat farre inward, that you may not see them on the sides. In these Scenes, although some haue painted personages therein like supporters, as in a Gallery, or doore, as a Dog, Cat, or any other beasts: I am not of that opinion, for that standeth too long without stirring or mouing; but if you make such a thing to lie sleeping, that I hold withall. You may also make Images, Histories, or Fables of Marble, or other matter against a wall; but to represent the life, they ought to stirre. In the latter end of this Booke I will shew you how to make them.

Sebastiano Serlio's set design for a tragedy

Four Books on Architecture *(top) Architectural pattern: Design of the Corinthian Order from Book I; (middle and bottom) Architectural possibilities: Design for the Palazzo Valmarana.*

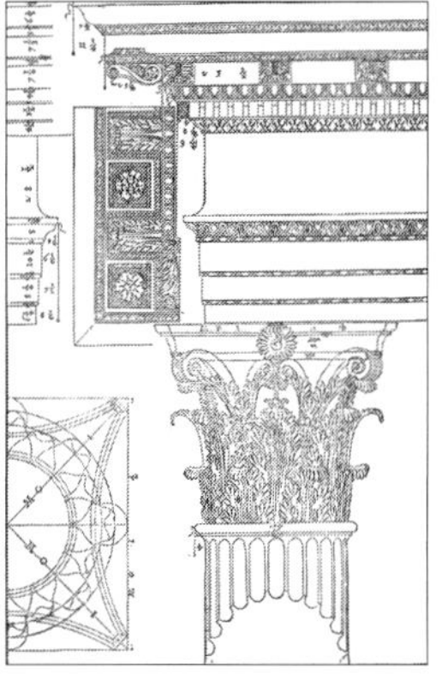

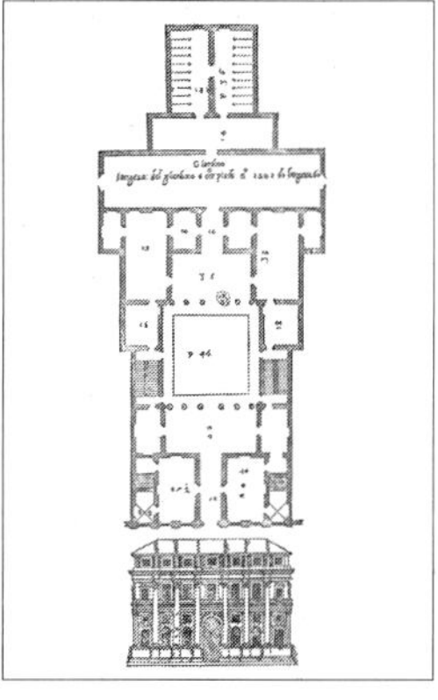

PALLADIO AND PALLADIANISM

In the sixteenth century, another world-renowned Italian architect, Andrea Palladio, published his *Four Books on Architecture*—probably the most influential single work in the history of architecture. In it, Palladio published woodcuts with plans and elevations of villas and palaces he had designed over the course of his career. The format he chose, which combines architectural detail with designs of buildings, was clearly a key to the success of his ideas and the lasting influence they exerted. Palladio's basic format is the one that has been used for pattern books ever since.

Once again, the organizational approach Palladio applied to the content of his books helps us devise an effective structure for modern pattern books. Palladio's first book describes materials and techniques for construction, including structural systems, before presenting the five orders (the three classical orders plus the Tuscan and Composite orders developed by the Romans) in detailed drawings and formulas for their correct application. Palladio concludes the first book with drawings of "mechanical" elements such as stairways. In effect, the book presents a kit of parts for building correct buildings.

The second and third books contain a portfolio of Palladio's work, demonstrating the way in which the kit of parts presented in the first book can be used effectively to create a wide variety of structures. The second book deals with residences, both urban palaces and country villas; the third, with public buildings.

In the fourth book, Palladio presents precedents as well as detailed drawings of ancient Roman buildings that he found instructive and on which he based his architectural designs.

Palladio introduced two major innovations. In his work, we see for the first time the elements of classical architecture applied to domestic architecture on this scale. Also, the format of the book sets the stage for all pattern books that followed. The format Palladio created departs from earlier examples in that it combines plans, elevations, and details with theory, making his rationale clear and the designs very easy to replicate. Because the drawings are both specific and general, they can be interpreted in many different ways and thus adapted to different building traditions and climates.

Published in 1570, Palladio's work was immensely popular and spread throughout Europe. By 1616, the Queen's House in Greenwich, England, built by Inigo Jones following Palladio's principles, had created a sensation. A great admirer of Palladio, Jones, by the time of his death, had collected a total of

240 of Palladio's drawings and had prepared plates for his own treatise, which was never published. All of this preceded the actual publication of Palladio's *Four Books* in England; the books were published in France, and these volumes were, in turn, copied for the first British edition. Over the course of the next 150 years, several editions were published, most definitively the Leoni Edition under the sponsorship of Lord Burlington, himself an architect.

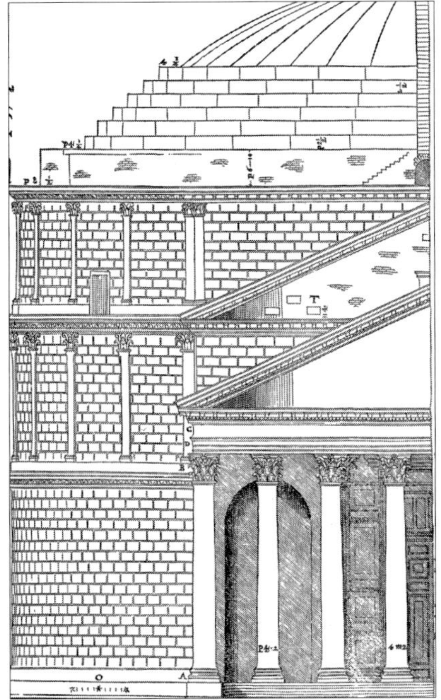

Four Books on Architecture
(top) Precedent: Elevation and section study of the Pantheon; (bottom left) Villa Trissino, Meledo; (bottom middle) Villa Ragona, Ghizzole; (bottom right) Precedent: Details of the Temple of Jupiter.

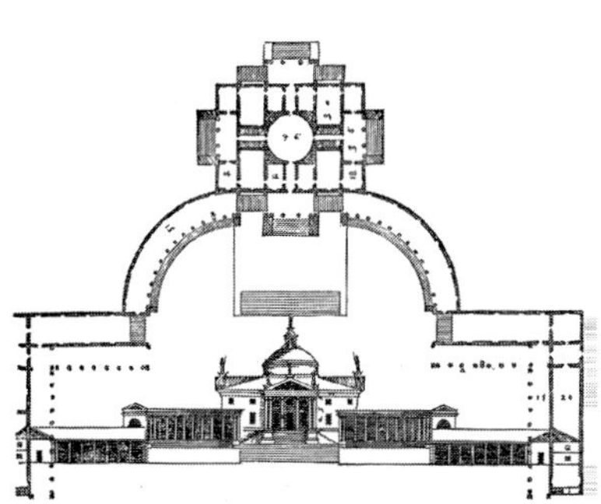

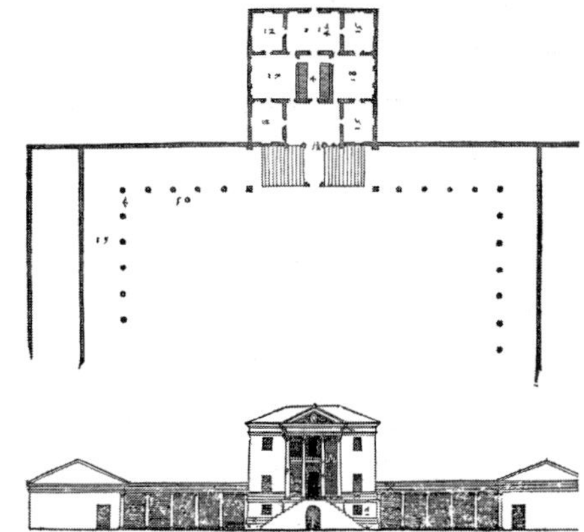

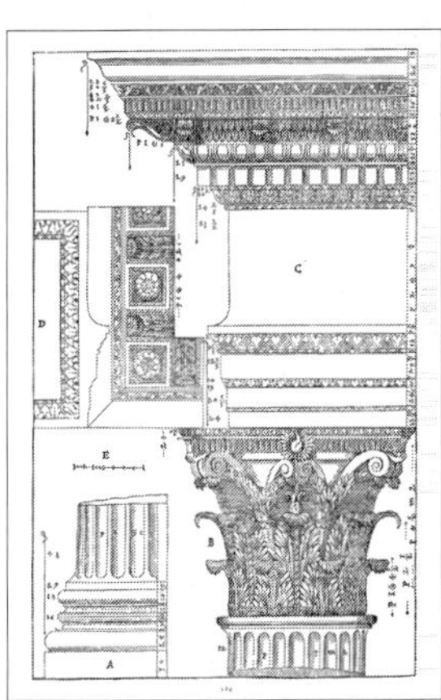

EARLY URBAN ASSEMBLY KITS: GEORGIAN LONDON

Other books on classical design principles, such as Colen Campbell's *Vitruvius Britannicus*, were used extensively in the course of a series of great building booms and urban expansions in London and other British cities. These books played a role in the development process — a process that has interesting parallels with that of the present day.

Large tracts of land in London were held by single landowners who acted as master developers. They prepared a plan, often with a range of house sizes, often including one or more squares. Lots were sold, either individually or in groups, to a variety of developers, ranging from large operations to craftsmen who had scraped together enough money to be able to start a company. The level of skill and design sensibilities of this diverse group ranged from amateurish to highly sophisticated.

The London townhouse is a simple box. Although it may vary in size, it is nearly always a simple arrangement of two rooms per floor with stairs and support spaces adjacent. The flush facades on the public side are elegant and composed, while the rear facade is often irregular, with add-ons. It is to this standard, repetitive, and mass-produced house type that architectural elements were applied.

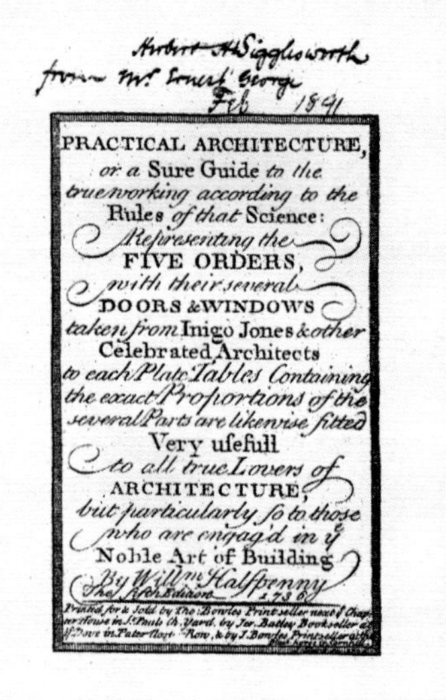

Feb 1891

PRACTICAL ARCHITECTURE,
or a Sure Guide to the
true working according to the
Rules of that Science:
Representing the
FIVE ORDERS,
with their several
DOORS & WINDOWS
taken from Inigo Jones & other
Celebrated Architects
to each Plate Tables Containing
the exact Proportions of the
several Parts are likewise fitted
Very usefull
to all true Lovers of
ARCHITECTURE,
but particularly so to those
who are engag'd in ye
Noble Art of Building
By Willm. Halfpenny
The Fifth Edition 1736

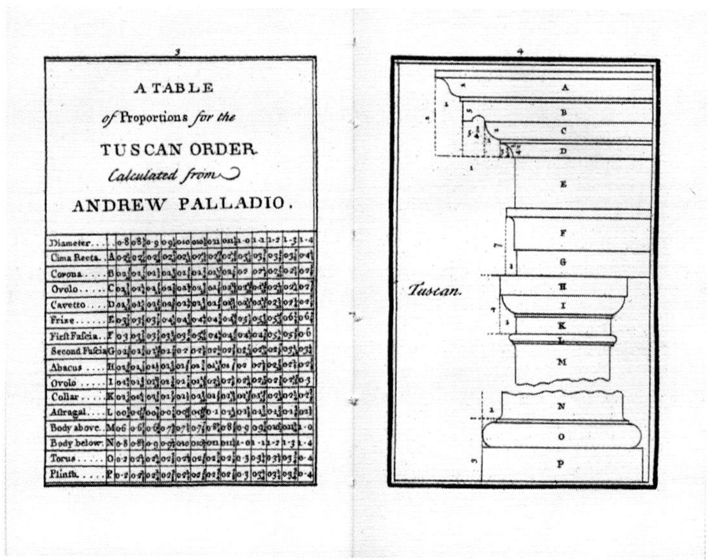

A TABLE
of Proportions for the
TUSCAN ORDER
Calculated from
ANDREW PALLADIO.

Diameter . . .		0·8	[illegible]	0·9	[illegible]	0 10	[illegible]	0 11	[illegible]	1·0	1·1	1·2	1·3	1·4
Cima Recta. .	A	[illegible]	[illegible]	[illegible]	[illegible]	[illegible]	[illegible]	[illegible]	[illegible]	[illegible]	[illegible]	[illegible]	[illegible]	[illegible]
Corona	B	[illegible]	[illegible]	[illegible]	[illegible]	[illegible]	[illegible]	[illegible]	[illegible]	[illegible]	[illegible]	[illegible]	[illegible]	[illegible]
Ovolo	C	[illegible]	[illegible]	[illegible]	[illegible]	[illegible]	[illegible]	[illegible]	[illegible]	[illegible]	[illegible]	[illegible]	[illegible]	[illegible]
Cavetto	D	[illegible]	[illegible]	[illegible]	[illegible]	[illegible]	[illegible]	[illegible]	[illegible]	[illegible]	[illegible]	[illegible]	[illegible]	[illegible]
Frize	E	[illegible]	[illegible]	[illegible]	[illegible]	[illegible]	[illegible]	[illegible]	[illegible]	[illegible]	[illegible]	[illegible]	[illegible]	[illegible]
First Fascia. .	F	0 3	[illegible]	[illegible]	[illegible]	[illegible]	[illegible]	[illegible]	[illegible]	[illegible]	[illegible]	[illegible]	[illegible]	0·6
Second Fascia	G	[illegible]	[illegible]	[illegible]	[illegible]	[illegible]	[illegible]	[illegible]	[illegible]	[illegible]	[illegible]	[illegible]	[illegible]	[illegible]
Abacus	H	[illegible]	[illegible]	[illegible]	[illegible]	[illegible]	[illegible]	[illegible]	[illegible]	[illegible]	[illegible]	[illegible]	[illegible]	[illegible]
Ovolo	I	[illegible]	[illegible]	[illegible]	[illegible]	[illegible]	[illegible]	[illegible]	[illegible]	[illegible]	[illegible]	[illegible]	[illegible]	0 3
Collar	K	[illegible]	[illegible]	[illegible]	[illegible]	[illegible]	[illegible]	[illegible]	[illegible]	[illegible]	[illegible]	[illegible]	[illegible]	[illegible]
Astragal	L	[illegible]	[illegible]	[illegible]	[illegible]	[illegible]	[illegible]	0·1	[illegible]	[illegible]	[illegible]	[illegible]	[illegible]	[illegible]
Body above. .	M	0 6	[illegible]	[illegible]	[illegible]	[illegible]	[illegible]	[illegible]	0 8	0·9	[illegible]	[illegible]	[illegible]	1·0
Body below.	N	0·8	[illegible]	0·9	[illegible]	0 10	[illegible]	0 11	[illegible]	1·0	[illegible]	1·2	1·3	1·4
Torus	O	0·2	[illegible]	[illegible]	[illegible]	[illegible]	[illegible]	[illegible]	[illegible]	0·3	[illegible]	[illegible]	[illegible]	0·4
Plinth.	P	0·2	[illegible]	[illegible]	[illegible]	[illegible]	[illegible]	[illegible]	[illegible]	0·3	[illegible]	[illegible]	[illegible]	0·4

Title page and plates from William Halfpenny's Practical Architecture

By providing a collection of correct Palladian details, the Georgian pattern books ensured a consistent quality to the as-built character of houses of the period. Elements addressed in these pattern books include cornices, window and door surrounds, special windows (e.g., bay windows, Serlian windows, and thermal windows), and porticos that could be applied to the standard box. These pattern books also coincided with developments in mass production of building elements. The details were used as the patterns for shopmade windows and ornamentation. New manufactured products, such as Coades Stone, enabled builders to provide ornament at a more affordable price. And of course, the designs were consistent with those found in the pattern books.

The results of this process, which we see throughout London and many British cities, are a series of handsomely proportioned streets and squares lined with elegant townhouses. Although very similar in form (and in some cases architectural character), the houses that create these spaces display a rich variety of details that make the spaces memorable. The variety, however, is within a very controlled range and usually used to create a large-scale, palace-like form. For example, Bedford Square in London has identical houses, with a pedimented house in the center of each side and corner articulation at the ends. The result is an expression of the leasehold system in which the assertion of individuality is within a controlled system. In that way, it is very different from the American experience.

Other pattern books, such as those produced by William Halfpenny, dealt with practical aspects of building and construction as well as with styles other than the Palladian.

EARLY URBAN ASSEMBLY KITS: J.N.L. DURAND AND PARIS

During the time of Napoleon, Jean Nicolas Louis Durand was an engineer teaching at the polytechnical school that trained engineers. Durand had worked with Claude Nicholas Ledoux and Étienne-Louis Boullée and had built a few buildings. Durand had also published *Recueil et parallèle des édifices de tous genres anciens et modernes,* (Collection and Parallel of Edifices of All Kinds, Ancient and Modern), a comparative analysis of the orders and their application. Then Napoleon decided that architects needed to be trained to build in a systematic and practical way in order to implement his visions of building the city. Durand was put in charge of training architects in the engineering school.

Durand's lectures were published in various forms, including summaries of his *Précis of the Lectures on Architecture*. In these books, he provides a direct and simple approach to architecture. In the introduction to Volume One, Durand says that there are so many different building types and conditions that it would be impossible to teach how to do them all individually. But, by identifying the elements of buildings and the way in which they can be put together, it is possible to provide skills that will enable the architect to design anything.

Durand's system begins with parts and pieces of buildings, especially the orders, all rigorously presented. Then building types are diagrammed in simple line drawings, with symbols to represent various elements such as arcades, pediments, etc. The parts and pieces are then applied to the diagrammatic plans to illustrate various combinations. With this methodology, the first true urban assembly kit was born.

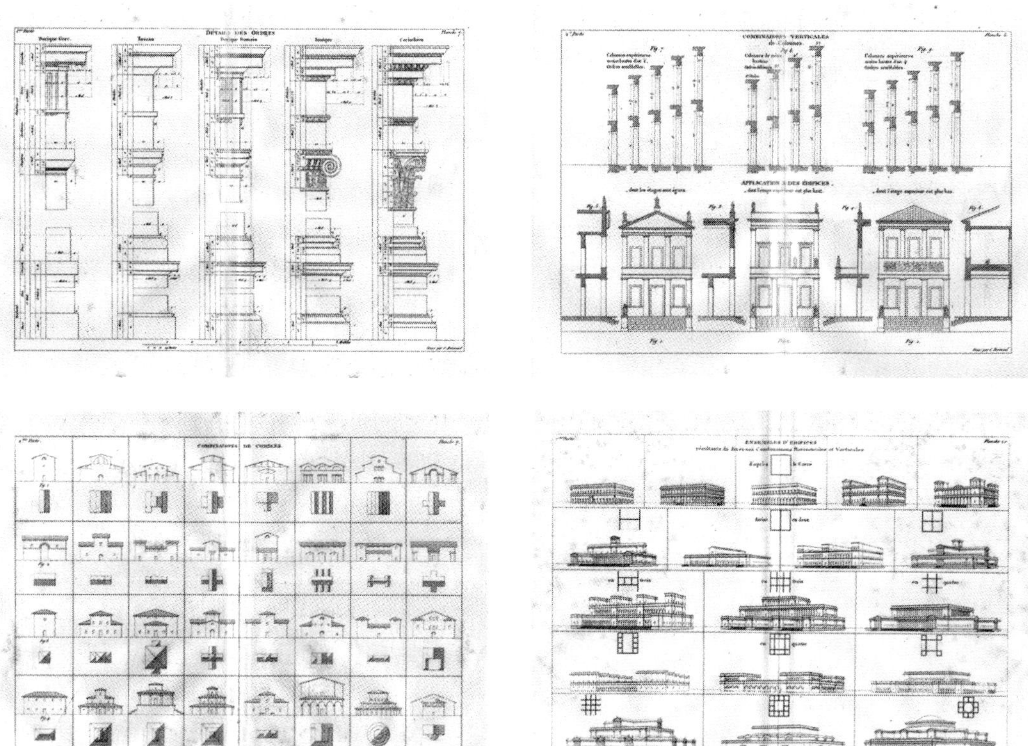

Plates from J.N.L. Durand's Précis Des Leçons D'Architecture

EARLY AMERICAN PATTERN BOOKS

It is not unusual in places that would have been remote from cities on the frontier of colonial and early federal America to find exquisitely proportioned and detailed houses. How did they come to be built in such a faraway spot? The answer is simple. The local craftsmen used pattern books that provided them with the essential details of a correct house.

American pattern books included a number of different types. Some were direct descendants of the English ones, which included both the classical treatises and practical "builder's companions" or carpenter's manuals. The classical treatises continued to be refined, culminating at the end of the nineteenth century in *The American Vignola: A Guide to the Making of Classical Architecture* by William R. Ware. Pattern books then took on new forms: as plan books that could be replicated; as catalogs for building products that could be used; and even as plans for premanufactured houses.

With all of these types, the format is as important as the content because, by this time, pattern books had become both an educational tool, helping the builders build architecturally "correct" houses, and a marketing tool, used to sell houses. In this way, consistency is created between the technique of building and the objectives of the developer. The specifying of a particular window or porch detail is tied directly to an understanding of the house's appeal in the marketplace. This was not a discipline imposed on builders, but rather a tool helpful to them in achieving a successful development.

Most pattern books, whether using elements of classicism or introducing a new style, contained a very high level of architectural design. Well-trained architects contributed designs, and, because they worked in traditional vocabularies, objective bases were established on which to evaluate the results.

Early American houses, built in the seventeenth and early eighteenth centuries, followed traditional techniques and methods already known to the immigrant tradesmen. Typically, the construction and design were very simple. For example, in both New England and Virginia during this period, houses started with a one-room box and attached chimney; and evolved into two rooms with a stair and loft; later, lean-tos were added for kitchen and buttery functions. This Colonial house type was largely produced through the acquired knowledge of the builder/craftsman, generally without reference manuals of any sort. Environmental circumstances and limited resources in the early settlements produced houses and buildings built from wood—heavy timber post-and-beam framing with wood siding instead of the masonry construction techniques that immigrant tradesmen had been accustomed to using in the old world. This adaptation produced a uniquely American house type with its roots in medieval house construction.

As the settlements matured, more craftsmen appeared on the scene and access to resources increased. The building craft began to move from basic shelter needs and concerns to a somewhat more refined and developed trade in the colonies. As wealth and capital began to increase, the demand for more sophisticated buildings emerged. Wealthy landowners had a tendency to import already-carved elements for interior and exterior components such as lintels and doorways. These were added to thc locally constructed houses and buildings. Some of the tradesmen coming over from England also had experience in building classically detailed buildings in and around London. These details began showing up in brick and masonry buildings built as civic structures, such as the original buildings for the College of William and Mary or the 1701 Capitol building in Boston. These details began to be used in residential applications as well in the early 1700s.

The first examples of houses being built using the compositional rules documented in translations of the older architectural treatises developed by Palladio and Serlio date to the mid-eighteenth century. Tradesmen in this period began to have access to a growing number of early pattern books being published in England. (Documented availability of architectural books in America can be found in several great resources such as *Architectural Books in Early America* by Janice G. Schimmelman and *A List of Architectural Books Available in America Before the Revolution* by Helen Park.) As the availability of books grew, the transformation of the earlier vernacular buildings into a kind of American Classicism accompanied them. Interestingly, the influences exerted by these books differed from region to region. Drayton Hall in South Carolina (built in 1738) was adapted from a Palladio design and features a deep porch to mitigate the intense sun and heat, while in New England, buildings from the same period were without porches but incorporated more elaborate door surrounds and detailing.

These early resource books fell into two categories. The larger, more expensive treatises, multivolume works, and books were relatively rare. In addition to Palladio's *Four Books*, these included James Gibbs's *A Book of Architecture* (1728) and *Rules for Drawing the Several Parts of Architecture* (1732); William Kent's

Designs of Inigo Jones (1727); Abraham Swan's *The British Architect: Or, The Builder's Treasury* (1745); Batty Langley's *Treasury of Designs* (1745); Robert Morris's *Select Architecture: Being Regular Designs Of Plans and Elevations Well Suited to Both Towns and Country* (1755); William Halfpenny, John Halfpenny, and Robert Morris's *The Modern Builder's Assistant: Or a Concise Epitome of the Whole System of Architecture* (1742); and William Salmon's *Palladio Londinensis* (1734). These books and others provided resources for the American builders in the mid- and late eighteenth century.

Many less expensive, pocket-sized versions, such as William Pain's *The Practical House Carpenter* (1796) and pamphlets with selected plates, also were available for tradesmen.

These books, designed primarily for craftsmen and the trade, were largely organized by details illustrated on plates and used by builders as references for details. The books also presented composed facades and were a source for the overall form and composition of the house. All of these books were based on the Roman and Palladian classicism and were used as the correct reference on the architecture created by English architects and builders such as Inigo Jones and Robert and James Adam. Jefferson was famous for referring to Palladio, Serlio, Morris, Gibbs, Campbell, Freart de Chambray, and others in his architectural work on the Capitol, Monticello, and other projects. Early American architects—Charles Bulfinch, John McComb, and Benjamin Henry Latrobe, for example—used these same precedents.

This "high style" reference material trickled down to the everyday application for houses, churches, and civic buildings throughout the colonies and the newly declared states after the revolution. The builder's companion/carpenter's manual

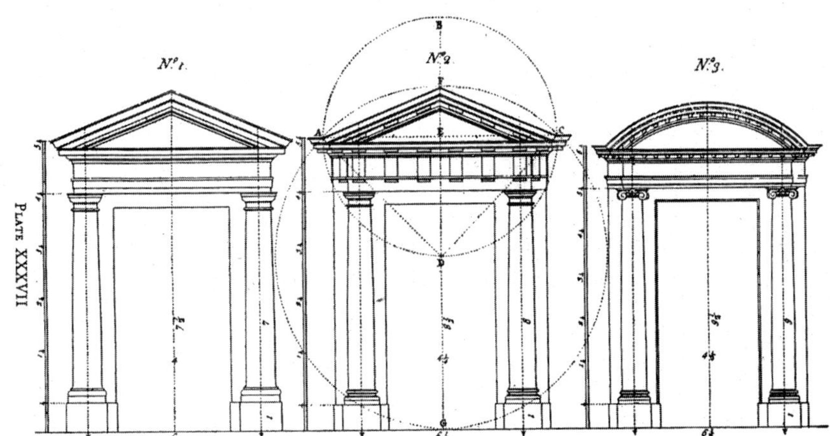

Plates from James Gibbs' Rules for Drawing the Several Parts of Architecture

trend continued steadily into the nineteenth century with the publication of books by American builder/architects. These volumes include Asher Benjamin's *The Country Builder's Assistant* (1797) and *American Builder's Companion* (1806), and Owen Biddle's *The Young Carpenter's Assistant* (1805). These books still referenced English details that were adaptations of the Roman models. The details were often translated to wood detailing for application in the American context. They were applied as embellishments and detailing to standard vernacular house forms rather than as part of a composed, holistic design.

The second wave of builder's companion resource books focused on Greek precedents as the new reference for details and house forms. John Haviland's three volumes of *The Builder's Assistant* published between 1818 and 1822, Asher Benjamin's 1827 publication *The American Builder's Companion,* and Minard Lafever's *The Modern Builder's Guide* (1833) were key publications that documented Grecian components, proportions, and detailing for American builders. This trend in Grecian detailing and proportioning spread pretty quickly and pretty far afield—New York, Ohio, Pennsylvania, Wisconsin, Vermont, North Carolina, and Virginia all benefited from the rapid dissemination, through these books, of techniques and style. This phase really established a kind of "national style" for the rapidly growing and prospering country—a style that lasted well into the mid-1800s.

The third wave of pattern books presented a new kind of resource designed more for use by the owner or patron than as an exclusive resource of the builder. These books introduced the emerging Romantic styles and building designs. For the first time, the books illustrated a complete picture of the house and its key details in the form of a montage of elevations, perspectives, plans, and a page of details. Alexander Jackson Davis published the first such book—*Rural Residences, Etc. Consisting of Designs . . . for Cottages, Farm-Houses, Villas, and Village Churches* (1837). This work was followed by many additional volumes including several by Andrew Jackson Downing, who dominated the market for Romantic designs for cottages and houses. Trained as a horticulturist, Downing published several books; the first one in particular, *Cottage Residences: or, A Series of Designs for Rural Cottages and Cottage Villas, and Their Gardens and Grounds* (1842), proved to be popular.

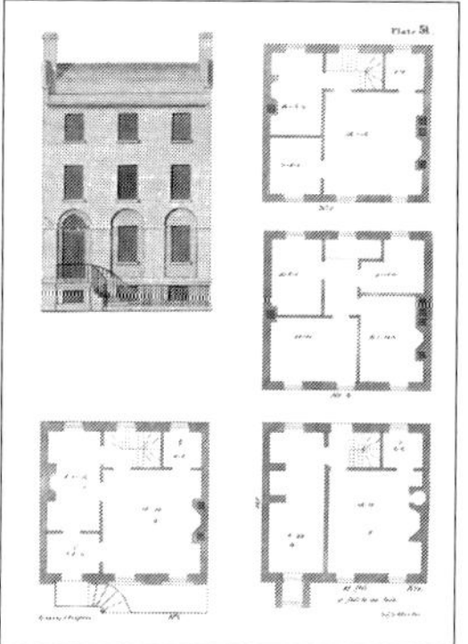

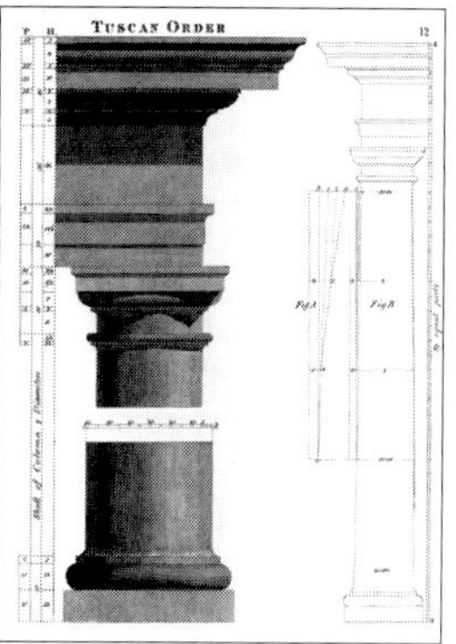

(above) Cover and two plates from Asher Benjamin's The American Builder's Companion; *(bottom right) Architectural possibility: Plate from Minard Lafever's* The Modern Builder's Guide

These new books were still based on English precedents and English books but were adapted to the growing demand for country homes and cottages in the United States. Many original designs from American architects were featured in these books; Davis, Downing, and others promoted their own original work. The sources were Gothic and Italianate, based on the Picturesque principles developed in the eighteenth- and nineteenth-century England that encouraged connections between landscapes and buildings that would strike the imagination with the force of a painting.

These designs coincided with another national trend in house design and production. The development of sawmills and lighter framing techniques enabled the Picturesque-style house to flourish as a predominantly wooden building type with delicate cut ornament, exuberant and light forms, and complicated massing types. These production and construction techniques continued as new styles, including the Queen Anne and Stick styles, emerged toward the end of the nineteenth century.

Samuel Sloan's 1852 book, *The Model Architect*, covered a broad range of building types, including designs for houses, schools, and churches, as well as good practice points and technical data for the builder. This was probably the most complete pattern book that had been published to date.

In addition to the gothic inspiration, other exotic architectural influences began to be introduced as the publication of pattern books flourished in the latter part of the nineteenth century. For example, Calvert Vaux included French-inspired Mansard roofs, building designs, and details in his 1857 publication *Villas and Cottages*. By this time, pattern books had become an effective marketing tool for architects to use to promote residential design

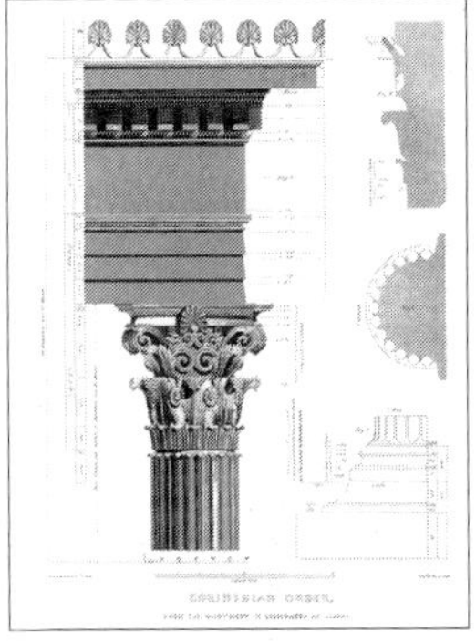

Minard Lafever's The Modern Builder's Guide

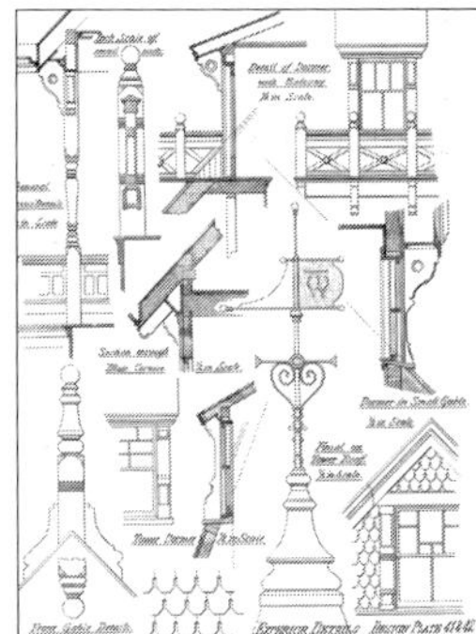

William T. Comstock's Victorian Domestic Architectural Plans and Details

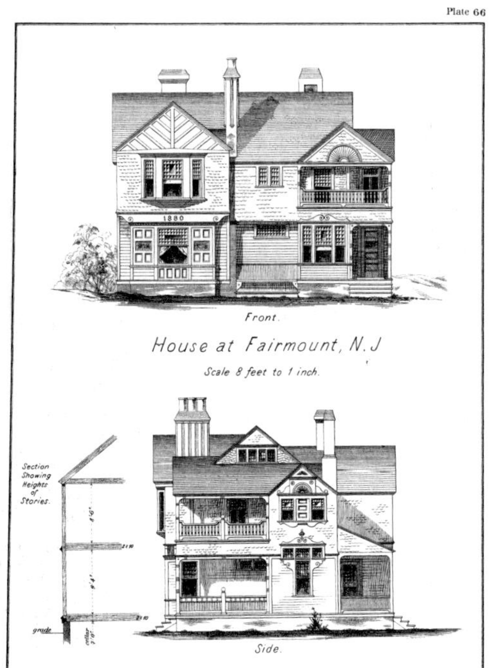

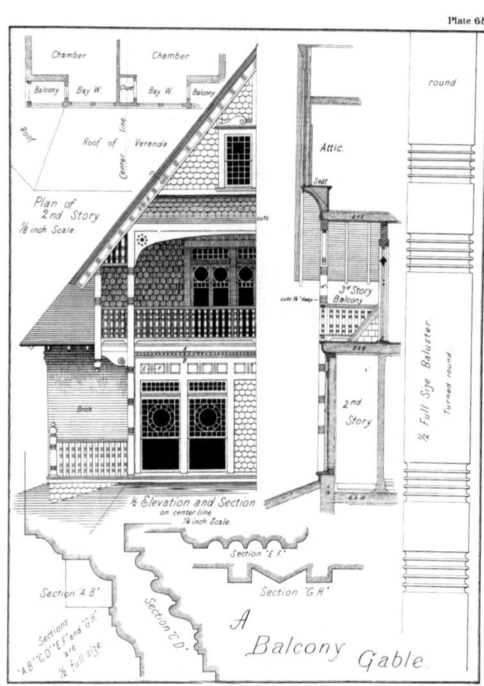

Plates from William T. Comstock's Modern Architectural Designs and Details

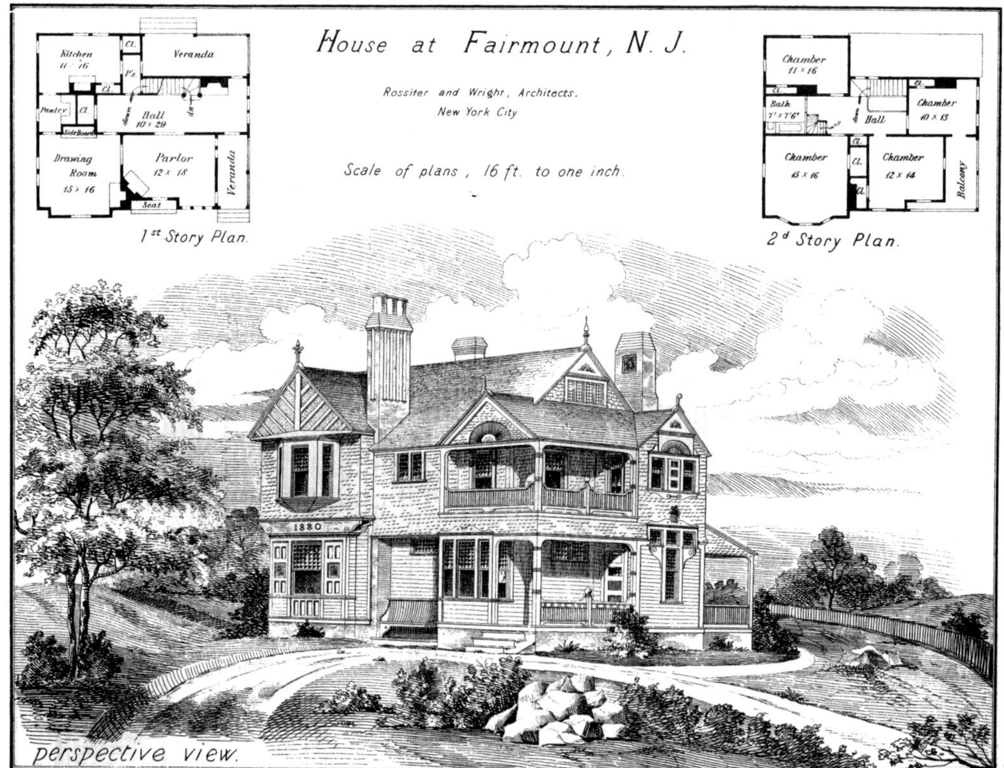

services, and Calvert Vaux used his own pattern book extensively to market his design services.

A refinement to previous pattern books emerged in the 1860s. Pattern books of this era began to feature large-scale, clearly drawn details that were easier to measure and replicate than the smaller drawings produced in the earlier versions. Publishers such as Amos J. Bicknell and M. F. Cummings pioneered the reformatting of pattern books to make them more usable and legible. There were also many publications that started to include such things as specifications and model contracts. This mix of selling house plans and design services continued in earnest by firms such as Palliser, Palliser & Co., an architectural production firm based in Connecticut. Their catalogs contained perspectives and plans with a large advertising section of manufacturers for housing components and products.

(inset) House design from Sears, Roebuck and Company's Honor Bilt Modern Homes; *(below) R. W. Shoppell's* Turn-of-the-Century Houses, Cottages and Villas

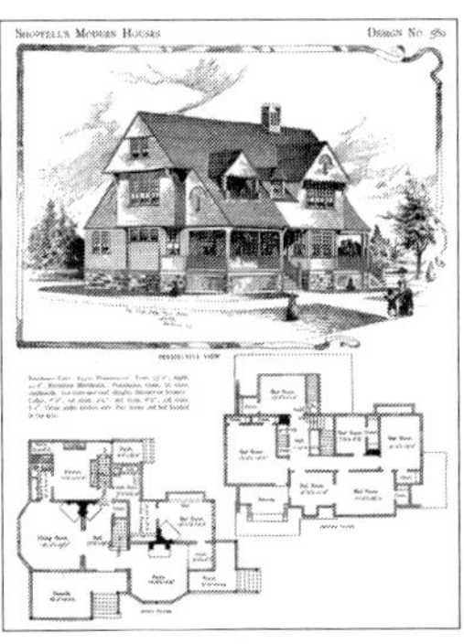

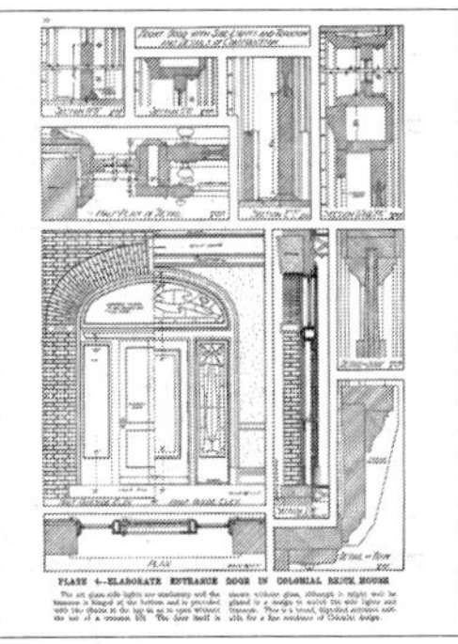

In the late nineteenth century, "plan books" became the next trend in the evolution of pattern books. R. W. Shoppell's Co-operative Building Association, for example, published house plan catalogs starting in 1881 and eventually began publishing house plans in a quarterly "magazine" that continued into the 1900s. Many of these were copied by local builders who did not actually order the plans, but the books became very popular. William Radford, who owned a lumber business in Wisconsin, created a widely used plan book series in the early 1900s. The series included a broad range of stylistic variations and massing types that continued to evolve as the popularity of particular styles changed. The houses ranged from cottages and bungalows to rather large and more elaborate houses.

The Chicago House Wrecking Company was the first organization to use the sale of house plans to sell building materials *directly* to the purchaser. Later, this format was adapted by companies such as Sears and Roebuck, Alladin, and Standard, and became a major business across the United States. By the 1920s, traditional pattern books had been replaced by catalogs of houses that could be purchased and shipped to the owner's site or by plan books that sold full sets of drawings and specifications.

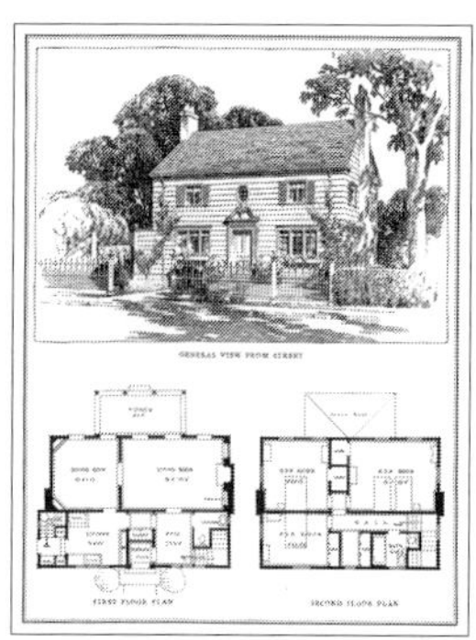

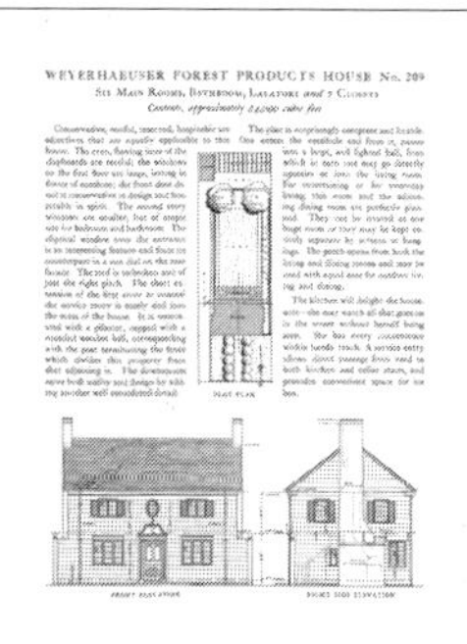

(*top, middle, and inset*) *Weyerhaeuser's* A Dozen Modern Small Houses; (*bottom*) *Cover of the February 1922* White Pine Series of Architectural Monographs

WEYERHAEUSER AND THE WHITE PINE SERIES

In order to promote the use of lumber, the Weyerhaeuser Company supported a series of plan books in the second two decades of the twentieth century. The White Pine series was a collection of journals, some of which documented historic American architecture to the same level of detail with which previous generations had documented the architecture of ancient Rome. This brought a new respect for America's historic legacy, a legacy that had been undervalued in a culture that still viewed itself as new.

Other White Pine issues published the results of design competitions. Many of the best architects in the country competed to design the best house for a preset dollar amount, or the best vacation house. The top several proposals were published in the journal. The drawings followed a similar format to that used for the historic houses: there was a site plan to show how the building should relate to its context, followed by plans, and some typical details. The cover was usually a three-dimensional representation such as a perspective drawing or a photograph. The plan books were conceived as marketing tools as well as educational texts and, as such, generally included an order form for detailed construction documents available for a relatively modest cost.

In 1923, the winning house was built on the Mall in Washington, D.C. as a demonstration of the importance of house design to American culture. The impact of these books and projects was considerable. They raised the standard for the design of low-cost, mass-market house production. The beautiful and straightforward graphic design of these books was an integral part of their success and clearly informs the format of the current pattern books illustrated in this volume.

PATTERN BOOKS AND AMERICAN URBANISM

Whereas English and French pattern books were used to create uniform and harmonious urban ensembles, the American sensibility has been to celebrate individuality. This significant difference between American urbanism and European urbanism has an impact not only on the built results, but also on the pattern books.

Less so in the colonial period, but with increasing intensity after the American Revolution, the expression of individuality—a different architecture for each house—became a dominant purpose and theme. Therefore, as pattern books evolved, they provided more and more variety. As a result, in many neighborhoods, no two houses were created identically. Houses might have the same floor plan and the same basic box structure, but they were dressed up in different architectural styles, with different special elements such as porches, and a variety of details and colors.

So, paradoxically, by providing standardized patterns in America, pattern books became the means of producing an extraordinarily diverse array of urban architecture. The combination of an underlying harmony among the buildings that define the street spaces of our neighborhoods with a diversity of architectural detailing resulted in some of the most beautiful urban spaces the world has known.

A traditional neighborhood street

(above and opposite) Late 20th century houses and neighborhood streets: tradition lost.

CHAPTER

2

The Decline and Revival of Pattern Books

THE DECLINE

By the end of the twentieth century, American residential development practices had produced some of the worst urbanism the world has known. How did this happen? How could we have fallen from producing the best neighborhoods to creating some of the worst?

Much has been written about the forces at work in the post–World War II period that created the sprawling suburban environments in which the concept of subdivision replaced that of neighborhoods. A series of differences between pre-war and post-war development practices arose that resulted in the deterioration of the way in which neighborhoods are developed.

First came the standardization of the building industry to respond to a sudden and voracious appetite for new houses.

Second, the dividing up of the development process into a series of specialized professions without effective communication among them broke the links that had previously existed between the various participants in the development process. In this process of becoming "efficient," the design of streets, the installation

of utilities, the assembly of land, and the design of construction were seen as separate steps in an assembly line process, rather than as part of the integrated process of creating whole places.

Third, the consensus that had once existed regarding the form of neighborhoods and neighborhood streets began to deteriorate. In place of interconnected grids, with the street as a social as well as a traffic place, increased street width and the proliferation of cul-de-sac street patterns produced isolated enclaves with such low density that the social quality diminished. The next step in this process was the elimination of the elements of houses that contributed to sociability, such as porches, replacing them with two- and three-car garages that effectively transformed streets into exceptionally wide and well-landscaped alleys.

Fourth, the imposition of standardized zoning policies and codes that were not based on a physical vision of a place, but rather on preventing undesirable things from happening, resulted in the low-density, cookie-cutter environments that consume so much land in the United States.

Fifth, the estrangement between the architectural profession and the building industry resulted in a lower quality of design in pattern books as well as in builder houses. The Modern Movement, in its rejection of traditional architectural vocabulary, attempted to change public taste—to "educate" and convince the American public that it should buy modernist houses and reject traditional architecture. No one bought this. For most families, a house is their biggest single investment and represents the largest single item in their net worth. For this reason, most homebuyers look for something that feels solid and stable, something that is part of an ongoing tradition, rather than something that could easily turn into a fad. Therefore, in the course of the 1950s, '60s, and '70s, fewer and fewer of the most talented architects participated in the homebuilding industry. Architecture schools stopped providing training in mass-produced residential design. Prior to World War II, the most talented architects all provided designs for pattern books, including innovators like Frank Lloyd Wright, as well as traditional architects.

And so the problems that we face today are a combination of poorly conceived urban form, uncoordinated legislative and implementation processes, and a lack of communication among the design professions and the building industry.

NEW URBANISM AND THE REVIVAL OF PATTERN BOOKS

The New Urbanist movement, beginning in the 1980s, began to address these problems with a revival of traditional urbanism. Seaside, in Florida, was created as a model town to demonstrate how a wide range of architectural styles could create a traditional town. Kentlands, in Maryland, and others used traditional architectural vocabularies to create neighborhoods and towns that have succeeded because of the appeal of a real community. The increasing use of these practices has produced some of the most successful developments around the country; that, in turn, has had a very positive impact on the building industry. Many New Urbanist practitioners have revived the practice of preparing standardized house plans as a way of bringing back consistently high-quality design to production housing.

Different firms have different approaches to re-establishing urbanism and designing neighborhoods in which each house contributes to the quality of the neighborhood, rather than constructing subdivisions. This book presents the approach used by Urban Design Associates, which resulted in the revival of pattern books in current practice. UDA's approach evolved over time, beginning 15 years prior to the start of New Urbanism as a movement.

The firm's central interest has always been the design of the public realm and environments that support the creation of social capital. Therefore, our firm's interest in housing moves from the outside-in. How can the architecture of houses create a congenial street or square?

All of our work, especially in existing cities and towns, is done in the context of a broad-based public process, and therefore attempts to respond to the interests of the people in the community. Without exception, there has been dissatisfaction with current development practices and great enthusiasm for traditional neighborhoods, irrespective of their physical and social conditions. Many of our early projects were neighborhood revitalization plans in which modern houses and developments had been proposed and rejected. During that period, we saw the emergence of the now common practice of communities organizing themselves to protect their neighborhoods from the ravages of modern architectural and development practices. The next few sections chronicle the evolution of UDA's particular approach to, and use of, pattern books as a means of responding to these problems.

PRESERVATION AND HISTORIC INFILL IN THE 1970S

In the 1970s, UDA was involved in a number of communities just when the preservation movement was gaining momentum. Originally focused on historic buildings, the movement began to include whole districts that had value as an overall collection of buildings. UDA was commissioned to prepare the National Register Guidelines for York, Pennsylvania, the largest such district in the United States at the time. In the course of that work, we photodocumented every house and made recommendations for remodeling and improvements that would be consistent with the original architecture. To do so required that we study the traditional architectural vocabularies used in the neighborhoods. And we began to analyze street elevations of many of the blocks of housing. That analysis revealed the extraordinary complexity of the architecture. Within the simple system of row houses, variety was produced by adding bay windows and porches, or changing the roof line, or using different windows, or through color. This experience completely changed our practice. UDA realized that production housing could be seen as a kit of parts. The building plans and basic volumes were all the same, but a series of interchangeable architectural elements made it possible to create a wide range of different buildings and therefore neighborhood streets of different character.

In the late 1970s, we began work on an infill development in the Shadyside neighborhood of Pittsburgh. The developer was very concerned that the architecture be traditional, and originally suggested that we use the vocabularies of a recently constructed Georgian row house development nearby. We proposed an approach that would use the architectural style of the houses in the immediate area, which were more Victorian in character. These houses used a combination of various gable treatments, roof dormers, bay windows, and porches to create both consistency and variety. We began to experiment with the basic townhouse plan, in two versions—three stories and three-and-a-half stories. To these basic boxes we began applying different architectural elements. We called this approach using a kit of parts to assemble the houses.

Elevation analysis of historic row houses in York, Pennsylvania

In 1978, UDA began a plan for the redevelopment of the Randolph neighborhood in Richmond, Virginia. The redevelopment plan was for a cleared portion of this traditional neighborhood. A previous plan had been prepared proposing a series of suburban-style "projects," each for a different income group. In the public process, members of the community expressed both concern about this approach and their desire to rebuild a traditional neighborhood. This resulted in what was perceived to be a "radical" plan, but in fact was simply returning to traditional urbanism. The plan consisted of streets, lined with houses that had front yards and back yards. The streets were designed as an interconnected network that included three parks and a number of community facilities. Although different parts of the neighborhoods were funded differently, for different incomes, no physical distinction was to be made between them — at least none in terms of urban form.

All houses were to be constructed for the minimum budget, so it was necessary to keep the building forms simple and standardized. At the same time, it was essential to convey the sense of quality and permanence that was (and still is) found in the parts of the neighborhood that had continued to thrive. These were brick-fronted houses, some detached and some attached, built in the 1920s from pattern books. Although the house plans were standardized, there was great variety in the way in which the facades were treated. Predominantly red brick with white trim, the houses gained variety from bay windows, roof details, porch details, and window placement.

The plan recommended continuing this tradition and included a series of sketches that illustrated the way in which standard house plans could be treated with different street facades. In the plan, these were intended to be design guidelines that developers would use in the design of houses. This did not work. The quality of design was not consistent with the goals of the community, so UDA was asked to design every house. We refused, because we felt it would be too much like a project. Urbanism can only be the result of many voices, not one. Instead, we proposed to develop a pattern book that would provide correct details for the street facades of houses. In order to be effective, it was necessary

Pattern book house elevations, Richmond, Virginia

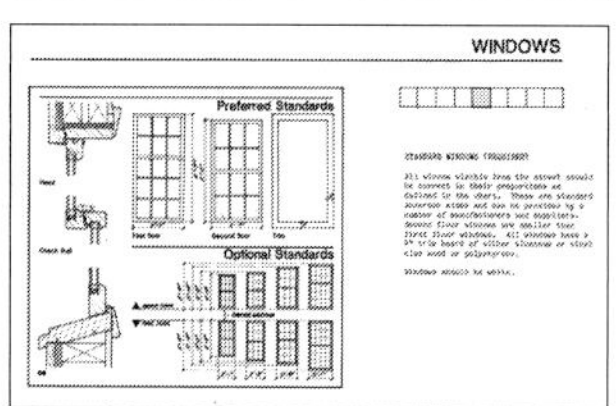

Pattern book and built results, Middletowne Arch, Norfolk, Virginia

to provide construction document–level information for the facades, porches, and exterior details. In that moment, the UDA Pattern Book was born.

NEW NEIGHBORHOODS IN NORFOLK: 1980S

In 1986, UDA prepared a master plan for a neighborhood in Norfolk, Virginia, now known as Middletowne Arch. It was the site of a failed public housing project with a very negative reputation. The city had originally proposed that the site be redeveloped as an industrial area, but the adjacent neighborhood protested and convinced the city leadership to redevelop it as a homeownership neighborhood. There was great skepticism that this would work in such a location. To be successful, the UDA plan would have to create a new image for the area.

We used the semi-circular plan forms found in some of the most admired Norfolk neighborhoods. The plan was to be built by a number of small homebuilders, following design guidelines we were asked to provide. The real estate marketing professionals firmly asserted that, in such a pioneering location, the architecture should be traditional and comfortable. In that region, the most popular style among builders and homebuyers was Williamsburg. UDA's analysis of the conventional new housing being built under this label made it clear that it was very far from being an authentic representation of the style. To remedy that, UDA developed a simple pattern book to be used by production homebuilders. In the process of creating the pattern book, we discovered that there were relatively few items that we could specify with any certainty of having them followed. So the question we asked ourselves was, "If we can have five things done correctly, what would they be?" The answer guided the content we developed for the pattern book—content that specifies:

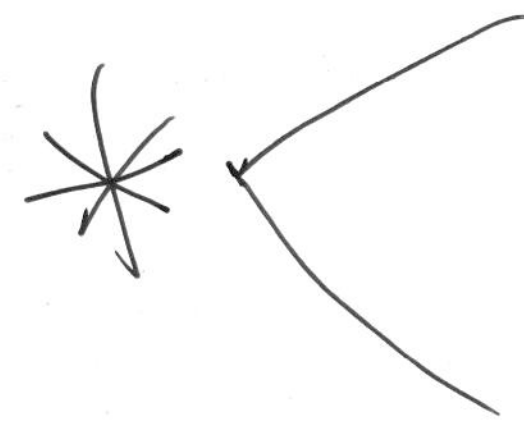

1. Massing, including roof pitch and eave details
2. Facade composition, including window and door placement
3. Window and door types and proportion
4. Materials on the street facades
5. Position on the site of houses, front yards, and front door location

The builders embraced the pattern book because it reinforced their marketing objectives (i.e., "Williamsburg" style), provided assurance that the other builders would keep the same quality, and gave them the freedom to do whatever they wanted with the interiors of the houses.

One year later, we were asked to prepare a master plan, in collaboration with Jonathan Barnett and the economist Philip Hammer, for the Ocean View community in Norfolk. Once again, we were working with a neighborhood that had developed a bad reputation despite its location on Chesapeake Bay and inventory of waterfront properties. The plan included a development called Pinewell-by-the-Bay. Instead of developing a high-density condominium on this waterfront site, the city chose to develop three blocks of small, single-family house lots, in the hope of attracting people to build large expensive houses. This was part of a redevelopment strategy that called for upgrading the marketing image of Ocean View.

The plan created 50' x 75' lots configured to provide maximum views of the bay. It called for an architecture that continued some of the forms of traditional beach houses in the area, such as living levels on the second floor and wrap-around porches. The narrow sites led to a house type similar to the Charleston single house, which has a long, multi-story side porch. Although some sites were sold to production builders, most sites were to be sold to individual homebuyers. Consequently, some concern existed that houses conform to design standards that would create a harmonious character for the neighborhood. UDA was asked to prepare a pattern book that provided patterns for massing, windows, porches, materials, and colors. In this project, the pattern book idea was more fully developed, but with less emphasis on architectural detail.

(above left) Pinewell-by-the-Bay, Norfolk, Virginia; (below) Sample pattern book pages

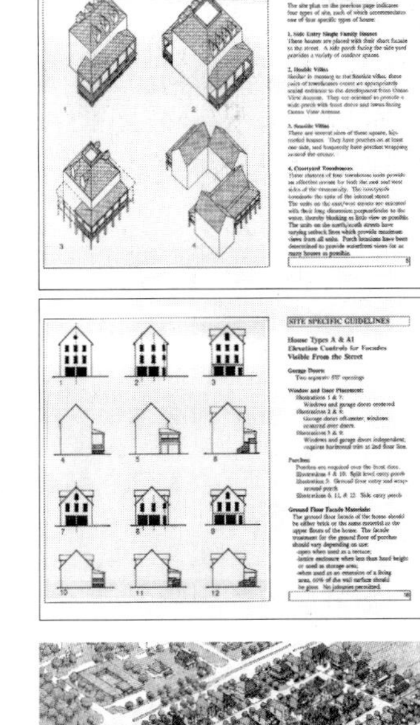

INTRODUCTION

SITE SPECIFIC GUIDELINES

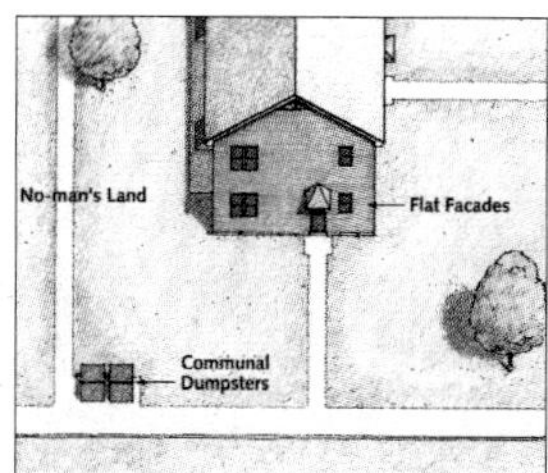

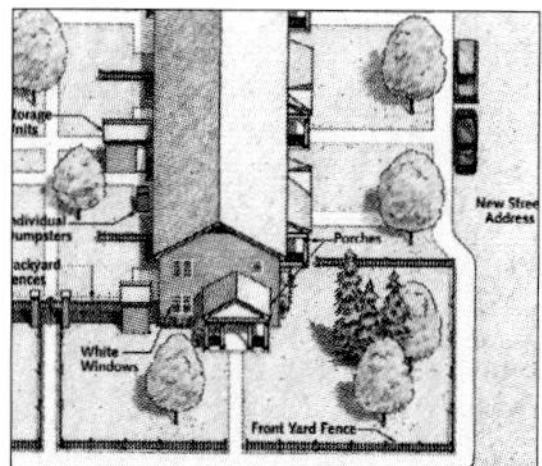

(top left) Existing site with no community patterns; (top right) Remodeled site with community patterns; (bottom) Diggs Town, Norfolk, Virginia before exterior remodeling and after exterior remodeling

SOCIAL IMPACT OF THE NEIGHBORHOOD PUBLIC REALM

In the early 1990s, two projects contributed to the evolution of UDA Pattern Books—Diggs Town in Norfolk, Virginia, and Crawford Square in Pittsburgh, Pennsylvania.

Diggs Town is a public housing "community." By the early 1990s, it had become infamous for its high crime rate. Most of the residents lived in fear of the gang wars that took place in the common areas. Children and house plants were kept indoors because the outdoor spaces were deadly. David Rice, the executive director of the Norfolk Redevelopment and Housing Authority, asked UDA to develop some ideas for physical improvements that might help remedy this desperate social situation. He asked if the standard modernization funds could make a more substantial change to the quality of life than simply putting in new windows. It was clear that, without such change, improvements would merely be akin to rearranging deck chairs on the Titanic.

The design process began with engaging the residents so that we could try to understand the problems they faced and the ways in which the physical form of the project contributed to its dysfunction. We learned that residents felt unable to control the open space around their units, space that had been taken over by gangs. The housing "units" lacked either a front yard or a back yard. There were neither porches nor fences. Many units faced pedestrian "greens" (usually brown) instead of streets.

The residents dreamed of having houses with porches, front yards with front yard fences, back yards with back yard fences, and streets where they could park in front of their houses. With these elements of a traditional neighborhood,

Crawford Square, Pittsburgh, Pennsylvania

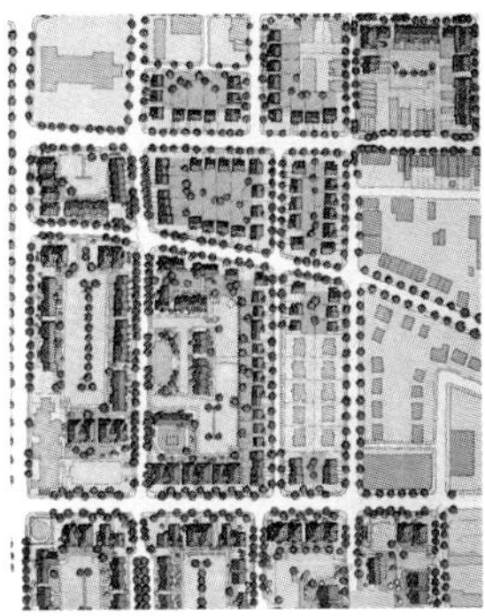

residents felt they could take back the neighborhood from the gangs and make it their own. The design provided those elements, construction was done between 1993 and 1995, and by mid-1994 the residents had taken control. Crime rates dropped precipitously, performance in school improved, and employment increased.

The changes dealt entirely with the zone between the house and the street and with the back yard. By establishing a traditional neighborhood form for the public spaces, it was possible to provide an environment in which the residents could succeed.

This experience reinforced UDA's resolve to elevate awareness of the public realm as the most important (and most neglected) aspect of building neighborhoods.

Crawford Square is a new neighborhood immediately adjacent to downtown Pittsburgh. It was built between 1990 and 1998 on 20 acres of vacant land in a failed urban renewal area. At the edge of the Hill District in Pittsburgh, Crawford Square is in an area that for many years had been perceived to be unsafe. When the developer, Richard Baron of McCormack Baron Associates, proposed a mixed-income neighborhood, he was greeted with skepticism by the real estate community, who considered it inconceivable that middle- or upper-income people would invest or rent in the area. The design that emerged in a public process called for a traditional Pittsburgh neighborhood, with tree-lined streets, front porches, and back yards. A pattern book set the building types, massing, window and door types, and special elements such as porches and bay windows. It was used to design both the rental buildings and the for-sale houses. The result is a diverse collection of houses that, though new, resemble those in highly regarded Pittsburgh neighborhoods.

The sense of stability created by this image and the quality of the public realm contributed to the success of Crawford Square in attracting both renters and homebuyers in a wide range of income groups. From this experience, UDA learned the role that pattern books can play in the development of mixed-income neighborhoods, especially in locations perceived to be risky.

NEW TOWNS

Baxter, Fort Mill, South Carolina

New towns, larger in scale than urban infill projects, can use pattern books to create the balance of diversity and harmony of real towns. New towns resemble the great building booms of London and Paris in which large tracts of land were developed in a short period of time using a number of different builders and architects, often working in close proximity to one another.

In UDA's experience, pattern books have served to bring all of the various players together by first graphically describing the desired image of a community, which in turn is the key to the way in which the new community will be marketed. To achieve that image, the architecture of each house and building must contribute to the overall quality of the public realm. The prescribed patterns relate directly to that image and are understood to be not only supportive of the marketing program, but essential to its success.

This worked for small new neighborhoods and towns such as Mason Run in Monroe, Michigan, and the Ledges in Alabama, as well as for large towns such as Celebration and WaterColor in Florida, and Baxter in South Carolina. It also has proven to be successful in large-scale rebuilding of city neighborhoods such as Park DuValle in Louisville, Kentucky.

(above and next page top) Mason Run, Monroe, Michigan

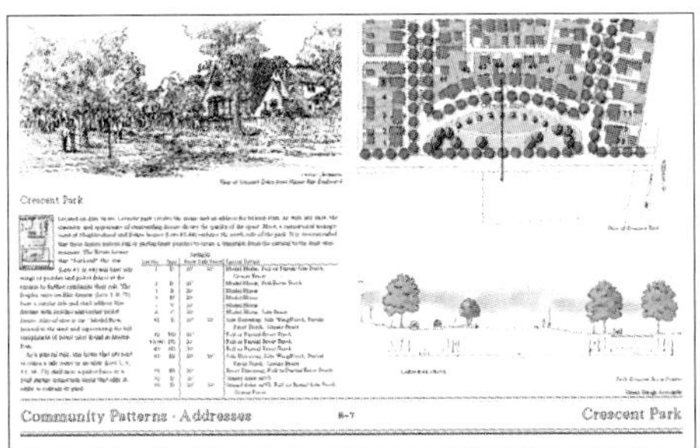

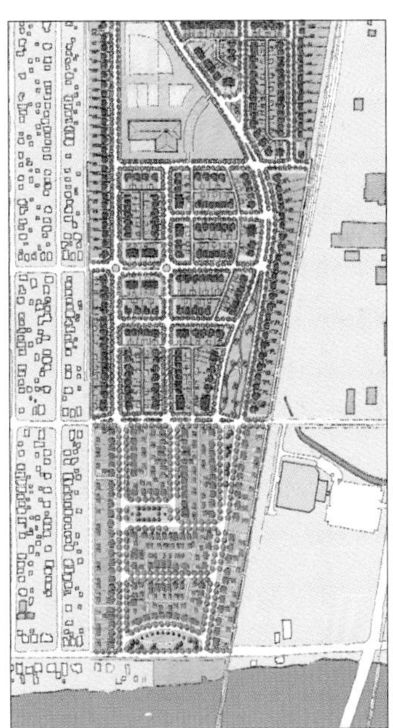

The present format and content of UDA's pattern books evolved significantly over the course of creating pattern books for several new towns. Because the right marketing image is so essential for the success of a new town, the first section of the pattern books we create — the Overview section — became of increasing importance in our approach. In the Overview, photographs, drawings, and text portray the concepts and desired quality of development. If the developers and builders respond to and support this section, they will be more likely to follow the pattern book's recommendations.

CITIES AND REGIONS

Pattern books can also be prepared for cities and regions. For example, the City of Norfolk would like to raise the quality of new construction in existing historic neighborhoods so that it enhances rather than diminishes the existing character of these areas. And for newer neighborhoods without much architectural character, the city's goal is to encourage construction that creates a richer, more "Norfolk" character. UDA is also preparing the first in a series of pattern books for the Yorkshire region of England with the goal of coordinating the many persons and entities involved in development there to enhance the quality of the public realm. City-wide and regional pattern books are intended to be broad-based educational tools, rather than a means for implementing specific projects.

PATTERN BOOKS FOR URBANISM

The approach to creating pattern books described and illustrated in the chapters that follow has developed and been refined over time as a product of these various experiences. The common theme among these is the need to communicate the goals of the development to the diverse team of individuals involved in building it, and to establish a consensus among all participants on the means and methods of achieving those goals. Therefore, pattern books are both manual and textbook.

As must be clear from the history of pattern books summarized in Chapter 1, we can all draw inspiration from the efforts of the past. In recent years, other firms have also embraced the pattern book as a tool both in the United States and elsewhere. In Great Britain, for example, Robert Adam, inspired by the traditional pattern books, has created pattern books for various developments for the Duchy of Cornwall, Poundbury among them.

The format of UDA Pattern Books includes elements of those historic antecedents. For example:

→ Each UDA Pattern Book begins with concern for site location and the form of streets, as did those of Vitruvius and Serlio.

→ Precedents of both community and architectural patterns are the key references for establishing the patterns. The classical treatises developed this approach with great sophistication.

→ UDA Pattern Books combine details with images in both two and three dimensions as did most of the Victorian and twentieth-century pattern books, especially the White Pine Series.

UDA Pattern Books differ from their predecessors in that ours focus on urban space and the creation of a cohesive public realm as their prime goal. Prior ages were graced with a much greater consensus about the quality of the public realm, perhaps because it took so much longer to build cities and towns. Therefore, both the process of producing a pattern book and its format can be a means of overcoming our present lack of consensus. By working together, as the medieval builders did, all parties can work within a shared vision of the public realm.

C H A P T E R

3

The Purpose and Structure of a Pattern Book

The central message of the modern pattern book is that the character and quality of urban spaces is created through careful attention to detail at three scales: the overall plan for the development; the image of typical urban spaces within that plan; and the individual buildings with their architectural details. How often we see spaces that may have been beautiful in plan, but fail to delight the eye because of poorly proportioned building forms, or a lack of windows, or dark and dreary materials and colors! Pattern books provide criteria and patterns that ensure a degree of harmony among elements at all three scales.

These scales respond to the challenges of building urbanism today by:

→ Enabling the diverse group of specialists involved in building towns and cities to work together within a shared vision for the physical form of the development, which is rooted in the qualities of the specific region in which it is located.

→ Establishing the physical and visual form of the public spaces and community patterns that each individual building effort can help to create.

→ Providing a primer on the patterns and elements of architectural styles appropriate to the unique character and traditions of the place in which the development is located.

The modern pattern books described and illustrated in this book were prepared to serve this mission. Many were prepared for specific development projects, commissioned by either a private-sector master developer or a public agency acting in that capacity. Regardless of whether the client came from the public or private sector, the pattern books served to coordinate a large and complex development to be built over time by many different individual builders.

The pattern books illustrated herein are the result of the evolution described in the previous chapter and respond to the challenges of current development practices discussed in the next. The format and content of these books were developed collaboratively with stakeholders of each development in a process that is presented in Chapter 5.

Different from their predecessors, these pattern books focus on the public realm, rather than on the elements of a particular architectural language or style (although they do include architectural patterns in a variety of styles). In contrast with design guidelines, these modern-day pattern books provide a systematic method for placing buildings on sites and for using specific architectural elements.

Design guidelines are often viewed by the development industry as cruel and unusual punishment that forces builders to follow what seem to them to be arbitrary regulations. However, these pattern books, conceived in the tradition of the builders' companions discussed previously, are designed to help builders fulfill the marketing objectives of the development, gain consensus to support the approvals process, and expedite the development process.

Frequently, these pattern books function as "instruments of service," that is, they guide the construction of buildings and public spaces as part of a contractual arrangement among the parties involved. Created out of consensus among the parties involved and backed up by the terms of the contract between them, these pattern books have often formed part of the deed restrictions for transfer of land from one party to another.

In this way, pattern books differ from zoning ordinances or codes, even New Urbanist codes, which can be incorporated into public legislation, thereby providing development controls by law. Pattern books rely on their ability to be persuasive and compelling in presenting both the overall vision of a development and the specific detailed requirements necessary to build that vision. In some cases, they have helped streamline the approval and entitlement process for developers since agreements with the municipalities can often be achieved with a shorter process when the patterns in the pattern book are used correctly.

THE CONCEPT OF AN URBAN ASSEMBLY KIT

Pattern books can be conceived as a kit of parts that gives designers and builders the flexibility to create a wide range of houses while still maintaining the distinct characteristics of traditional neighborhood design inherent in the particular region.

The metaphor of the classic children's toy, Mr. Potato Head, describes this approach well. The toy provides several choices for eyes, noses, mouths, and ears, enabling children to create a number of different characters by the choices they have among the available facial features. The basic shape is known — a potato — and the general location of each feature is known: pairs of eyes and ears have correct placement, as do the nose, mouth, mustache, and bow tie. The sequence of content presented in the Architectural Patterns section of a well-constructed pattern book does the same thing. The massing page sets the basic shape (the potato). A selection of windows and doors, like eyes and ears, have correct locations on facades. Porches and other special features, like noses and mustaches, have a prominent setting in the front. And the main door (the mouth) finds its place underneath them.

This simplified approach to architectural form is designed, as we will see in the next chapter, to respond to the demands of standardized production techniques in the building industry, while providing architectural coherence and form.

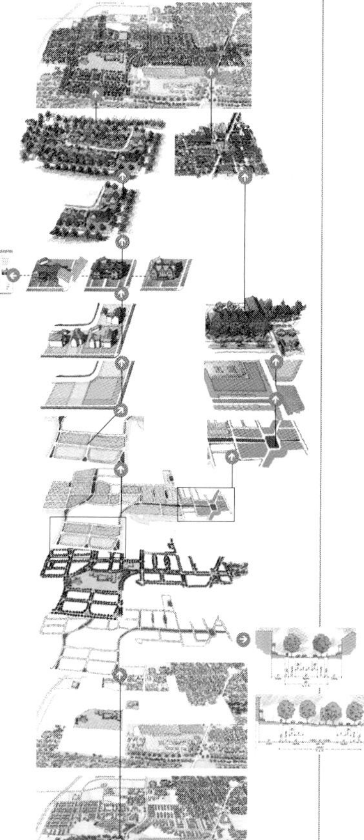

Architectural patterns, however, are only one element in a large-scale approach to urbanism. Neighborhoods and cities are complex systems that are an assemblage of elements. These elements include a framework of streets, public open space, blocks, lots, and buildings. The exploded perspective drawing of the Park DuValle neighborhood in Louisville, Kentucky (shown at right) illustrates these various elements. Thus, this same technique is applied to the Community Patterns contained in a pattern book as a means of setting the character of public space and the role buildings play in them. The Architectural Patterns extend that approach to the details of buildings.

While this approach provides a system for creating urbanism, it is designed to create unique environments in each location that respond to local traditions, culture, and aspirations. It is a means of navigating the perils of the development process, while infusing the development with local character. The approach provides all involved with an overall means of understanding urban space since local interpretation of an architectural style varies from one region to another.

Similarly, while there are general qualities and patterns common to most modern pattern books, it is the specific ways in which these elements are adapted to each local condition that we believe is the most important means of reviving and continuing the unique richness of American urbanism.

THE STRUCTURE

Typically, modern pattern books contain three sections:

I. Overview
II. Community Patterns
III. Architectural Patterns

Exemplars of each of these sections are presented in Part 2 of this book. In some cases, additional sections are provided — for example, on landscape design, appendices, or a glossary of terms.

I. Overview

The Overview section describes the essential qualities of the development for all participants. It is a means of establishing consensus among all those involved in the process. It also serves as the objective basis for the specific requirements called for in the pattern book.

To accomplish this, the Overview contains visual images that describe the intended character and image of the proposed development. The specific content of this section is unique to each pattern book, but generally includes the following:

Description of the Overall Development. If the pattern book is for a specific development, the Overview or Introduction begins with the master plan and marketing criteria. If the pattern book's purpose is to provide guidance for neighborhood improvements, it emphasizes those attributes that the community would like to have reinforced.

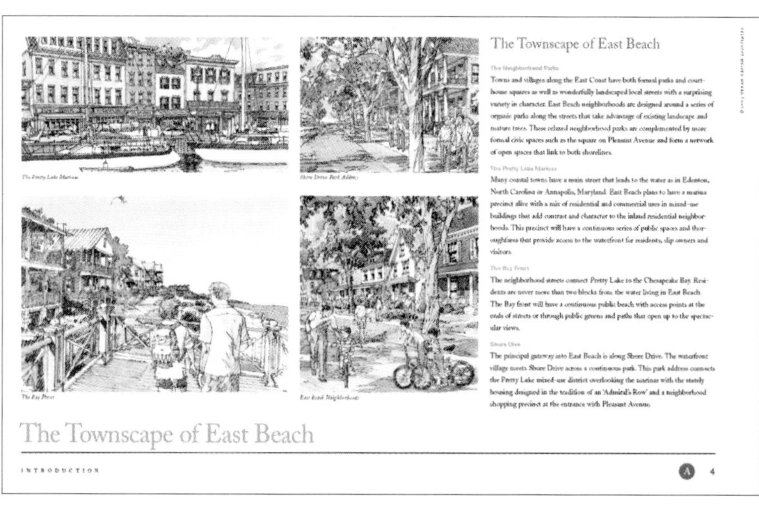

The Townscape of East Beach

The Neighborhood Parks

Towns and villages along the East Coast have both formal parks and courthouse squares as well as wonderfully landscaped local streets with a surprising variety in character. East Beach neighborhoods are designed around a series of organic parks along the streets that take advantage of existing landscape and mature trees. These relaxed neighborhood parks are complemented by more formal civic spaces such as the square on Pleasant Avenue and form a network of open spaces that link to both shorelines.

The Pretty Lake Marinas

Many coastal towns have a main street that leads to the water as in Edenton, North Carolina or Annapolis, Maryland. East Beach plans to have a marina precinct alive with a mix of residential and commercial uses in mixed-use buildings that add contrast and character to the inland residential neighborhoods. This precinct will have a continuous series of public spaces and thoroughfares that provide access to the waterfront for residents, slip owners and visitors.

The Bay Front

The neighborhood streets connect Pretty Lake to the Chesapeake Bay. Residents are never more than two blocks from the water living in East Beach. The Bay front will have a continuous public beach with access points at the ends of streets or through public greens and paths that open up to the spectacular views.

Shore Drive

The principal gateway into East Beach is along Shore Drive. The waterfront village meets Shore Drive across a continuous park. This park address connects the Pretty Lake mixed-use district overlooking the marinas with the stately housing designed in the tradition of an 'Admiral's Row' and a neighborhood shopping precinct at the entrance with Pleasant Avenue.

The Townscape of East Beach

INTRODUCTION A 4

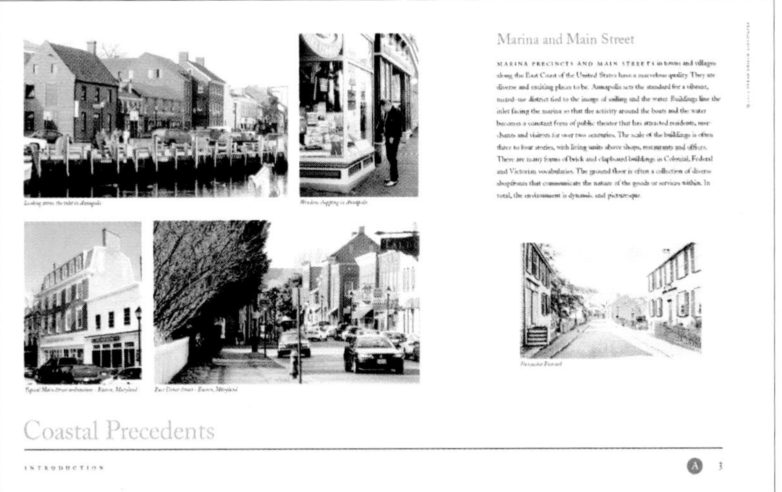

Marina and Main Street

MARINA PRECINCTS AND MAIN STREETS in towns and villages along the East Coast of the United States have a marvelous quality. They are diverse and exciting places to be. Annapolis sets the standard for a vibrant, mixed-use district tied to the image of sailing and the water. Buildings line the inlet facing the marina so that the activity around the boats and the water becomes a constant form of public theater that has attracted residents, merchants and visitors for over two centuries. The scale of the buildings is often three to four stories, with living units above shops, restaurants and offices. There are many forms of brick and clapboard buildings in Colonial, Federal and Victorian vocabularies. The ground floor is often a collection of diverse shopfronts that communicate the nature of the goods or services within. In total, the environment is dynamic and picturesque.

Coastal Precedents

INTRODUCTION A 3

EAST BEACH IS A NEW NEIGHBORHOOD on Norfolk's Chesapeake Bay that draws upon southeastern building types and town planning practices to create a unique waterfront village rooted in the traditions of the region. It is intentionally and distinctly *Tidewater* in feeling, from its overall layout and landscape design to the details of its buildings, pathways and parks.

The plan of East Beach is a response to the historic pattern of neighborhood forms and specific natural features and contrasting qualities of the site. Pedestrian-scaled streets, hidden gardens, sheltered porches, narrow alleys and overhanging roofs have been brought together to provide a sense of familiarity, stimulation and ease.

This sense of wholeness is underscored by the interweaving of natural and built elements, each reinforcing an appreciation of the other. Mature shade trees and parks set the address for many intimate neighborhood streets while uses along Pretty Lake to the south provide a delightful contrast and a destination for residents. Residents and guests can walk from these neighborhoods out to the long stretch of preserved dunes and beaches along the Chesapeake Bay. Interspersed among and giving form to this distinctive local landscape are strongly vernacular Southern buildings of varying size, finish and color – all of which underscore the strong regional character of the place. The two pages that follow are samples of the regional precedents that help form the design of East Beach.

East Beach Character

INTRODUCTION A 1

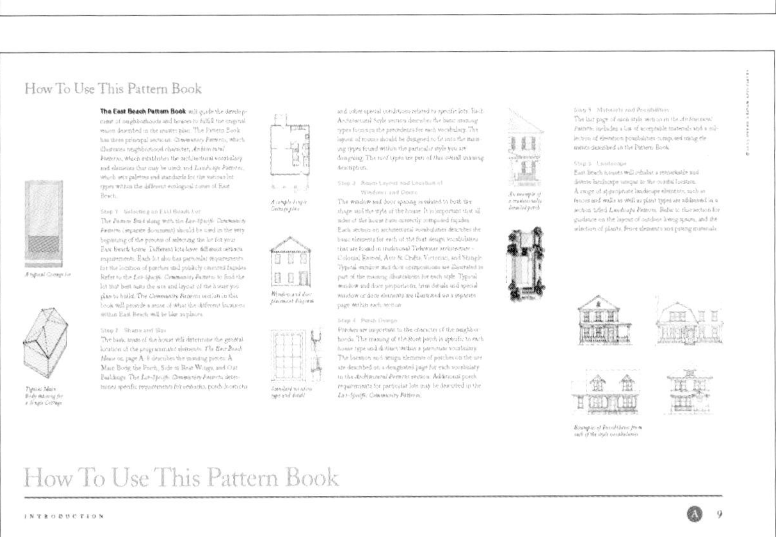

How To Use This Pattern Book

How To Use This Pattern Book

INTRODUCTION A 9

Description of Context and Precedents. To inspire and inform the users of the pattern book, this description includes: the qualities of the site itself; the natural systems to which it is connected; adjacent neighborhoods, towns, and development; the urban and architectural traditions of the community and region in which the site is located; dimensions of streets and sidewalks, setbacks for buildings, architectural styles, dominant materials and colors, and landscape palettes.

Description of Essential Qualities and Character. This summary of the detailed provisions that follow can include images of typical addresses, prototype buildings, and key details. It identifies the patterns that are the most appropriate for the development and the essential attributes that respond to both local traditions and current market demands.

How To Use The Pattern Book. Step-by-step instructions are graphically described for various ways in which the book should be used.

II. Community Patterns

Based on research on local building traditions, the Community Patterns section of a pattern book describes the essential qualities of the public spaces of the development, the various building types used to create those spaces, and the way in which they are placed on their lots. Although this section is unique to each pattern book and can vary in length, it generally includes the following:

Plan with Requirements. An overall plan indicates the urban requirements diagrammatically and identifies the key addresses and public spaces of the plan. The proposed form of streets and public spaces is illustrated with plans and sections that indicate setbacks, facade properties, building height, and the character of the landscape treatment in both the public and private areas.

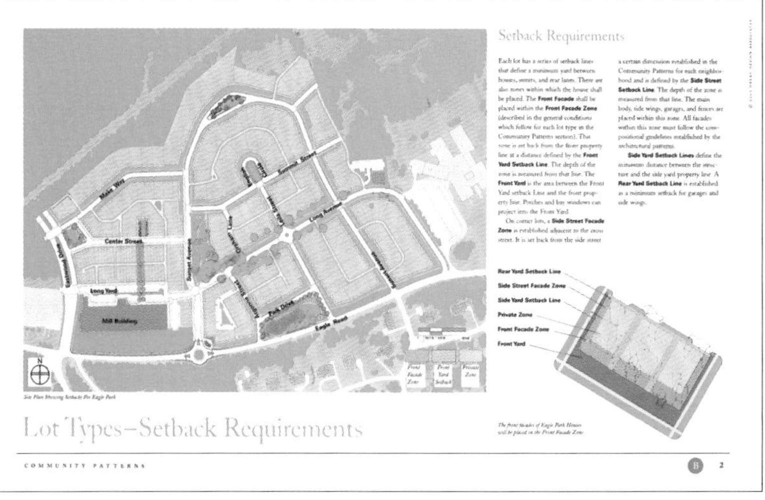

Address. This section also describes and illustrates different addresses within the community. Each distinct address may be described on a page with a plan of lots having specific house placement criteria for that particular neighborhood. An eye-level perspective and a street section generally accompany the plan drawing to help create a full picture of the intent.

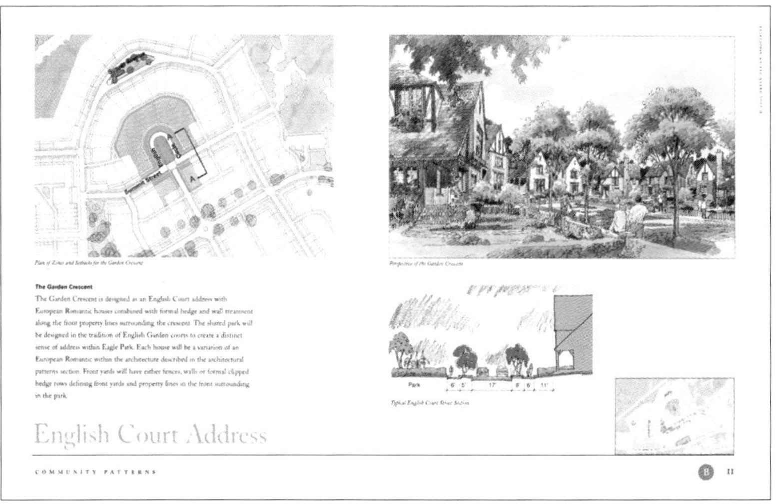

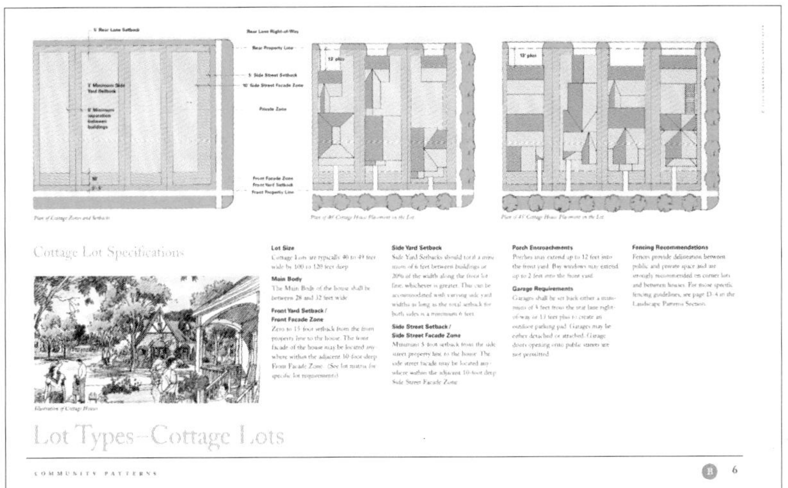

Cottage Lot Specifications

Lot Size
Cottage Lots are typically 40 to 49 feet wide by 100 to 120 feet deep.

Main Body
The Main Body of the house shall be between 28 and 32 feet wide.

Front Yard Setback / Front Facade Zone
Zero to 15-foot setback from the front property line to the house. The front facade of the house may be located anywhere within the adjacent 10-foot-deep Front Facade Zone. (See lot matrix for specific lot requirements.)

Side Yard Setback
Side Yard Setbacks should total a minimum of 6 feet between buildings or 20% of the width along the front lot line, whichever is greater. This can be accommodated with varying side yard widths as long as the total setback for both sides is a minimum 6 feet.

Side Street Setback / Side Street Facade Zone
Minimum 3-foot setback from the side street property line to the house. The side street facade may be located anywhere within the adjacent 10-foot-deep Side Street Facade Zone.

Porch Encroachments
Porches may extend up to 12 feet into the front yard. Bay windows may extend up to 2 feet into the front yard.

Garage Requirements
Garages shall be set back either a minimum of 3 feet from the rear lane right-of-way or 13 feet plus to create an outdoor parking pad. Garages may be either detached or attached. Garage doors opening onto public streets are not permitted.

Fencing Recommendations
Fences provide delineation between public and private space and are strongly recommended on corner lots and between houses. For more specific fencing guidelines, see page D-4 in the Landscape Patterns Section.

Lot Types—Cottage Lots

COMMUNITY PATTERNS B 6

Lot Types. For each of the Descriptions of the various lot types within the development, these pages set the location of individual buildings, their volume, and any areas that are suggested to receive special design attention.

Landscape Styles in Gardens

Three garden styles have been developed for East Garrison that reflect the rich and diverse landscape traditions of Monterey Bay and the peninsula.

The Mediterranean Garden

The Mediterranean Garden will reflect the coastal climate with a mix of arid and exotic plantings in a courtyard setting. Lush vertical plantings such as vines on the porches and flowering trees set in the ground plane plantings of groundcovers, perennials, and succulents can be symmetrical or informal in design emphasizing the entry to the house. Walls and gates can define a private entry courtyard which is a hallmark of this garden type.

The Cottage Garden

The cottage garden is the most prevalent in the region. Picket fences, arbors, and trellises define entries and front yards. Plantings are lush and primarily perennials and annuals with a scattering of ornamental shrubs and small flowering trees as accents. These gardens are characterized an explosion of color and layered with a variety of texture.

The Arts & Crafts Garden

Another regional garden type, the Arts & Crafts style is more formal and organized. As is typical of English border gardens, hedges formally define the edges of the garden and the more natural landscape patterns beyond the hedges. Ornamental shrubs and small trees are used as accents, plant palettes include groundcovers, and annuals and perennials. Elements of "Good," "Better," and "Best" gardens are documented on the following pages.

Landscape Styles for Front Yard Gardens

LANDSCAPE PATTERNS D 4

Landscape and Site Design Elements. If there is no separate landscape section, these pages describe patterns for fences, alley structures, and landscape elements. When appropriate, this section may also include lighting specifications and, for commercial pattern books, will often also include style guidelines or specifications for amenities for public spaces (e.g., benches, waste receptacles, bike racks, etc.).

III. Architectural Patterns

The Architectural Patterns section defines the architectural style(s) selected for the project. The number and type of styles vary with each pattern book. The selection of styles is a result of both the precedent research and a collaborative process among all parties to determine those most appropriate to create the desired quality of town or neighborhood.

Each architectural style is presented on a series of pages, the first of which describes the essential qualities of that style, its history, and character. On the succeeding pages, patterns for the elements of that particular style are identified and described.

These pages represent a kind of assembly kit, consisting of the basic massing of the house, on which windows and doors are placed, and to which special elements such as porches can be added, with a palette of materials and colors that are appropriate for that style.

The number of pages for each style also varies from pattern book to pattern book, with as few as three pages and as many as eight. The sequence, however, remains the same and includes the following:

History and Character. The history and key characteristics of the style are described in order to identify the essential elements that should be respected and built correctly. In any building process, there is a limit to the number of different aspects that can be controlled, so it is critical to ask for the ones that are most important. Four to six of these attributes are listed, illustrated, and described.

The Tidewater Shingle Style in the East Beach Pattern Book illustrates a typical History and Character page. In this region, the styles are often complex combinations of various time periods and changes made to alter the original forms of houses. This style is based on simple forms that can be detailed in either a Colonial or Victorian-era palette. Its attributes include simple volumes, symmetrical composition of windows within each volume, simplified Colonial or Victorian details, gabled or shed dormers, simple one- or two-story porches, cut shingle siding, and white trim.

Tidewater Vernacular Architecture

Tidewater Vernacular Architecture

INTRODUCTION

A 6

History and Character

Tidewater Shingle

ARCHITECTURAL PATTERNS

C 8

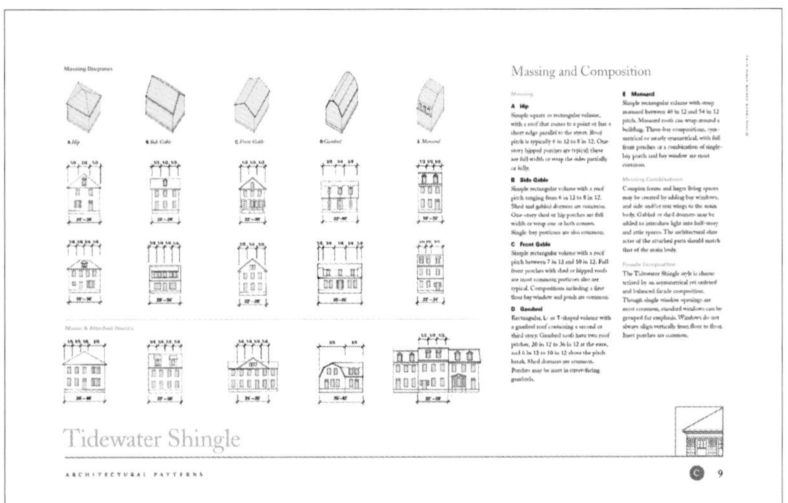

Massing and Composition. The massing of the house includes a main body in which the front door is located and side wings for more complex houses. Patterns for massing establish the roof pitch, height, and overall form of the buildings. Facade composition, especially the placement of windows, is closely related to building massing. For example, windows within the main body of the house are typically placed in a three-bay or five-bay composition.

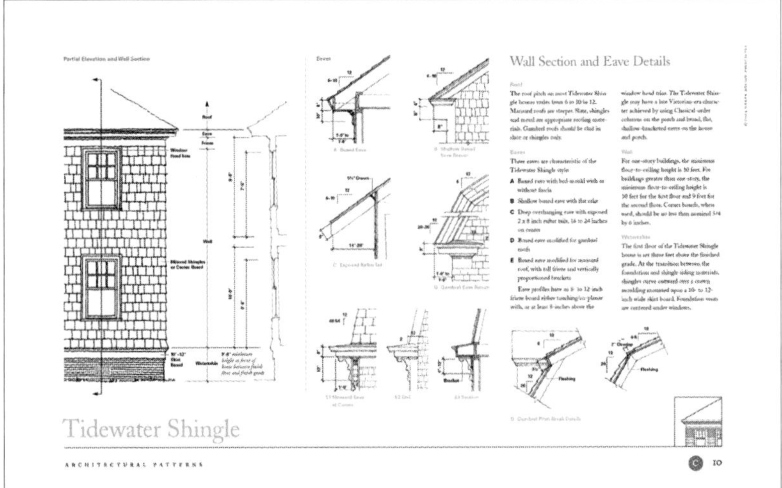

Massing and Eave Details. The massing of the house is articulated with eave and soffit details that are particular to each style. In the Tidewater Shingle example, the roof pitch is typically between 6 in 12 and 8 in 12. Gambrel types of compound slopes and mansard roofs are detailed as another option. The roof overhang varies, but can be as much as 20 inches in the Victorian detailing, or only 12 inches with a boxed soffit in the Colonial detailing.

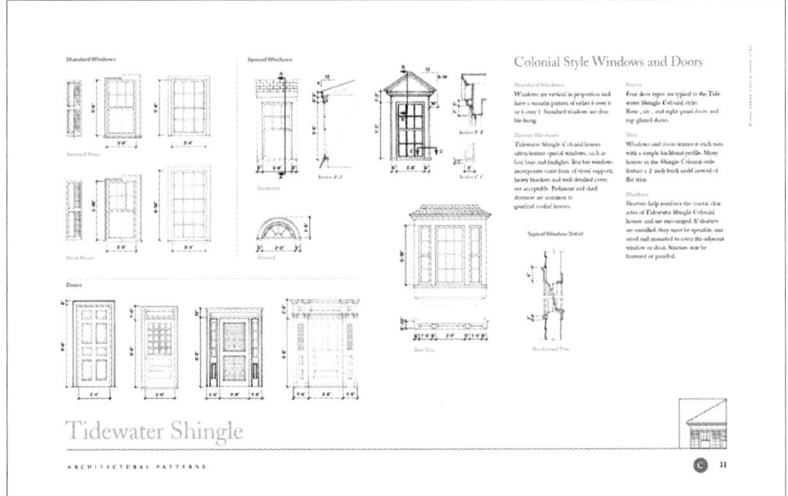

Windows and Doors. The pattern book establishes both the proportions of windows and the principles for placing them on the mass of the house.

The Tidewater Shingle style uses two basic window types — a Colonial-style window (6-over-9 or a 6-over-1 muntin pattern) or a Victorian-style window type (2-over-1 muntin pattern). Typically, ground-floor windows are taller than second-floor ones.

Porches. The porch is the special element most associated with the Tidewater Shingle style. It can be either one or two stories tall and can have a variety of roof and column configurations. The drawings on this page indicate the way in which porches are placed on the various massing types of the style, and include correct details and components such as railings and column types.

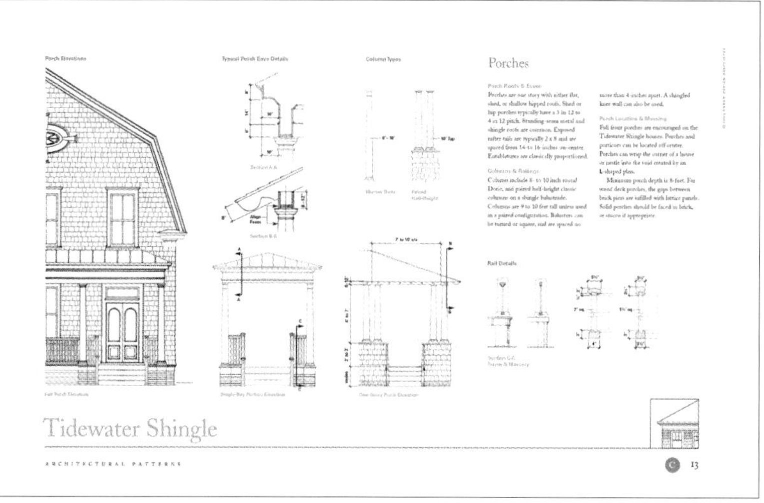

Materials, Colors, and Possibilities. A materials list is provided. Appropriate color palettes are typically specified in a separate color palette book. A number of possible house elevations are illustrated to demonstrate the wide range of possible house designs that can be created by using combinations of the massing patterns, facade compositions, windows, doors, special elements, materials, and colors of the style.

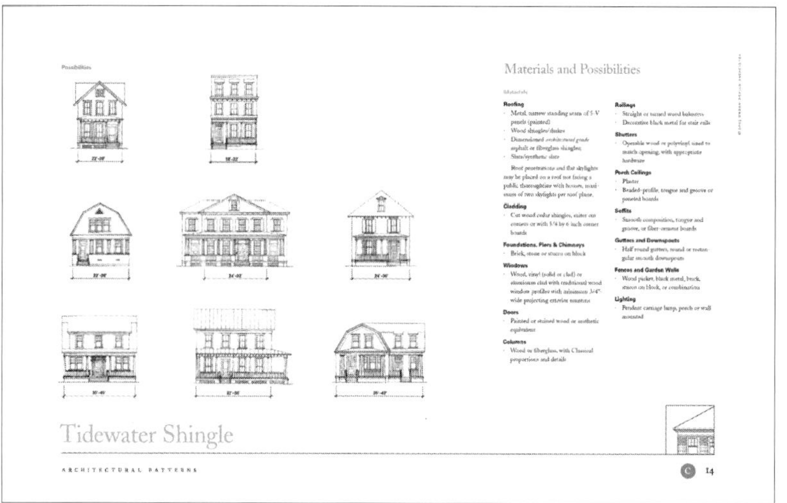

These are all single-family houses. When the same elements of style are applied to other building types, such as townhouses, small apartments, and duplexes, the possibilities multiply. Typically, in each development, there are at least three different architectural styles. As a result, the new neighborhoods that are built with this approach have the diversity and richness of traditional, well-established ones.

An Appendix may include excerpts from relevant building codes, developer guidelines and requirements, etc.

THE PATTERN BOOK COVER

The last part that gets created for a pattern book is its cover. As with any book, the cover must engage the reader in an inviting way. Consequently, careful attention should be paid to selecting powerful, attractive, iconic images. UDA Pattern Books include three scales of image on the cover.

The cover images emphasize the interrelationships among the overall vision for the development, the design of the public spaces that enable that vision to be experienced, and the details of individual buildings that will make the vision a reality.

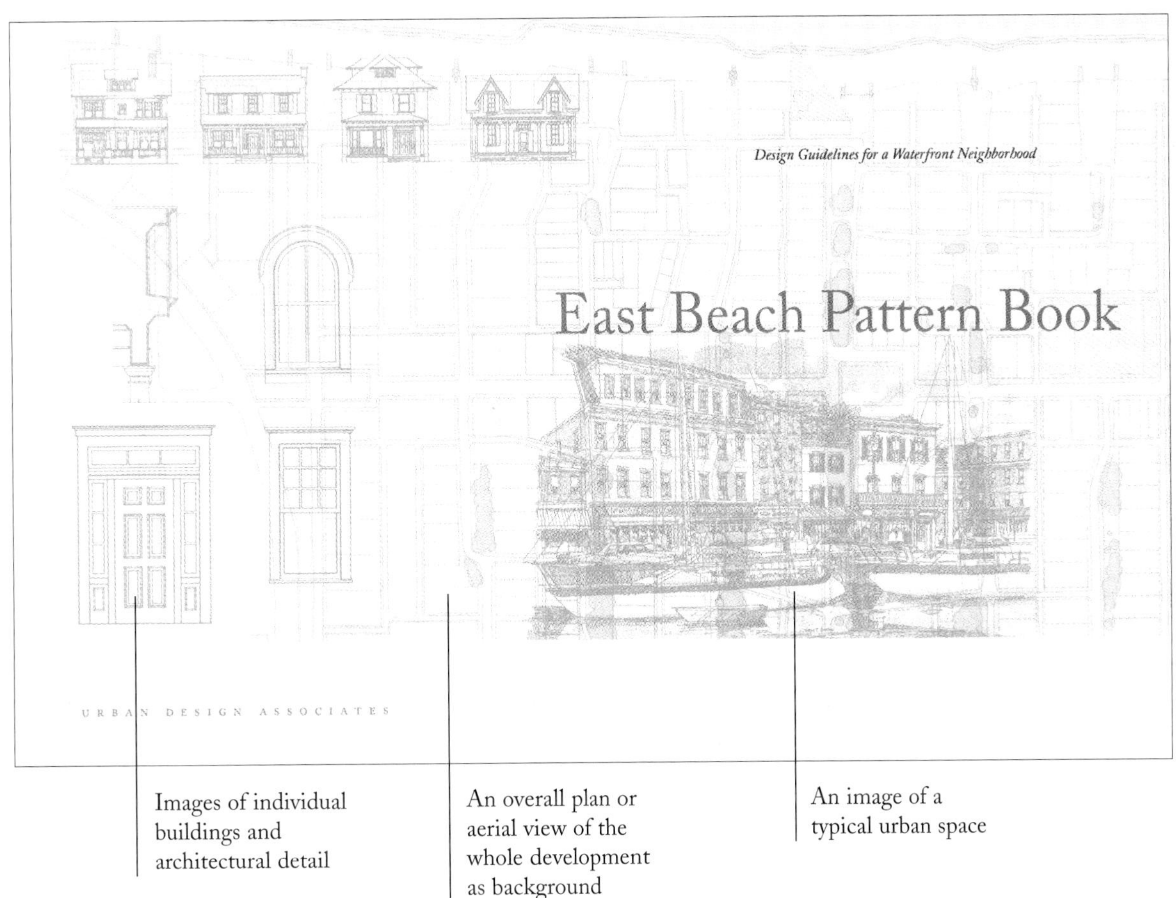

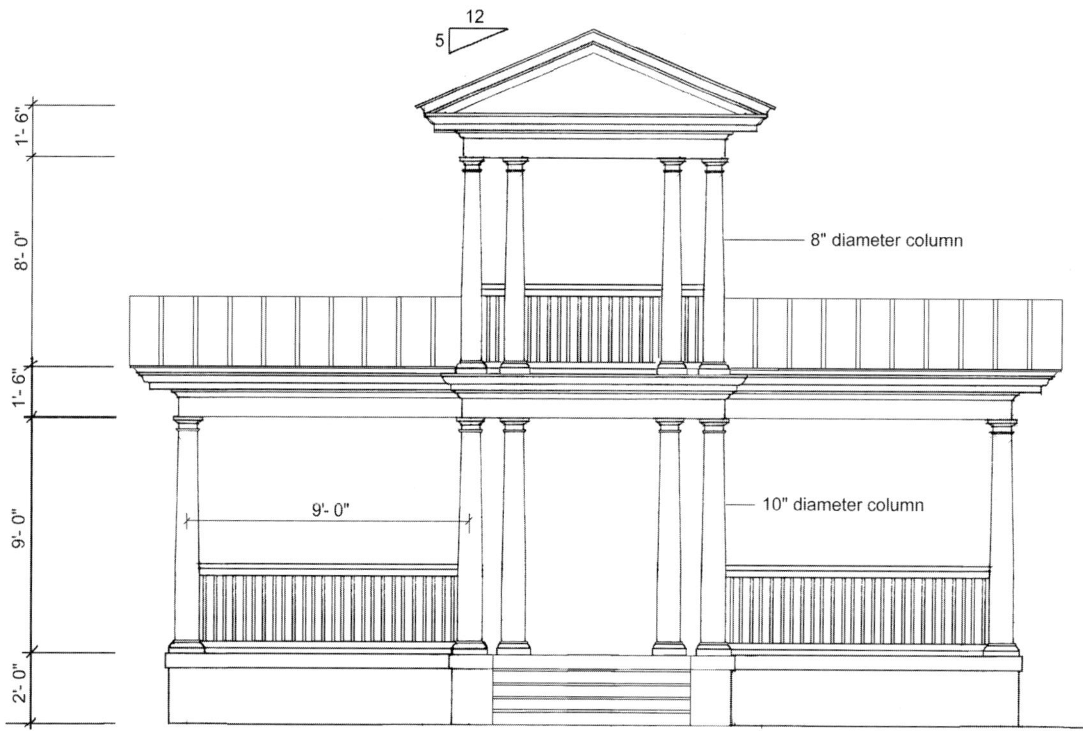

Baxter, Fort Mill, South Carolina, Classical architectural pattern and built result

CHAPTER

4

The Value of Pattern Books to Current Practice

The pattern book method provides a means of addressing the key issues that development teams must cope with in the design of neighborhoods and new towns. In this chapter, we will first summarize the problems encountered when current development practices are used to create urbanism, then describe the ways in which pattern books can solve those problems by providing helpful guidance and encouraging collaboration among all parties, and conclude with examples of neighborhoods and towns that have been built using this approach.

CURRENT DEVELOPMENT PRACTICE

Development is a risky business. Developers work to minimize their exposure in the planning and predevelopment phases of a project and prefer to work in predictable situations with relatively few surprises and contingencies. To be successful, the development must respond to a series of challenges, the most significant of which are described below.

The Market. The first and most essential challenge is to respond to the market. The master plan for a development must be created based on a clear understanding of market potential. The quality of public spaces, the distribution and type of units, the mix of commercial, residential, and other uses—all must meet the needs of the market that the development is trying to attract. Therefore, the master plan, and the way in which it is presented, should be a key part of the marketing program. And certainly, in order to create urbanism, the development must fulfill the vision that is delineated in the master plan.

Precedent

Pattern book possibility

House design

Built result

This need to be successful in the market is often a perceived risk for the development team. Current practice often groups building types and similar-size houses together based on the selling price and the tenure type—i.e., rental, condominium, or detached for sale. This creates a clear segregation within a new development that is positioned to send a specific message to the buyer or renter about cost and quality. This pattern runs counter to the basic principles and character of many traditional neighborhoods and towns, where a much more liberal mix of building types, tenure, sizes, uses, and prices exists. From the developer's perspective, this clear delineation by product type sets up a very straightforward selling proposition to the buyer. A more organic pattern that blurs the distinction between these standard categories presents a different challenge to the sales and marketing team.

While designers may understand the relationships and inherent qualities of the places within the master plan, most people don't read plans very well, nor do they share the same sense of what a place will be like once it is constructed. It is important in the development strategy to communicate the essential qualities of the place in ways that resonate with potential buyers and builders. Many new places are marketed through the use of two-dimensional master plan drawings, house elevations, and photographs that are designed to create positive associations. However, it is almost impossible for the prospective buyer or tenant to predict what the place will actually feel like once it is built from these reference materials alone.

Flexibility. There is an inherent risk in master plans in which the mix and type of buildings is rigidly fixed beyond a foreseeable period of time. This is particularly true in New Urbanist developments, which can change the market once the first phases are built. By creating an attractive environment with a strong sense of place, these developments often appeal to a broader and more diverse population than conventional development. Many plans are developed that depend on a particular market to create the sense of place and build out the master plan. One of the recurring issues in many mixed-use developments is their ability to successfully attract the types and projected square footage of uses envisioned in the master plan. Often a plan has to be completely reworked if the assumptions don't materialize as anticipated. Therefore, it is

Community pattern

Built result

important to have a means of responding to changes in the market, such as the flexibility to change the mix of unit types and prices, without compromising the integrity of the master plan.

Standardized Production. In most development efforts, pressure exists to standardize the process in order to minimize risks, expense, and time. Builders and developers generally prefer to use house plans that they have used in the past and know to be successful. In production housing, the budgets are very tight and there is little time for individual custom design to modify already-tested house plans to fit the master plan.

Over the course of the past several decades, large-scale residential development has been dominated by national and regional production builders able to deliver a large number of housing units with enough efficiency to generate profits. The architecture of the houses is primarily derived from floor plans that the builder has found, through trial and error, to work well with various market segments of targeted buyers or renters. Interior finishes, kitchen and bath layouts, and the feeling of large interior spaces are the focus of the design of these plans. Once the plan is set, the walls and roof forms are wrapped around it. The architecture that results tends to be a random set of volumes on which components from the catalog of favored suppliers are casually placed in an effort to create a more or less traditional image.

Community pattern

Built result

In this context, houses are thought of as production units, often referred to as products. The process of construction is a production line, with a set of specific operations—using a selection of predetermined components often selected by the developer's or builder's procurement department (not the architect or designer)—designed to bring the house to the market within a projected budget. Additionally, the builder is looking for repetitive details that are applied to each house to cut down on mistakes and to increase the speed of construction.

The challenge then, is to find a way of working within the demands of standardized production and construction techniques to create houses

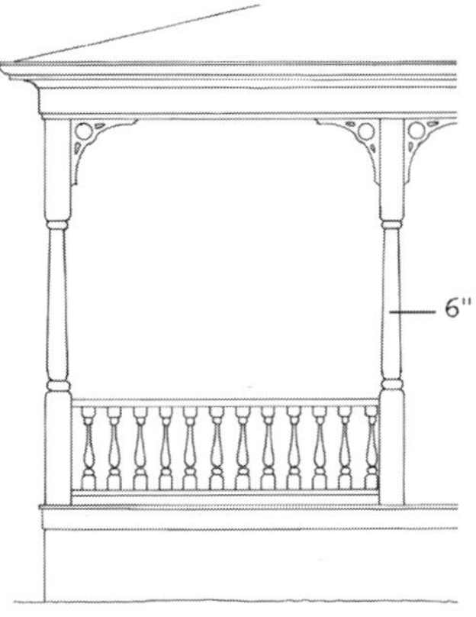

Architectural pattern

Built result

Precedent

House design

Built result

that respond to local traditions and conditions and produce an architectural form of sufficient quality to create the desired image for the community. A balance must be found between those elements that can be mass-produced and standardized, and those that must be specifically designed to create a unique place that is appropriate to its location.

Approvals and Politics. Every project is dependent on zoning and planning approvals. That means the project must be based on some degree of public consensus and support. This further complicates the developer's situation because, while trying to standardize production, move quickly, and be able to respond to an ever-changing market, the developer must also respond to the concerns of local citizens, local administrators, and the political environment in which large projects take place. Once again, the need for a level of certainty that gives everyone confidence in the program must be balanced with the need for flexibility. Local officials typically want guarantees and are less interested in the opportunities for change over time, regardless of the market response to the development. Approvals are often viewed as fixed promises to deliver exactly what is proposed. Additionally, many of the current standards, such as zoning regulations, street standards, parking requirements, and so on, run counter to the expressed desires of the public and the planning authorities. This means that many of the standards have to be modified to grant approval to a development proposal that adheres to the principles of making good urban places and local patterns found in the best traditional neighborhoods. This added level of negotiation and modification of existing standards can be costly and defeating to a well-intended and wonderfully designed plan.

Community pattern

Built result

Current approval processes usually result in an adversarial relationship between the developer, the public officials, and the existing community. Master plans are typically presented to the public administrative bodies and planning officials in a more or less finished state. When this occurs, there is little room for accommodation or response to different issues, and the result, frequently, is a tense and difficult negotiation that takes places after the development team has already expended a considerable amount of effort and expense. This standard plan approval process almost inevitably sets up this kind of confrontation, no matter what the proposal. Under these circumstances, the risk potential is very high for the development team, and the additional requirements for approval are negotiated in a highly charged political environment.

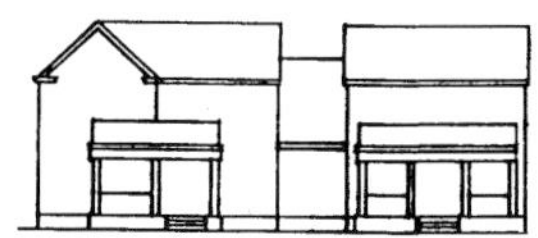

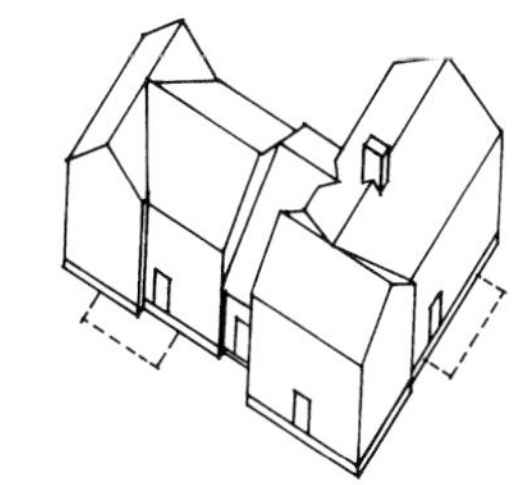

Architectural patterns

Built result

Physical Conditions. The physical context for the project creates its own set of demands. The form and character of the landscape can be a major determinant of neighborhood form and the relationship of buildings to each other and to the site. Among the questions to be considered are: How does a tight grid of streets and blocks with alleys work in a rolling terrain? How do uphill and downhill lots work? How does the goal of preserving existing environmental features such as mature stands of trees or wetlands relate to the grading plan for the pattern of streets and lots shown in the master plan? The physical constraints or attributes of a site are often the least understood elements early on in the planning and design process. These physical attributes are important to understand in three dimensions early on in the process, as they are critical to place-making, building types, access, and the form of the plan.

Implementation. Another important consideration is the local capacity for implementation. Urbanism requires the cooperation of many different specialists who must be coordinated and who must perform well. So the developer is faced with a series of questions: Which homebuilders are capable of maintaining the quality and schedule? How does the infrastructure (e.g., streets, utilities, and public open space) get built? What is the depth and experience of the development team? How will the phasing occur? What is the capacity and quality of the local design talent? The answers to all of these questions vary from place to place, but it is certain that the quality of talent is not consistent across all disciplines. Many projects are designed without a clear understanding of how the implementation process will occur. The strategy and the tools for implementation vary substantially depending on the implementation strategy. Many plans are created that cannot be successfully implemented given the capacity and method of land disposal, construction coordination, participation, and control.

Community pattern

Built result

Community pattern

Built result

Quite often, a master plan is fully developed and approved, lots are sold to builders, and then everyone discovers how things are really fitting on the site. Grading plans are often produced to create a flat building pad on each lot without thinking about the desired character and quality of each shared street or park address. Builders are often stuck with lots that don't accommodate the building footprints. Engineering is separated from landscape design which is separated from urban design which is separated from the design of houses, and so on. The result is that the buildings never contribute to the sense of place as it was originally envisioned.

THE BENEFITS OF THE PATTERN BOOK METHOD

Pattern book possibility

Built result

Pattern books can provide a mechanism for resolving these problems by serving as a means of communicating the goals of a development to all involved in building it. Traditionally, pattern books, such as the builders' companion books, provided helpful advice for building well-designed houses in correct architectural styles. Modern pattern books respond to the greater challenges faced by current development practitioners by providing a critical link between the vision or concept for a place, the master plan, the implementation strategy, and the market. This applies in much the same way for both private and public development interests, although the latter often introduce additional complexities.

The core value of a pattern book given the current development process is the ability to link all participants in the development process together as the vision of a place is translated to the built environment. The participants include developers, marketing professionals, engineers, architects, governing and administrative stakeholders, the public, homebuilders, and the media.

In the early stages of the work, it is important to involve many of these professionals as data is collected, and local precedents and existing conditions are documented. Focus groups, interviews, field research activities, and on-site

Architectural pattern

Built result

working sessions and charrettes provide multiple opportunities for gathering input from all stakeholders and participants in the development process. This builds a shared set of values for the image and character of the design. Later in the process, there is a rigorous testing of the master plan with all of these interest groups participating. In the course of this testing, the master plan is often refined to create places consistent with, and complementary to, the original vision and sense of place.

The Market. The most successful efforts have been ones where careful analysis and understanding of various market segments have been correlated with appropriate building types, sizes, and costs; neighborhood character; amenities; and mix of unit types. The process of developing a pattern book brings together the place-making qualities of a proposed plan, the projected market needs, building types and sizes, landscape design, and architectural vocabulary. The refinement of the plan is a central part of the process that tests the mix of unit types and refines the details and elements required to create specific addresses within the plan. Once these different elements are brought together, the resulting places created by the master plan and the mix of building types and landscape elements can be illustrated. This detailed understanding of the place is highly effective in communicating the unique qualities of the built environment to the public and to the development team. Prospective buyers, public officials, and other stakeholders can understand the specific qualities that result from the various elements within the plan. The concepts and images in the pattern book must be perceived by all participants to be essential to the marketing success of the program. When they are appreciated in that way, the pattern book is accepted as a useful tool to help achieve success, rather than viewed as an obstacle to implementation.

Pattern book possibility

Built result

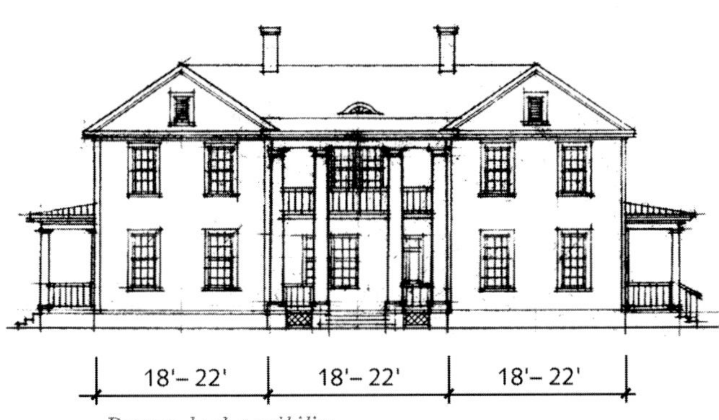

Pattern book possibility

Built result

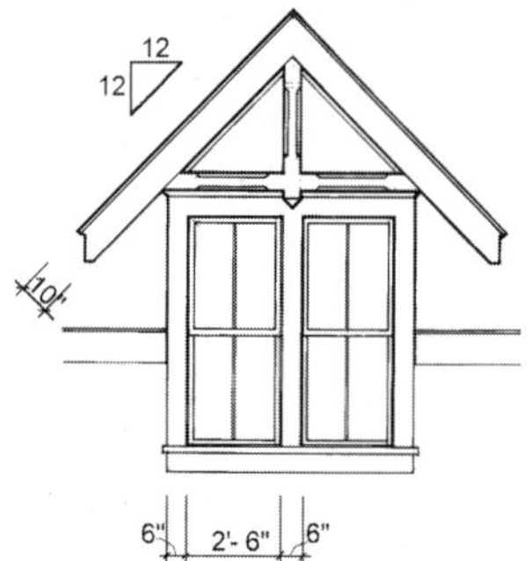

Architectural pattern

Built result

Flexibility. As mentioned in the previous discussion on current practices, flexibility in responding to different market trends and responses is important to most development efforts, particularly when there are significant numbers of units absorbed over a long period of time. In a pattern book process, typically the initial phases are developed in detail. Community patterns are set for a certain area that will typically have a two- to five-year implementation period. Later phases may have the same street and open space patterns as set forth in the master plan, but may have a different mix of building types or unit sizes that responds more to the market or development preferences that emerged during the course of the initial phases. Often, the community patterns are developed as a series of chapters created as the project moves forward. The principal elements of street types, parks, block types, and architectural vocabulary may remain constant, while the flexibility to respond to evolving markets is preserved.

Often, building types are redefined to respond to the market and to create the desired quality of place. Condominium or apartment buildings can take on either the character of large houses when placed in a neighborhood or that of more urban building types when sited downtown. Place-making does not have to be tied to the unit type; rather, the creative process of understanding the appropriate character is one that takes advantage of adapting market forces to place-making. The Urban Assembly Kit process developed by UDA takes the approach of designing blocks and building types within a master plan to create flexibility and diversity. This process identifies specific components of the master plan—street types, blocks, parks, building types—as a kit of parts that can be combined in different ways to create diverse addresses throughout the plan. The kit approach allows building types to be switched or modified without changing the pattern of streets and blocks, and enables the design to respond to changes in the marketplace.

Community pattern

Built result

Pattern book possibility

Built results

The framework of public space is the most essential element in creating memorable neighborhood addresses. The kit approach includes criteria and images for the facades of buildings that define those spaces. For example, the Community Patterns section describes both the quality of space and specific patterns for the placement and massing of buildings along it. It does not, however, specify a single unit or house type. As the market changes, different building types can be placed according to the same patterns, thereby simultaneously responding to changing needs and preserving the character of place.

Standardized Production and Local Architectural Character. The pattern book process re-establishes the concept of using specific local architectural vocabularies to create the image and character defined in the master plan. Both the process of collecting precedents, which involves the builders and developers, and the format of the book itself are intended to establish the value of local traditions. Pattern books illustrate the key elements of a particular architectural vocabulary so that a builder team can incorporate the strategy in the design and production process.

The next step is to work with builders' standard plans to demonstrate ways in which the architectural vocabularies can be most easily applied to their own "products." These transformations are done collaboratively with each builder's design team to establish a positive working relationship and trust among team members. The developer then knows that only certain aspects of its standard products will need to be modified and can evaluate the implications for both costs and production methods.

This approach often enables the team to make a significant change in the conventional builder design/production process. Instead of working in a rather freeform way where the interior relationships are worked out without regard to the compositional and massing elements, the design team begins with the

Community pattern

Built result

Architectural pattern

Built result

basic massing types set forth for specific styles in the pattern book and the corresponding door and window compositions. The evolution of the plan relationships is then worked out in response to one of the basic massing types. The detailing and applied elements—such as bays and porches, trim, and cornices—become a much more manageable series of design and construction problems to solve. Typically, a production builder will want to generate at least two different houses using the same plan form. Many traditional houses consist of simple forms that have other simple forms added to them, i.e., a main body and wings. Basic massing types can often be developed as different architectural vocabularies with changes to eaves, roof pitch, and window and door styles, as well as trim and porch details. And once again, the assembly kit facilitates the process by making it clear which elements are fixed and which are variable. It is the "Mr. Potato Head" approach to design at work. The result is a specifically local and correct traditional architecture accomplished within the rigors of mass-production homebuilding.

Approvals and Politics. The pattern book is central to building consensus among community stakeholders, political leaders, administrative departments, builders, and the development team. Zoning and planning approvals, which are key to so many development efforts, are important factors integrated into the process. The relationship between abstract zoning criteria and the character of a neighborhood street or park is illustrated in three dimensions through models and perspective drawings so that everyone understands the connection between the underlying patterns and the quality of the place. That way, when variances or changes to legislation are required, they are accomplished with a full understanding of the result.

Again, the Urban Assembly Kit approach is useful. By taking the various elements of the design and pulling them apart to be visualized as separate

Architectural pattern

Built result

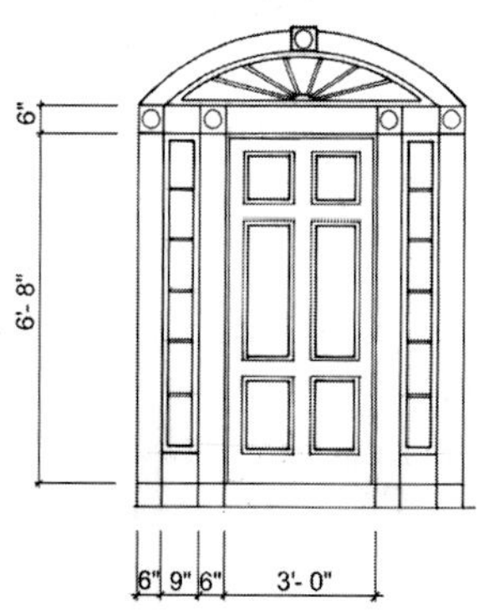

Architectural pattern

Built result

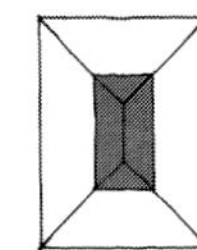

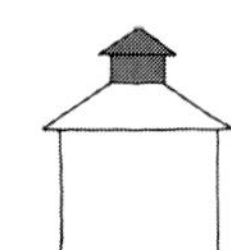

elements, it is possible for each to be evaluated, approved, and funded. For example, the design of streets and public parks, once conceived integrally with the design of buildings, and the resulting quality of place can then be separated and submitted for approvals. This method helps resolve the issues that arise with perceived density as well. Once the proposed building types are illustrated in the context of place-making within the plan, the issues about numbers of units per acre or sizes of lots are less important than the resulting pattern and character of the address. This is very helpful in demonstrating the application of the proposed building types and mix of uses, street widths, and types to public officials and the general public.

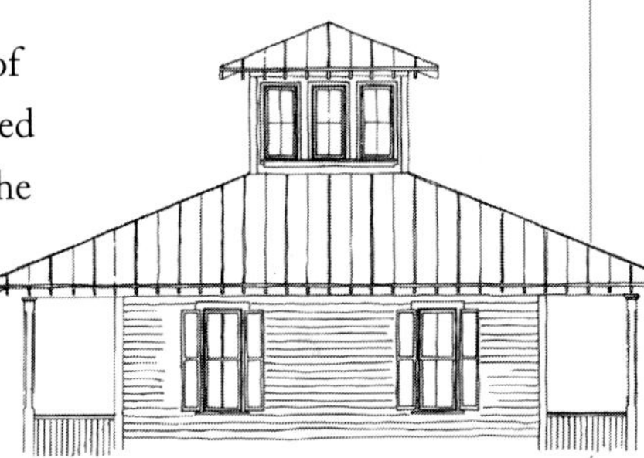

Architectural pattern

Built result

Physical Conditions. A central component in the method of producing pattern books described here is the testing and refinement of the master plan in response to local precedents, detailed landscape design, topographic conditions, architectural vocabularies, and building types and mix. The pattern book chapter relating to the character of the neighborhoods, Community Patterns, is developed in response to the market projections for sizes and types of units, how these units will fit on their sites, and the assembly of these components within the plan. These elements are tested in a 1" = 20' scale model with accurate building types fabricated to reflect the architecture, building types, and sizes.

The model is used to develop specific places within the plan, then recorded and illustrated. The plan is modified as needed to accommodate the testing and to produce the desired spatial quality modeled and illustrated for the pattern book.

Implementation. Pattern books enable builders, architects, and the development, sales, and marketing team to understand the proposed character of the place. Engineering decisions and landscape design decisions about street alignments, planting and pavement options, setbacks, and curb types and radii are seen in the context of place-making instead of as isolated components. This can eliminate months of time from the final engineering and implementation program by having the team together to analyze the elements of the plan using the modeling technique. This process creates the basis for a more detailed understanding of what will be required from builders as well as from the developer to produce the desired results. Each lot and building site can then be detailed as needed with

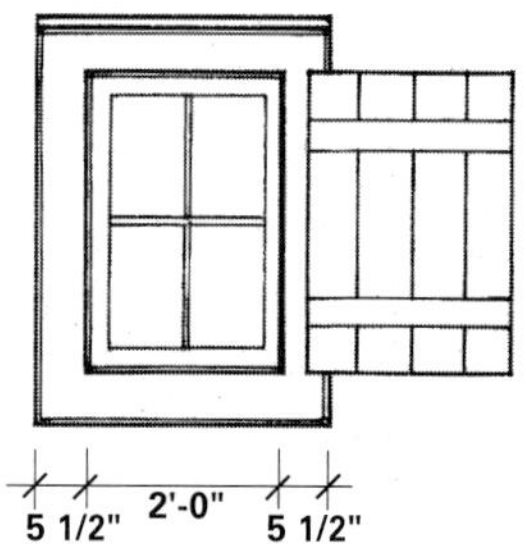

Architectural pattern

Built result

special characteristics or standard conditions as appropriate. Each park or street may have a specific landscape palette that works to create the sense of a unique environment that adds to the appeal of diverse locations within the plan.

EXAMPLES OF THE BUILT RESULTS

The following images in this chapter illustrate the original architectural patterns and details included in a number of UDA Pattern Books and some of the built results from the field. The projects illustrated include:

→ Baxter, a mixed-use village being developed in Fort Mill, South Carolina by the Clear Springs Development Company. Baxter has a mix of production and custom builders.

→ The Ledges, in Huntsville, Alabama, a residential neighborhood built by custom builders and developed by The Ledges of Huntsville, LLC.

→ Park DuValle, in Louisville, Kentucky, a HOPE VI initiative led by the City of Louisville and the Louisville Housing Authority with Community Builders, a private development firm. Park DuValle is a mixed-income, mixed-finance redevelopment effort.

→ WaterColor, a mixed-use community being developed in the Florida panhandle by St. Joe/Arvida with custom builders based on a master plan by Cooper Robertson.

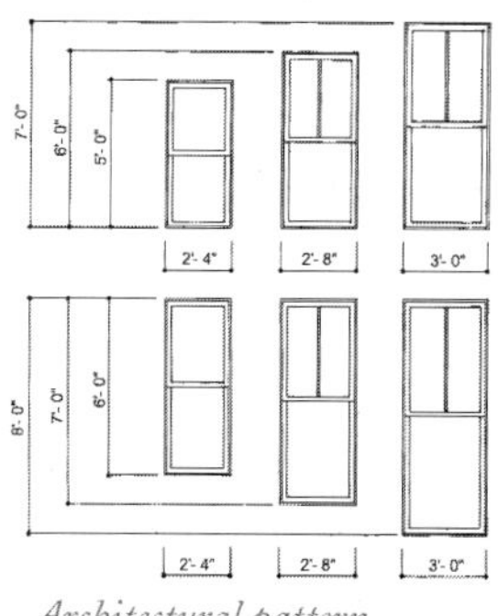

Architectural pattern

Built result

On any given project, the goal of the pattern books is to ensure that the architects and builders engaged to create homes for a particular site will have the tools they need to design houses that will create the quality and character of neighborhoods and public spaces envisioned in the urban design.

Like their nineteenth-century ancestors, each of these modern pattern books was designed to be an effective marketing tool. Because pattern books relate the architectural patterns to the marketing themes for a given development, the book enables prospective homebuyers to see the overall vision for the neighborhood and appreciate how their new home will fit within that context. Rather than being a "code" that tells people what they can't do, pattern books help homebuyers envision what they can do—what their new dream house can look like. As such, pattern books are proactive, providing a collection of details and methods for building houses that spark the imagination and support the design concept for the neighborhood or town.

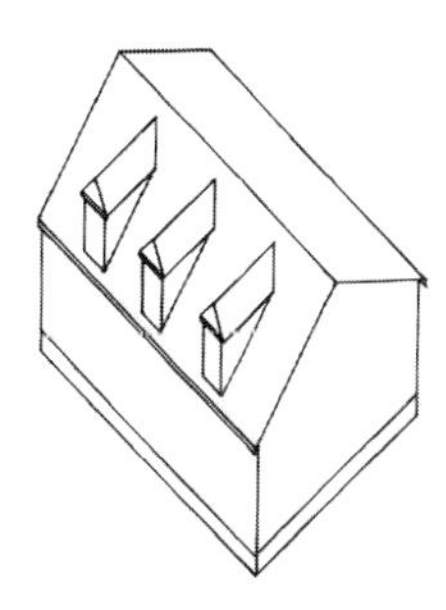

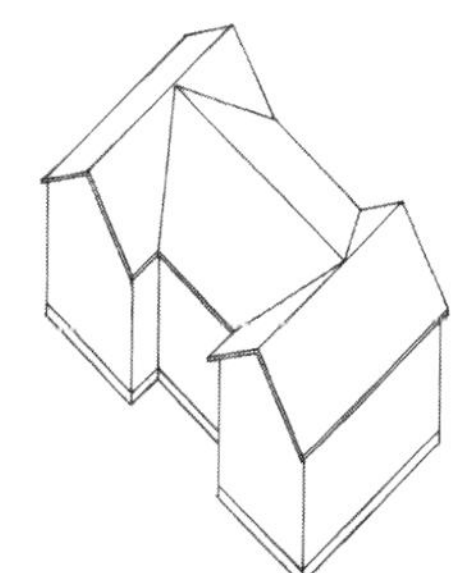

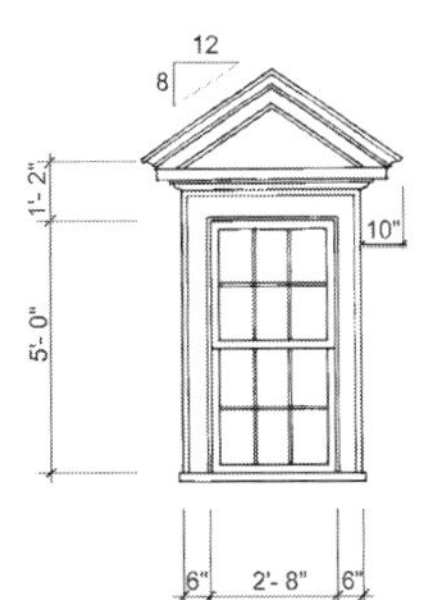

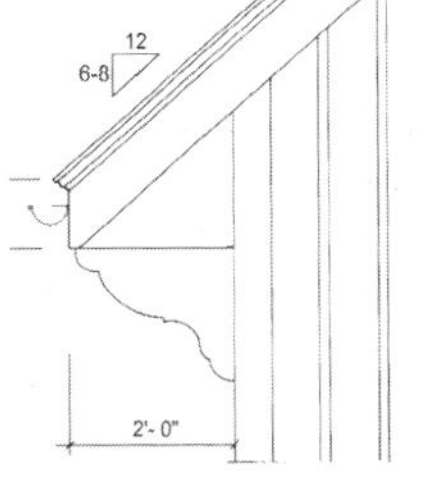

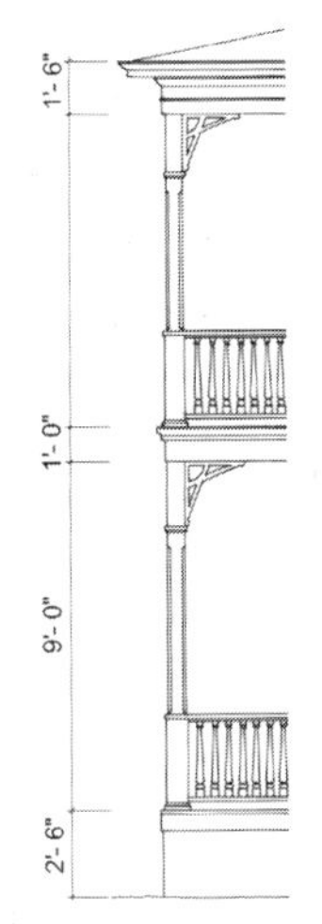

Architectural patterns and built results

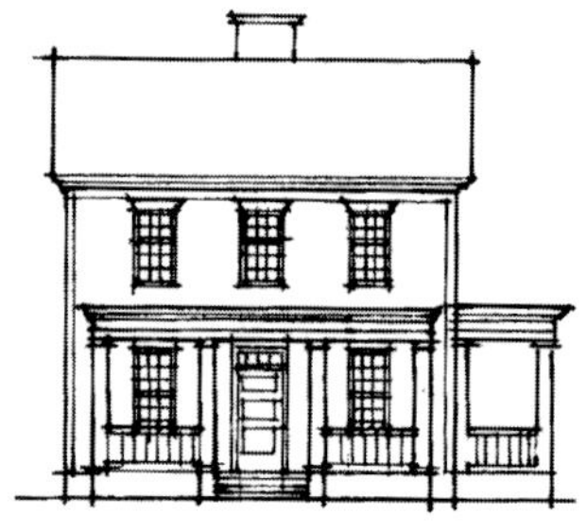

Architectural patterns and built results

CHAPTER

5

The Process for Creating a Pattern Book

The process for creating a pattern book has several phases:

- → **Phase One:** Understanding the Context — Past and Present
- → **Phase Two:** Developing the Palette — Documenting Characteristics
- → **Phase Three:** Defining the Patterns — Community, Architecture, and Landscape
- → **Phase Four:** Production — Producing the Pattern Book

It helps to work closely with a graphic designer who can establish a format for the pattern book and assist the pattern book development team with content, design, production, and printing issues. Additionally, a professional writer can help craft and edit the text. The typical process takes about six months and includes the following steps:

PHASE ONE: UNDERSTANDING THE CONTEXT

Past and Present

The most effective pattern books grow out of an understanding of the regional character of a place. Thus, the design process should begin with researching traditional towns or neighborhoods in the region surrounding the project, including the houses and buildings that create their public spaces. It is important to pay close attention to the precedents that clients and the urban design team have used to develop an image and character for the proposed master plan. Whether you are collaborating on a master plan or implementing one you developed, be sure to document the appropriate regional (and sometimes

Tidewater precedents and details

national) precedents that are appropriate to the vision and character of the site and project.

At the first meeting with the client and the development/design team on site, strive to understand the design, the precedents, the market, the phasing, and the process for building. Spend two to three days with your client documenting area precedents. Have a team equipped with cameras, measuring tapes, and notepads. Explore the area, noting dominant building types, architectural styles, and materials. Pay careful attention to what is fundamental to the overall fabric of the area—its prevailing style(s)—as well as to the more exotic styles that add spice to various neighborhoods. To understand local community patterns, measure and photograph street cross-sections, house setbacks, lot widths and depths, and landscape character. Take care to photograph and document actual house and building types, identifying their architectural style, massing configurations, and key details. Draw the dimensions and qualities of individual neighborhood streets and public spaces in a series of cross-sections that show the relationships between house facades and street space.

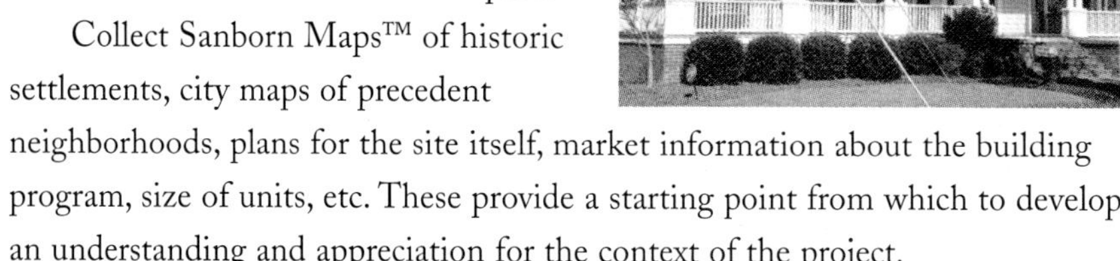

Collect Sanborn Maps™ of historic settlements, city maps of precedent neighborhoods, plans for the site itself, market information about the building program, size of units, etc. These provide a starting point from which to develop an understanding and appreciation for the context of the project.

At the same time, working with standard plans from a number of developers can help you understand the forms with which they work and learn the qualities that they feel are important for successful marketing. In this way, the developer/builder's input is part of the process. This helps re-establish the collaboration between architects and builders that once existed. When this is done, it's time to go back to your office and begin sorting out what the palette might be.

Typical street cross-section

PHASE TWO: DEVELOPING THE PALETTE

Documenting Characteristics

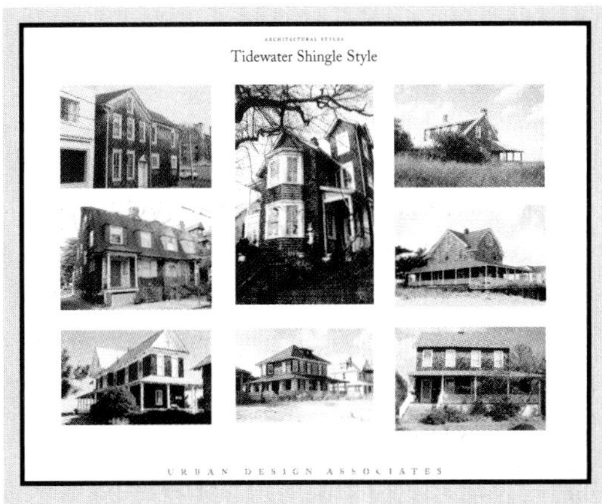

Precedent studies

Phase Two begins with cataloging the documented neighborhoods into categories, either digital or hard-copy prints. To understand the neighborhood character, sort images by place. Prepare figure–ground drawings of the precedent neighborhoods and key them to cross-sections of streets and park spaces with their building setbacks. Then begin to develop block patterns, building typology images based on the development program and the historic character of appropriate buildings.

At this point, you can start developing a first draft of an architectural palette. Sort the full inventory of photographs and the collection of historic documentation about the regional development patterns into general families of styles or vocabularies. This process requires a series of selected images and refinement of the different types, key elements, and characteristics. This includes preparing precedent boards for building types and for architectural styles using photographs and cross-section drawings as well as neighborhood plans collected as community precedents. These can be used in a second working session with the development team to test the palette and its applicability to the proposed community.

For the East Beach Pattern Book, for example, the UDA design team researched the character and form of towns and neighborhoods in a region along the eastern seaboard that served as precedents for East Beach, a new neighborhood along the Chesapeake Bay in Norfolk, Virginia. The team visited ten towns, photographing and documenting houses, building types, and architectural styles in each of them. From an initial inventory of eight potential architectural styles, the inventory was reduced to four styles that were appropriate for East Beach: (shown at right, top to bottom) Tidewater Shingle, Tidewater Colonial Revival, Tidewater Victorian, and Tidewater Arts & Crafts.

As is often the case, the distillation process for East Beach identified key signature elements for each style or vocabulary that seemed to be unique to the region. Often elements found in exemplars were combined and emphasized to produce a coherent series of guidelines and essential qualities that communicated the distinctive character. For East Beach, many of the proposed styles were

Building a Pattern Book House

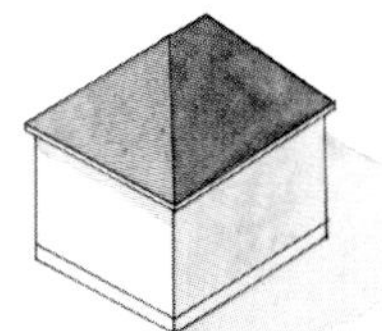

Main Body

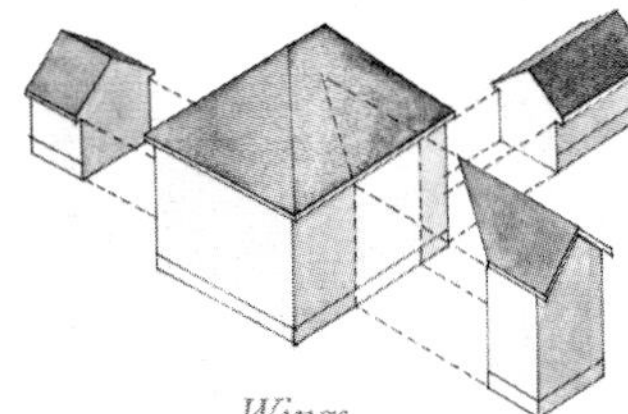

Wings

Door and Window Composition

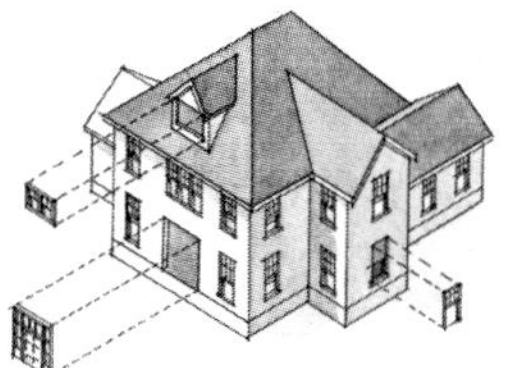

Doors and Windows

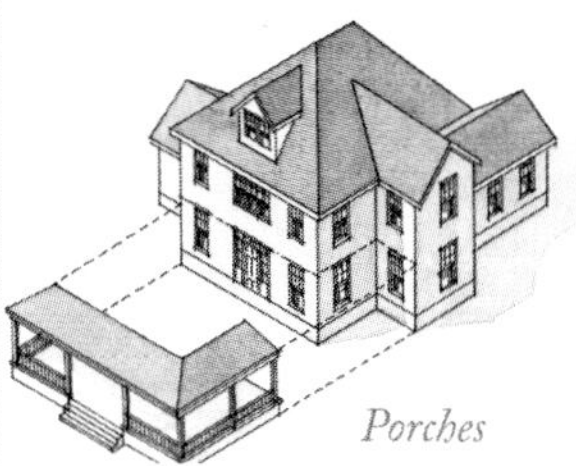

Porches

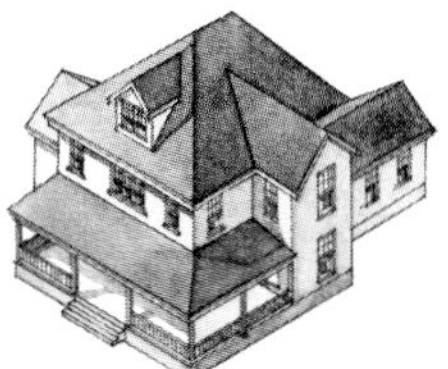

Final House Assembly

extrapolated from regional precedents and edited to emphasize the coastal, maritime nature of the earlier settlements, which had pretty much been replaced in the immediate region of the site. This emphasis was developed as part of the comprehensive strategy to reconnect the site with the origins of a coastal village long replaced by more generic patterns of development and building practices.

When necessary, engaging specialists in particular architectural styles is useful for obtaining detailed design criteria. Once that research is complete, you can begin developing a series of house and building types based on the proposed market types for the new development and applying the key massing types found within each proposed style. Prepare axonometric drawings as input to the model makers. These drawings should include key porch elements and garages that may or may not be integrated into the primary house massing type. In articulating massing for each style, you'll begin to see how the community patterns and the architectural patterns are coming together, and you'll discover where you need to work further to refine your ideas.

Once you reach consensus with the development team on the palette, you can proceed with another round of more focused documentation for architectural style characteristics. Have the team return to the locale to photograph details and architectural elements within each of the designated styles. These include:

- → Front elevations for door and window compositions
- → Cornices and eaves
- → Window and door types and placement
- → Porch types and details
- → Massing and materials

At this point, you're likely to be ready to draft the architectural palette that will be displayed subsequently at the on-site model charrette that takes place during Phase Three of a pattern book project. Have the project team edit the collected data and begin to select models for key details such as cornices, window types, trim elements, porch railings, column types, eaves and entablatures, special windows and doors, materials, chimneys, and other details. This process involves accurate sketches of key details, as well as the dimensional and proportional aspects of the various elements. Drawing standards are established based on agreed-upon pattern book techniques to ensure consistency among all participants in the project, including other contributors such as landscape architects, perspectivists, and so on.

PHASE THREE: DEFINING THE PATTERNS

Community, Architecture, and Landscape

At the start of Phase Three, the team prepares a page-by-page outline of the book. Create a 1" to 20' scale base map of the site plan and 1" to 20' scale wooden models of each prototype house in each category. Set the model up in-house and have the entire team review it together, noting any weaknesses and correcting those that are within your purview to correct before you take the model on site.

The base map and scale models are then taken to the community and used to test the plan during an on-site model charrette. In addition, draw perspective images of key addresses so that during the charrette you can work toward achieving consensus regarding the desired image, lot patterns, and building mix.

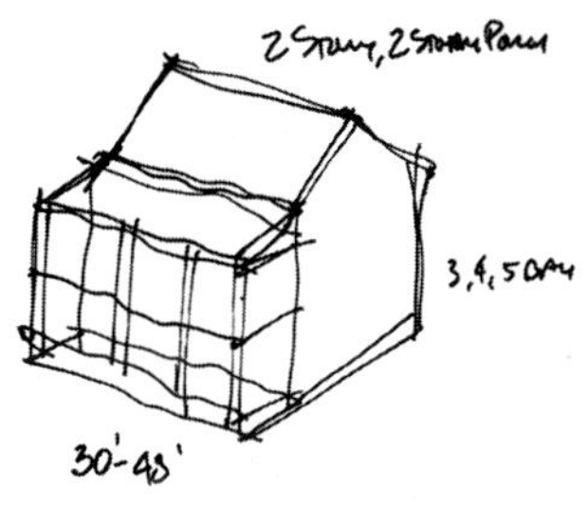

The charrette is extraordinarily revealing to clients because it is usually the first time they will have seen a three-dimensional version of their master plan. Because the model exposes weaknesses in the master plan, refinements are often made during the model charrette. Review the community patterns, architectural patterns, and landscape patterns during the course of the charrette. Assess and adjust setbacks; lotting; specific design criteria by lot type, such as a tower on a corner house; street alignments; landscape details; parks, monuments, open space ideas; and so forth. This is a very labor-intensive process because you should go

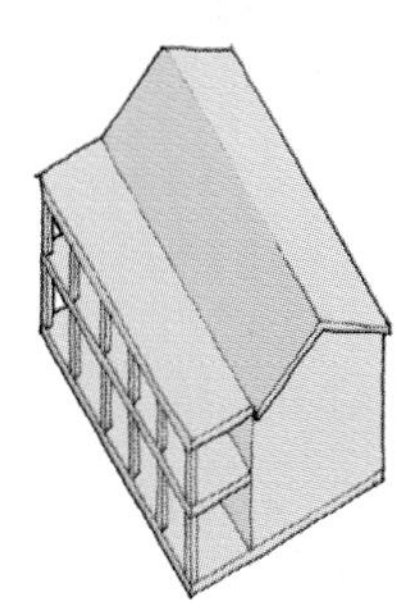

Community pattern from drawn from model

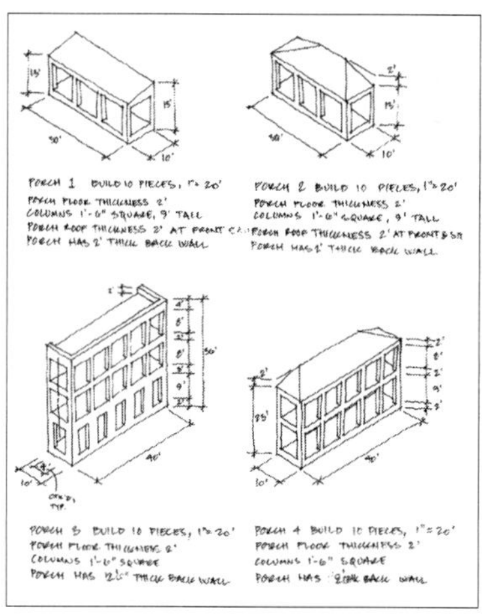

Model specifications

through the plan, lot by lot, documenting any changes made directly on the base map. The documentation becomes the source material for descriptions of each of the specific addresses in the Community Patterns section of the pattern book.

It is also important to involve the full range of consultants on the development team, including the civil engineers, environmental engineers, landscape architects, etc., in this process so that all team members have a full understanding of the form and character of the various addresses. By refining the plan at 1" = 20' in three dimensions, the engineering components can be evaluated and tested, and the new alignments/adjustments to the plan can be confirmed. Also, the refinement and illustration of the plan is part of an inclusive process where everyone understands the rationale and the physical vision of how the various components—architecture, landscape design, civil engineering, marketing, and implementation—come together.

In addition to the core consulting team, it may be useful to bring candidate builders into the process at this point so that they can participate and begin to understand the many different facets of the planning for the new community and see the relationships between the architecture, the building types, and the mix of uses that create the sense of place. This helps everyone begin to understand the bigger vision of the place and provides an opportunity for them to ask questions, understand how the process affects their own operational methods and techniques, and begin to identify opportunities for their companies.

While this step sets the stage for the pattern book production, it also sets the stage for completing the construction documents and final design elements for the master plan. It is important to note that the public or civic spaces within the plan are designed by the development team in concert with the emerging details and design elements that grow out of the original master plan vision. The focus is on specific addresses and details that the pattern book process identifies and illustrates. It is equally important that the pattern book guidelines for building and the master plan design for streets, parks, and open spaces reinforce each other so that the illustrated quality of places within the plan is incorporated into the various components of the plan that are implemented by the master development team.

PHASE FOUR: PRODUCTION

Producing the Pattern Book

Following the model charrette where you will have tested and refined the addresses within the plan, it's time to develop a more detailed storyboard for the entire pattern book, page by page, identifying which drawings will be required and where they will be used. Typically, the project manager does this task in consultation with the principal-in-charge.

At the same time, final decisions should be made about which photographs and drawings will be used. Each pattern book will likely mix freehand drawings and hardline drawings. The type of drawings and the scale for different details should be established now, at the very beginning of the production of the draft pattern book, and communicated to the entire team (including external contributors to the pattern book) before work commences on the drawings.

The overall quality of the finished pattern book will be far better as a result of the team working closely with a graphic designer and print production personnel to set up the document within the firm's prescribed parameters for pattern book layout and drawing and text specification standards.

Now it's time to begin producing the book. Based on the feedback you've received during the charrette, your team can develop a full draft of the pattern book for review by your client.

Once the draft has been developed and reviewed in-house, including a thorough proofreading, it is ready to go to the client for comment. You may choose to send it also to builders and architects to test it out before the final version is produced and distributed.

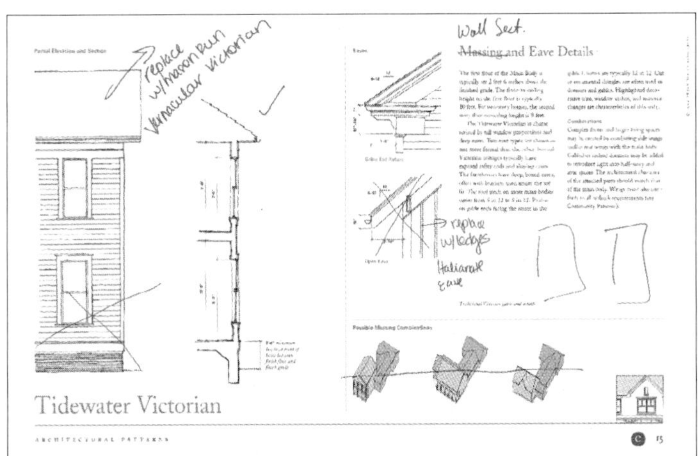

Sample page of a working layout

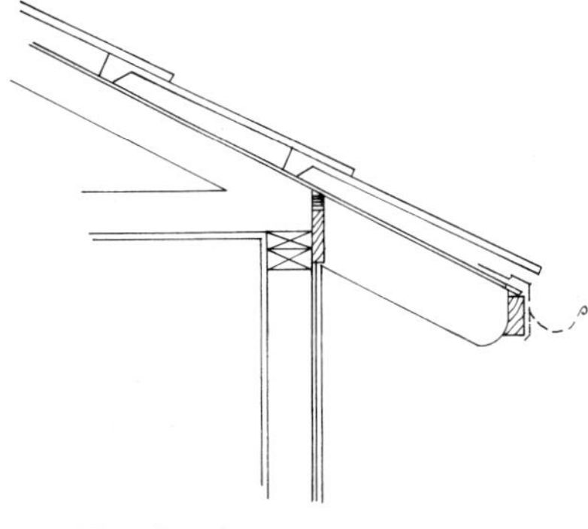

Hard line drawing

PART 2: UDA PATTERN BOOK EXEMPLARS

This section of the book presents a series of pages from pattern books that UDA has produced over 10 years. The organization of Part 2 parallels the recommended three-chapter structure of a pattern book as set forth in Chapter 3. Chapter 6 contains sample Overview section pages; Chapter 7 contains Community Patterns examples; and Chapter 8 contains sample Architectural Patterns pages.

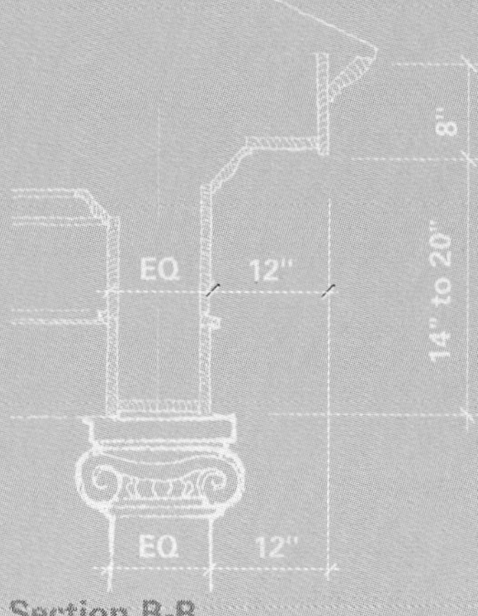

The examples of pattern book pages in chapters 6 through 8 represent an array of project types, including new towns, new neighborhoods in old cities, and developments in rural settings:

- *East Beach* is a development in the Ocean View neighborhood of Norfolk, Virginia. East Beach includes a range of addresses from beach front to bay front with a traditional neighborhood in between. The neighborhood's themes were developed from analysis of Tidewater and Atlantic oceanfront towns, up and down the east coast.
- *WaterColor*, a new town on the Florida Panhandle, creates a series of public spaces that are finely tuned to the natural setting of the town between the ocean and a wooded lake. The patterns create a sequence of addresses from the oceanfront, through the woods, to the lake.
- *Baxter*, a new town in Fort Mill, South Carolina, is designed to continue the local traditions of the South Carolina Upcountry, both in the quality of its public spaces and the architectural style of its houses and buildings.
- *Park DuValle*, a neighborhood in Louisville, Kentucky, has been transformed from a low-income public housing area to a diverse, mixed-income neighborhood. The pattern book was instrumental in successfully revitalizing Louisville's west end by creating a traditional neighborhood with both community and architectural patterns that are easily recognized as being based on the most admired addresses in the city.
- *Eagle Park*, an infill project in Belmont, North Carolina, where the pattern book includes a mix of live/work uses, a business center and housing in a restored mill, new townhouses, and single-family detached houses.
- *Ducker Mountain (Biltmore)*, a development on the Biltmore property near Asheville, North Carolina, where the image of the development is based on a detailed understanding of the architectural traditions of the lodges and resorts built at the close of the nineteenth century.
- *Liberty*, a new town on the shores of Lake Elsinore, California, envisions a series of neighborhoods designed around an extensive parks and open space network on reclaimed land adjacent to the lake. The architecture and character of the neighborhoods was developed from extensive research of both coastal and southern California towns and neighborhoods.

- → *Norfolk, Virginia*, where a pattern book for the entire city was designed to assist all residents in building new houses or remodeling existing ones to enhance the quality of urban space in their neighborhood.
- → *Mason Run*, a new neighborhood in Monroe, Michigan, combines the redevelopment of a brownfield site and the goal of providing market-rate, affordable housing in a way that reinforces the surrounding neighborhoods. The design of the site plan is based on the creation of a series of addresses, many around small neighborhood parks and a linear park designed to accommodate storm water in a natural conveyance system. The design of new infill housing is based on the inherited architecture found throughout this diverse and historic town.
- → *Génitoy Est*, a 2500-unit precinct that will complete the ambitious new town of Bussy St. Georges, east of Paris. The challenge was to establish a marketable image for upper-market single-family houses in a mixed-income new town with a high percentage of multifamily and attached houses. The design created a park way which extends the proposed Génitoy Park to the open agricultural landscape at the edge of town. These will be lined with "villas" that, although they are attached houses, have the image of the large villas most often found on the edges of towns in this region.
- → *East Garrison*, a new community on the former military post, Fort Ord, in Monterey County, California. The plan for the development is based on early church camp settlements found in the region as well as the small agricultural towns that dot the valley. A very dense mix of 1500 units of detached and attached housing is integrated into a mix of artists studios, preserved natural habitat, and regional recreation facilities. The pattern book defines a series of interpreted house styles and vocabularies found in the towns surrounding the site.

CHAPTER

6

Overview Pages

The primary purpose of the pattern books advocated in this volume is to assist designers and developers to build buildings that create beautiful addresses and urban space. To accomplish that, it is essential to provide a full understanding of the goals of the development and its marketing objectives. In that way, all participants—whether homebuilders, architects, traffic engineers, park designers, or public officials—share a common understanding of the overall goals.

Therefore, the first section of each pattern book should provide an overview of the goals of the development and include images that describe the most important qualities that the built development should have when completed. This Overview provides a context within which the various specific patterns can be described.

Each pattern book is different because each should respond to the goals of the specific development for which it is created. Some pattern books are for new towns in which the marketing image of the development is a key factor. In most cases, the natural setting and the traditions of the region in which the development is located will be the basis for the development and architectural themes. For developments within existing cities, local buildings should be examined in detail to provide specific patterns.

The Overview also provides a place to explain to its readers how to use the pattern book.

East Beach / Tidewater precedents: (top) Annapolis, Maryland, (bottom) Edenton, North Carolina

CASE STUDY: EAST BEACH

Norfolk, Virginia

East Beach is a new infill neighborhood being developed as part of an overall plan for the Ocean View area of Norfolk, Virginia. Ocean View is situated on the Chesapeake Bay on a narrow peninsula of land that stretches almost four miles along the coast. The surrounding area was primarily redeveloped during the past fifty years as low-quality apartment housing and inexpensive motels to serve the large military population adjacent to the naval base situated on the north end of Ocean View.

The vision for East Beach portrays the new neighborhood as an authentic coastal Virginia settlement with a mix of uses, housing types, and sizes. The immediate context yields very little to draw on in terms of precedents and examples of community character. The natural environment plays a large role in determining planting materials and setting street and park character. The site will preserve existing stands of mature coastal trees and plant types. Sources for neighborhood character were identified along the eastern seaboard from North Carolina to the Maryland eastern shore as a region of distinct character that shared building types, cultural and physical attributes, and environmental context. The team documented a series of villages and towns as part of the distillation process to link the master plan design with the sense of an authentic place evolving from the inherited patterns in the Tidewater region. The site and development plan identified a series of very particular places: the Chesapeake Bay frontage; the inland neighborhood; the marina frontage along Pretty Lake inlet on the western shore of Ocean View; and the park entrance along Shore Drive as one enters East Beach. The research of precedent places helped establish a distinct character for these unique places within the plan.

In addition to the overall character of the coastal settlements, the precedent research yielded a palette of architectural vocabularies that were found most consistently throughout the region. Norfolk, while having examples of all these vocabularies in the nineteenth-century neighborhoods, had lost much of the older coastal types over the years. The Overview for the pattern book presents a palette of four distinct architectural vocabularies: Tidewater Colonial Revival, Tidewater Shingle, Tidewater Victorian and Tidewater Arts & Crafts. Additionally, the pattern book defines a mixed-use commercial building type. The East Beach Overview also describes the essential components of a typical East Beach house and the relationship it has to its lot. Porches and overhangs are important in this coastal environment and for that reason are emphasized as a component of these houses. There is a section on how to use the pattern book to design a house in relationship to the lot, using one of the Tidewater vocabularies.

East Beach Character

INTRODUCTION

EAST BEACH IS A NEW NEIGHBORHOOD on Norfolk's Chesapeake Bay that draws upon southeastern building types and town planning practices to create a unique waterfront village rooted in the traditions of the region. It is intentionally and distinctly *Tidewater* in feeling, from its overall layout and landscape design to the details of its buildings, pathways and parks.

The plan of East Beach is a response to the historic pattern of neighborhood forms and specific natural features and contrasting qualities of the site. Pedestrian-scaled streets, hidden gardens, shuttered porches, narrow alleys and overhanging roofs have been brought together to provide a sense of familiarity, stimulation and ease.

This sense of wholeness is underscored by the interweaving of natural and built elements, each reinforcing an appreciation of the other. Mature shade trees and parks set the address for many intimate neighborhood streets while uses along Pretty Lake to the south provide a delightful contrast and a destination for residents. Residents and guests can walk from these neighborhoods out to the long stretch of preserved dunes and beaches along the Chesapeake Bay. Interspersed among and giving form to this distinctive local landscape are strongly vernacular Southern buildings of varying size, finish and color – all of which underscore the strong regional character of the place. The two pages that follow are samples of the regional precedents that help form the design of East Beach.

Norfolk, Virginia

Edenton, North Carolina

Edenton, North Carolina

Nantucket Postcard

Neighborhoods

THE CHARACTER AND QUALITY of the historic villages and towns along the East Coast of the United States have been studied carefully as a resource and guide to the planning and building of East Beach. The coastal character is expressed in the architecture which has been modified by local architects and builders over time to respond to the environment in subtle ways. It can be seen in the structure of the town, the street layout and public spaces, and in the landscape elements and materials. Towns and villages along the East Coast have both formal parks and courthouse squares as well as wonderfully landscaped local streets with a surprising variety of character. The green in Edenton, North Carolina is a great example of a public space surrounded by houses from different eras and a courthouse which looks east toward the sea. Many coastal towns have a main street that leads to the water as in Portsmouth, Virginia or Annapolis, Maryland.

Coastal neighborhoods have a variety of house types and architectural vocabularies. The Freemason and Ghent neighborhoods in Norfolk represent two distinct eras of building tradition, both of which are oriented to the water. Ghent is defined by a formal public edge along the inlet fronted by a mix of houses and civic uses such as the museum and opera. Freemason is characterized by narrow, cobblestone streets lined with a variety of attached townhouses and formal Colonial era houses. Many villages such as St. Michaels and Easton on Maryland's Eastern Shore have small cottages on narrow lots that give the village a delicate scale. Annapolis combines attached houses and mixed-use commercial buildings around the harbor to create an active and dynamic sense of place that is unique to the waterfront marina setting.

Historic settlements further north along Cape Cod and Nantucket are characteristic of the refined sense of place that results from the combination of the coastal landscape, neighborhood form and architectural materials.

The neighborhoods of East Beach will draw on these images and forms to establish a unique sense of living on two waterfronts in the Tidewater region.

Coastal Precedents

INTRODUCTION

A 2

Looking across the inlet in Annapolis

Window shopping in Annapolis

Marina and Main Street

MARINA PRECINCTS AND MAIN STREETS in towns and villages along the East Coast of the United States have a marvelous quality. They are diverse and exciting places to be. Annapolis sets the standard for a vibrant, mixed-use district tied to the image of sailing and the water. Buildings line the inlet facing the marina so that the activity around the boats and the water becomes a constant form of public theater that has attracted residents, merchants and visitors for over two centuries. The scale of the buildings is often three to four stories, with living units above shops, restaurants and offices. There are many forms of brick and clapboard buildings in Colonial, Federal and Victorian vocabularies. The ground floor is often a collection of diverse shopfronts that communicate the nature of the goods or services within. In total, the environment is dynamic and picturesque.

Typical Main Street architecture - Easton, Maryland

East Dover Street - Easton, Maryland

Nantucket Postcard

Coastal Precedents

INTRODUCTION

A 3

The Pretty Lake Marinas

Shore Drive Park Address

The Bay Front

East Beach Neighborhoods

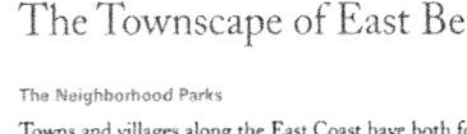

The Townscape of East Beach

The Neighborhood Parks

Towns and villages along the East Coast have both formal parks and courthouse squares as well as wonderfully landscaped local streets with a surprising variety in character. East Beach neighborhoods are designed around a series of organic parks along the streets that take advantage of existing landscape and mature trees. These relaxed neighborhood parks are complemented by more formal civic spaces such as the square on Pleasant Avenue and form a network of open spaces that link to both shorelines.

The Pretty Lake Marinas

Many coastal towns have a main street that leads to the water as in Edenton, North Carolina or Annapolis, Maryland. East Beach plans to have a marina precinct alive with a mix of residential and commercial uses in mixed-use buildings that add contrast and character to the inland residential neighborhoods. This precinct will have a continuous series of public spaces and thoroughfares that provide access to the waterfront for residents, slip owners and visitors.

The Bay Front

The neighborhood streets connect Pretty Lake to the Chesapeake Bay. Residents are never more than two blocks from the water living in East Beach. The Bay front will have a continuous public beach with access points at the ends of streets or through public greens and paths that open up to the spectacular views.

Shore Dive

The principal gateway into East Beach is along Shore Drive. The waterfront village meets Shore Drive across a continuous park. This park address connects the Pretty Lake mixed-use district overlooking the marinas with the stately housing designed in the tradition of an 'Admiral's Row' and a neighborhood shopping precinct at the entrance with Pleasant Avenue.

The Townscape of East Beach

INTRODUCTION  A 4

The Plan of East Beach

The Park Streets

The plan for East Beach features a series of unique addresses, each with a distinctive character and mix of houses. A series of informal park streets extends from the Chesapeake Bay to Pretty Lake. Mature trees that exist on the site become the focal points of the park streets and create a sense of a mature neighborhood. Each street has a different form, character and sequence of park spaces to create a rich inventory of neighborhood streets.

The Bay Front

The northernmost address is the Bay address with a mix of large and small houses flanking parks that look out to the Bay. The views from the ends of the park streets are preserved by the bay front parks that also provide public access to the beach. Houses along the Bay will feature deep porches and will build on the tradition of Tidewater Shingle Style waterfront architecture as the dominant image.

Pleasant Avenue is the heart of the new neighborhood and provides a strong identity for East Beach. A village square, adjacent to Shore Drive, anchors Pleasant Avenue creating a memorable address. The square will be lined with a mix of residential over shops at Shore Drive, manor houses, and a mix of house sizes in the westernmost blocks.

Pretty Lake Avenue is the primary address running east–west along the marina precinct. Near the Shore Drive intersection, the intended character of Pretty Lake is that of 'Little Annapolis' – a reference to the scale, character and mix of uses and buildings found in historic marina districts like Annapolis. This location and mix of uses will create a vibrant place to live, work and shop in East Beach.

The Plan of East Beach

INTRODUCTION  A 5

Tidewater Vernacular Architecture

THE TIDEWATER INFLUENCE in East Beach is clear in its architecture. Houses are simple, low-key and defer to one another and to the indigenous qualities of the landscape. The regional building traditions, which over the years have evolved to take advantage of shade and capture breezes, will be seen in the porches, overhanging eaves, shuttered windows, and screened doors, the traditional use of shingle and clapboard siding, and the picket fenced yards and gardens. The architectural goal is a simple elegance derived from well proportioned massing and fenestration, a rich color palette and details that are derived from the building traditions throughout the region.

Tidewater Vernacular Architecture

INTRODUCTION

6

Tidewater Colonial Style

Tidewater Shingle Style

Tidewater Victorian Style

Tidewater Arts & Crafts Style

The Houses of East Beach

EAST BEACH HOUSES WILL DRAW on four primary architectural languages that have a unique regional and coastal character appropriate to this site along the Chesapeake Bay. These four languages include:

Tidewater Colonial Houses

These houses have roots in the Colonial and Classical traditions of the region. Later Colonial Revival houses derived their forms from more expressive Classical motifs with Ionic and Doric order columns and entablatures on the porches, deeper eaves and cornices, and a wider variety of house massing and window and door elements. The coastal adaptation of Colonial Revival features deep porches and a more relaxed composition of windows and doors.

Tidewater Shingle

Houses designed in this style have roots in the country's New England coastal villages. Houses are generally simple, elegant forms clad in cut shingles. In the South, many of these houses were built with deep porches and windows under shade to protect from the summer sun. Windows, doors, porches and trim can have either simple colonial trim details or Victorian era proportions and details typically painted in white.

Tidewater Victorian

In many towns, these Victorian houses are the principal 'spice' elements in a neighborhood. Steeply pitched gable roofs facing the street, deep porches and decorative trim combine with vertical proportions to create an endearing style. The coastal variations include many full façade, one- and two-story porches as well as deep eaves and ornate porch trim.

Tidewater Arts & Crafts

Arts & Crafts houses were based on the English tradition of summer cottages and became popular in this country in the late nineteenth century. Deep eaves, robust porch elements and shaped rafter tails are signature elements of this language. Windows tend to be wide in proportion and combined to take advantage of the light in living areas. An asymmetric composition and massing is part of this vocabulary.

©2003 URBAN DESIGN ASSOCIATES

East Beach Architecture

INTRODUCTION

A 7

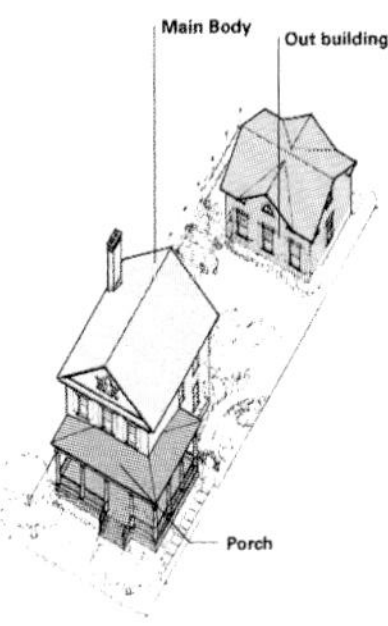

An East Beach House
Simple, dignified massing with large porches and overhanging roofs

Elements of an East Beach House
The Main Body is the largest and most visible element with the most specific design requirements. Side or Rear Wings, Porches, and Out buildings provide a wide range of options for homebuilders.

The East Beach House

EAST BEACH HOUSES WILL CREATE the backdrop for the many distinct addresses within the neighborhood. As in traditional Southern towns, the houses define the character of the public space and reflect the individual composition of the private realm behind the porch or front door.

In these traditional neighborhoods, the front portion of the house is the most public and must be responsive to the character of the neighborhood and the adjacent houses. The landscaping of the front yard, the setbacks from the street, the size and placement of the house on the lot and the front porch are all shared elements that form the public realm.

The houses in East Beach are based on the traditional vernacular architecture of the East Coast, using regional house types with style elements applied. The four house styles for East Beach are defined by the character and shape of the Main Body which can draw from any of the six types shown at left.

Principal Elements

The East Beach House includes these principal elements:

The **Main Body** of the house, which is the principal mass and includes the front door.

Side or Rear Wings, which are one or two stories connected to the Main Body. These optional additions have smaller massing than the Main Body and are set back.

Porches are encouraged on the Main Body of the house. These include full-façade front porches, wraparound porches and side porches. Some architectural styles have inset porches into the Main Body of the house.

Out Buildings are optional structures that include carports, garages, storage, carriage buildings, and work studios. Typically, Out Buildings must be placed behind the Main Body.

Towers, Cupolas and Widow's Walks are optional elements that allow distant views from certain lots.

East Beach Roof Types

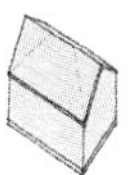

Side Gable House

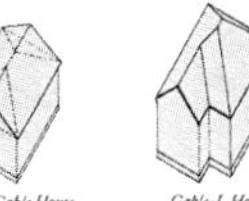

Front Gable House

Gable-L House

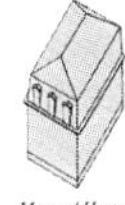

L-Shaped House

Gambrel House

Mansard House

The East Beach House

How To Use This Pattern Book

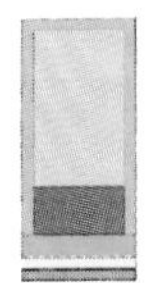

A typical Cottage lot

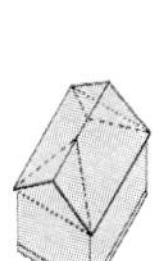

Typical Main Body massing for a Single Cottage

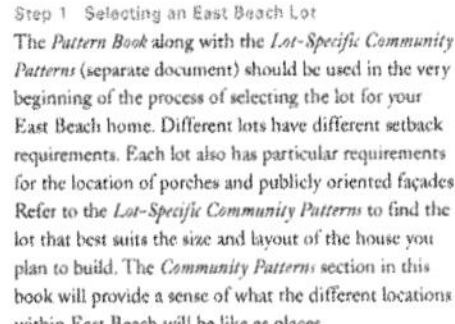

The East Beach Pattern Book will guide the development of neighborhoods and houses to fulfill the original vision described in the master plan. The Pattern Book has three principal sections: *Community Patterns*, which illustrates neighborhood character; *Architectural Patterns*, which establishes the architectural vocabulary and elements that may be used; and *Landscape Patterns*, which sets palettes and standards for the various lot types within the different ecological zones of East Beach.

Step 1 Selecting an East Beach Lot

The *Pattern Book* along with the *Lot-Specific Community Patterns* (separate document) should be used in the very beginning of the process of selecting the lot for your East Beach home. Different lots have different setback requirements. Each lot also has particular requirements for the location of porches and publicly oriented façades. Refer to the *Lot-Specific Community Patterns* to find the lot that best suits the size and layout of the house you plan to build. The *Community Patterns* section in this book will provide a sense of what the different locations within East Beach will be like as places.

Step 2 Shape and Size

The basic mass of the house will determine the general location of the programmatic elements. *The East Beach House* on page A-8 describes the massing pieces: A Main Body, the Porch, Side or Rear Wings, and Out Buildings. The *Lot-Specific Community Patterns* determines specific requirements for setbacks, porch locations and other special conditions related to specific lots. Each Architectural Style section describes the basic massing types found in the precedents for each vocabulary. The layout of rooms should be designed to fit into the massing types found within the particular style you are designing. The roof types are part of this overall massing description.

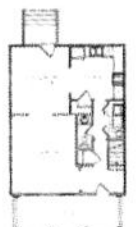

A sample Single Cottage plan

Window and door placement diagram

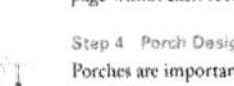

Standard window type and detail

Step 3 Room Layout and Location of Windows and Doors

The window and door spacing is related to both the shape and the style of the house. It is important that all sides of the house have correctly composed façades. Each section on architectural vocabularies describes the basic elements for each of the four design vocabularies that are found in traditional Tidewater architecture – Colonial Revival, Arts & Crafts, Victorian, and Shingle. Typical window and door compositions are illustrated as part of the massing illustrations for each style. Typical window and door proportions, trim details and special window or door elements are illustrated on a separate page within each section.

Step 4 Porch Design

Porches are important to the character of the neighborhoods. The massing of the front porch is specific to each house type and distinct within a particular vocabulary. The location and design elements of porches on the site are described on a designated page for each vocabulary in the *Architectural Patterns* section. Additional porch requirements for particular lots may be described in the *Lot-Specific Community Patterns*.

An example of a traditionally detailed porch

Step 5 Materials and Possibilities

The last page of each style section in the *Architectural Patterns* includes a list of acceptable materials and a collection of elevation possibilities composed using elements described in the Pattern Book.

Step 6 Landscape

East Beach houses will inhabit a remarkable and diverse landscape unique to the coastal location. A range of appropriate landscape elements, such as fences and walls as well as plant types are addressed in a section titled *Landscape Patterns*. Refer to this section for guidance on the layout of outdoor living spaces, and the selection of plants, fence elements and paving materials.

Examples of Possibilities from each of the style vocabularies

How To Use This Pattern Book

Nature, Art and Southern Character

WATERCOLOR IS A NEW COMMUNITY on Florida's fabled Emerald Coast that embraces nature, draws upon traditional Southern building and town planning practices, and fosters support for a variety of local artistic and cultural activities, both as observer and participant. It is intentionally and distinctly Southern in feeling, from its overall layout and landscape design to the details of its buildings, pathways and parks.

The plan of WaterColor is a response to the specific natural features and contrasting qualities of the site and to the best aspects of traditional vernacular place making found in the American South. Pedestrian-scaled streets, scented gardens, shuttered porches, narrow alleys and overhanging roofs, vivid as well as pale colors, deep shades and bright surfaces have been brought together to provide a sense of familiarity, stimulation and ease.

This sense of wholeness is underscored by the interweaving of natural and built elements, each reinforcing an appreciation of the other. Marshes, creeks and wooded frontages around the quietly reflective waters of Western Lake provide a variety of complementary but contrasting settings to the long stretch of dunes and dazzling white beaches. Interspersed among and giving form to this distinctive local landscape are strongly vernacular Southern buildings of varying size, finish and color—all of which underscore the strong regional character of the place.

Nature, Art and Southern Character

INTRODUCTION

I

The Landscape of WaterColor

THE LANDSCAPE OF WATERCOLOR is extraordinary, a rare and magical configuration of plant communities found only along this stretch of the Florida beachfront. Here the dark, leaf-stained freshwater lakes and waterlily sloughs lie next to the aquamarine surf of the Gulf of Mexico. Two beautiful ecosystems, adjacent yet intact, create between them a remarkable, diverse environment, where one encounters many distinct and identifiable plant communities, including dry upland pine stands, freshwater marshes, cypress depressions, beach dunes with coastal scrub, and sawgrass needle-rush wetlands. Numerous endangered or threatened plant and animal species inhabit these overlapping ecosystems. Because it is such an exceptional environment, and is wooded throughout, very special care has been taken to preserve both the existing vegetation and the animal habitat as integral parts of the new community.

Wind, temperature, sea-salt, soil and, most importantly, water, determine what can grow in WaterColor. And because water is central to everything about this environment, it is embraced, protected and celebrated at WaterColor.

The Landscape of WaterColor

INTRODUCTION

A 2

WaterColor's Town Center

A view of The Lawn

Western Lake Drive

An intimate neighborhood street

The Townscape of WaterColor

The Parks

In the best Southern communities, parks tend to be associated with the most prominent public buildings. Thus, at WaterColor, a framework of public spaces—large and small public parks and squares—defines the plan, with the largest of these open spaces, The Lawn, serving as the front door to the community. This broad public space is not only the heart of WaterColor, but provides a long 'water axis' that connects the beach front and main entrance to the highest point of land on the other side of Western Lake. The lawn also creates a visual corridor through the site, from gulf to lake and unites the wooded upland with the white beaches of the Gulf, integrating two quite different places in a direct and powerful way.

The Main Residential Drive

Many Southern towns have a main street, a communal spine, on which the largest and most prominent homes are situated. Western Lake Drive can be seen as a 'land axis'—it links the three residential areas that surround Western Lake, connecting the entrance lawn at the western end of WaterColor to County Road 395 to the east.

The Neighborhoods

WaterColor is comprised of neighborhoods that use a regional palette of landscape and architecture. Houses are oriented toward the street with deep front porches that convey a sense of neighborhood and civic responsibility. Regardless of their size, houses are unpretentious and defer to the landscape and the street. Low fences or hedges provide a subtle delineation between the public zone of the street and the semi-private zone of the front yard and porch. The predominant public image is of shaded porches nestled within a richly textured native landscape.

The Townscape of WaterColor

INTRODUCTION

A 3

The Architecture of WaterColor

THE VERNACULAR 'SOUTHERNNESS' of WaterColor is clear in its architecture. Houses are simple, low-key and defer to one another and to the connective tissue of the landscape. The regional building traditions, which over the years have evolved to take advantage of shade and capture breezes, will be seen in the porches, 'dogtrot' passages, overhanging eaves, shuttered windows, and screened doors, as well as the traditional use of wood siding, metal roofs and exposed rafter tails. The architectural goal is a simple elegance derived from well proportioned massing and fenestration, a rich color palette and details that catch the sun and create shadows—a sinuous profile on a rafter tail, a delicately turned porch post, the subtle sheen of a cast bronze door knob.

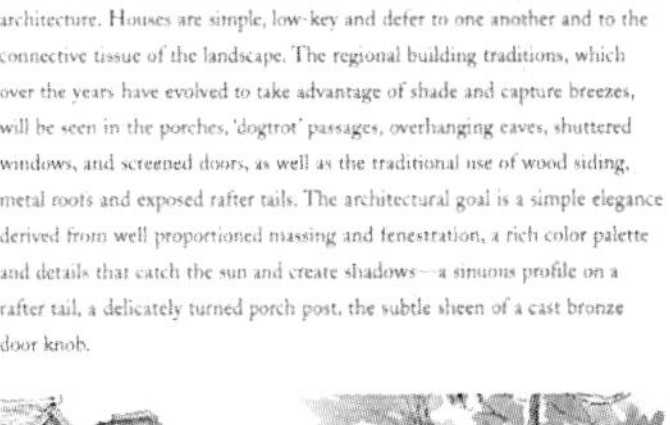

The Architecture of WaterColor

INTRODUCTION

A 4

Town Center – *The heart of WaterColor, with shops, civic buildings, and residences arranged around The Lawn.*

Park Row – *Cottages overlooking Grayton Beach State Park.*

Sunset Ridge – *Tall houses with two-story porches look across the street to the lake, past lakeside houses set back in the trees.*

Rose Garden Mews – *An intimate street that connects the lake to the beach. A garden surrounded by cottages forms its center.*

The Lake District – *A gently curving road, lined with prominent houses, that serves as the main residential street.*

The Cottage District – *An intimate street, defined by the front porches of cottages, connects the lake to the beach.*

Rainbow Row – *A block-long street of colorful cottages.*

Sunrise Ridge – *Larger houses along a common green have views to the lake, while smaller cottages face the tennis courts.*

Beach Lane – *Cottages connected by a pedestrian path have direct access to the beach.*

Addresses within the First Phase

THE CHARACTER OF SOUTHERN TOWNS and neighborhoods that one most admires did not happen by accident. Towns and neighborhoods were laid out according to standard surveying practices. Civic spaces were defined, lots were created and building setbacks established. Houses and buildings filled in the plan over the course of many years, the massing and setbacks following what had come before.

Similar tools are used to describe distinct addresses within the community. While houses employ a consistent architectural language throughout the community, each address will be defined by its particular arrangement of house types, use of landscape elements and building coloration.

Phase I is surrounded by water, spanning from the beach to Western Lake.

One of WaterColor's addresses is Rose Garden Mews, with cottages surrounding a public garden.

Sunrise Ridge is an address characterized by larger houses facing a common green.

Addresses within the First Phase

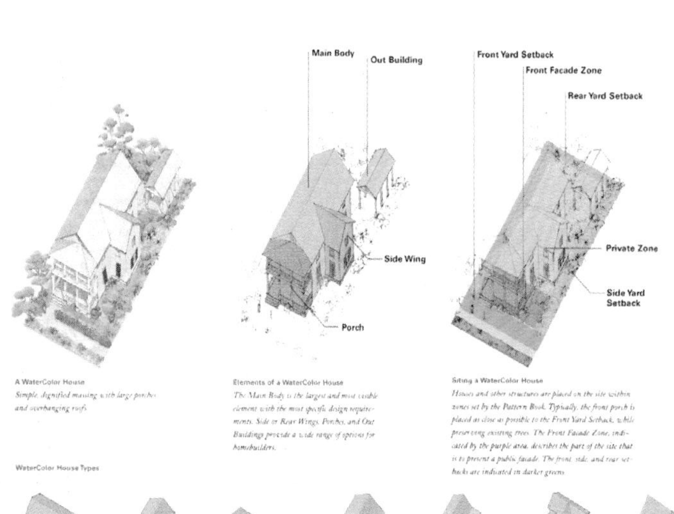

A WaterColor House
Simple, dignified massing with large porches and overhanging roofs.

Elements of a WaterColor House
The Main Body is the largest and most visible element with the most specific design requirements. Side or Rear Wings, Porches, and Out Buildings provide a wide range of options for homebuilders.

Siting a WaterColor House
Houses and other structures are placed on the site within zones set by the Pattern Book. Typically, the front porch is placed as close as possible to the Front Yard Setback, while preserving existing trees. The Front Facade Zone, indicated by the purple area, describes the part of the site that is to present a public facade. The front, side, and rear setbacks are indicated in darker greens.

WaterColor House Types

Center Hall House · *Side Hall House* · *Creole Cottage* · *Single Cottage* · *Sideyard House* · *T-Shaped House* · *Spraddle-Roof Cottage*

The WaterColor House

WATERCOLOR HOUSES WILL CREATE the backdrop for the many distinct addresses within the town. As in traditional Southern towns, the houses define the character of the public space and reflect the individual composition of the private realm behind the porch or front door.

In these traditional neighborhoods, the front portion of the house is the most public and must be responsive to the character of the neighborhood and the adjacent houses. The landscaping of the front yard, the setbacks from the street, the size and placement of the house on the lot and the front porch are all shared elements that form the public realm.

The houses in WaterColor are based on the traditional vernacular architecture of the Florida panhandle, using regional house types. The house types are defined by the character and shape of the Main Body.

Using traditional architectural elements, a type of carport was invented for WaterColor called a 'porch cochère'. This parking structure is to be an extension of a porch; greater detail can be found on the Parking Structures page, C-6.

Principal Elements

The WaterColor House includes these principal elements.

The **Main Body** of the house, which is the principal mass and includes the front door.

Side or Rear Wings, which are one or two stories connected to the Main Body. These optional additions have smaller massing than the Main Body and are set back behind the Front Facade Zone.

Porches are required to be added to the Main Body. These include full-facade front porches, wraparound porches and side porches. Some architectural styles have porches that are inset into the Main Body.

Out Buildings are optional structures that include carports, garages, storage buildings and work studios. Typically, Out Buildings must be placed behind the Front Facade Zone, with the exception of 'porch cochères'—carports that are designed and detailed as a continuation of the front porch.

Towers, Cupolas and Widow's Watches are optional elements that allow distant views from certain lots. See page C-7 for requirements.

The WaterColor House

How to Use this Pattern Book

The WaterColor Pattern Book will guide the development of neighborhoods and houses to fulfill the original vision described in the master plan. The Pattern Book has three sections. *Community Patterns*, which establishes guidelines for placing the house on its lot and defining neighborhood character; *Architectural Patterns*, which establishes the architectural patterns and elements that may be used; and *Landscape Patterns*, which sets palettes and standards for the various lot types and ecological zones.

A typical Cottage lot

Step 1 Selecting a WaterColor Lot

The Pattern Book should be used in the very beginning of the process of selecting the lot for your WaterColor home. Some lots require two-story houses; other lots require one- or one-and-a-half-story houses. Different lots have different setback requirements. Each lot also has particular requirements for the location of porches and publicly oriented facades. Refer to the Community Patterns section to find the lot that best suits the size and layout of the house you plan to build.

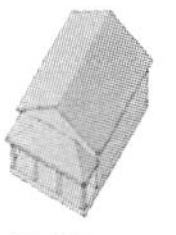

Typical Main Body massing for a Single Cottage

Step 2 Shape and Size

The basic mass of the house will determine the general location of the programmatic elements. The Pattern Book addresses the appearance of the house and the yard from the street or public space. The portions of the house that are not visible from the public areas can accommodate a broader range of elements and may not follow the compositional patterns found on the public faces of the house.

A sample Single Cottage plan

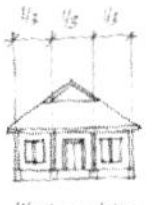

Window and door placement diagram

The WaterColor House on page A-6 describes the massing pieces: Main Body, Porch, Side or Rear Wing, and Out Building. House Types are determined by the shape of the Main Body and the location of porches. The Address pages specify which house types are permitted on each lot, and whether the house is to be one story or two.

Depending on the house type, the Main Body will be a simple rectangular volume oriented perpendicular to the street or parallel to the street, or a simple T-shape, of one or two stories. The Main Body massing for each house type is described on page C-2.

Step 3 Room Layout and Location of Windows and Doors

The window and door spacing is related to both the shape and the width of the house. It is important that all sides of the house that are exposed to public view have correctly composed facades. On facades with porches, window and door spacing should relate to porch bays. Some possible facade compositions are shown on page C-2. Window and door designs are described on page C-5.

Step 4 Porch Design

Porches are important to the character of the neighborhoods. The massing of the front porch is specific to each house type. The location of porches on the site is described in the Building Placement pages (B-3 through B-8). Additional porch requirements for particular lots are described in the Address pages (B-9 through B-14). Porches must be at least 8 feet deep. Page C-4 specifies column types, handrail and eave profiles to use in designing the porches.

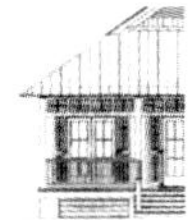

An example of a traditionally detailed porch

Typical window head/sill profile

Step 5 Materials

As outlined in Section C-7, Materials and Possibilities, WaterColor houses will use materials traditional to this region: wood board-and-batten or drop siding, metal roofs and brick or stucco pier foundations.

Step 6 Details

Before lumber yards and building products manufacturers took over the design of windows, doors and columns, builders distinguished themselves by inventing signature eaves, handrails and columns. The Architectural Patterns section (Section C) documents some of the typical details found in the best traditional examples of Southern vernacular architecture.

Step 7 Color

Each address within WaterColor will be described by a particular color palette. Refer to Section E when selecting the colors for your house.

Step 8 Landscape

WaterColor houses will inhabit the landscape with the least possible disruption to the site. Refer to Section D for guidance on the layout of outdoor living spaces, and the selection of plants and paving materials.

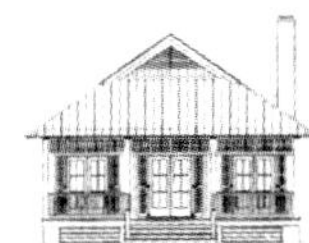

How to Use this Pattern Book

INTRODUCTION A 7

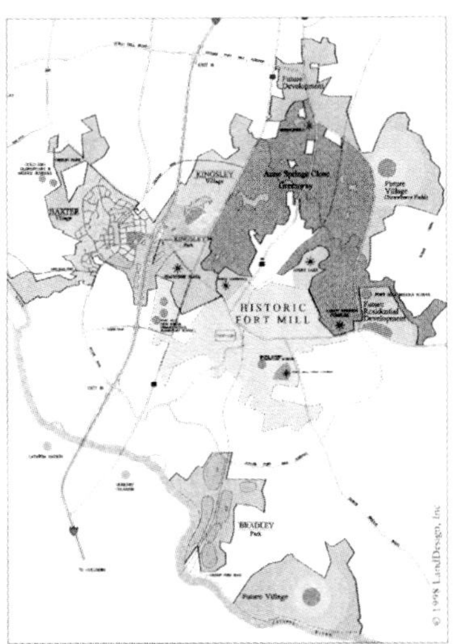

The Clear Springs Plan

Clear Springs and Upcountry Traditions

Clear Springs, a 6,200-acre development being undertaken by the Close family in Fort Mill, South Carolina, embodies a remarkable concept for how to make a great place to live, work, raise children, enjoy the natural environment and participate in building community. Clear Springs is a constellation of villages, each with its own distinctive character surrounding historic Fort Mill. Neighborhoods are designed in the tradition of South Carolina's Upcountry towns complete with tree-lined streets, neighborhood parks, and gracious houses with architectural details such as deep front porches that face the street and convey a sense of neighborhood and civic place.

The Close family has dedicated over 2,300 acres surrounding Fort Mill as an environmental preserve and greenway. The Anne Springs Close Greenway features over 26 miles of hiking and horseback riding trails, three lakes, the Leroy Springs recreation complex and restored historic buildings. Each of the villages is linked to this greenway system and residents will enjoy access to this resource as well as to a wide variety of civic parks and recreational amenities.

The design of each village is based on the treasured legacy of Upcountry towns and villages that developed during the nineteenth century and into the early part of the twentieth century. These places are admired today for their character and quality of architecture. The pattern of development is an expression of the democratic ideals of civic responsibility and participation. Each neighborhood, street, park, or public space is designed using the regional palette of landscape and architecture ensuring a continuation of the best traditions and sense of identity that is unmistakably Upcountry.

The Anne Springs Close Greenway provides over 2300 acres of preserved natural environment for the residents of Fort Mill and the Clear Springs villages.

Clear Springs neighborhoods and houses will be designed in the tradition of the region. The Springs' Founders House in Fort Mill is an example of Victorian-era architecture found throughout the region.

Clear Springs Development Company, LLC reserves the right to change the plans, landscaping, and buildings at their sole discretion and without notice. All renderings, plans and maps are artists' conceptions and are not intended to be an exact depiction of the landscaping or buildings.

Urban Design Associates

Introduction · Baxter A-1 Clear Springs & Upcountry Traditions

Neighborhood streets have a variety of lot widths, setbacks, and landscape

Neighborhood parks bring nature into the heart of the community

Upcountry Towns and Villages

Neighborhoods

One of the most consistent features of the Upcountry neighborhoods is the pattern of houses on a street. Big houses are mixed with small houses; large lots will often interrupt a pattern of narrow lots; setbacks may vary from one side of the street to the other. There are seldom fences between properties and yards often flow into one another. The predominant image is of white, frame houses sitting within a deep green band of trees and lawn. Streets are generally narrow with parking on both sides. Sidewalks with trees and lawns of varying widths give neighborhoods an informal and diverse character. This loose fit, predicated on pockets of generous lawns within relatively modest lot sizes, creates the charm of the small town.

Main Streets

Main Streets have a unique character in the Upcountry region. The pattern is a series of two- and sometimes three-story buildings, often attached but many times separated slightly to form the fabric of the downtown. The vocabulary is a mix of Victorian-era detailing and proportion as well as a more classical building vocabulary. The most successful towns have centers. The square in Chester is an example of a Main Street that ends at the top of the hill in an enclosed space.

Civic Buildings

Davidson, Chester and York all have excellent examples of civic architecture. In towns of this scale, there are a series of small-scale buildings such as the town hall, the courthouse, the library and institutional buildings such as the masonic halls and churches. These are typically set within the normal pattern of lots and blocks with the exception of a city hall or courthouse sometimes fronting on a public space as in Chester. These buildings are scaled down to reflect the character of the single-family house with the exception of the churches, which historically use spires and bell towers to mark the skyline and provide orientation. The dominant style for the public buildings is Classical.

Parks and Open Space

In the smaller towns, the parks tend to be associated with either the most prominent public buildings as formal squares or front lawns or as community parks with recreation facilities within them. There is also the rural edge – the distinct line between farmland, woodlands and the compact pattern of houses within a village. Charlotte's best neighborhoods, developed in the 1920's, have a sophisticated sequence of neighborhood parks. This pattern can be integrated into the small town to create another layer of richness in the Upcountry character.

Gracious lawns are a hallmark for corner lots

A classic Upcountry retail street

Urban Design Associates

Introduction · Baxter A-2 Upcountry Towns & Villages

Upcountry Classical-Adams/Federal Style

Upcountry Classical Revival Style

Upcountry Colonial Revival

Upcountry Colonial Revival with full front porch

Upcountry Victorian

Upcountry Victorian Carpenter Gothic Cottage

Upcountry Architecture

The historic settlements in the Upcountry region of North and South Carolina were largely built by Irish, Scotch and German settlers migrating from Pennsylvania through the Shenandoah Valley. These settlements were frontier settlements in the late 1700s and early 1800s. They were agricultural in nature and grew into villages and towns serving regional populations. Today the predominant architectural styles found in Upcountry towns include Classical, with houses designed in the Adams/Federal and Greek Revival styles. These include a mix of red brick and clapboard exteriors with slate and metal roofs. During the early 1900s, Colonial Revival houses were built that provided a vocabulary complementary to the Classical-era styles. Colonial Revival is also a pervasive style. The Victorian-era houses typically add 'spice' to the neighborhood fabric. They were largely built as either large Italianate mansions in urban locations, or Carpenter Gothic cottages in village neighborhoods or farmhouses.

This palette of architectural styles has limitless variations and creates a varied and interesting neighborhood character. This mix is the distinguishing character of neighborhoods in towns like York and Chester and sets them apart from later developments where the vocabulary is more eclectic and discordant. Houses built in Clear Springs will be designed in one of the three architectural vocabularies. While there are pre-approved house plans available to builders and homeowners, this *Pattern Book* ™ contains a series of design guidelines for architects to use when designing individual houses in one of the three styles. Since the *Pattern Book*™ is not an exhaustive or definitive manual for each style, architects and designers may also draw on historic Upcountry precedents as a basis for new house designs.

Houses in Baxter will be designed in one of the three Upcountry styles.

Urban Design Associates

Introduction · Baxter A-3 Architectural Precedents

Phase II Plan of Baxter

The Pattern Book and Baxter Neighborhoods

The character of the towns and neighborhoods that we most admire did not happen by chance. The builders used pattern books from England and the colonies to design and build sophisticated houses and civic buildings without the aid of architects in areas remote from the urban centers. Towns and neighborhoods were laid out according to set surveying practices. Civic spaces were defined, lots were created and building setbacks established. Houses and buildings filled in the original plan over many years. While the architectural styles changed over the years, the common elements of streets and public open space as well as setbacks and massing followed what had come before.

The building of Baxter, the first village to be built in the Clear Springs Plan, will also be guided by similar tools. Each village in Baxter will have its own distinct character formed by the rolling topography, woodlands, the design of the streets and neighborhood parks and the placement and design of houses on the lots. This *Pattern Book* describes guidelines for placing houses on lots and for designing and building houses in the Upcountry traditions. The *Community Patterns* section of the book describes the range of setbacks for houses and ancillary structures, the width of streets, parks and location of sidewalks and tree lawns for each neighborhood. The common areas of streets and parks are carefully designed as shared gardens and civic spaces – some formal and some informal. Indigenous plants, traditional landscape treatments found in historic Upcountry towns and neighborhoods serve as models for the design of Baxter. The *Architectural Patterns* section describes the range of architectural styles found in Upcountry neighborhoods with key elements defined for architects and builders.

The following pages provide a sense of what the finished neighborhood character might look like using both the architectural styles described in the Architectural Patterns section and the setbacks and landscape elements described in the Community Patterns section.

View along Colonel Springs Way

Baxter Square

Typical Baxter Neighborhood Street

Houses look out across neighborhood parks

Urban Design Associates

Introduction · Baxter A-4 The Site

A. The **Main Body** of the house placed within a defined **Front Facade Zone**.

B. Smaller one-story or one- and one-half-story. **Wings** are added to the sides and the back. The faces of the house visible from the street create the **Front Facade**.

C. **Front Porches** add an essential element of character and contribute to the intimate scale of the neighborhood.

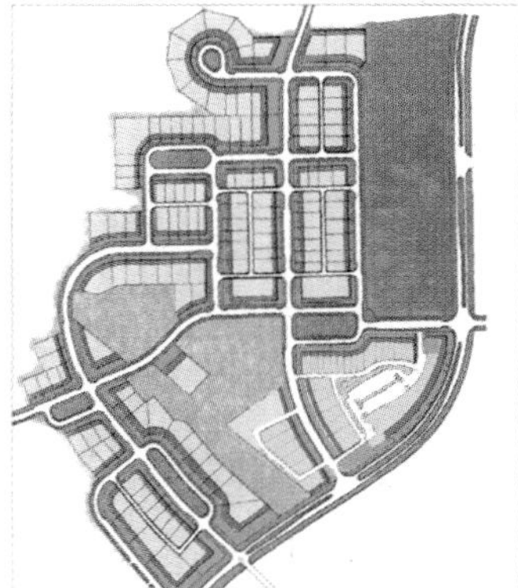

Partial plan of Baxter

Baxter Houses

Building a house in Baxter is part of building a neighborhood. Each house contributes to the overall character and quality of a particular street or park address. Houses will relate to one another within a given address – setbacks will be consistent, landscaping will be coordinated, and massing will be similar.

The public face of the house, the **Front Facade**, is an important element that defines the neighborhood character. Porches, windows and doors, correct proportions and traditional 'detailing' are important facets that contribute to the character of Baxter. The private areas of the back yard will be screened from public view by the siting of the house and the relationship between houses.

The **Front Facade** of each house includes all the sides of a house that are visible from the street or public spaces.

Traditional houses have three major elements that make up the house form including:

- The **Main Body,** the largest mass of the house, contains the front door and has a composed window and door pattern.
- **Side wings** are one- or one-and-one-half stories set back from the front facade of the Main Body. These are typically smaller in scale than the Main Body.
- **Porches** can include full-facade, one- and two-story structures, side porches on Colonial Revival houses, or smaller porticos surrounding the front door.

Corner houses have public facades on two streets. These houses use side wings and fences to create a formal composition on the side street, and to screen the private world of the backyard from public view. Each lot has zones within which the Front Facade of the house can be placed. These are described on page B-2.

Urban Design Associates

Introduction · Baxter A-5 Baxter Houses

Aerial perspective of the new Park DuValle neighborhood

The New Park DuValle Neighborhood

THE NEW NEIGHBORHOOD IS DESIGNED to become a mixed-income, mixed-use, compact and pedestrian-friendly community with many activities of daily life within walking distance.

The Park DuValle neighborhood is comprised of several distinct Addresses, each with its own character. It includes a wide range of housing types and a sequence of public open spaces and parks linking the parts of the neighborhood together and to nearby amenities such as Algonquin Park. A new front door for the entire neighborhood will be established with single-family houses along Algonquin Parkway and at several points along Wilson Avenue.

Within the neighborhood are a series of institutions and community facilities, including a Village Green. Lined with buildings that combine public uses, retail shops, and residential uses, the Village Green will become a new heart for the neighborhood. The system of parks and parkways provide appropriate settings for civic and religious buildings that will be reinforced as anchors for the community.

The Park DuValle Plan

INTRODUCTION

 1

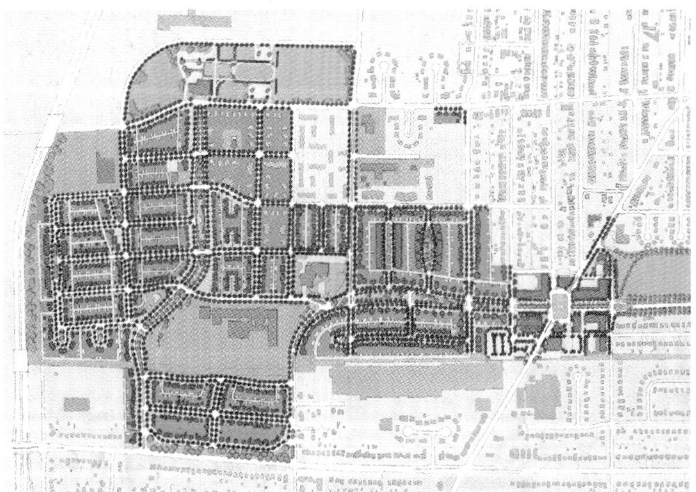

The Plan as Framework

THE PLAN PROVIDES AN INTERCONNECTED network of streets and public open space. They define blocks within which a wide variety of individual lot types are accommodated. Placement of alleys and front yard set-backs are fixed but can accommodate lots of varying widths. The plan will be developed over time, in market conditions which may change. Therefore, this flexible system of blocks and lots provides the capacity to respond to changing conditions.

In order to create marketable, mixed-income development, however, it is essential to create a series of attractive Addresses, each with its own character. The plan calls for developing these Addresses by following Louisville's great traditions of neighborhood development. The architecture of individual houses and the image of Park DuValle's public spaces should recall the best and most stable of Louisville's neighborhoods.

Research in preparing this Pattern Book identified a number of well known residential 'Addresses' in Louisville which have served as models for the guidelines. Three of them are illustrated on the following pages: Old Louisville, Olmsted's Parkway designs, and the Cherokee Triangle area.

The Plan as Framework

INTRODUCTION

 2

© LOJIC - Louisville/Jefferson Information Corporation

St. James Court

The Grid City - Old Louisville

Louisville's finest early neighborhoods were built upon a grid of streets and small urban parks and squares. The plan of Park DuValle reflects this pattern of streets in a pedestrian-oriented loose grid as well as parkways which wind through the site. Parks, courts, and public gathering spaces play a large role in the formation of the community.

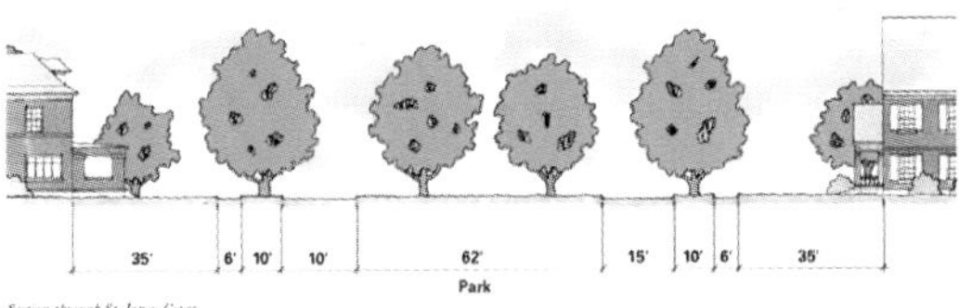

Section through St. James Court

Community Precedents

INTRODUCTION

3

Cherokee Parkway © LOJIC Louisville/Jefferson Information Corporation

Algonquin Parkway

Olmsted's Parkways

The Parkways form an armature of green space linking Louisville's three major Olmsted-designed parks. New park drives in Park DuValle, which reflect this traditional linkage of green spaces, wind through the site and link to Algonquin Parkway as well as Algonqion Park.

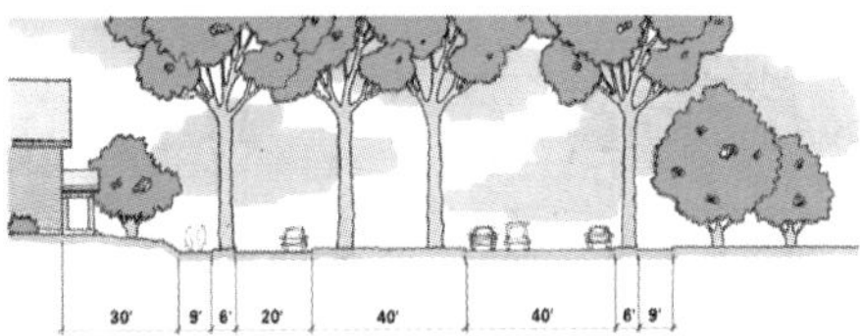

Section through Cherokee Parkway

Community Precedents

INTRODUCTION

4

Cherokee Triangle, Crescent Hill and The Highlands

The establishment of Cherokee, Iroquois, and Shawnee Parks at the turn of the century provided an attractive setting for the development of new 'suburban' neighborhoods. Built largely between 1890 and 1930, Cherokee Triangle, Crescent Hill, and The Highlands neighborhoods most clearly express the influence of Olmsted's design principles in their picturesque street layout and expanses of community green space.

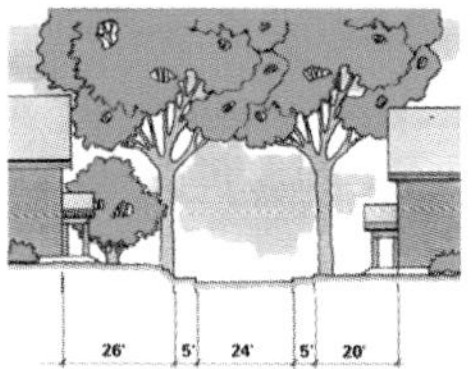

Section through Edgeland Avenue

Community Precedents

The Park DuValle Pattern Book

THE PARK DUVALLE PATTERN BOOK contains design guidelines for both community character and architectural character. The section that follows, *Community Patterns*, describes the general principles for placing houses on their lots, as well as specific requirements for lots within the different neighborhoods. These principles include setbacks, overall massing of the house, locations for fences and ancillary structures and access from driveways or alleys. The third section, *Architectural Patterns*, describes the palette of architectural styles for Park DuValle and includes guidelines for designing the parts of the house that are visible from a street or public space.

Once a lot has been selected, the guidelines for placing the house on the lot can be determined by turning to the page that describes the general conditions for the lot type and then the page that describes specifics for the particular neighborhood in which the lot is located. For instance, if you decided to build a Victorian house on a Cottage Lot along Von Spiegel Avenue, you would first turn to B-2 to determine the general setbacks and width of the house. You would then turn to B-12 to determine what specific variations or additional site guidelines might apply.

The specific house design would then be developed or selected in accordance with the Victorian style described in the Architectural Patterns section.

The Park DuValle Pattern Book

View of renovated mill building and new live/work buildings from the proposed town square park

Colonial Revival house in Belmont

European Romantic house in Charlotte

New residential street lined with Colonial Revival, European Romantic and Craftsman houses

Eagle Park

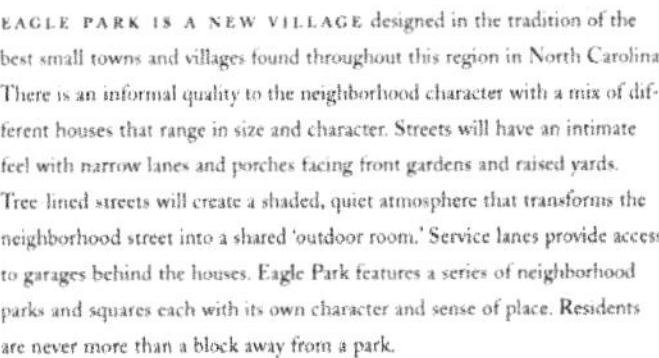

EAGLE PARK IS A NEW VILLAGE designed in the tradition of the best small towns and villages found throughout this region in North Carolina. There is an informal quality to the neighborhood character with a mix of different houses that range in size and character. Streets will have an intimate feel with narrow lanes and porches facing front gardens and raised yards. Tree lined streets will create a shaded, quiet atmosphere that transforms the neighborhood street into a shared 'outdoor room.' Service lanes provide access to garages behind the houses. Eagle Park features a series of neighborhood parks and squares each with its own character and sense of place. Residents are never more than a block away from a park.

The western neighborhoods in the village will feature a restored mill with loft housing and offices as part of the village center which will have live-work houses and attached houses combining to create an active precinct to complement the neighborhoods. The Pattern Book serves as a guide to the creation of special neighborhoods and houses designed and built to make an authentic place to live, work and play.

Overview of Eagle Park

INTRODUCTION  1

Arts & Crafts House

Informal Garden in Pinehurst

Belmont Front Yards

North Carolina Villages

THE CHARACTER OF villages and small towns in the region provides precedent for the neighborhood design in Eagle Park. The design of the new district surrounding the historic mill in Eagle Park draws on the commercial centers of villages like Belmont, Davidson, Southern Pines and Pinehurst. These precedents combine the small-scale character and softness of a residential street address with commercial uses. The treatment of sidewalks, landscape and building character will be reflected in the design for Eagle Park. The neighborhoods of Eagle Park are also drawn from these small towns and villages as well as historic neighborhoods in Charlotte. The character found in Belmont neighborhoods features front lawns raised above the street, often with a sloped lawn or short wall. Small-scale wrought iron fences and hedges reinforce the pattern of a seperation between the public street and the front yard. Many neighborhoods have cottages combined with larger houses on corners and along the Main Street. Many houses were influenced by the romantic periods of domestic architecture available from Pattern Books and catalogs early in the twentieth century.

Pinehurst

Historic Sanborn map of Belmont, South Carolina

Regional Precedents

INTRODUCTION  2

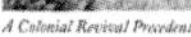

A Colonial Revival Precedent

A Craftsman Precedent

A European Romantic Precedent

A Mixed-Use Building Precedent in Belmont

The Architecture of Eagle Park

EAGLE PARK HOUSES WILL DRAW on three primary architectural languages that have a unique regional character appropriate to the context of Belmont. These three languages include:

Belmont Colonial Revival Houses

These houses have roots in the Colonial and Classical traditions of the region. Later Colonial Revival houses derived their forms from more expressive Classical motifs with Ionic and Doric order columns and entablatures on the porches, deeper eaves and cornices and a wider variety of house massing and window and door elements. The regional adaptation of Colonial Revival features deep porches and a more relaxed composition of windows and doors.

Belmont Craftsman Houses

Arts & Crafts houses were based on the English tradition of summer cottages and became popular in this country in the late nineteenth century. Deep eaves, robust porch elements and shaped rafter tails are signature elements of this language. Windows tend to be wide in proportion and combined to take advantage of the light in living areas. An asymmetric composition and massing is part of this vocabulary.

Belmont European Romantic

Houses designed in this style have roots in the country's interpretation of English and European cottages around the first quarter of the twentieth century. Houses designed in this Romantic style became hallmark images for aspiring homeowners. In the South, many of these houses were built as interpretations of the original stone or stucco precedents found in England using cut shingles and clapboard siding. There are many brick examples with half-timbered accents as well. Houses are generally simple, elegant forms with asymmetric compositions and a variety or casement or double-hung windows.

A Belmont Colonial Revival House

A Belmont Craftsman House

A Belmont European Romantic House

Eagle Park Architecture

INTRODUCTION

A 3

The overall Master Plan for North Ducker showing neighborhoods surrounding the golf course

North Ducker will have a system of streets and open space similar to these found in Biltmore Forest

NORTH DUCKER LIES just south of the historic Biltmore House and is part of the original 125,000 acre estate established by George Washington Vanderbilt. Ducker Mountain is a geographic landmark in the region encircled by the French Broad River and rising over 600 feet above the river valley. From the mountain, you experience spectacular views over the rugged and beautiful western North Carolina landscape including the estate grounds, Pisgah National Forest and the town of Biltmore Forest. North Ducker continues the heritage of carefully designed landscapes and villages commissioned by the Vanderbilt family.

North Ducker encompasses 1,000 acres of woodland forest crossed with streams. It has been designed to accommodate houses tucked into the forest overlooking an 18-hole championship golf course. Mountain lanes wind up the slopes along the original trails that followed courses of minimal disturbance to the mountain terrain. Houses on North Ducker will be designed to take advantage of the views while preserving the woodland character of the mountain site. The mountain lanes, private drives and garden landscaping are all elements that build on the inherited patterns of the Olmsted-inspired plan for Biltmore Forest.

Biltmore Arts & Crafts

Biltmore Colonial Revival

Biltmore European Romantic

North Ducker

INTRODUCTION

A 1

Parks in Biltmore Forest

View of the terrace overlooking the golf course at the Biltmore Country Club

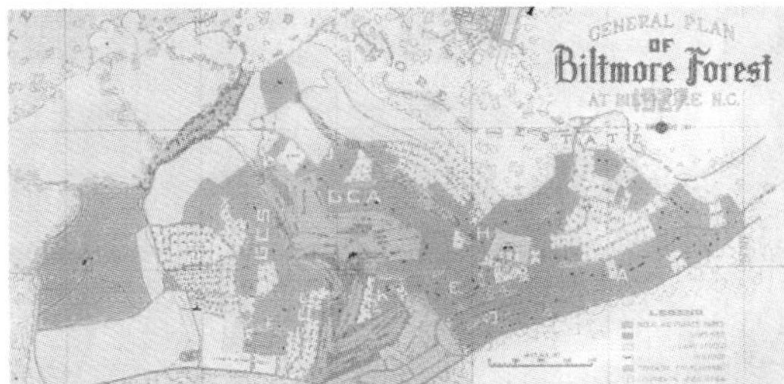

Plan of Biltmore Forest

Houses in Biltmore Forest

IN THE EARLY 1900S, the Vanderbilt family commissioned the design of a village adjacent to the estate, Biltmore Forest, which eventually became incorporated as a town. The Frederick Law Olmsted-inspired plan for the village was based on concepts of creating organic, garden neighborhoods nestled into the woodland foothills flanking the estate. A compact and elegant golf course, designed by Donald Ross, creates a social and recreational center to the plan. A village center was constructed adjacent to the Forest neighborhoods to provide neighborhood shopping and services. Biltmore Forest provides a strong precedent for the design of North Ducker. Narrow, winding streets are positioned to take advantage of the natural topography and define a network of private parks and woodland vistas that create a strong sense of place reflective of the western North Carolina landscape.

The use of low stone walls as edging for many of the streets complements the Arts & Crafts light fixtures and the dense forest landscape flanking the streets. Houses are set deeply into their lots with significant stands of trees in a natural woodland setting acting as a green veil between the private realm of the house and the more public realm of the street or park. The best house sites have a series of landscaped terraces to create a proper setting for the house on a steeply sloped lot. Driveways are narrow and unobtrusive. Often they are flanked by stone walls to provide a gracious arrival and minimal disturbance to the forest landscape. The golf course creates open vistas for residents across the rolling hills. These elements form the basis for the North Ducker addresses.

The Biltmore Forest Legacy

INTRODUCTION  2

The Legacy of the Biltmore Estate

THE RUGGED BEAUTY OF ASHEVILLE'S rural terrain instantly bewitched George Washington Vanderbilt, and it is here that he decided to fulfill his long time vision of an estate that was to be modeled after the immense land baronies he had seen in Europe. They not only served as cherished retreats, but also as self-supporting businesses. It had been suggested to Vanderbilt that commercial forestry represented a good investment, so he purchased 125, 000 acres, and began taking the first steps toward his goal.

Vanderbilt called the estate 'Biltmore' – from Bildt, the Dutch town where his ancestors originated, and 'more', an old English word for open, rolling land. He then commissioned architect Richard Morris Hunt and landscape architect Frederick Law Olmsted to collaborate on the estate's design. For Olmsted, this was his last private commission, and it is said to have been a summation of all his ideas.

Vanderbilt later hired Gifford Pinchot to help restore the forests of Biltmore at Olmsted's request. Pinchot was one of the first people in the United States to start thinking about forest health and management. His work helped to establish the Biltmore School of Forestry and what is now part of Pisgah National Forest as the Cradle of Forestry in America.

Much of Biltmore's lush woodland, the first forest in the country to be managed scientifically, was planted in the 1890s; today it covers some 4,500 acres. Although some improvements have been made to improve the quality of soil, water and wildlife habitats, the harvesting of mature trees, as well as selective thinning and pruning, remain a vital part of current forest management practices.

Portrait of Olmsted painted by John Singer Sargent on display in the Biltmore House

Landscape Precedents of Biltmore Estate

INTRODUCTION  3

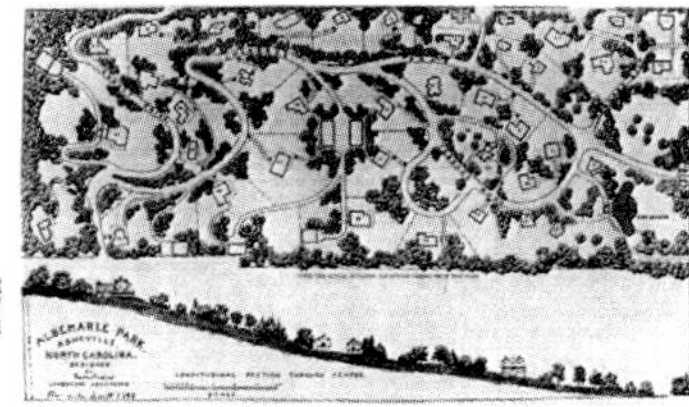

The Neighborhoods of Asheville

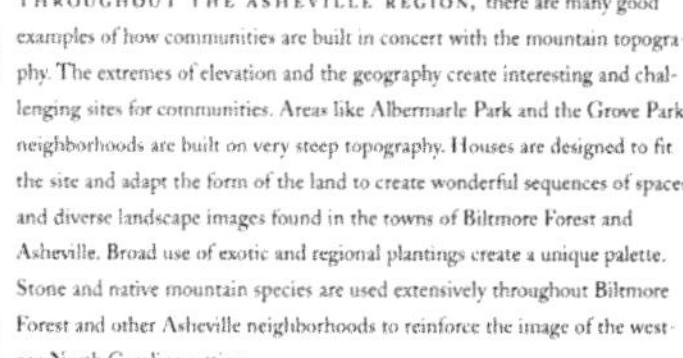

THROUGHOUT THE ASHEVILLE REGION, there are many good examples of how communities are built in concert with the mountain topography. The extremes of elevation and the geography create interesting and challenging sites for communities. Areas like Albermarle Park and the Grove Park neighborhoods are built on very steep topography. Houses are designed to fit the site and adapt the form of the land to create wonderful sequences of spaces and diverse landscape images found in the towns of Biltmore Forest and Asheville. Broad use of exotic and regional plantings create a unique palette. Stone and native mountain species are used extensively throughout Biltmore Forest and other Asheville neighborhoods to reinforce the image of the western North Carolina setting.

Landscape Precedents

INTRODUCTION  4

Mountain Shingle Precedent

Classical Precedent

Mountain Shingle Precedent

European Romantic Styles with English and French Elements

English Romantic Precedent

Colonial Revival Precedent

Mountain Architecture

ONCE THE RAILROAD CONNECTED Asheville to the east coast network of cities and towns in 1880, the region became a magnet for people drawn to the mountain environment for recreation, health benefits and respite from the urban centers in the northeast. With this growth and influx of people, the character of the region's architecture was transformed rapidly in the late 1800's with such projects as the Biltmore Estate. The prominent architect Richard Morris Hunt drew on strong European influences for his work and brought with him an interest in the current architectural influences developing in the northeastern region of the country. Architects such as Richard Sharp Smith, who came to Asheville to supervise the Biltmore construction, contributed many civic and residential buildings to the Asheville region. A unique architectural language that used combinations of different styles and architectural elements developed within the region. This trend is evident in many of the area's historic neighborhoods such as Montford and Albemarle Park. Significant variations of the Arts & Crafts style and the European Romantic styles are found throughout Asheville and the surrounding region. Classical and Colonial Revival houses provide a balance to the more exotic architectural varieties.

North Ducker houses will be designed using the incredible variety found in four dominant style families: the Biltmore Mountain Shingle style, the Biltmore Colonial Revival, the Biltmore English Romantic style, and the Biltmore Classical style. The Pattern Book establishes design patterns for houses in each of the style categories. Each style builds on the unique elements found in the inherited stock of fine quality houses in the region.

Architectural Elevation of Asheville House from Richard Sharp Smith

Architectural Precedents

INTRODUCTION  5

The Southern Appalachians

THE SOUTHERN APPALACHIANS contain extraordinarily diverse landscapes and rare forest types. As a result of this inherent natural beauty, the Southern Appalachians have been attracting visitors for centuries. In the late 19th century, Asheville was a popular health resort due to the availability of mineral springs, a pleasant climate and fresh air. Today, as the Blue Ridge Parkway and the Great Smoky Mountain National Park traverse the Appalachians, millions of visitors are exposed to the unique natural wonders of the region.

The Appalachian Mountains rise to a maximum of 6,684 feet, and diminish to less than 1,000 feet. As a result of this elevation change, highly varied climates and environments appear. The lower regions are filled with mixed deciduous woods throughout the dry zones and pines in the shaded, moist environments. As the topography rises, oak/hickory forests flank the slopes of the mountains leading to boreal and transitional forests on the ridge tops, representing almost every eastern forest type in America.

At the heart of the Southern Appalachians, these habitats converge seamlessly allowing visitors to hike from a deciduous forest in the lowlands to a spruce-fir forest on the ridge-tops to habitats at or near sea level, all within a matter of hours. However, these forest types are not easily distinguishable due to the moderating effects of the humidity level.

Resulting from the variation and multitude of forest types, the southern end of the Blue Ridge Mountains in North Carolina possesses the greatest number of tree species in North America. Many of the species proliferate in record proportions and are among some of the oldest in North America.

Landscape Character of North Ducker

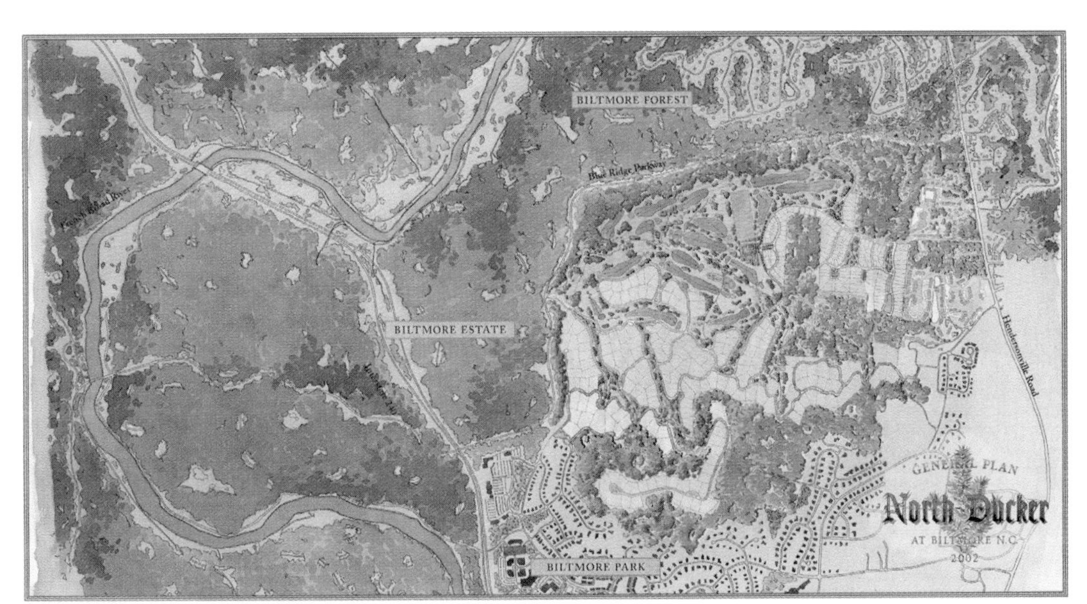

The Site in Context

The Golf Course

The Village (Hamlet, Terrace & Neighborhood Lots)

Woodland Preserve Lots

Mountain Estate Lots

North Ducker Master Plan

A Site in Nature

THE DESIGN OF THE NORTH DUCKER community is both a response to the inherited quality and character of the neighborhoods in Biltmore Forest and the diverse and unique landscape of the mountain. The design principles include the celebration of the natural stream corridors as preserved parks linking the mountainside neighborhoods to the golf course which traverses the lowland areas of the site adjacent to the Blue Ridge Parkway. Access to the mountain slopes is patterned after the pre-existing trails and roadways to minimize disturbance to the woodland environment. Houses sited on the slopes are carefully planned to preserve the woodlands and minimize grading and clearing. These neighborhoods are organic in form and follow the natural contours of the slope. Specific design criteria for how houses are designed to meet these slopes are detailed in the Landscape Patterns section of this Pattern Book. A village centered on the Clubhouse and recreational amenities offered by the Club builds on the traditional pattern found in the original Biltmore Village. Houses front tree-lined, neighborhood streets and parks on land that is suited for a village environment. A range of lot and house sizes are provided in the North Ducker Plan as well as a diverse selection of neighborhoods, each with its own character and charm.

Architectural styles are also carefully chosen for North Ducker. These styles are found throughout the Asheville region and are particularly appropriate in Biltmore Forest and the North Ducker environment.

North Ducker Master Plan

INTRODUCTION A 8

Looking across Lake Elsinore toward the Santa Ana Mountains

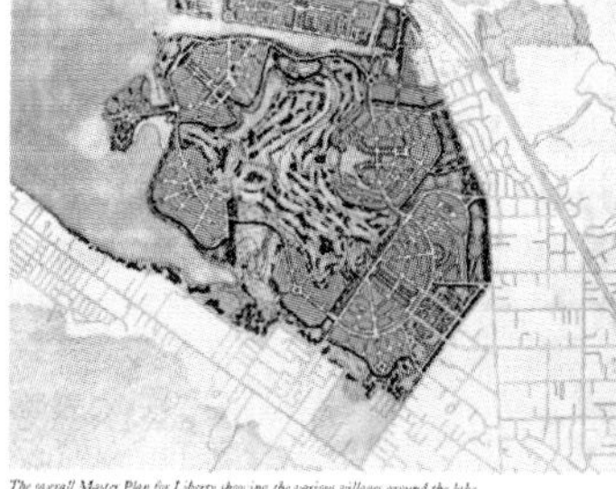

The overall Master Plan for Liberty showing the various villages around the lake

LIBERTY IS A 2900-ACRE DEVELOPMENT nestled in the Santa Ana mountains along the eastern shoreline of Lake Elsinore. This 3300-acre natural lake creates a spectacular setting for a series of villages that will look out over the lake toward the mountains. The villages are designed on principles of historic town planning and environmental conservation. Each village is linked by a 1300-acre preserved open space that will have wildlife preservation areas, protected marshlands, and recreation amenities such as golf courses and walking trails.

The design of each village is based on the tradition of Southern California resort communities and towns. Lake Elsinore was a prominent resort area in the early 1900s and attracted visitors to the remarkable views and lake setting. The Liberty Master Plan, developed by Cooper, Robertson & Partners, builds on the character and unique quality of Inland Empire towns, coastal villages, and historic Southern California resorts. The neighborhoods, streets, boulevards, parks, and town center are connected to the shoreline, the parklands, and the view of the mountains so that every resident enjoys the natural amenities. Each village is designed with a village center containing shops, restaurants, offices, and apartments within walking distance of the surrounding residential neighborhoods.

Liberty neighborhoods will have a character similar to historic settlements such as this neighborhood in Orange.

Classic

Craftsman

Victorian

European Country

Monterey Ranch

Spanish Revival

Liberty and California Traditions

INTRODUCTION A I

Streets in the Belmont Shores neighborhood take you to the water. The blend of streetscapes and private gardens creates a distinctly nautical character.

Colonial Revival houses sit comfortably next to Craftsman, Spanish Revival, and European houses with front yards that are gardens for the street.

The downtown historic district in Riverside contains a variety of mixed-use buildings designed in the Spanish Revival and Mission styles.

Plan of historic neighborhood in Riverside

Inland Empire and Coastal Towns

SOUTHERN CALIFORNIA HAS A VARIETY of town forms that serve as precedents for Liberty. One distinct form can be found in coastal towns, such as Coronado Island, Corona Del Mar, Venice, Long Beach, and Balboa Island, where narrow streets and nautical imagery lead you to the water's edge. These are quirky and delightful environments with a variety of different house types, streetscapes, and water edge conditions. Some neighborhoods are built on canal frontages, such as Venice and Naples. Others, such as Balboa, create another kind of public address along the beach. A common trait is the informal nature of the street and yard configuration and the sense of being near the water, even on inland streets.

Another form is represented by valley settlements such as Riverside, Orange, and Pasadena — established neighborhoods with a distinct character quite different from that of the Coastal precedents. Many of these places developed at the turn of the century and have marvelous neighborhoods from the early 1900s. Places like Madison Heights in Pasadena and Floral Park in Orange are models of beautiful public spaces and street designs that create settings for a varied collection of houses of all different sizes, styles, and prices. The common element is the unique mix of landscape, garden, and regional adaptation of architecture. Some neighborhoods were built at one time as compositions in a single style, like the bungalow courts in Craftsman or European Romantic styles. Others are a diverse collection of styles built over many years.

Southern California Towns and Neighborhoods

INTRODUCTION

A 2

American Classic houses include California adaptations of Colonial Revival.

California Craftsman houses from the early 1900s

Victorian-era farmhouses and cottages

European Country styles use English and French elements.

Spanish Revival houses from the early twentieth century

Monterey Ranch houses are a unique California house type.

Southern California Architecture

THE TRADITIONAL ARCHITECTURE of Southern California neighborhoods includes a wide variety of styles built in different time periods and with unique regional adaptations to styles as well as housing types. While Spanish Revival architecture has been a signature style for so many recent developments throughout the region, the traditional towns and villages have a much more varied palette of styles and materials. Craftsman houses, Victorian farmhouses, Monterey Ranch houses, and varieties of American Colonial houses dominated many early town and neighborhood patterns in the Inland Empire as well as the coastal towns. This variety and diversity has been lost in recent years and will be re-established in Liberty. Six styles have been adapted and re-introduced. These include: Liberty Classic, which draws on Colonial Revival precedents; Liberty Craftsman; Liberty Victorian; Liberty European Country; Liberty Monterey Ranch; and Liberty Spanish Revival.

Architectural Precedents

INTRODUCTION

A 3

Perspective views of various street and park addresses in the North Neighborhood

Master Plan for Village One in Liberty

The Pattern Book and Liberty Neighborhoods

THE CHARACTER OF SOUTHERN CALIFORNIA towns and neighborhoods that we most admire did not happen by accident. Early in this century, builders used Pattern Books from England and later plan books and magazine publications such as *Pencil Points* and *The Bungalow* as resources to design and build sophisticated houses in emerging Southern California settlements. Towns and neighborhoods were laid out according to standard surveying practices. Civic spaces were defined, lots were created, and building set-backs established. Houses and buildings filled in the original plan over the course of many years. While the architectural styles changed according to current fashion, the massing and set-backs followed what had come before.

The building of Liberty will be guided by similar tools. *The Liberty Pattern Book* is a device developed for guiding the development of neighborhoods and houses consistent with the original vision described in the Master Plan. The Pattern Book has three sections: *Community Patterns*, which establishes guidelines for placing the house on its lot and defining neighborhood character; *Architectural Patterns*, which establishes architectural precedents for six particular styles in Liberty; and *Landscape Patterns*, which sets palettes and standards for the various lot types and house styles.

The Site

INTRODUCTION

 4

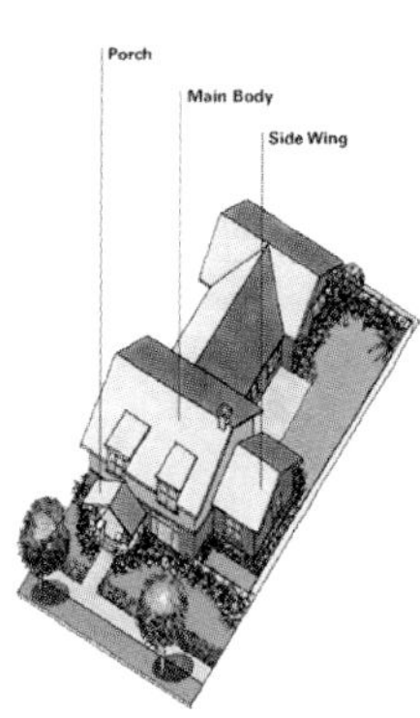

The first diagram illustrates the finished house on its lot with the Main Body screening the private world of the backyard from the most public areas.

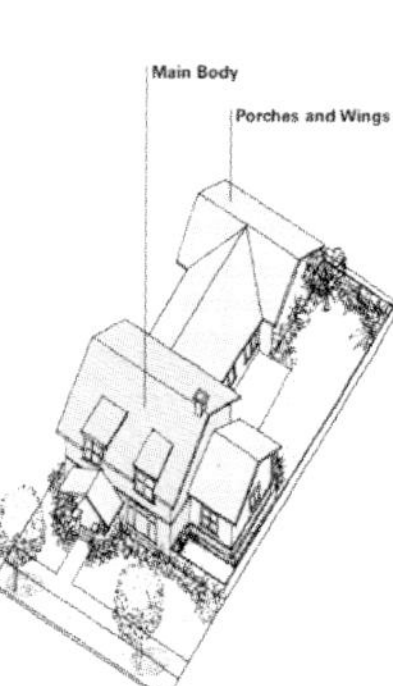

The second diagram highlights the principal components of the house including the Main Body, Side and Rear Wings, and Porches.

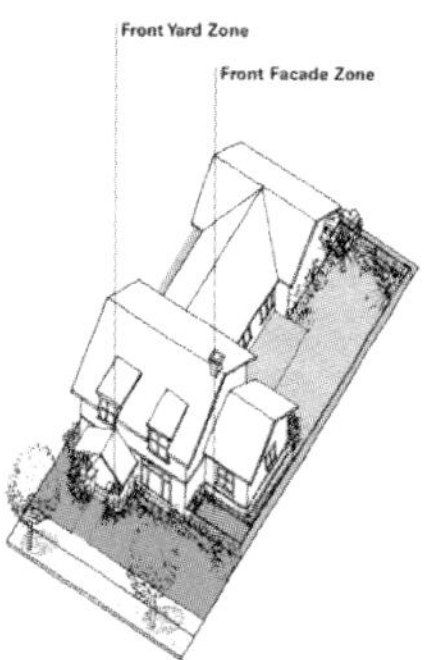

The third diagram illustrates the house placement guidelines in Liberty. The Front Facade Zone indicates a general area within which the Main Body can be placed. Liberty Houses will have varied set-backs depending on location, neighborhood character, and adjacent buildings.

Liberty Houses

LIBERTY HOUSES WILL CREATE the backdrop for the many distinct neighborhoods within the village. As in traditional California towns and villages, the houses define the character of the public space and signal the individual character of the private realm behind the porch or front door.

In these traditional neighborhoods, the front portion of the house is the most public and must be responsive to the character of the neighborhood and the adjacent houses. The landscaping of the front yard, the set-backs from the street, the size and placement of the house on the lot, and the front porch, courtyard, or verandah are all shared elements that form the public realm.

Three Elements

The Liberty House includes three principal elements.

The **Main Body** of the house, which is the principal mass and includes the front door.

Side Wings, which are one or one-and-one-half stories connected to the Main Body. These are set back from the front facade of the Main Body the same depth as the length of the wing.

Porches are typically additive to the Main Body. These include porticos, side porches, full-facade front porches, or wraparound porches. Some architectural styles have porches that are inset into the Main Body.

The Liberty House

INTRODUCTION

 5

Purpose of the Norfolk Pattern Book

Norfolk has a rich architectural heritage that has created a collection of neighborhoods, remarkable for their diversity and unique character. The architectural style of the houses varies from neighborhood to neighborhood, especially in the traditional neighborhoods built between 1850 and 1950. In recent years, the distinctly different quality of the traditional architectural styles has been affected by the mass production of houses that seem the same wherever they are located. Also, homeowners often have a difficult time finding builders, architects, or materials and components that are in keeping with the period and detailing of their original house.

The Department of Planning and Community Development has commissioned *A Pattern Book for Norfolk Neighborhoods* to provide a resource for homeowners, builders, and communities as they repair, rebuild and expand their houses and preserve their neighborhoods. From remodeling a front door, adding a wing to your house, building a new house, to building a whole new housing development, you will be able to find the appropriate patterns to help guide the process of designing and building in ways that are consistent with the traditional Norfolk architecture and are compatible with the neighborhood character.

Overview of the Norfolk Pattern Book

This Pattern Book is organized in four sections: The Overview, Neighborhood Patterns, Architectural Patterns, and Landscape Patterns. Each section is designed to provide key information to help you make design and site planning decisions about a planned renovation or new house construction. The Neighborhood Patterns section provides a description of the various types of Norfolk neighborhoods by era. Building setbacks, the character of the streets, landscaping, and architectural diversity are described for each type. This gives owners a sense of what key elements to look for when planning to build or renovate a house in one of these neighborhoods.

The Architectural Patterns section presents guidelines for building or renovating a traditional Norfolk house within a specific architectural style. Six different traditional styles found throughout the Norfolk neighborhoods are illustrated with key details, materials and shapes to help owners determine the appropriate design elements for their house.

The Landscape Patterns section illustrates specific examples of fencing, walls, paving, and driveway types for Norfolk houses.

An Appendix listing materials resources and reference materials is also included.

Neighborhood Patterns

Architectural Patterns

Landscape Patterns

A Pattern Book for Norfolk Neighborhoods

A Norfolk neighborhood pattern

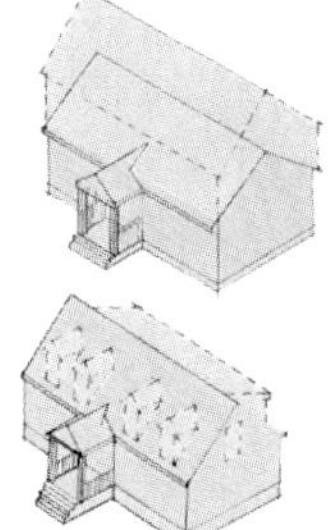

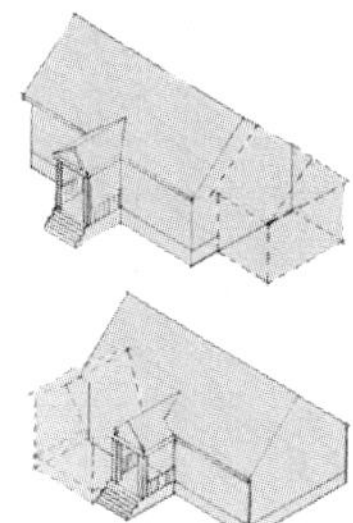

Designing and Renovating a Norfolk House

How To Use The Norfolk Pattern Book

The following is a step-by-step outline which describes how to use the Pattern Book for both homeowners who are interested in renovating or adding on to their house, and individuals who are interested in constructing a new house.

STEP 1 Identify Your Neighborhood

Whether you own an existing house or are building a new house, refer to the Neighborhood Patterns section of the Pattern Book (pages B6 through B15) and review the three eras of neighborhood building.

If you already own a house, select the era which your neighborhood most closely resembles. Read about the individual components – such as the typical front yard depth, streetscape character, house spacing, landscape treatments (both public and private) – that define your neighborhood.

If you are searching for a lot on which to build your new house, the Pattern Book can also be helpful. The Neighborhood Patterns section provides an overview of the unique characteristics of each era of neighborhood building and a listing of many Norfolk neighborhoods that fall within each era. This introduction can direct you to the neighborhoods that have characteristics that interest you.

Refer to directly to Step 4 if you are constructing a new house. Otherwise, continue to Step 2.

STEP 2 Identify the Architectural Style of your House

Once you've familiarized yourself with the era of your neighborhood, identify the architectural style that most closely resembles your house.

The Overview of Architectural Styles in the beginning of the Architectural Patterns section (pages C16 and C17) describes in visual form the predominant architectural styles found in Norfolk. The Table of Roof Pitches on page C22 in the Additions and Renovations section might also be helpful.

If your house does not have an identifiable style or is a mix of two styles, select one for it that would work best with its massing and height.

STEP 3 For Additions and Renovations

For information on appropriate means of modifying your house (whether historic or post-war) refer to the Additions and Renovations section (pages C22 and C23). This section describes strategies for adding on extra rooms or garages as well as changing or replacing exterior components such as windows, doors and materials.

STEP 4 For New Construction

If you are planning on constructing a new house, please refer to the "Building a Norfolk House" and "Siting a Norfolk House" sections (pages C18 through C21).

The "Building a Norfolk House" section outlines the step-by-step process of composing a Norfolk House and relates the individual elements, such as windows, doors, and porches, to the architectural style sections (as described in Step 5).

"Siting a Norfolk House" explains how to locate your house, garage, ancillary structures, and landscaping on your lot in a manner appropriate to the neighborhood context.

Also refer to the "House Lot Diagram" which is shown for every era of neighborhood in the Neighborhood Patterns section. The diagram describes the typical "zones" of a house lot, such as front yard, front facade, side yard, and private zone, all of which vary depending on the era.

STEP 5 Review the Architectural Style Sections

Six architectural styles found in Norfolk are documented in the Pattern Book: Classical Revival, Colonial Revival, European Romantic, Arts & Crafts, Victorian, and Coastal Cottage.

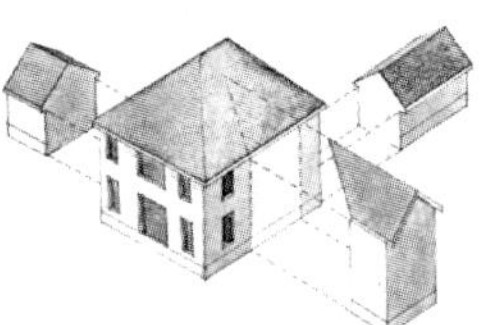

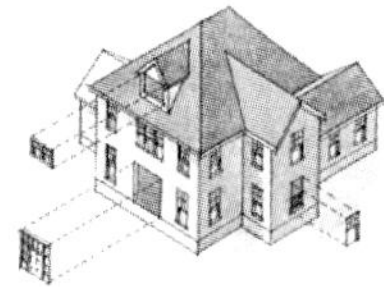

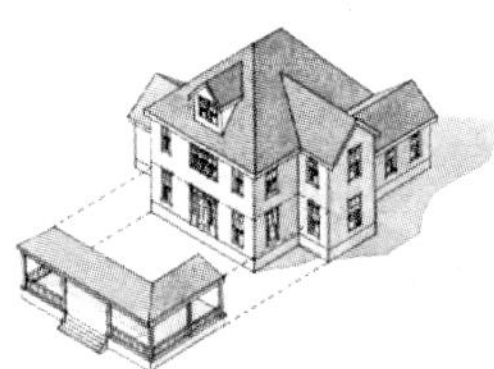

Assembling the elements of a Norfolk house

4 OVERVIEW

Character sketch of a Norfolk Arts & Crafts house

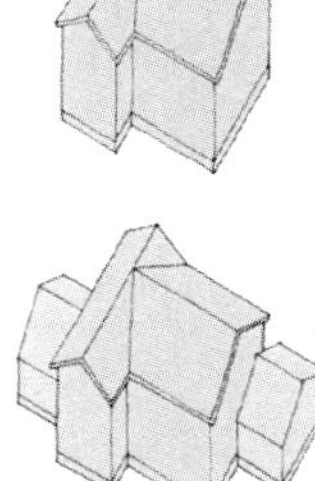

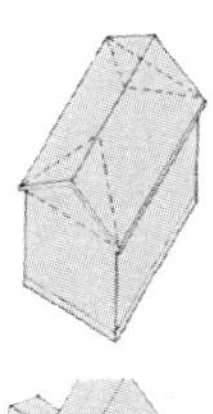

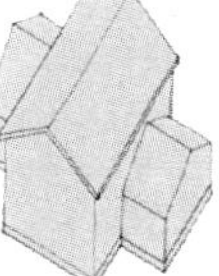

Massing and composition diagrams

HISTORY & CHARACTER PAGE

The first page of every architectural style section begins with a brief description of the style and its history. Photos of relevant examples of the style in Norfolk have been documented and are shown along with the essential qualities of each style. A partial elevation drawing and measured cross-section relay the critical dimensions and elements of the facade.

MASSING & COMPOSITION PAGE

This page describes the basic massing types or shapes of houses found in the Norfolk precedents for each architectural style. Each massing type is shown as a 3D image with a corresponding elevation diagram showing potential additions. The layout of rooms should be designed to fit into the massing types found within the particular style you are designing. The roof types are part of this overall massing description.

WINDOWS & DOORS PAGE

The window and door spacing is related to both the shape and the style of the house. Typical window and door compositions are illustrated as part of the massing illustrations for each style. Typical window and door proportions, trim details and special window or door elements are illustrated on a separate page within each section.

PORCHES & CHIMNEYS PAGE

Porches are essential elements of the character of many Norfolk neighborhoods. The location and design elements of porches are covered on this page. The massing of the front porch is specific to each house type and distinct within a particular style.

Chimneys are a key element in the composition of the elevation for several styles. Massing and details such as chimney caps are outlined on this page.

MATERIALS &D APPLICATIONS PAGE

This page of each style section in the Architectural Patterns includes a list of acceptable materials and their application. Also included on this page are hand-drawn elevation "possibilities" composed using elements described in the Pattern Book to illustrate the end result achieved if one follows the guidelines of the Pattern Book.

GALLERY OF EXAMPLES PAGE

This last page of each style section contains both a collection of photos of Norfolk houses in that style as well as detail photos of porches, doors and windows.

STEP 6 Review the Materials & Components List in the Appendix

Please review the list of materials and components such as doors, windows, columns, and moldings. Keyed to the appropriate architectural style, the list can serve as a reference or resource when searching for the appropriate building supplies from local sources.

STEP 7 Review the Reference List in the Appendix

For those who are interested in learning more about Norfolk's residential architecture, architectural styles in general, Norfolk's history, or available resources from the City of Norfolk, this list provides a handy reference.

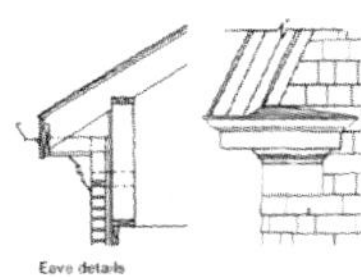

Eave details

Style examples

Identifying or selecting a porch

Identifying or selecting a window

Material options example

WaterColor built results

CHAPTER 7

Community Patterns Pages

Community patterns typically establish two important elements for a master plan—the fundamental design parameters for different building types related to their lots, and guidelines that establish character for different addresses within the plan. Once the specific program of different building types and lot sizes has been identified by the development team and incorporated into the final version of the master plan, the pattern book can define the key setbacks, coverages, and relative sizes of houses and buildings related to lot width and depth. Typically, these guidelines create a flexible framework for placing buildings on their lots so that variation can occur in different locations and contexts. In the examples shown in this chapter, the guidelines appear on pages entitled "Lot Types—General Conditions." These conditions may be supplemented with specific design or setback criteria within the second section of the Community Patterns chapter, where neighborhood addresses are described.

Neighborhood addresses are designed as a result of testing the master plan in a three-dimensional modeling exercise. During this part of the design process, the design and development team participates in a series of working sessions over the course of two or three days to refine the addresses within the plan. This work includes identifying special conditions that help create a desired effect or character of place intended by the plan. Particular architectural elements, setbacks, building types, or landscape elements may be identified to create these distinct addresses. These conditions are coded and integrated into the pattern book guidelines for individual lots and buildings. Each different address is illustrated with perspective drawings, typical setback plans, and street sections to communicate the essential relationships that set the character.

Community patterns built results, Baxter, Fort Mill, South Carolina

CASE STUDY: BAXTER

Fort Mill, South Carolina

The Community Patterns section of the pattern book for Baxter identifies a series of residential lot types that include two- and three-unit attached houses, townhouses, 45' x 100' cottage lots, 55' x 120' village lots, and 70' x 120' estate lots. Some of the lot types—cottage, village, and estate—have both front driveway conditions and alley-serviced conditions. These lot types formed the principal single-family types; however, the plan also includes apartments, live/work units, and mixed-use buildings that are handled outside of the pattern book lot types.

Baxter is designed as a traditional village in the "Upcountry" region of South Carolina. Villages within this region have a relaxed and diverse pattern of house types, mixing large and small houses on the same street. Also, there is no legacy of conventional townhouse building types, since that is a more urban condition. Townhouses in Baxter needed to appear in a building type that would be consistent with the informal character of Upcountry neighborhoods. Additionally, the plan of Baxter had to be modified to reflect this mix of various sizes of lots and houses on the same street. There was some randomness to the setbacks and sidewalk locations in the traditional patterns. This choreography of a mix of setback conditions was part of the refinement and guideline development for the Baxter Community Patterns section. Attached houses were defined in the pattern book such that they either appear to be large houses or form a central public space and take on the character of small college buildings found throughout the region's many small towns. The Community Patterns also set the sense of landscape character and architecture for the various neighborhoods in Baxter. Each address and each lot is coded for specific setback and/or architectural requirements where needed.

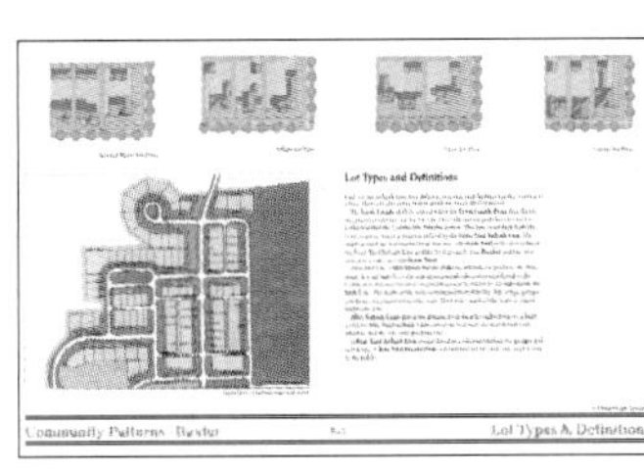

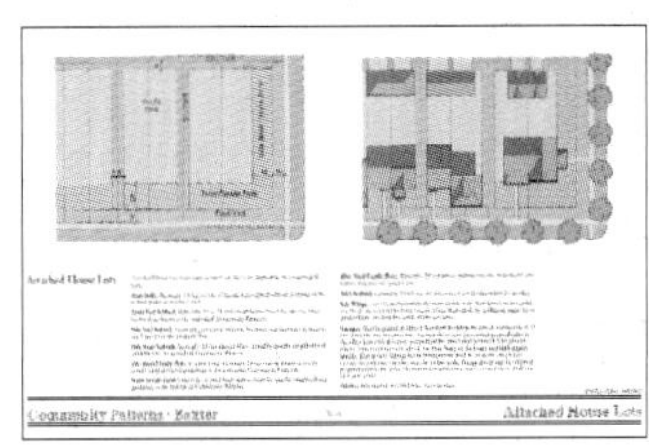

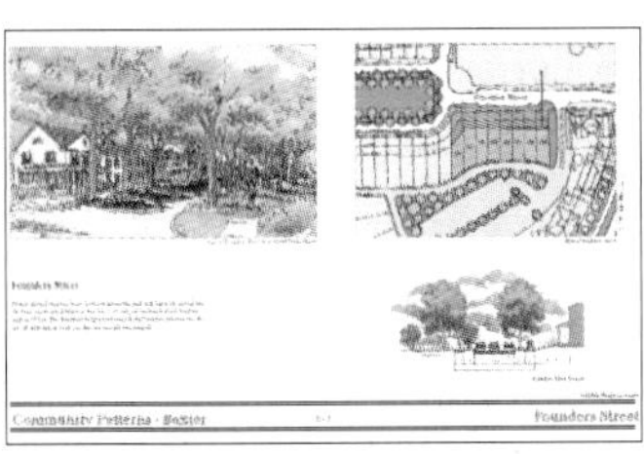

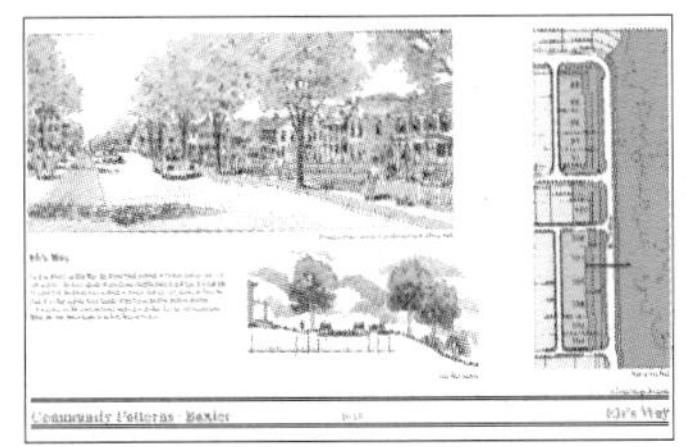

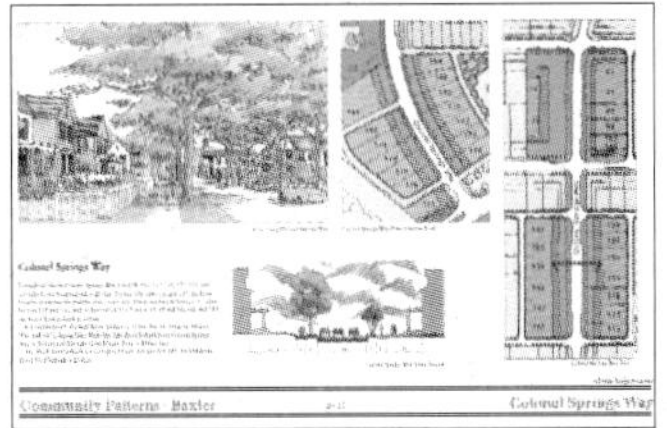

View of Baxter Square

Baxter Square

For lots 115–117 the minimum Front Yard Setback is 25 feet. For lot 115, the Side Street Setback is 15 feet minimum for the Main body of the house and 8 feet for the detached garage. The minimum Front Yard Setback for lots 118–120 is 20 feet. The minimum Front Yard setback for lots 122 and 123 is 35 feet and for lot 121 the minimum Front Yard setback is 28 feet. For corner lot 123, the Side Street Setback is 17 feet for the Main Body of the house and 10 feet for the detached garage.

For lots 149–158, the minimum Front-Yard Setback is 20 feet. For corner lot 149, the Minimum Side Street Setback is 10 feet. Two-story (minimum height) houses are required on all lots.

Community Patterns · Baxter B-8

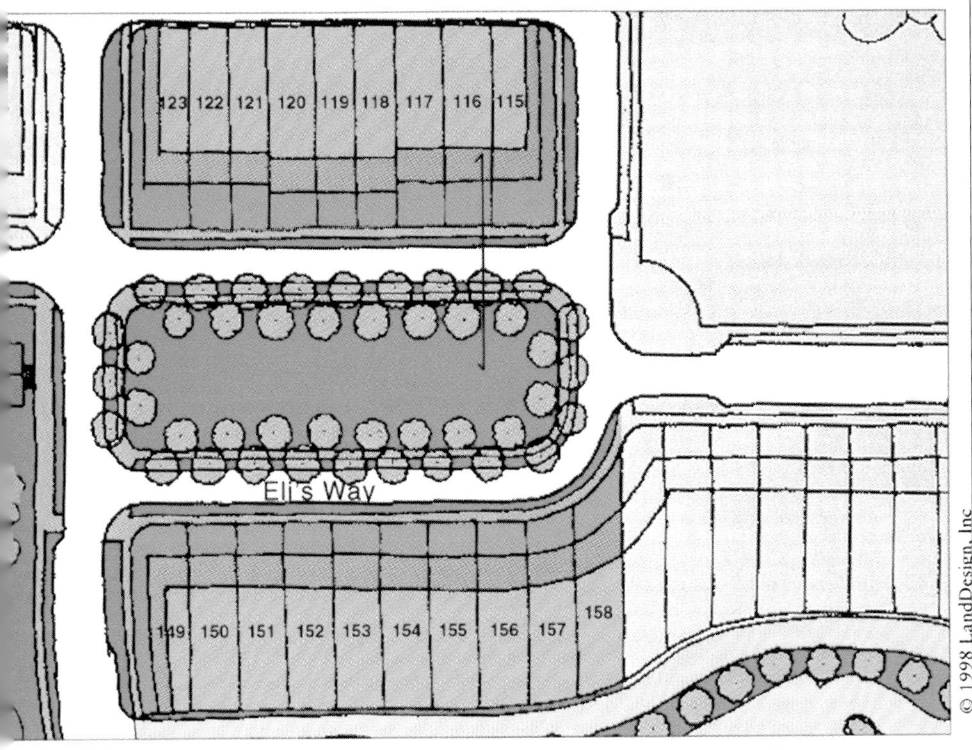

Plan of Baxter Square

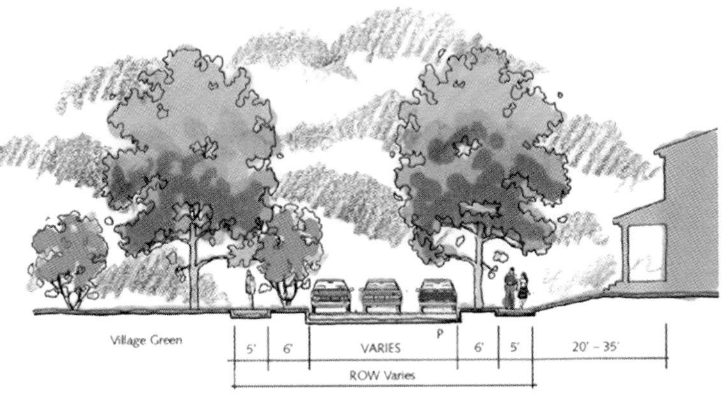

Baxter Square Section

Baxter Square

BAXTER

Fort Mill, South Carolina

The character for Baxter is patterned after the small towns found throughout the "Upcountry" region of South Carolina. This particular region is distinct due to its agricultural characteristics, soil and plant types, cultural migration and settlement patterns, and the resulting settlement character. Baxter Square was developed as an address for multi-family housing and the community center building. The small towns in the region have no legacy of townhouses or larger multi-family buildings. The square was designed to reflect the civic character of places like Cheraw, South Carolina or Davidson, North Carolina. The community center is patterned after a small town hall and the housing is designed as large houses with additions made over time.

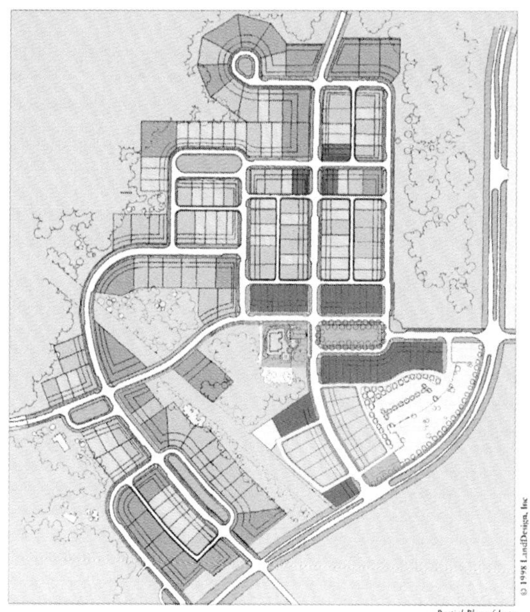

Partial Plan of Lots

Lot Types

Baxter offers a variety of lot types and locations. Attached house lots vary in width to accommodate a range of housing types including townhouses, three-unit and four-unit houses. Cottage lots are typically 45 to 55 feet wide and 110 to 130 feet deep and are either served by alleys or driveways off the street. Detached houses may be constructed on these lots. Village lots are typically 65 to 80 feet wide by 110 to 130 feet deep. These lots are served by alleys and some lots have front driveway access. Estate lots vary but are generally 90 feet wide by 120 to 150 feet deep and are typically accessed by driveways off the street.

Baxter Square will have the greatest mix of building types including proposed small office buildings, attached houses, mews townhouses and civic buildings with possible neighborhood retail uses on the ground floor. This pattern of mixed lot sizes is a traditional neighborhood pattern found throughout the Upcountry region.

The mix of large and small houses provides great variety in character along neighborhood streets. Corner lots are particularly important to the image of the neighborhood. These lots have generous front yards facing two streets. Houses on these lots are important landmarks.

Cottage Lots
45 – 55 feet wide

Estate Lots
90 feet wide

Village Lots
65 – 80 feet wide

Attached House Lots *Varied width*

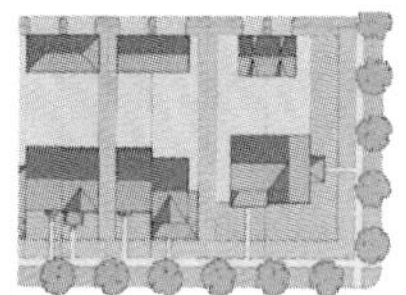
Attached House Site Plans

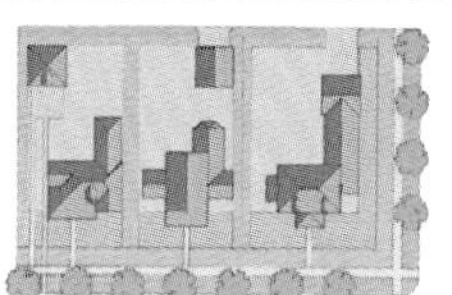
Village Site Plans

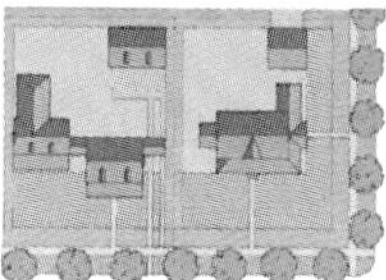
Estate Site Plans

Cottage Site Plans

Partial plan of setback areas and zones

Lot Types and Definitions

Each lot has setback lines that define a minimum yard between houses, streets and alleys. There are also zones within which the house shall be placed.

The **Front Facade** shall be placed within the **Front Facade Zone** described in the general conditions for the lot type and in the specific guidelines for the lot location within the Community Patterns section. This zone is set back from the front property line at a distance defined by the **Front Yard Setback Line**. The depth of the zone is measured from that line. The **Front Yard** is the area between the Front Yard Setback Line and the front property line. **Porches** and bay windows can project into the **Front Yard**.

On corner lots, a **Side Street Facade Zone** is established adjacent to the cross street. It is set back from the side street a certain dimension established in the Community Patterns for each neighborhood and is defined by the **Side Street Setback Line**. The depth of the zone is measured from that line. Side wings, garages and fences are placed within this zone. The Front Facade of the house is placed within this zone.

Alley Setback Lines define the distance from the alley right-of-way to a built structure. **Side Yard setback Lines** define the minimum distance between the structure and the side yard property line.

A **Rear Yard Setback Line** is established as a minimum setback for garages and side wings. A **Rear Yard Facade Zone** is established for lots with rear yards visible to the public.

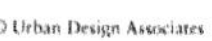

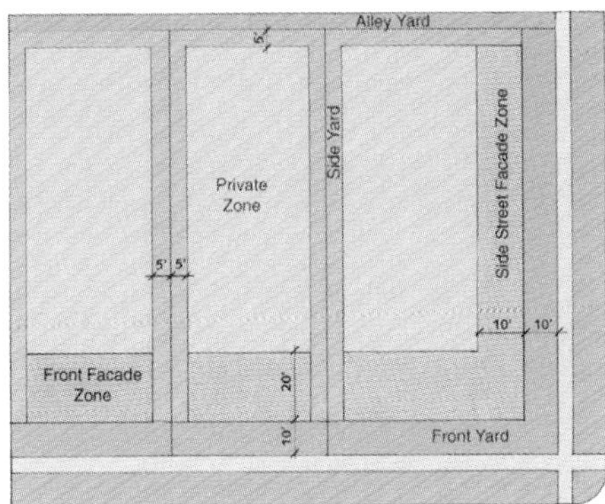

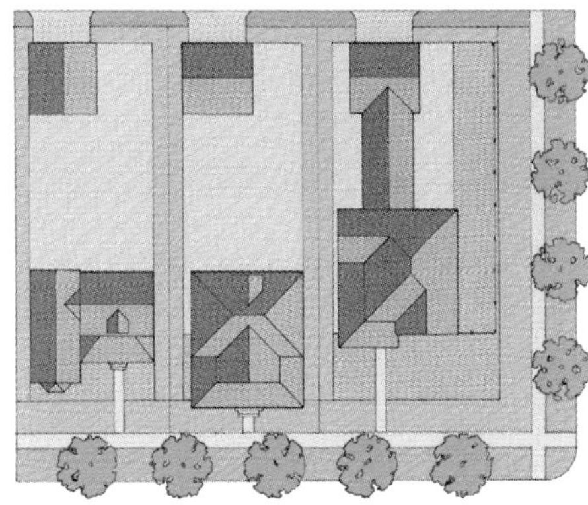

Cottage Lots

Cottage Lots are typically 45 to 55 feet wide by 110 to 130 feet deep. They may vary in size from lot to lot depending on location.

Main Body Width: Generally 32 feet or less within the Front Facade Zone.

Front Yard Setback: 10 feet except where noted by specific neighborhood guidelines in the individual Community Patterns.

Side Yard Setback: Minimum setbacks for all structures are 5 feet.

Side Street Setback: Generally 10 feet except where noted by specific neighborhood guidelines in the individual Community Patterns.

Side Street Facade Zone (Corner Lots): Generally 10 feet except where noted by specific neighborhood guidelines in the individual Community Patterns.

Front Facade Zone: Generally 20 feet except where noted by specific neighborhood guidelines in the individual Community Patterns.

Alley Yard Facade Zone: Generally 20 feet where indicated in the individual Community Patterns for specific lots.

Alley Setback: 15 feet for all structures from center line of alley.

Side Wings: 1 or 1½ stories within the Front Facade Zone. Side wings should generally be set back from the Front Facade of the Main Body by a distance equal to, or greater than, one-half the width of the side wing.

Garages: Shall be placed at either 5 feet from the property line or a minimum of 15 feet from the rear property line. Garage doors may be oriented perpendicular to the alley. Lots with driveway access from the street shall have garages placed behind the front facade of the Main Body of the house and shall require specific plan review. Garage doors facing streets shall be no wider than 9 feet. Garage doors facing the alley may be 18 feet wide. Garage doors may be oriented perpendicular to the alley. On corner lots with alley access, garage doors shall not face side streets.

Porches may extend into the Front Yard Setback.

Community Patterns · Baxter B-3 Cottage Lots

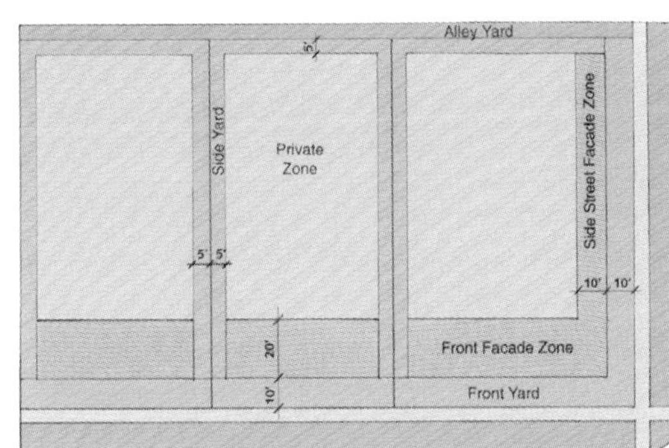

Village Lots

Village Lots are typically 65 or 80 feet wide by 110 to 130 feet deep. They may vary in size from lot to lot depending on location.

Main Body Width: Generally 40 feet or less.

Front Yard Setback: Generally 10 to 30 feet except where noted by specific neighborhood guidelines in the individual Community Patterns.

Side Yard Setback: Minimum setbacks for all structures are 5 feet.

Side Street Setback: Generally 10 feet except where noted by specific neighborhood guidelines in the individual Community Patterns.

Side Street Facade Zone (Corner Lots): Generally 10 feet except where noted by specific neighborhood guidelines in the individual Community Patterns.

Front Facade Zone: Generally 20 feet except where noted by specific neighborhood guidelines in the Community Patterns.

Alley Setback: Generally 15 feet for all structures from the center line of the alley.

Rear Yard Setback: Generally 5 feet for all structures.

Side Wings: 1 or 1½ stories within the Front Facade Zone. Side wings should generally be set back from the Front Facade of the Main Body by a distance equal to, or greater than, one-half the width of the side wing.

Garages: Shall be placed at either 5 feet from the property line or a minimum of 15 feet from the rear property line. Lots with driveway access from the street shall have garages placed behind the front facade of the Main Body of the house. Garage doors facing streets shall be no wider than 9 feet. Garage doors facing an alley may be 18 feet wide. Garage doors may be oriented perpendicular to the alley. On corner lots with alley access, garage doors shall not face side streets.

Porches may extend into the Front Yard Setback.

Community Patterns · Baxter B-4 Village Lots

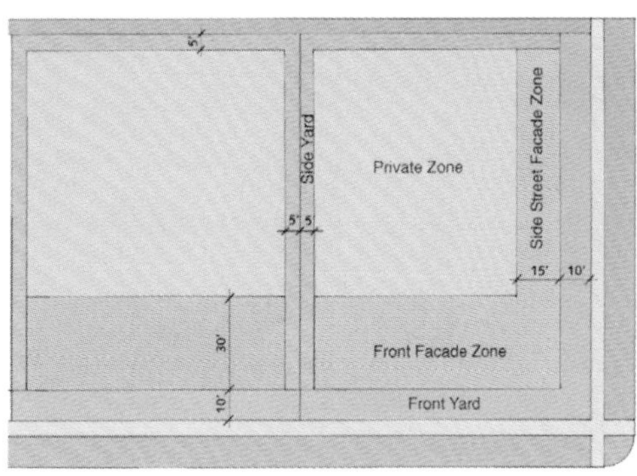

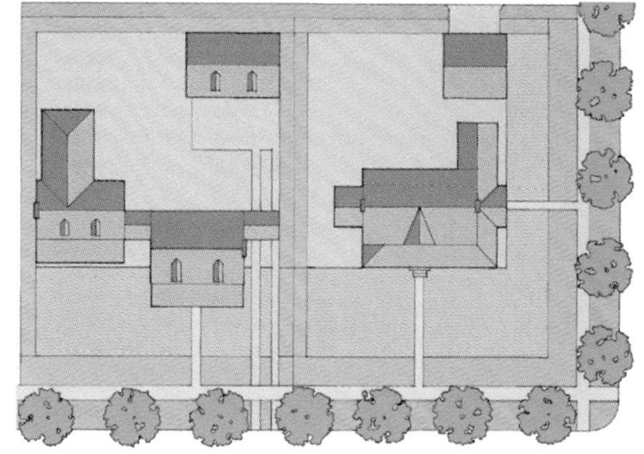

Estate Lots

Estate Lots are typically 90 feet wide by 120 to 150 feet deep. They may vary in size from lot to lot depending on location.

Main Body Width: Generally 48 feet or less.

Front Yard Setback: Generally 30 feet except where noted by specific neighborhood guidelines in the individual Community Patterns.

Side Yard Setback: Minimum setbacks for all structures are 5 feet.

Front Facade Zone: Generally 30 feet except where noted by specific neighborhood guidelines in the individual Community Patterns.

Alley Setback: Generally 15 feet for all structures from the centerline of the alley.

Rear Yard Setback: Generally 5 feet minimum for all structures.

Side Wings: 1 or 1½ stories within the front facade zone. Side wings should generally be set back from the Front Facade of the Main Body by a distance equal to, or greater than, one-half the width of the side wing.

Garages: Shall be placed at either 5 feet from the property line or a minimum of 15 feet from the rear property line. Lots with driveway access from the street shall generally have garages placed behind the front facade of the Main Body of the house and shall require specific plan review. Garage doors facing streets shall be no wider than 9 feet. Garage doors facing an alley may be 18 feet wide. Garage doors may be oriented perpendicular to the alley. On corner lots with alley access, garage doors shall not face side streets.

The maximum width of a garage with doors facing the street is 24 feet.

Porches may extend into the Front Yard Setback.

Community Patterns • Baxter — B-5 — Estate Lots

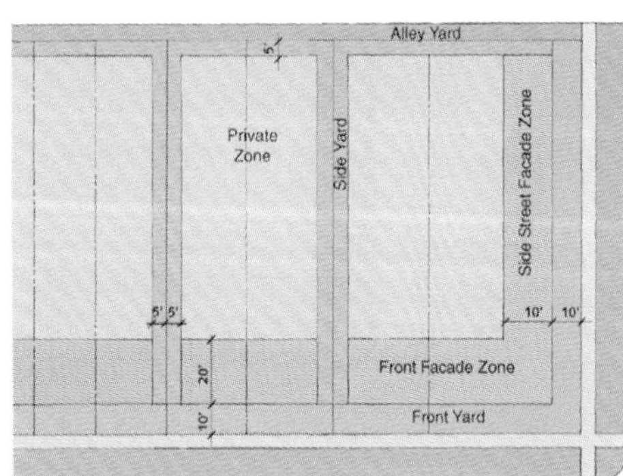

Attached House Lots

Attached House Lots may vary in size from lot to lot depending on location and type.

Main Body: Generally 50 feet or less of facade is permitted without a change in the vertical plane of at least 6 feet.

Front Yard Setback: Generally 10 to 25 feet except where noted by specific neighborhood guidelines in the individual Community Patterns.

Side Yard Setback: Generally, minimum setbacks between attached unit structures are 5 feet from the property line.

Side Street Setback: Generally 10 feet except where noted by specific neighborhood guidelines in the individual Community Patterns.

Side Street Facade Zone (Corner Lots): Generally 10 feet except where noted by specific neighborhood guidelines in the individual Community Patterns.

Front Facade Zone: Generally 20 feet except where noted by specific neighborhood guidelines in the individual Community Patterns.

Alley Yard Facade Zone: Generally 20 feet where indicated in the individual Community Patterns for specific lots.

Alley Setback: Generally 15 feet for all structures from the centerline of the alley.

Side Wings: 1 or 1½ stories within the front facade zone. Side wings should generally be set back from the Front Facade of the Main Body by a distance equal to, or greater than, one-half the width of the side wing.

Garages: Shall be placed at either 5 feet from the property line or a minimum of 15 feet from the rear property line. Garage doors may be oriented perpendicular to the alley. Lots with driveway access from the street shall generally have garages placed behind the front facade of the Main Body of the house and shall require specific plan review. Garage doors facing streets shall be no wider than 9 feet. Garage doors facing the alley may be 18 feet wide. Garage doors may be oriented perpendicular to the alley. On corner lots with alley access, garage doors shall not face side streets.

Porches may extend into the Front Yard Setback.

Community Patterns • Baxter — B-6 — Attached House Lots

View of Founders Street from North Sutton Road

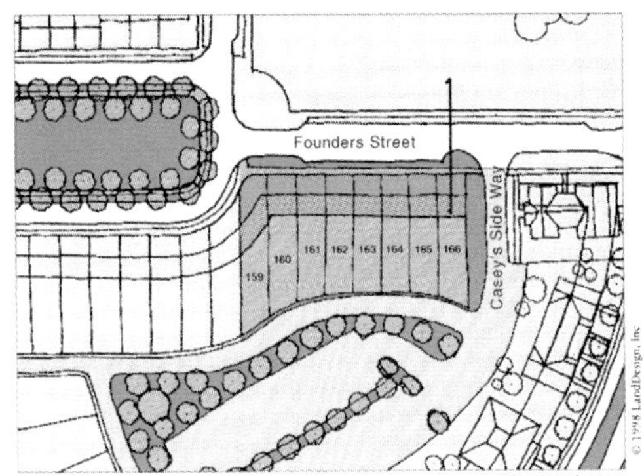

Plan of Founders Street

Founders Street

Houses along Founders Street look out across the park and frame the arrival into the heart of the neighborhood. For lots 159–166, the minimum Front Yard Setback is 15 feet. The minimum height for houses along Founders Street is two stories. Double-height front porches are strongly encouraged.

Founders Street Section

Community Patterns · Baxter B-7 **Founders Street**

The close provides an intimate setting for residences along Sonny's Way

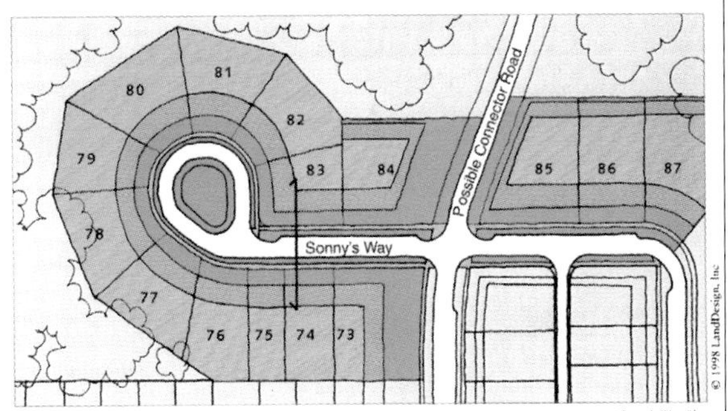

Sonny's Way Plan

Sonny's Way

For typical lots on Sonny's Way, lots 74–83, the Front Yard Setback is 20 feet. Houses on these lots shall have a one-and-one-half story or two-story Main Body and are strongly encouraged to have two-story porches. For lot 73, the Front Yard Setback is 40 feet. For lots 85–87, the Front Yard Setback is 15 feet and a 3 foot high front yard fence shall be built at the front property line. No portion of the house, including the porch, can be built closer than 5 feet from the property line.

For lots 74–83 and 85–87, two-car garages are permitted to be built in the front yard provided the garage doors are perpendicular to the street and face a paved motor court in front of the Main Body of the house. A front yard fence, wall or hedge shall be built at the property line.

For corner lot 84, the Front Yard Setback is 20 feet and the Side Street Setback is 60 feet. For lot 85, the Side Street Setback is 20 feet. For both lots the Side Street Facade Zone is 20 feet deep. If the connector road is eliminated, the setbacks for 84 and 85 shall be revised.

Sonny's Way Street Section

Community Patterns · Baxter B-9 **Sonny's Way**

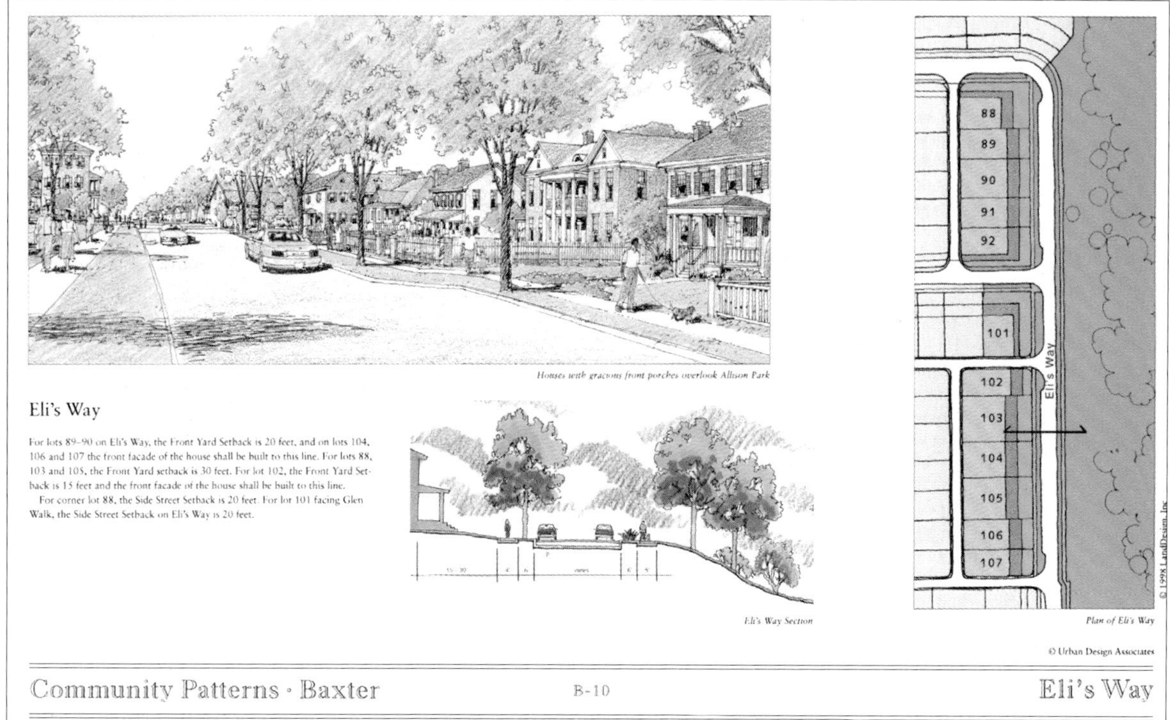

Houses with gracious front porches overlook Allison Park

Eli's Way

For lots 89–90 on Eli's Way, the Front Yard Setback is 20 feet, and on lots 104, 106 and 107 the front facade of the house shall be built to this line. For lots 88, 103 and 105, the Front Yard setback is 30 feet. For lot 102, the Front Yard Setback is 15 feet and the front facade of the house shall be built to this line.

For corner lot 88, the Side Street Setback is 20 feet. For lot 101 facing Glen Walk, the Side Street Setback on Eli's Way is 20 feet.

Eli's Way Section

Plan of Eli's Way

Community Patterns · Baxter B-10 Eli's Way

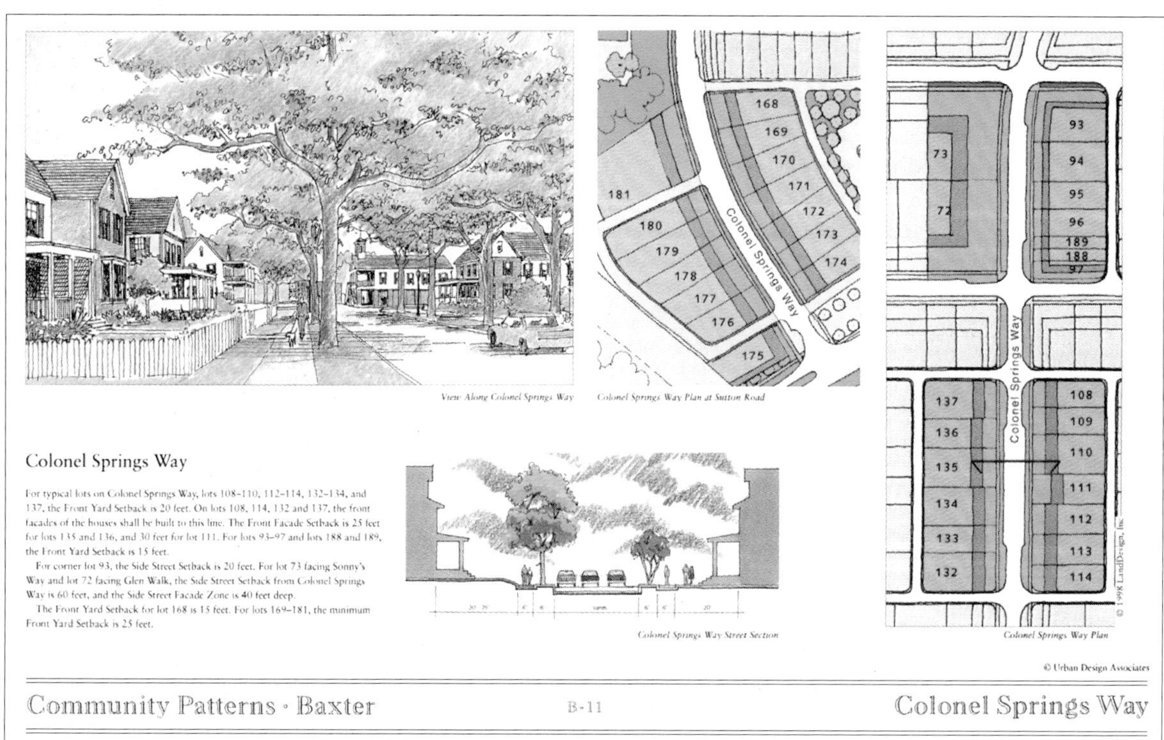

View Along Colonel Springs Way

Colonel Springs Way Plan at Sutton Road

Colonel Springs Way

For typical lots on Colonel Springs Way, lots 108–110, 112–114, 132–134, and 137, the Front Yard Setback is 20 feet. On lots 108, 114, 132 and 137, the front facades of the houses shall be built to this line. The Front Facade Setback is 25 feet for lots 135 and 136, and 30 feet for lot 111. For lots 93–97 and lots 188 and 189, the Front Yard Setback is 15 feet.

For corner lot 93, the Side Street Setback is 20 feet. For lot 73 facing Sonny's Way and lot 72 facing Glen Walk, the Side Street Setback from Colonel Springs Way is 60 feet, and the Side Street Facade Zone is 40 feet deep.

The Front Yard Setback for lot 168 is 15 feet. For lots 169–181, the minimum Front Yard Setback is 25 feet.

Colonel Springs Way Street Section

Colonel Springs Way Plan

Community Patterns · Baxter B-11 Colonel Springs Way

Community patterns built results, Baxter, Fort Mill, South Carolina

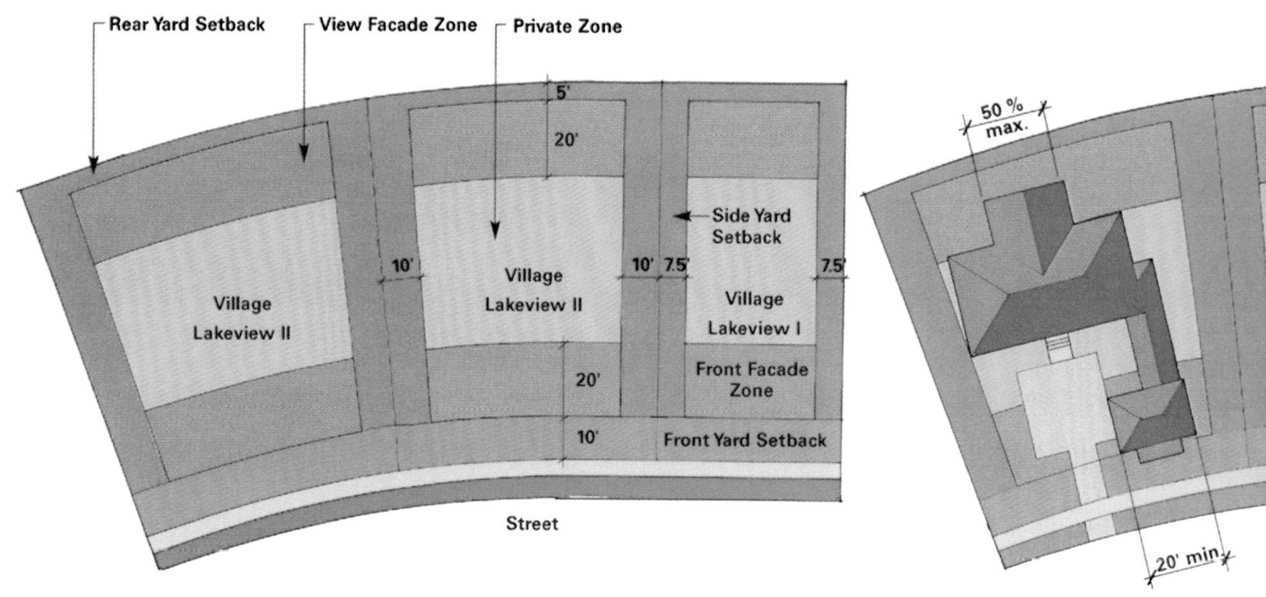

Village Lakeview Lots I and II Specifications

Lot Size
Village Lakeview I lots are approximately 50 feet wide. Village Lakeview II lots are approximately 70 feet wide.

Main Body
The width of the Main Body of the house shall be a maximum of 35 feet for Village I lots and 50 feet for Village II lots. The Main Body need not be placed in the Front Facade Zone. The house should be sited to preserve as many trees as possible.

Front Yard Setback / Front Facade Zone
The depth of the Front Yard is typically 10 feet from the front property line to the Front Yard Setback Line, unless noted otherwise in the Address section. The Front Facade Zone extends 20 feet from the Front Yard Setback Line. A minimum 20-foot-wide building mass at least one-and-one-half stories high and containing a living area shall be placed on the Front Yard Setback Line, while preserving as many trees as possible.

Side Yard Setback
Structures shall be set back a minimum of 7.5 feet from the side property line for Village Lakeview I lots and 10 feet setbacks for Village Lakeview II lots.

Side Street Setback / Side Street Facade Zone
Structures shall be set back a minimum of 5 feet from the side street property line. The Side Street Facade shall be defined by the side facades of the Main Body and any Rear Wings or Out Buildings. Where there is no building structure, the Side Street Facade shall be delineated by a fence or hedge.

Rear Yard Setback/ View Facade Zone
Structures shall be set back a minimum of 5 feet (unless noted otherwise in the Address section) from the rear property line, including porches and swimming pools. The View Facade Zone extends 20 feet from the setback line. The total width of the buildings within the View Facade Zone may be no more than 50 percent of the width of the lot at the rear property line. A full-facade, two-story porch, which may be partially or fully enclosed, is required on all Main Body or Rear W the View Faca

Encroachmen
Only porch ste Front Yard and Zone.

Out Building
Garages may b ings or one-an masses attache nection to the doors may not houses, garage may be placed Zone. 'Porch c designed to be porch) may be Facade Zone.

Building Placement – Village Lakeview

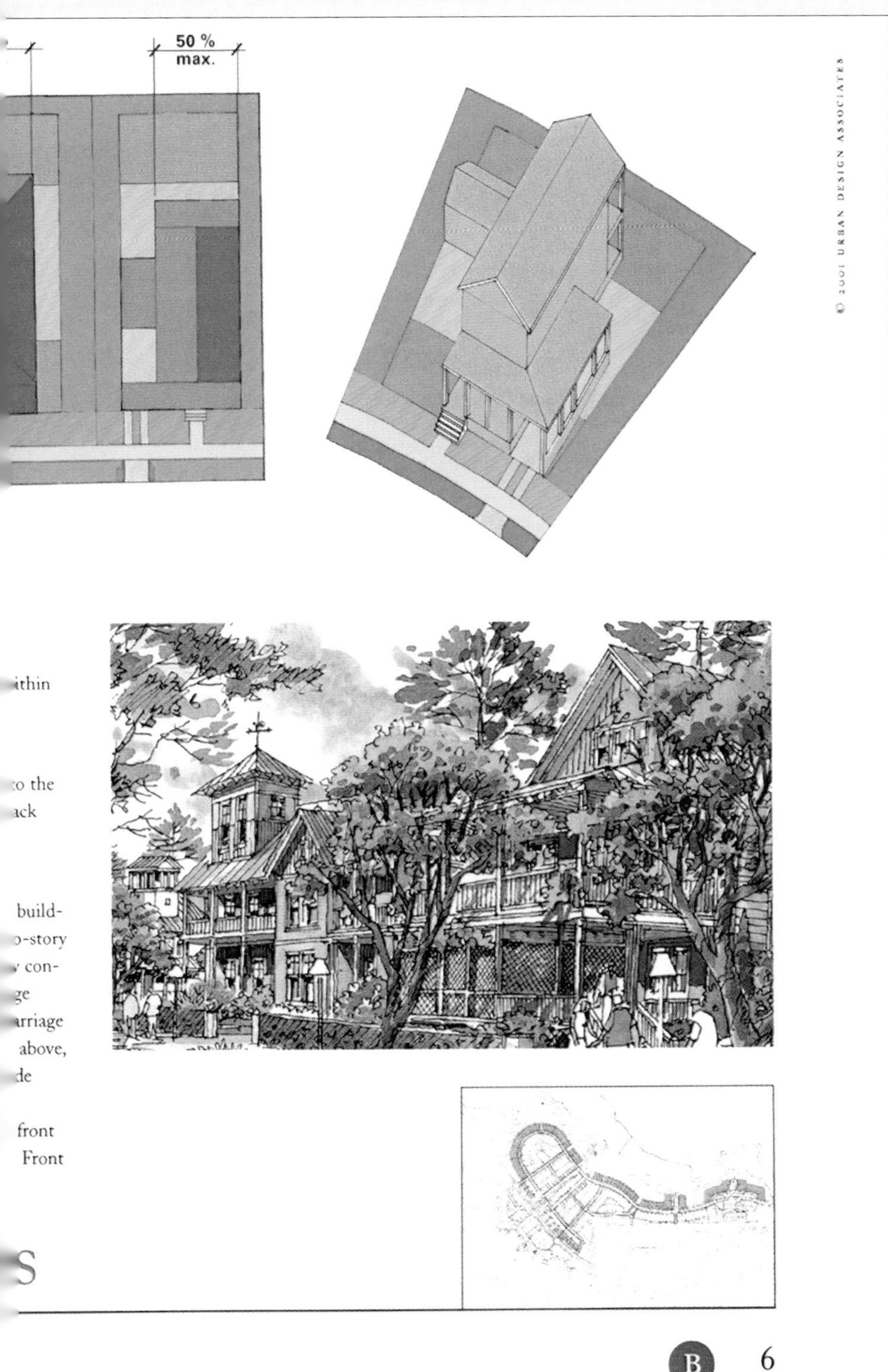

WATERCOLOR

Florida Panhandle

WaterColor has many different neighborhoods, each with its own unique character defined by the relationship to the natural, coastal environment and the design of the master plan. One challenge was the design of house and lot relationships where houses have both a street front and a waterfront. This page demonstrates the established guidelines for accommodating parking and garages on a fan-shaped lotting plan while maintaining a compelling street frontage and pedestrian-oriented approach. Facade zones help establish a front yard character that helps mitigate the presence of cars in the public realm.

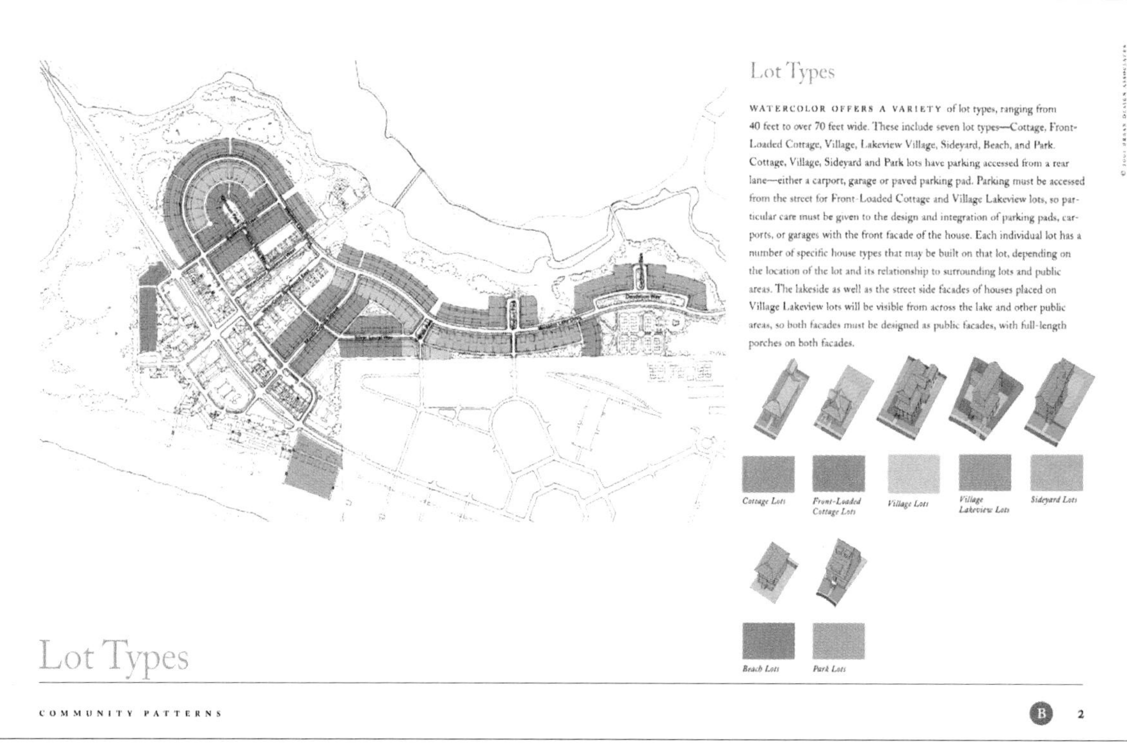

Lot Types

WATERCOLOR OFFERS A VARIETY of lot types, ranging from 40 feet to over 70 feet wide. These include seven lot types—Cottage, Front-Loaded Cottage, Village, Lakeview Village, Sideyard, Beach, and Park. Cottage, Village, Sideyard and Park lots have parking accessed from a rear lane—either a carport, garage or paved parking pad. Parking must be accessed from the street for Front-Loaded Cottage and Village Lakeview lots, so particular care must be given to the design and integration of parking pads, carports, or garages with the front facade of the house. Each individual lot has a number of specific house types that may be built on that lot, depending on the location of the lot and its relationship to surrounding lots and public areas. The lakeside as well as the street side facades of houses placed on Village Lakeview lots will be visible from across the lake and other public areas, so both facades must be designed as public facades, with full-length porches on both facades.

Lot Types

COMMUNITY PATTERNS

B 2

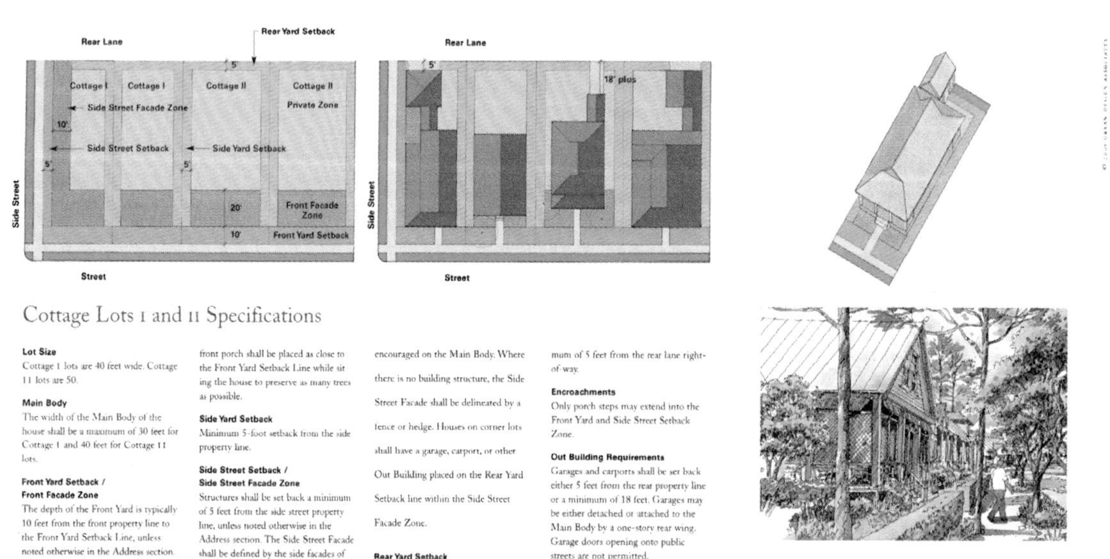

Cottage Lots I and II Specifications

Lot Size
Cottage I lots are 40 feet wide. Cottage II lots are 50.

Main Body
The width of the Main Body of the house shall be a maximum of 30 feet for Cottage I and 40 feet for Cottage II lots.

Front Yard Setback / Front Facade Zone
The depth of the Front Yard is typically 10 feet from the front property line to the Front Yard Setback Line, unless noted otherwise in the Address section. The Front Facade Zone extends 20 feet from the Front Yard Setback Line. The front porch shall be placed as close to the Front Yard Setback Line while siting the house to preserve as many trees as possible.

Side Yard Setback
Minimum 5-foot setback from the side property line.

Side Street Setback / Side Street Facade Zone
Structures shall be set back a minimum of 5 feet from the side street property line, unless noted otherwise in the Address section. The Side Street Facade shall be defined by the side facades of the Main Body and any Rear Wings or Out Buildings. Wraparound porches are encouraged on the Main Body. Where there is no building structure, the Side Street Facade shall be delineated by a fence or hedge. Houses on corner lots shall have a garage, carport, or other Out Building placed on the Rear Yard Setback line within the Side Street Facade Zone.

Rear Yard Setback
All structures shall be set back a minimum of 5 feet from the rear lane right-of-way.

Encroachments
Only porch steps may extend into the Front Yard and Side Street Setback Zone.

Out Building Requirements
Garages and carports shall be set back either 5 feet from the rear property line or a minimum of 18 feet. Garages may be either detached or attached to the Main Body by a one-story rear wing. Garage doors opening onto public streets are not permitted.

Building Placement – Cottage Lots

COMMUNITY PATTERNS

B 3

Rose Garden Mews

Rose Garden Mews consists of a crescent-shaped park with a walkway lined with brightly colored cottages, and a street, lined with similar houses, that leads to the water. The continuous porches and landscaping create an intimate neighborhood within the town. The ends of blocks and the corners of the Crescent are defined by two-story houses.

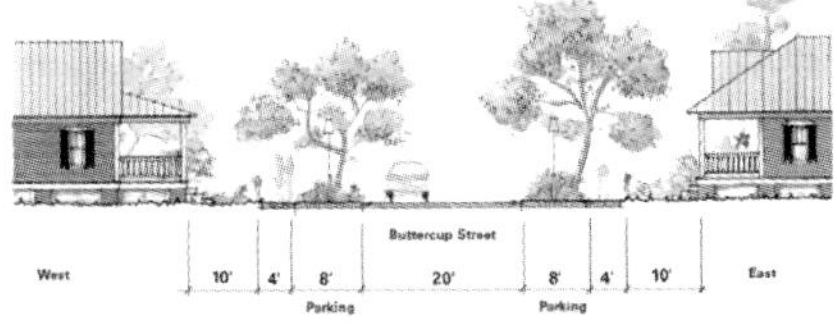

Crescent Frontage Lots
(Cottage Lots)

Main Body Types

For (**A**) lots, either one- or one-and-one-half-story Single cottages; for (**B**) lots, one-and-one-half-story Single cottages; and for (**C**) lots, two-story Side Hall or T-Shaped houses.

House Placement

Front porches should be set back 20 feet from the front property line, except for the **B** and **C1** lots where the Front Yard Setback and Side Yard Setback Lines are 10 feet from the front property line. Towers and tall elements should be used to mark corners on **C1** lots and along the pedestrian path (**C2**).

Colors

Warm vibrant tones of red, pink, yellow, and orange; see Section E.

Street Frontage Lots
(Cottage Lots)

Main Body Types

For (**D**) lots, either one- or one-and-one-half-story Single or Creole cottages; for (**E**) lots, two-story Side Hall or T-Shaped houses.

Placement

Front porches should be set back 10 feet from the front property line.

Colors

Buildings are a range of grays and neutral colors, with trim and special elements in bright colors. See Section E.

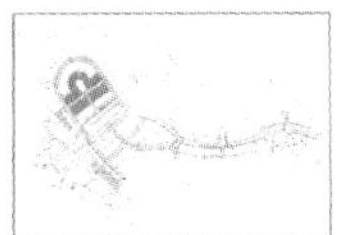

Addresses – Rose Garden Mews

Western Lake Drive

Western Lake Drive is WaterColor's main residential street which will connect the future neighborhoods of WaterColor to the Town Center. Along it are a variety of houses and neighborhood greens, each with a distinct character. Houses on the north side of the street have backyards which look across the lake or wetlands. They are designed to take advantage of those views while still providing view corridors for houses on the south side. There are a variety of house types along the street.

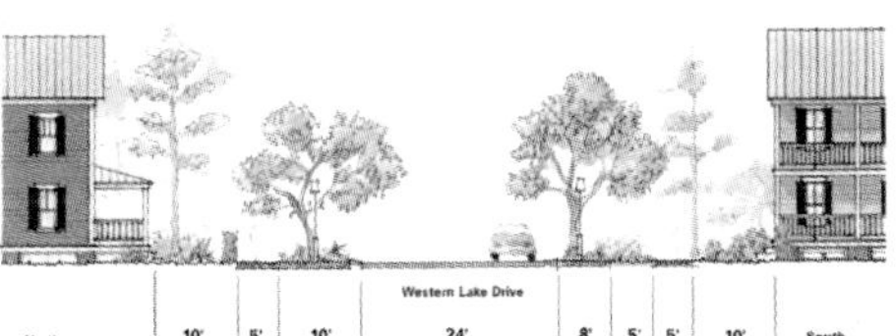

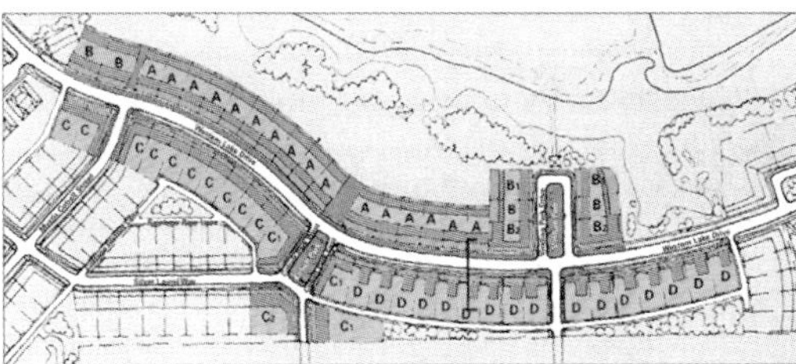

South Side Lots
(Village Lots and Sideyard Lots)

Main Body Types

For (**C**) lots, two- or two-and-one-half-story Side Hall houses, and for (**D**) lots, two-and-one-half-story Sideyard houses.

Placement

Lots on the western block (**C**) have a 12-foot Front Yard Setback on which front porches are to be placed. The eastern blocks (**D**) have a 10-foot Front Yard Setback. The front facades of these Sideyard houses are to be placed on the Front Yard Setback Line. **C1** and **C2** houses have 10-foot front and side yard setbacks. These houses should have wraparound porches and use other elements to provide a continuous facade around the park. The front facade of **C2** should address the park.

Colors

Limited to a few muted colors per house, with white trim in white; houses on Viridian Park have accents in red and darker sandtones; see Section E.

North Side Lots
(Village Lakeview Lots)

Main Body Types

For (**A**) lots, two- or two-and-one-half-story Side Hall houses for 50-foot lots, and for (**B**) lots, one-and-one-half-, two-, or two-and-one-half-story Center Hall houses for the wider lots.

Placement

Houses are to be set back a minimum of 10 feet from the front property line. **B** and **B1** lots have 20-foot rear lot setbacks. Towers and tall elements should be used on **B1** lots. Wraparound porches and other elements should be used at the corners on **B2** lots to define the public open spaces along Western Lake Drive.

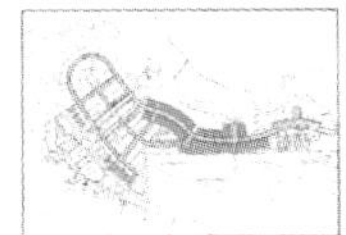

Addresses – Western Lake Drive

Character Sketch of Pretty Lake Waterfront

Typical Section of Pretty Lake Avenue (east of Little Annapolis)

Typical Section of Pretty Lake Aven

East Beach Addresses

COMMUNITY PATTERNS

Pretty Lake District

THE MARINAS ALONG PRETTY LAKE AVENUE create the backdrop for the character of a mixed-use waterfront district termed "Little Annapolis". The area adjacent to Shore Drive will have a mix of shops and residential units in the upper stories with broad sidewalks and a direct connection to the marinas along the shore. Further west, Pretty Lake Avenue will have a mix of attached and detached houses that look out to the marinas.

Images from Annapolis, Maryland

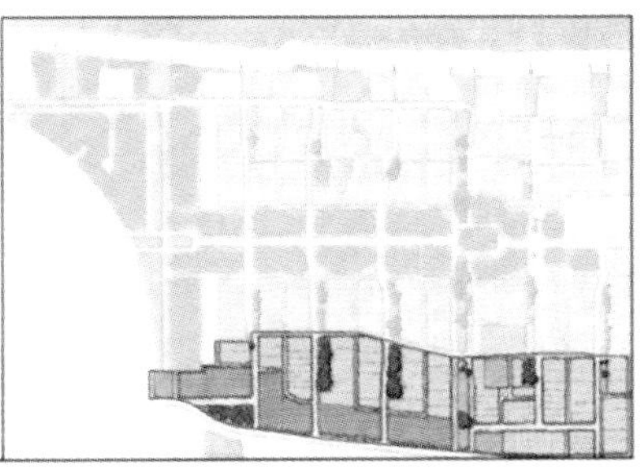

 3

EAST BEACH

Norfolk, Virginia

East Beach in Norfolk, Virginia has a remarkable site situated between the Chesapeake Bay and an inland lake and harbor called Pretty Lake. This dual frontage is connected by the new waterfront village only three blocks across. The Pretty Lake frontage is anchored at the western edge of the site by a proposed marina district based on the character and form of traditional waterfront settlements like Annapolis — a bit further north on the Chesapeake Bay. Building types, architectural character, and the relationship to the marina create a new public space for Norfolk.

East Beach Character

THE MASTER PLAN FOR EAST BEACH creates a series of distinct addresses that will be built over time. Each park space or street has a unique sense of place defined by the character of the civic space and the houses or buildings that form the neighborhood. This section of the *Pattern Book - Community Patterns* - illustrates examples of the intended character generated by the set-backs, placement and type of buildings and the architectural vocabularies described in the *Architectural Patterns* and *Landscape Patterns* sections of the *Pattern Book*.

Site Plan Delineating Principal Addresses

Shore Drive

The Bay Front

Pleasant Avenue

Pretty Lake

Addresses Within The Plan

Perspective view of Pleasant Avenue

Pleasant Avenue District

PLEASANT AVENUE IS THE HEART of the East Beach neighborhood. The street will have a mix of large and small houses, attached and detached to create a varied, rich character along its length. There are two public squares that define addresses along the Avenue. The westernmost square at Shore Drive is flanked by mixed-use buildings and serves as a gateway into the neighborhood. On the eastern end, the Avenue splits around a civic site framed by attached and detached houses. The site provides a prominent terminus for Pleasant Avenue while creating a unique address for this district. A series of parks along the north-south streets connect Pleasant Avenue to both waterfronts – Chesapeake Bay and Pretty Lake.

Images from Annapolis, Maryland (left) and Edenton, North Carolina (right)

Typical Section of Pleasant Avenue

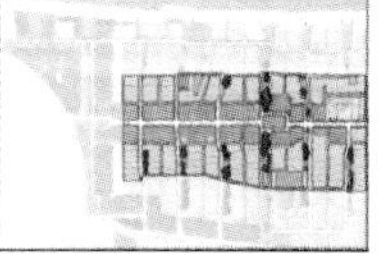

East Beach Addresses

Perspective view of typical neighborhood street

North-South Streets

THE NORTH-SOUTH STREETS within East Beach will have a marvelous character, each street different from the next. Many of these streets will have small, informal parks with mature trees and landscape. The character of the streets will also change from north to south. Some sections will have narrow cartways defined by soft edges and meandering walkways. A mix of cottages, attached houses and a variety of lot sizes and types will help create a sense of diversity and interesting character throughout the neighborhoods. These streets connect the Cheasapeake Bay to Pretty Lake providing easy walking access to both shores. Porches will be important elements for houses lining these streets.

Neighborhood images from Easton (left) and Annapolis (right) in Maryland

Typical Section (north of Pleasant Avenue)

Typical Section (south of Pleasant Avenue)

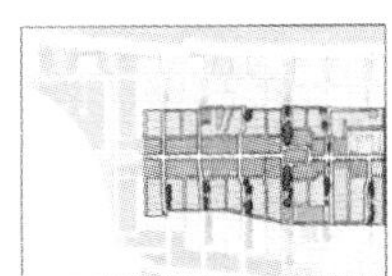

East Beach Addresses

COMMUNITY PATTERNS

B 5

Perspective view along Shore Drive

Shore Drive

THE ENTRANCE TO EAST BEACH is from Shore Drive, a major route linking all of Ocean View to the surrounding region. The image along this Drive is drawn from the precedent of an Admirals' Row of large houses, similar in character and scale, facing the drive across a linear park. This stately image will set the overall character of East Beach as residents and visitors cross the bridge to the bayfront.

Officers' Housing at the Presidio in San Francisco

Captains' Houses in Nantucket

Typical Section at Shore Drive

East Beach Addresses

COMMUNITY PATTERNS

B 7

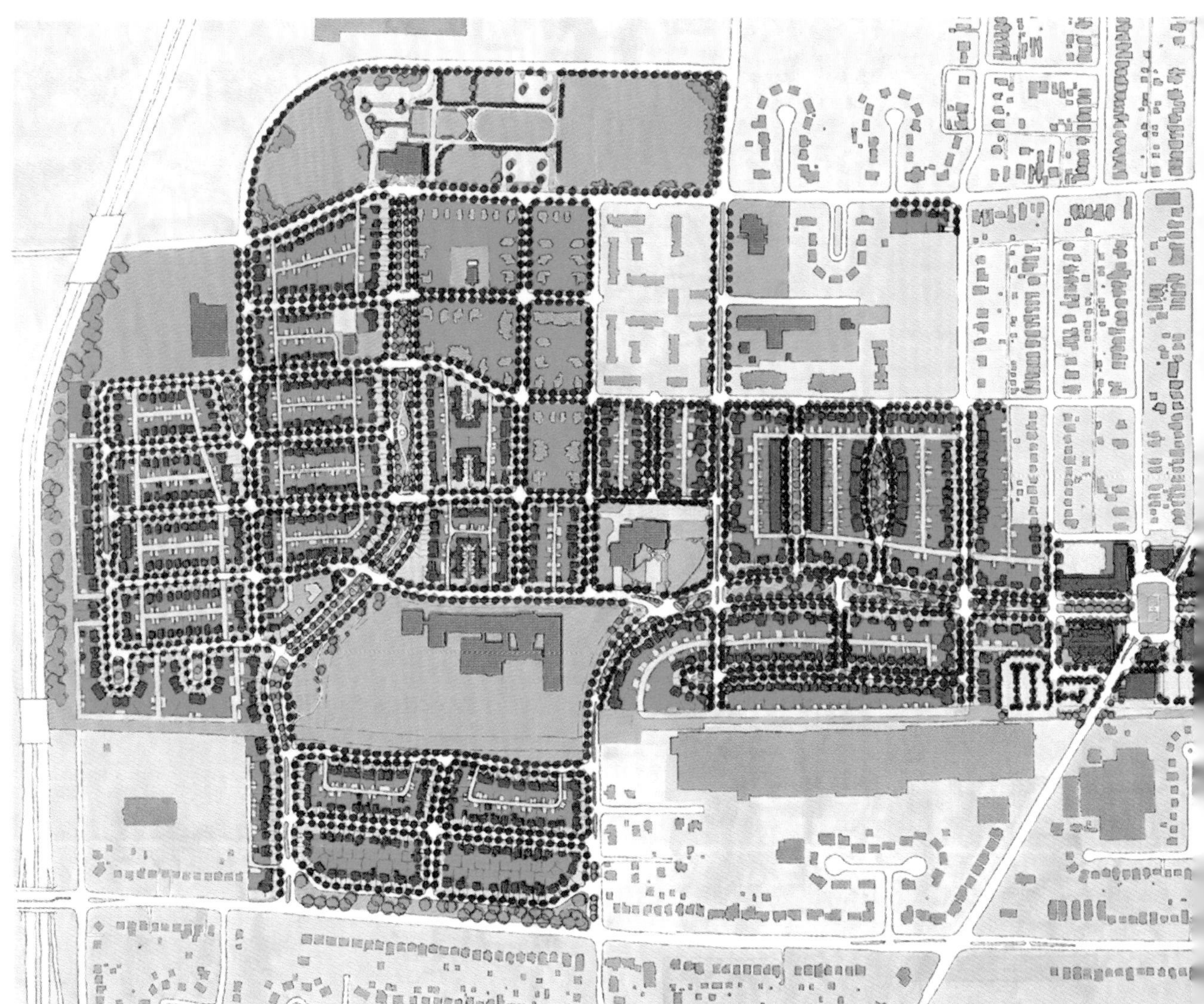

Park DuValle Lot Plan

Addresses

COMMUNITY PATTERNS

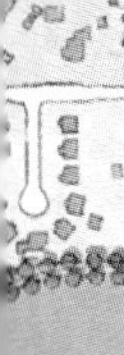

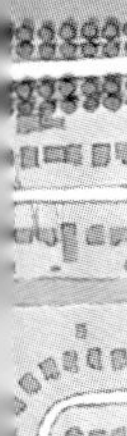

Creating Park DuValle Addresses

FOLLOWING LOUISVILLE'S GREAT TRADITIONS of neighborhood development, Park DuValle is created as a series of attractive addresses, each with its own character. Constant setbacks from property lines, building massing, and a mix of building types and architectural styles create the public spaces and streets of the addresses.

The addresses of Park DuValle include: Algonquin Parkway, Park Drive, typical Local Neighborhood Streets, and typical Community Streets. Architectural styles include: Victorian, Colonial Revival, and Craftsman.

B I

PARK DUVALLE

Louisville, Kentucky

Park DuValle is a public/private development initiative to rebuild a large area of deteriorated public housing and surrounding rental housing into a viable mixed-income neighborhood. The effort was guided by a public process and a pattern book that served to coordinate development within the master plan. Building types, block patterns, public open space and architecture are major components of the pattern book. A key component of the redevelopment is the design of distinct addresses throughout the plan that would change the former perceptions of the site. Each address is illustrated in perspective, plan, and section in the Community Patterns.

Lot Types

THE BLOCK PATTERNS INCLUDE GUIDELINES which establish setbacks for each lot. The plan calls for mixing lot types within each block as a means of replicating the character of Louisville's traditional neighborhoods. Therefore, in any given block, there could be a combination of all five of the lot types described on the following page. Common to all lot types are the setback lines, yard requirements and principles for placing buildings on them. The lot types include:

- 35-foot & 40-foot wide Cottage Lots
- 60-foot wide Neighborhood Lots
- 70-foot wide Estate Lots
- 100-foot wide Commons Lots
- Townhouse Lots
- Patio Lots

On the following pages, the general principles for placing buildings and landscaping on these lot types are described.

Lot Types Key

Commons Lots
Estate Lots
Neighborhood Lots
Cottage Lots
Patio Lots
Townhouse Lots

Lot Types

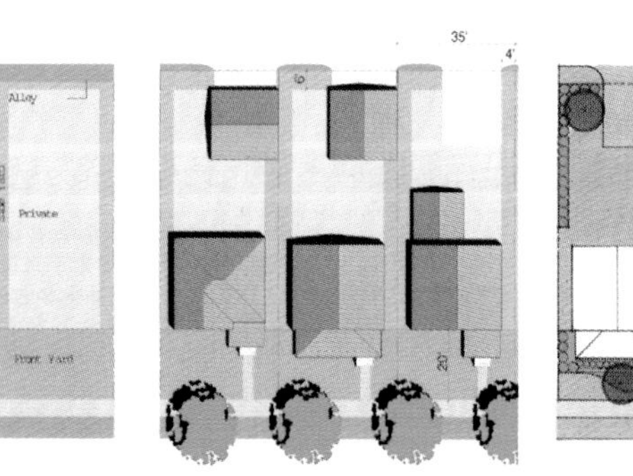

Yards and Setbacks

Placing the House on a 35-foot Lot

Landscape

Yards and Setbacks

Placing the House on a 40-foot Lot

Lot Size:
35-foot wide Cottage Lots are designed for single-family detached houses with a 24- to 27-foot Main Body. 40-foot wide Cottage Lots are designed for two-story detached houses with a 28- to 32-foot Main Body.

Front Facade Setback
20 feet from front property line.

Side Yard Setback
3 feet for adjacent lots and side alleys.

Alley Setback
6 feet from the rear property line.

Front Driveways
Front driveways are not permitted.

Porches
Porches may extend a maximum of 9 feet into the front or side street yards.

Garages
Garages can be placed at the Alley Setback and are allowed to be built on the property line between adjacent lots, subject to building code restrictions. Refer to Landscape Guidelines for placement of garages and parking pads.

Cottage Lot Landscape
In addition to the general landscape guidelines, one small ornamental tree shall be planted in the Front Yard. A minimum of one large ornamental or canopy tree shall be planted elsewhere on the lot. Lawn areas shall be fifty percent or less of the total area.

35-Foot and 40-Foot Cottage Lots

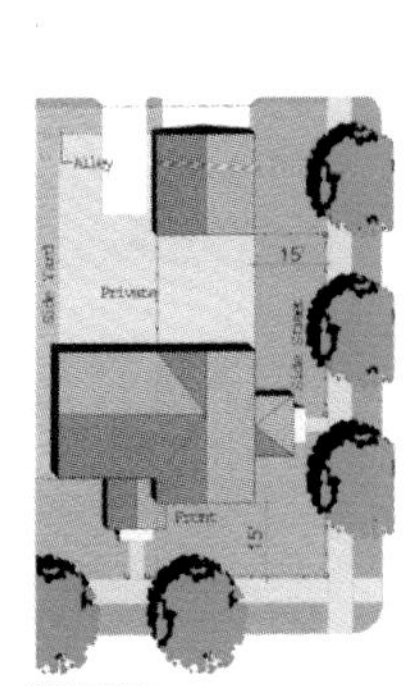

Yards and Setbacks

Placing the House on the Lot

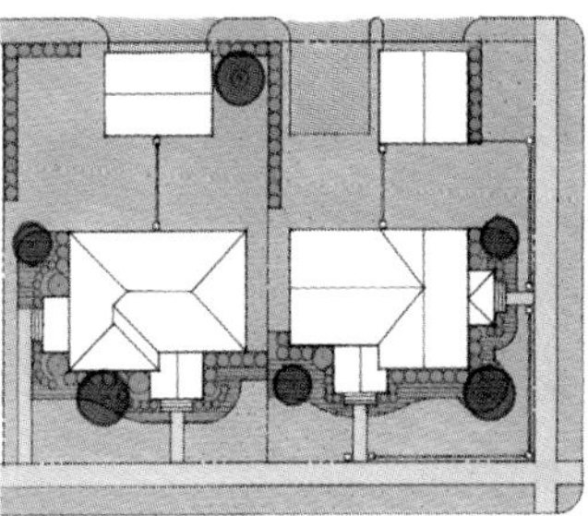

Landscape

Lot Size
The 60-foot wide Neighborhood Lots are also designed for two-family, semi-detached houses with a 40- to 42-foot Main Body. These can be mid-block or corner locations.

Front Facade Setback
20 feet from the front property line. On corner lots, the corner unit of a duplex may extend a maximum of 5 feet into the front yard.

Side Street Facade Setback
15 feet from the side street property.

Side Yard Setback
3 feet for adjacent lots and 5 feet for side alleys.

Alley Setback
6 feet from the rear property line.

Front Driveways
Front driveways are not permitted.

Porches
Porches may extend a maximum of 9 feet into the front or side street yards.

Garages
Garages can be placed at either the Alley Setback or 18 feet from the rear property line. If placed on the Alley Setback, garages are permitted to be built on the property line between adjacent lots. A garage is required for all corner lots, and shall be placed at the Side Street Setback. Refer to Landscape Guidelines for placement of garages and parking pads.

Neighborhood Lot Landscape
In addition to the general landscape guidelines, a minimum of one small ornamental tree and two large ornamental or canopy trees shall be planted. Lawn areas shall not exceed fifty percent of the total lot area.

60-Foot Neighborhood Lots – Duplexes

COMMUNITY PATTERNS

10

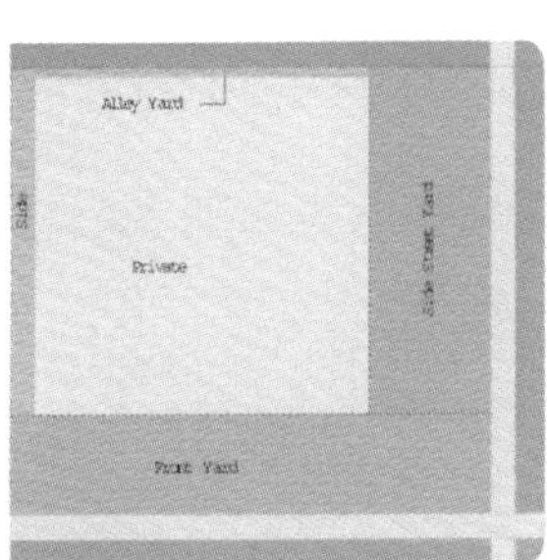

Yards and Setbacks

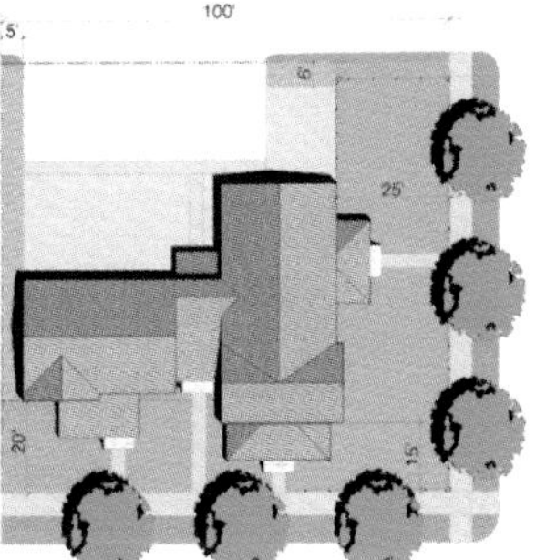

Placing the House on the Lot

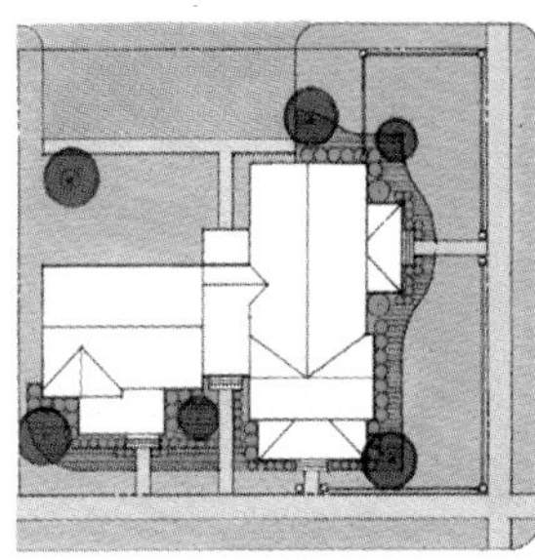

Landscape

The 100-foot-wide Commons Lots are designed for small apartment buildings of up to six units. These are always corner lots.

The maximum facade width without a change in horizontal plane of the facade is 35 feet. The change in facade plane shall be a minimum of 2 feet. A minimum of 70 percent of the street frontage of the lot, and 60 percent of the side street frontage, shall contain a residential structure.

Front Facade Setback:
20 feet from the front property line except where noted in the addresses section. The corner unit of a duplex may extend a maximum of 5 feet into the front yard.

Side Street Facade Setback:
25 feet from the side street property.

Side Yard Setback:
3 feet for adjacent lots and 5 feet for side alleys.

Alley Setback:
6 feet from the rear property line.

Front Driveways:
Front driveways are not permitted.

Porches:
Porches may extend a maximum of 9 feet into the front or side street yards.

Fences:
A Private Zone Fence shall be placed at the Side Street Setback to screen parking from public view.

Common Lots Landscape
In addition to the general landscape guidelines, a minimum of two small ornamental trees, one large ornamental tree, and one canopy tree shall be planted. Lawn areas shall not exceed 40 percent of the total lot area.

Common Lots

COMMUNITY PATTERNS

12

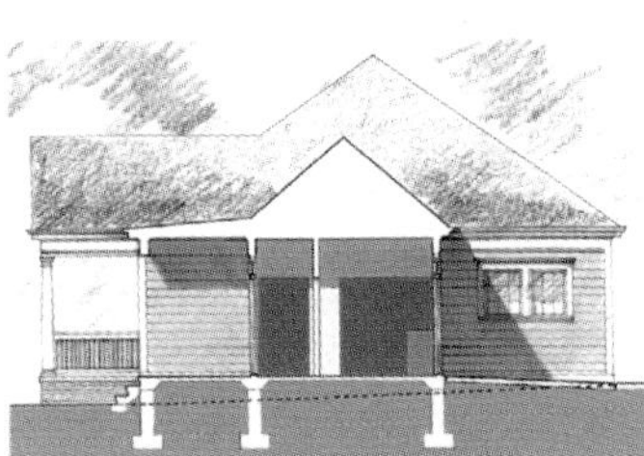

The grade of the site should enable the rear door to be level with the exterior grade. In this cross section, the dotted line indicates the alignment of the accessible route.

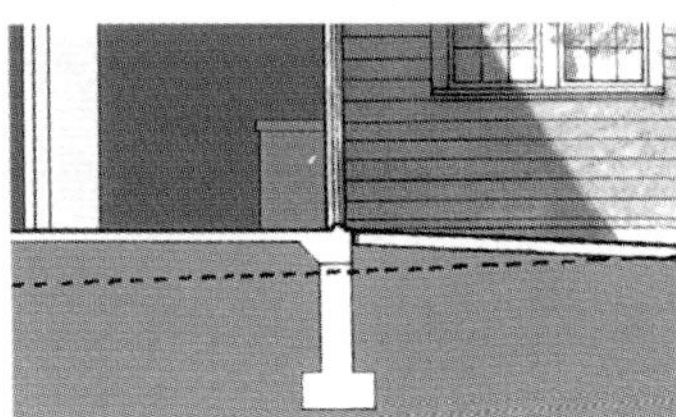

Raised slab construction allows an at-grade entrance to be at the same elevation as the interior floor. The accessible entrance door should allow 32 inches of clear passage.

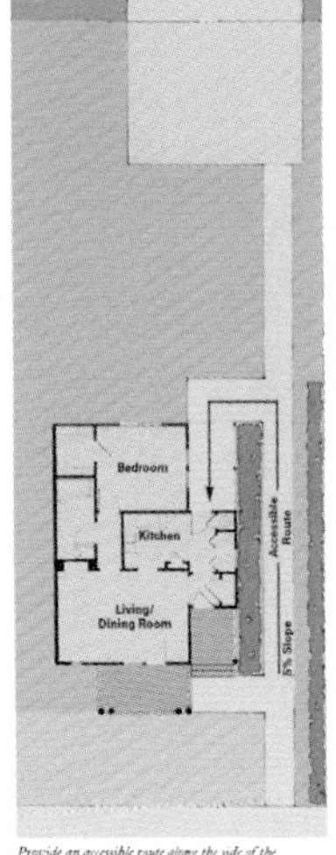

Provide an accessible route along the side of the house. When possible, use a front sidewalk with a grade of no more than 5% to access the side of the front porch.

Visitability Guidelines

PARK DUVALLE IS INTENDED to become a diverse, mixed-income, stable neighborhood. Contributing to its diversity will be the development of housing that is both accessible to persons with disabilities and marketable to all. 'Visitability' is loosely defined as making it possible for a disabled person to visit a friend's home and enjoy a meal, without having to be lifted up a step or be unable to get through the doorway. Therefore, house designs should provide at least one level access at grade without a step at the threshold.

Visitability can be accomplished by using raised slab foundation construction. This allows the rear entrance at grade to be at the same elevation as the interior floor. It also makes it possible to have a sloped walk along the side of the house with its change in grade taken up along the side of the foundation wall.

The house should also have a bathroom on the ground floor that can be used by a disabled person. In those cases in which it is a small powder room, this can be accomplished by simply employing an outward opening door yielding a 32-inch clear passage space and path inside.

Visitability not only permits disabled persons to visit their neighbors but can allow currently physically-able persons to age comfortably in their homes without the need for extensive renovations and the necessity for ungainly add-on ramps if disability should occur as part of the normal aging process.

Visitability Guidelines

COMMUNITY PATTERNS

15

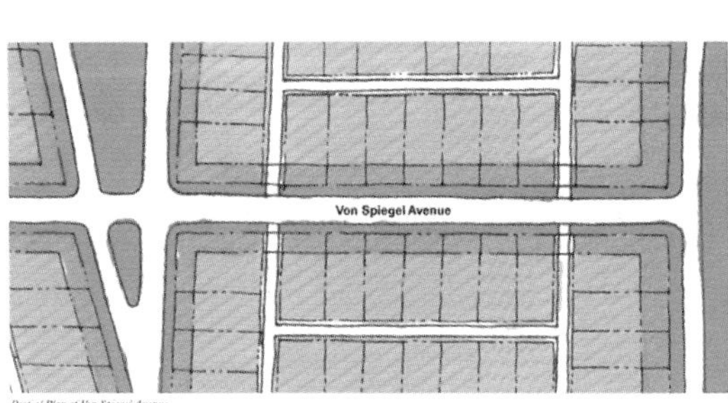

Partial Plan of Von Spiegel Avenue

View of Von Spiegel Avenue

Local Neighborhood Streets

THE MOST INTIMATE of neighborhood streets, local streets discourage high volumes of through-traffic and create a human, pedestrian scale. Cartways are narrow, with parking on both sides of the street, and houses are placed closer to the street to define a more enclosed space.

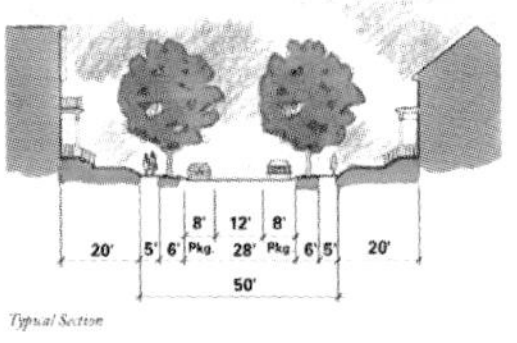

Typical Section

Local Neighborhood Streets

COMMUNITY PATTERNS

5

The Town Center area of the New Park Drive

View of the Town Center

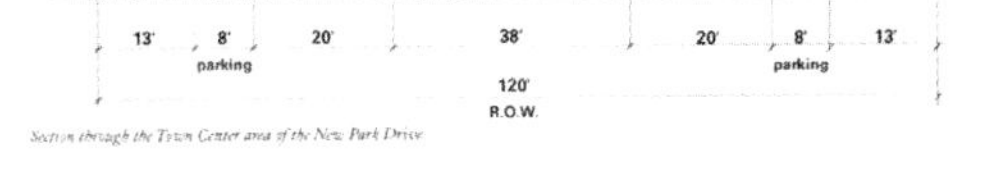

Section through the Town Center area of the New Park Drive

The Town Center

THE PARK DUVALLE TOWN CENTER is a mixed-use district of apartments and neighborhood retail, designed as a traditional shopping street. Buildings are brought up to the property line, with on-street parking in front and additional parking to the side or rear of the buildings. Wide sidewalks are delineated with street trees, lamp posts, and street furnishings.

Park DuValle Town Center

COMMUNITY PATTERNS

  6

Storefront Elements

- A Upper Facade
- B Lower Facade
- C Storefront
- D Cornice
- E Upper-Floor Window
- F Sign Band
- G Transom
- H Display Window
- I Entry
- J Piers
- K Bulkhead

Sign Types and Positions

1. Cornice Sign
2. Upper-Floor Window Sign
3. Transom Sign
4. Hanging Sign
5. Awning Sign
6. Lower Display Window Sign
7. Central Display Window Sign
8. Glazed Door Sign
9. Wall Sign for Upper-Floor Tenants

Town Center Guidelines

Retail Storefronts

Retail facades are to be traditional, with a very high degree of transparency. Store fronts should have a tripartite arrangement, with transoms and very low bulkheads. Glass should be clear, not tinted or reflective. Awnings should have a shallow slope, and project a minimum of four feet from the building.

Signage

Signs should be integrated into the architectural design of the building and should not dominate the facade or intefere with adjacent buildings. Installation must comply with applicaple city sign regulations.

Storefront-level signs should be primarily oriented to pedestrians and scaled appropriately. Place attached wall signs over the unadorned frieze of a cornice or along the top of the storefront below the sill of the second-story windows. Signs should project no more than five feet. Flush-mounted signs should be no more than three feet in height. They should be installed above the display windows and below the second-story window sills. Freestanding signs are not permitted.

Appropriate materials for signage include painted or carved wood signs, painted wall signs, sheet metal signs, and lettering applied to glass using gold leaf, paint, or etching. Plastic, over-scaled, or back-lit or internally-lit fluorescent signs or awnings are not permitted. Individual lettering and small logos may be illuminated within an opaque background. Neon may be used sparingly and judiciously.

Signs should be lit with concealed incandescent lighting. Bare spots or high-wattage metal halide lights are not permitted.

Town Center Guidelines

COMMUNITY PATTERNS

 18

View of Crescent Drive from Mason Run Boulevard

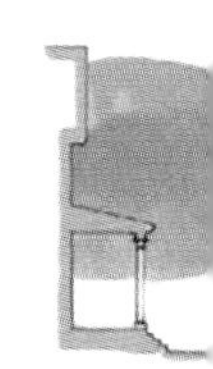

Crescent Park

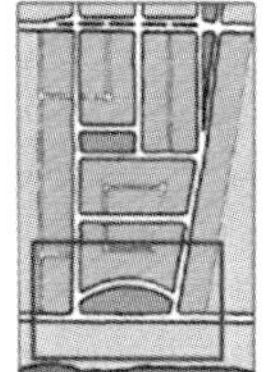

Located on Elm Street, Crescent Park sets the image and creates an address for Mason Run. As with any park, the character and appearance of surrounding homes dictate the quality of the space. Here, a symmetrical arrangement of Neighborhood and Estate houses (Lots 41-48) embrace the north side of the park. It is recommended that these homes possess full or partial front porches to create a transition from the natural to the built environment. The Estate houses that "bookend" this row (Lots 41 & 48) will have side wings or side porches and picket fences at the corners to further emphasize their role. The Duplex units on Elm Avenue (Lots 1 & 73) have a similar role and shall address the street with porches and corner picket fences. Also of note is the "Model Row," located to the west and representing the full compliment of house sizes found in Mason Run.

As a general rule, any house that sits next to either a side street or an alley (Lots 1, 6, 41, 48, 73) shall have a picket fence or a built garage connection along that edge in order to contain its yard.

Lot No.	Type	Setbacks Front	Setbacks Side Street	Special Details
1	D	20'	10'	Model Home, Full or Partial Side Porch, Corner Fence
2	D	20'		Model Home, Full Front Porch
3	E	20'		Model Home
4	N	20'		Model Home
5	V	20'		Model Home
6	C	20'		Model Home, Side Fence
41	E2	20'	10'	Side Driveway, Side Wing/Porch, Partial Front Porch, Corner Fence
42	N2	25'		Full or Partial Front Porch
43–46	N1	25'		Full or Partial Front Porch
47	N2	25'		Full or Partial Front Porch
48	E2	20'	10'	Side Driveway, Side Wing/Porch, Partial Front Porch, Corner Fence
71	E1	20'		Front Driveway, Full or Partial Front Porch
72	D	20'		Shared drive w/73
73	D	20'	10'	Shared drive w/72, Full or Partial Side Porch, Corner Fence

Community Patterns • Addresses

B-7

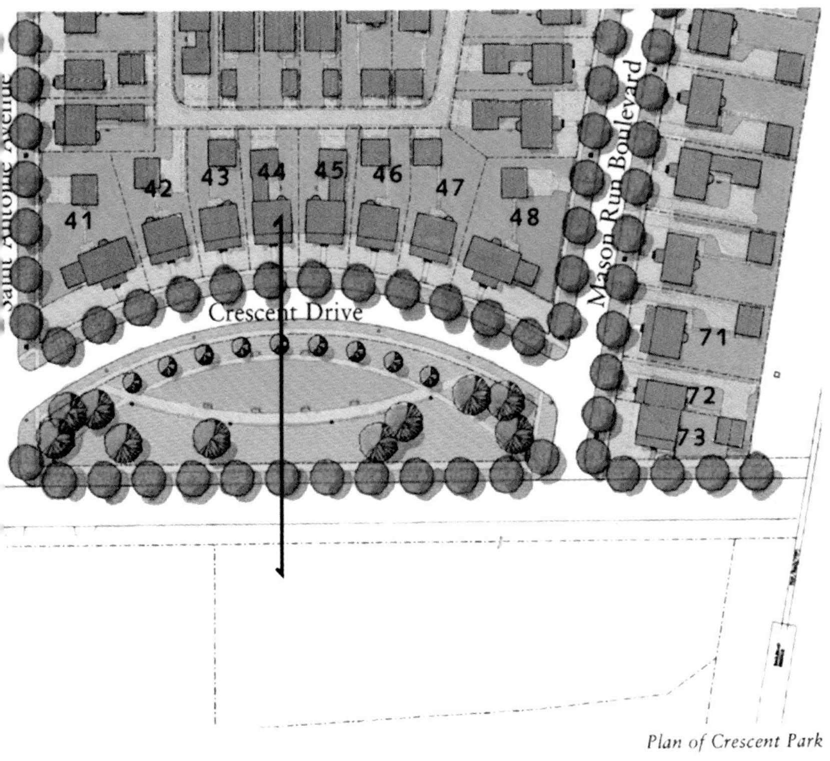

Plan of Crescent Park

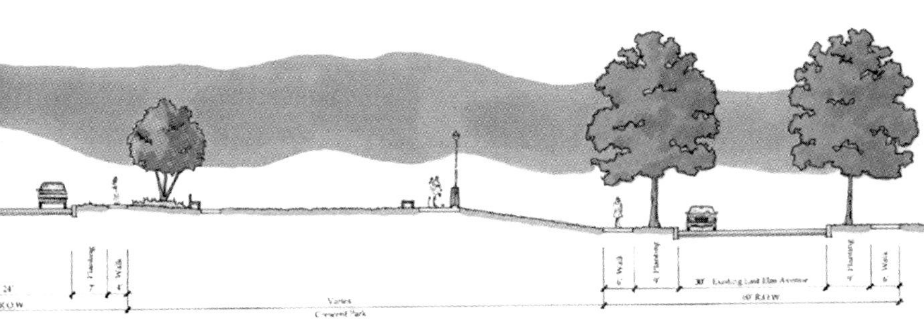

T DRIVE

ELM AVENUE

Crescent Park Street Section

Crescent Park

MASON RUN

Monroe, Michigan

The Community Patterns section for this initiative combine a perspective image of the proposed character of key places within the plan, a detailed site plan with lot designations, a typical section through the street or park, and a matrix with required setbacks or special conditions. The plan was developed by a private developer in concert with township officials as part of a brownfield site redevelopment strategy. Patterns are based on the surrounding neighborhoods and the diverse range of architectural styles and vocabularies found throughout the town.

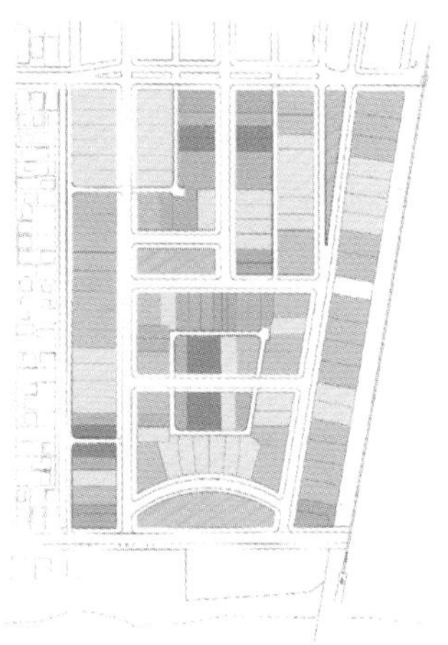

Plan Indicating Lot Types

Cottage Lots *32 – 35 feet wide*

Village Lots *35 feet wide*

Neighborhood Lots *40 – 50 feet wide*

Estate Lots *50 – 65 feet wide*

Duplex Lots *Varied width*

Townhouse Lots *Varied width*

Community Patterns

Lot Types

The Mason Run site plan contains a range of differently sized lots to accommodate the wide variety of house and unit types – from twenty-foot wide, rear-loaded, Townhouse lots, to 65 foot wide, front-loaded Estate lots. Lots are typically 100 to 110 feet deep and are either served by alleys or by driveways from the street.

The mix of large and small houses provides great variety along neighborhood streets. Corner lots with generous front and side yards are particularly important to the image of the neighborhood because they are highly visible and serve as important landmarks.

Setbacks and Zones

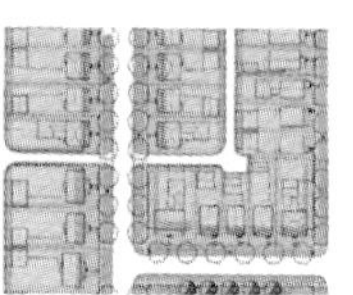

Partial Site Plan showing setback areas and zones

The overall image of a street is created by the way the houses and the landscaping work together to define space. Because the location of the house is crucial to creating the overall effect, each lot has setback lines that define minimum distances from front, rear and side lot lines. In addition, there are also a number of *setback zones* which allow a greater degree of flexibility in house placement.

Front Setback Line: Measured from the front property line.

Front Facade Zone: The zone in which the Front Facade must be placed. The zone begins at the *Front Setback Line* and continues a specified distance into the property. The Zone varies for each lot type and is subject to specific guidelines set out in this section.

Front Yard: The area between the front property line and the front facade of the house. Porches, Stoops and Bay Windows may encroach into the *Front Yard*.

Side Street Setback Line: Measured from the side property line on the street side.

Side Street Facade Zone: The zone in which the Side Street Facade must be placed. The zone begins at the *Side Street Setback Line* and continues a specified distance into the property. The Zone varies for each lot type and is subject to specific guidelines set out in this section.

Side Setback Line: Measured from the interior side property line.

Typical Lot Diagram showing setback areas and zones

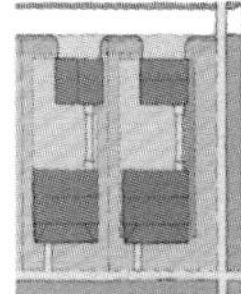

Typical Lot Diagram showing building placement on the site

Garage Setback Line: Garages facing alleys must be placed eight feet or sixteen feet or more from the rear property line, and a minimum of three feet from the interior side property line. (Sixteen feet provides enough driveway space for parking.)

Utility Easement Zone: Begins at the rear property line and extends six feet into the back yard. Only lawn, ground cover, annuals and perennials may be planted. (See Landscape Guidelines Section).

Architectural Variety

One of the things that people admire most about older, traditional neighborhoods is the architectural variety. When creating a new, traditional neighborhood it is extremely important to create and maintain variety in the streetscape. This can be done by creating a site plan that mixes different house types throughout the plan, and by establishing rules requiring diversity among facade elements. For example, if one house is brick with a full front porch and double windows, the adjacent house could be clad in siding with a partial porch and bay windows.

The *Architectural Patterns* section describes the basic principles of Mason Run residential architectural styles and provides the key elements for those parts of the house that face a public street or area.

In Mason Run there are four basic elements that contribute to the character and feel of a house facade: 1) Materials, 2) Color Palette, 3) Porch Design, and 4) Window Type

The Rule: In order to achieve architectural variety along the street, no one elevation may be repeated within a row of four houses, nor may it be repeated within the three elevations across the street. Within the row of four houses, each consecutive house must also differ in at least two of the four facade elements.

Community Patterns · Lots B-1 Lot Types, Setbacks & Zones

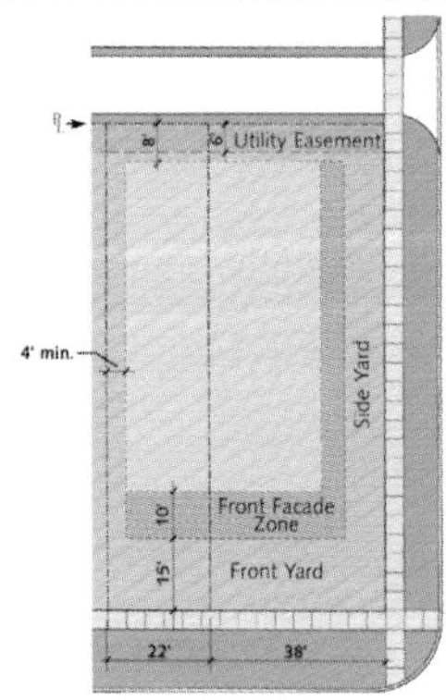

Duplex Lots

Duplex Lots are typically 22 and 38 feet wide by 100 to 110 feet deep. They may vary in size from lot to lot depending on location and type.

House Width: 18 and 24 feet typical.

Front Yard Setback: 15 feet (See Lot Information Table for specific setback information).

Front Facade Zone: 10 feet.

Side Yard Setback: 4 feet minimum (exterior side), 0 (zero) feet (interior side).

Side Street Setback: 10 feet minimum (See Lot Information Table for specific setback information).

Side Street Facade Zone: 5 feet.

Garage Side Setback: 3 feet.

Garage Size: One- and two-car garages permitted.

Side Street Fences: Picket fences are required on all corner lots. See Landscape Guidelines for specific rules about type and location.

Porches: May extend into the front yard and side yard a maximum of 8 feet.

Fireplaces: Must be located a minimum of 8 feet behind the front facade. Fireplaces on side street facade must have a chimney.

Rear (Alley) Access Lots

Utility Easement: 6 feet.

Rear Fence Line: 6 feet from the rear property line.

Garage Rear Setback: 8 feet, or 16 feet or more from the rear property line.

Garage Orientation: Garage doors must face the alley.

Front (Driveway) Access Lots

Garages: Garages on front access lots shall be positioned at least 16 feet behind the front facade of the house and no less than 3 feet from the rear property line.

Driveway: A maximum width of 8 feet maximum between curb and rear of house.

Rear Fence: Permitted along the rear property line.

Community Patterns · Mason Run B-6 Duplex Lots

View of Garrett Street from Central Park

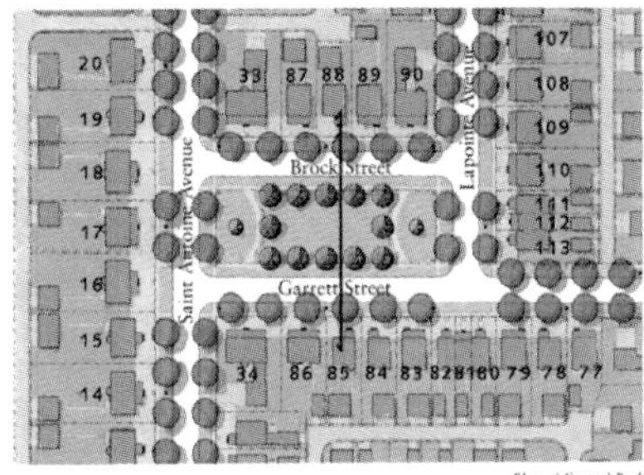

Plan of Central Park

Central Park

The simple form and classical layout of Central Park provide a distinct address for the houses that enclose it. Surrounding houses shall have either full or partial front porches in response to the open space. To add greater variation to the feel of Saint Antoine Avenue, some houses (Lots 16-18) are pulled farther back from the street. Meanwhile, full porches (Lots 16-18) or larger building masses (Lots 80-81, 111-113) are required at the termination of vistas. Corner yards (Lots 20, 33, 34, 90, 113) shall be contained with either picket fences or built connections to garages, such as breezeways.

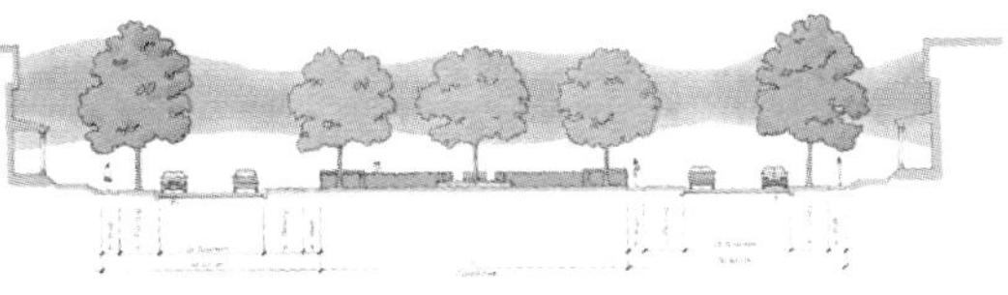

Lot No.	Type	Setbacks Front	Setbacks Side Street	Special Details
14	E	20'		
15	E	20'		
16	E	25'		Full Front Porch
17	E	25'		Full Front Porch
18	E	25'		Full Front Porch
19	E	20'		
20	E	20'		Side Fence
33	E	20'	10'	Full Front Porch, Corner Fence or Attached Garage
34	E3	20'	10'	Full Front Porch, Side Driveway, Corner Fence or Attached Garage
77		20'		
78		20'		
79		20'		
80-82		20'		
83		20'		
84-85		20'		
86		20'		
87		20'		
88		20'		
89		20'		
90		20'	10'	Side Driveway, Corner Fence or Attached Garage
107-109		20'		
110		20'		
111-112		20'		
113		20'	14'	Corner Fence

Community Patterns · Addresses B-8 Central Park

Houses with gracious front porches overlook Mason Run Boulevard

Mason Run Boulevard

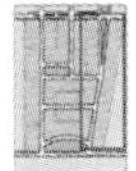

Mason Run Boulevard begins as a simple, neighborhood street and broadens into a lush, landscaped boulevard as it continues north to E. Noble Avenue. Of special note along Mason Run Boulevard are the houses on the western side, south of Garrett Street (Lots 49-51, 64, 74-76). Instead of mimicking the angle of the road, they remain orthogonal to the grid and "step" toward the linear park to the north, framing the view corridor. Further north along the park, some houses (Lots 116-119, 127-130) are moved closer to the street to contain the park area and emphasize that address. Finally, houses with corner lots (Lots 51, 64, 76, 114, 123, 124) shall have either a picket fence or a built connection (such as a breezeway) to the garage in order to contain the backyards.

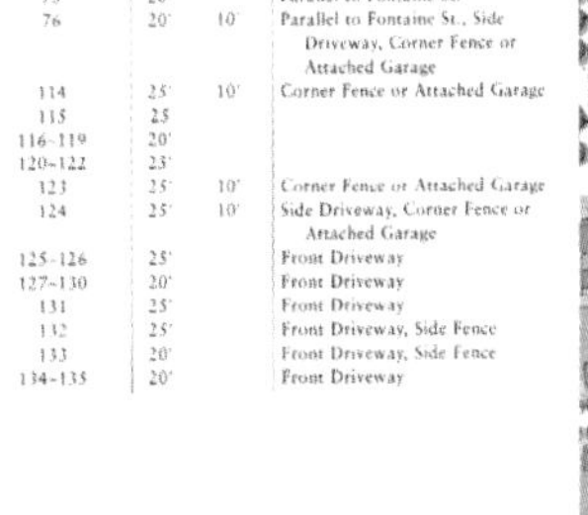

Lot No.	Type	Setbacks Front	Setbacks Side Street	Special Details
49	E1	20'		Parallel to Fontaine St.
50	N1	20'		Parallel to Fontaine St.
51	N2	20'	10'	Parallel to Fontaine St., Corner Fence or Attached Garage
64	E1	20'	10'	Parallel to Fontaine St.,Corner Fence or Attached Garage
65	E2	25'		Front Driveway, Full Front Porch
66	N2	25'		Front Driveway, Full Front Porch
67	N2	20'		Front Driveway
68-70	E1	20'		Front Driveway
74		20'		Parallel to Fontaine St.
75		20'		Parallel to Fontaine St.
76		20'	10'	Parallel to Fontaine St., Side Driveway, Corner Fence or Attached Garage
114		25'	10'	Corner Fence or Attached Garage
115		25		
116-119		20'		
120-122		23'		
123		25'	10'	Corner Fence or Attached Garage
124		25'	10'	Side Driveway, Corner Fence or Attached Garage
125-126		25'		Front Driveway
127-130		20'		Front Driveway
131		25'		Front Driveway
132		25'		Front Driveway, Side Fence
133		20'		Front Driveway, Side Fence
134-135		20'		Front Driveway

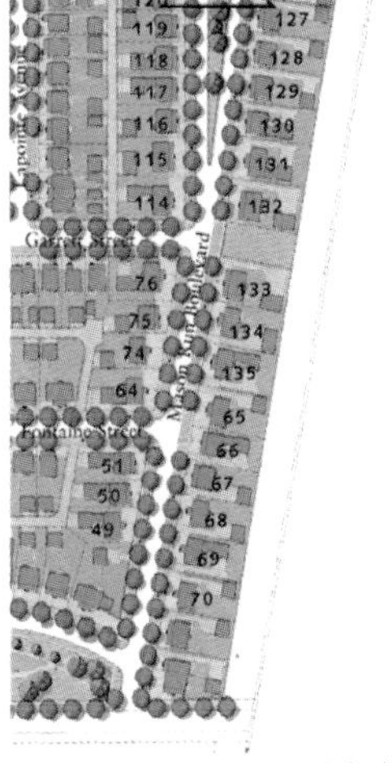

Plan of Mason Run Boulevard

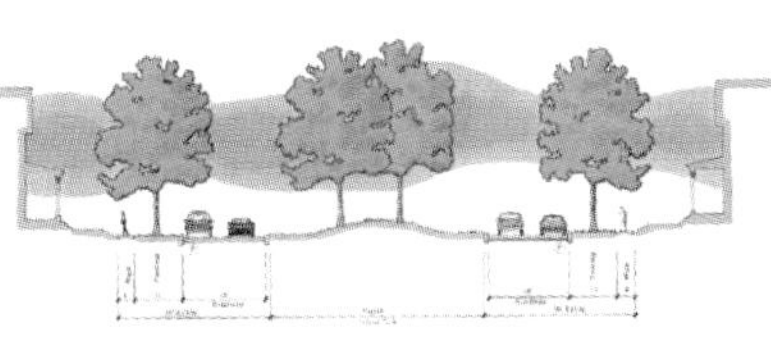

Community Patterns · Addresses B-9 Mason Run Boulevard

GÉNITOY EST: BUSSY SAINT GEORGES, FRANCE

Typical Block Plan

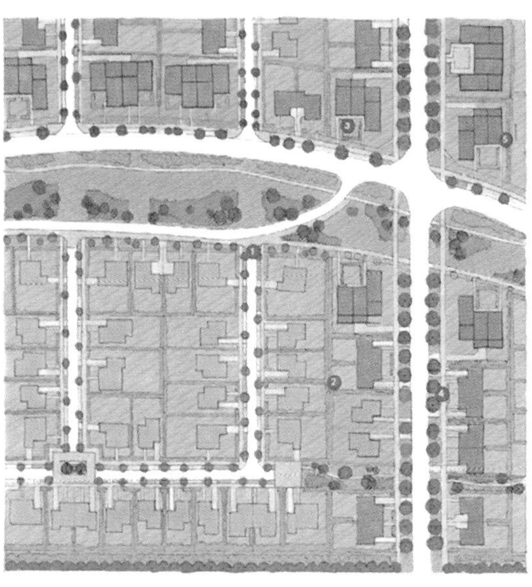

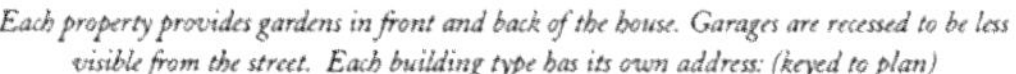

Each property provides gardens in front and back of the house. Garages are recessed to be less visible from the street. Each building type has its own address: (keyed to plan)

1. Single-family houses on the Park Way
2. Single-family houses on a residential lane
3. Small Villas (two attached houses) on a Park Way
4. Small Villas and houses on a neighborhood street
5. Large Villas (four or more attached units) on corners

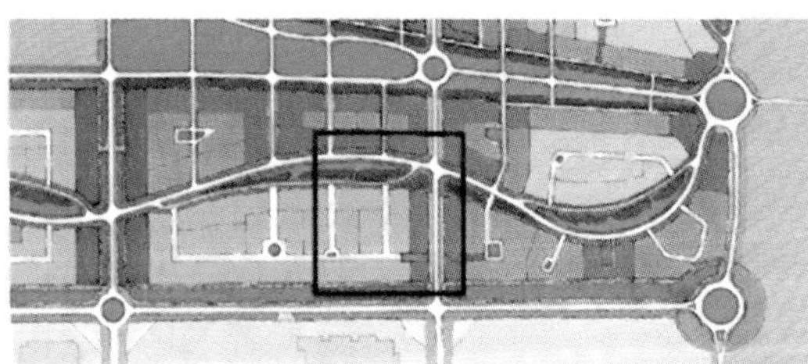

URBAN DESIGN ASSOCIATES
ERASME ÉTUDES URBAINES

JUNE 2002

Single-family houses and small villas face the Park Way and a neighborhood lane. They are compatible with the large villas which are placed on the corner of the block.

Each house has a clearly visible front door. The landscape elements and fencing define the yard without blocking views of the house. Garages are recessed.

GÉNITOY EST

Bussy St. Georges, France

The master plan for Génitoy is an extension of an existing new town outside of Paris. For this plan, the eastern extension was meant to be a return to more traditional French patterns of building types and architecture. The pattern book is a concise set of urban design and architectural patterns that establish a series of block and lot patterns, detailed building placement strategies, building types, and architectural style guidelines. These are combined in different ways throughout the plan to reestablish the sense of place and quality that is part of French traditional settlements in the region.

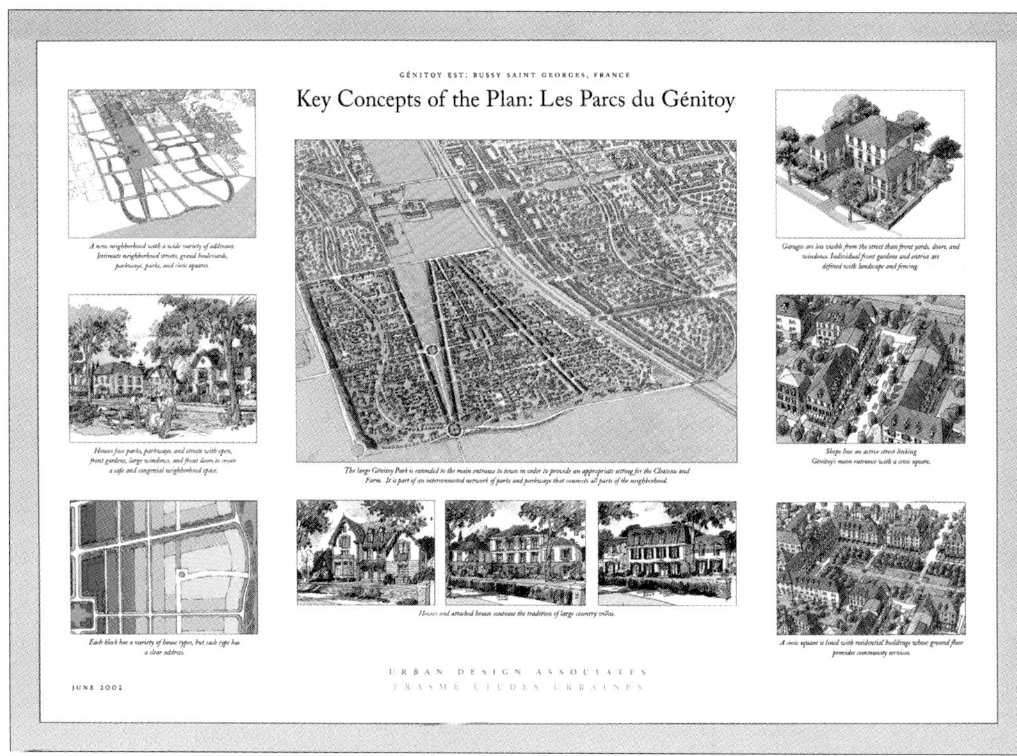
GÉNITOY EST: BUSSY SAINT GEORGES, FRANCE
Key Concepts of the Plan: Les Parcs du Génitoy
JUNE 2002
URBAN DESIGN ASSOCIATES
ERASME ÉTUDES URBAINES

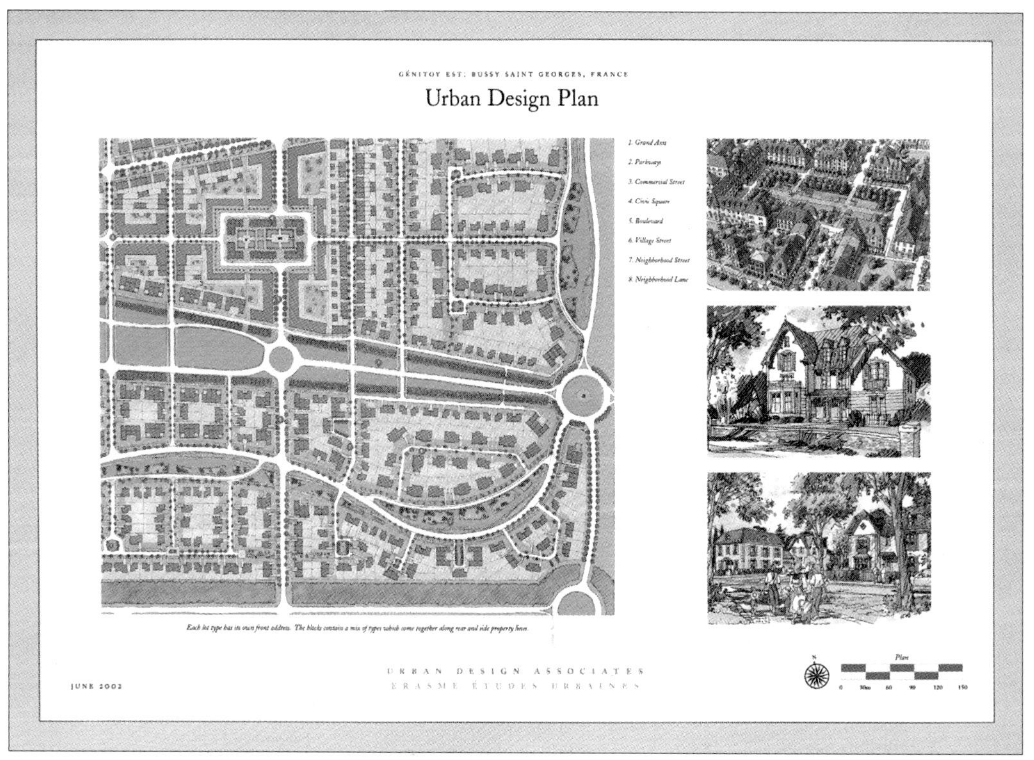
GÉNITOY EST: BUSSY SAINT GEORGES, FRANCE
Urban Design Plan
1. Grand Axis
2. Parkways
3. Commercial Street
4. Civic Square
5. Boulevard
6. Village Street
7. Neighborhood Street
8. Neighborhood Lane
JUNE 2002
URBAN DESIGN ASSOCIATES
ERASME ÉTUDES URBAINES
Plan

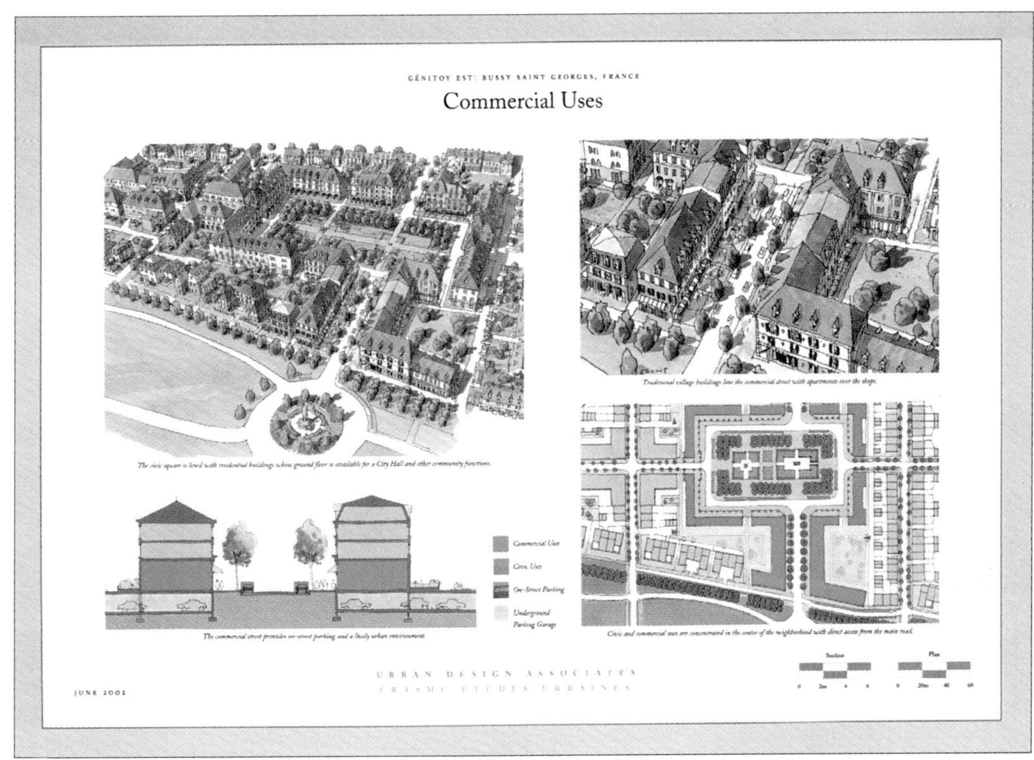
GÉNITOY EST: BUSSY SAINT GEORGES, FRANCE
Commercial Uses
The civic square is lined with residential buildings whose ground floor is available for a City Hall and other community functions.
Traditional village buildings line the commercial street with apartments over the shops.
Commercial Uses
Civic Uses
On-Street Parking
Underground Parking Garage
The commercial street provides on-street parking and a lively urban environment.
Civic and commercial uses are concentrated in the center of the neighborhood with direct access from the main road.
Section
Plan
URBAN DESIGN ASSOCIATES
ERASME ÉTUDES URBAINES
JUNE 2002

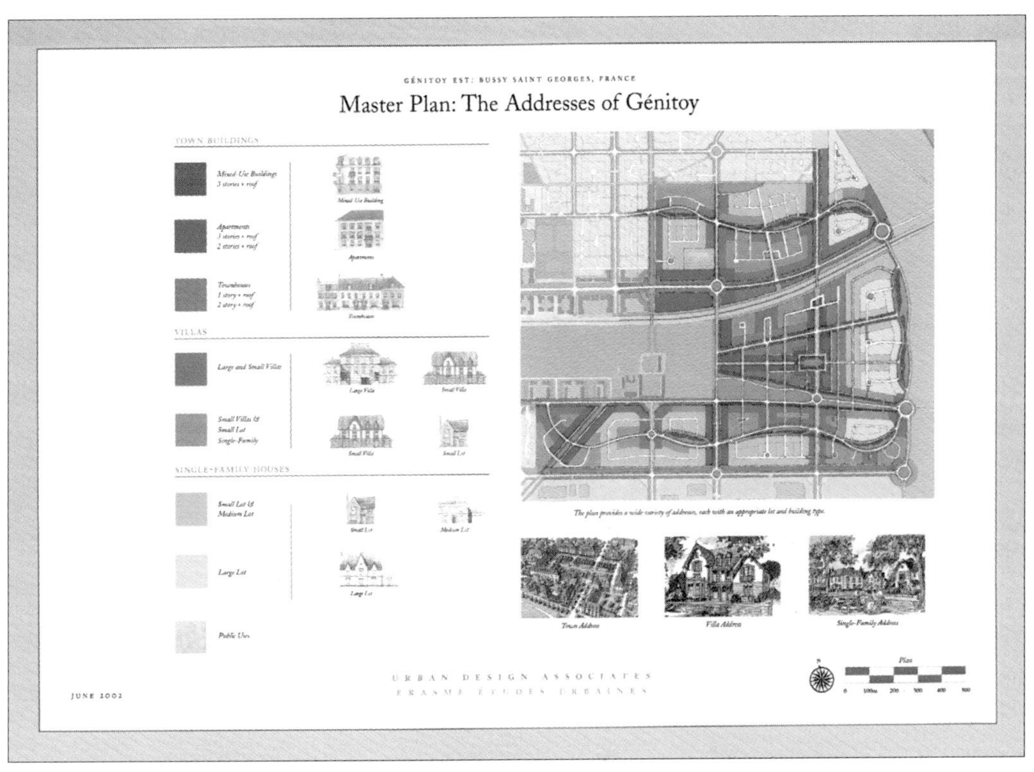
GÉNITOY EST: BUSSY SAINT GEORGES, FRANCE
Master Plan: The Addresses of Génitoy
TOWN BUILDINGS
Mixed-Use Buildings
3 stories + roof
Mixed-Use Building
Apartments
3 stories + roof
2 stories + roof
Apartments
Townhouses
1 story + roof
2 story + roof
Townhouses
VILLAS
Large and Small Villas
Large Villa
Small Villa
Small Villas &
Small Lot
Single-Family
Small Villa
Small Lot
SINGLE-FAMILY HOUSES
Small Lot &
Medium Lot
Small Lot
Medium Lot
Large Lot
Large Lot
Public Uses
The plan provides a wide variety of addresses, each with an appropriate lot and building type.
Town Address
Villa Address
Single-Family Address
Plan
URBAN DESIGN ASSOCIATES
ERASME ÉTUDES URBAINES
JUNE 2002

Tidewater Colonial Revival

CHAPTER

8

Architectural Patterns Pages

The Architectural Patterns section illustrates a series of specific architectural vocabularies or styles deemed appropriate for the proposed development and key to the creation of a regionally unique place. As discussed in Chapter 5, the identification of the principal architectural patterns comes out of an intensive process of documenting precedent neighborhoods within the region and distilling the dominant architectural vocabularies that form the core character of the particular places identified as relevant precedents. Once these character trends have been identified, photographed, and measured, the team can begin the process of identifying key components for each vocabulary, including: massing types; eave details; materials; standard windows and doors; special or unique components, methods, and details; and porches, columns, and roofs.

Each vocabulary often has locally unique qualities or signatures. Where this occurs, it is important to document the details or methods to incorporate within the relevant architectural style section. In most cases, pattern books will illustrate and define three to six different styles in the Architectural Patterns section. The process of preparing the drawings and content for each style or vocabulary requires detailed analysis and reference research to refine the patterns. These need not be historically accurate reproductions. Details and proportions, typical components, and assemblies are illustrated as a resource for architects and builders. In addition to the signature elements for each vocabulary, the examples shown in this chapter underscore the importance of translating the traditional vocabularies to ones that will work with current building practices and with the proposed lot sizes and types within the plan. Proportions were adjusted to fit current practices for floor-to-ceiling heights and available components from manufacturers, where applicable, such as windows, doors, columns, and trim. The pattern books define massing types for the houses, but leave floor-plan arrangements and interior detailing up to the individual user, builder, or architect. Plan arrangements have to work within the massing types and strategies in order to develop an architectural character consistent with a particular vocabulary. One recurring theme that cuts across most traditional architecture is the relatively simple massing found within each vocabulary.

The Architectural Patterns may be organized as five- to six-page sections that document the essential elements of a particular type or style. In the examplars presented in this chapter, the first architectural pattern page describes the history and character of the style with illustrations and photographs of examples. The second page documents four or five primary massing types that illustrate the principal forms (main bodies) and additive forms (wings). A third page deals with the primary form of the house and key eave and cornice options. This sets the floor-to-ceiling heights and the relationship to the first floor above the ground. A fourth page illustrates doors and windows; the fifth page illustrates porch types; and the last page defines typical materials and illustrates a series of elevation possibilities using the elements detailed in the pattern book.

The remainder of this book is devoted to presenting examples of Architectural Patterns pages derived from UDA Pattern Books. They have been grouped by architectural style so that you can see how, even within a particular architectural vocabulary, the designs vary from project to project, based on the objectives of the project and the prevailing precedents in the particular region. Five distinct styles are presented: Colonial Revival, Victorian, Arts & Crafts, Classical, and European Romantic.

The Ledges is a new neighborhood designed using key character elements found in the surrounding historic neighborhoods and villages around Huntsville, Alabama. The site is a remarkable vantage point atop the Cumberland Plateau overlooking the surrounding valleys. The design of each street, park, and precinct was carefully crafted in response to the inherited patterns of the site and the legacy of historic settlement patterns. A pattern book was created for the development team to guide architects and builders in the design and placement of houses as a continuation of regional architectural vocabularies.

COLONIAL REVIVAL STYLE

Comparative Analysis

The Colonial Revival variations are the bread-and-butter of most American neighborhoods that have a cross-section of architecture, particularly those built during the latter part of the nineteenth and early part of the twentieth centuries. While there have been many different "Colonial" revivals throughout this country's early development phases, most often the period documented in pattern books is later, 1900 through the 1930s. Royal Barry Wills was one of the premier American architects who helped define the elements of style for this particular revival. This architecture became a hallmark of a broad cross-section of the culture, from the most modest houses to the most affluent. The houses can be very simple with broad, gracious windows and simple porticos or surrounds calling out the front door. The more exuberant versions use exotic, heavy moldings and brackets in eave and cornice detailing, as well as at door surrounds and window openings.

As towns and cities began to grow out into the rural countryside in the early part of the twentieth century, Colonial Revival was often the choice for the houses. Many designs were developed for catalog sales for companies such as Sears, Alladin, and Standard House. Larger window proportions, often biased toward width; double window compositions; angled bay windows or gangs of double-hung windows; exuberant use of special windows and elements such as Palladian windows or arched upper-sash windows; expressive frieze detailing; and cornice articulation on simple gabled-roof house forms are common traits in this vocabulary. Oftentimes, traditional vernacular house forms were adapted to include the signature Colonial Revival elements.

Sample pages of the Colonial Revival style have been excerpted from the East Beach (Norfolk, Virginia), Liberty (Lake Elsinore, California), and Norfolk, Virginia pattern books.

Precedent photos

Elizabeth City, North Carolina

Portsmouth, Virginia

Edenton, North Carolina

Essential Elements of the Tidewater Colonial Revival

1 Simple, straightforward volumes with side wings and porches added to make more complex shapes.

2 An orderly, symmetrical relationship between windows, doors and building mass.

3 Simplified versions of Classical details and columns, occasionally with Classical orders used at the entry.

4 Multi-pane windows.

Tidewater Colonial Revival

Edenton, North Carolina

History and Character

THE TIDEWATER COLONIAL REVIVAL is based on Colonial Revival styles that were prevalent throughout the country in the late nineteenth and early twentieth centuries. During this era, elements from Classical and Colonial houses were combined with and modified to produce a new vocabulary that became popular in the latter part of the nineteenth century. This mixing of influences produced a wide variety of expression and form in the Colonial Revival house. Many of these houses have more elaborate entrances, cornice treatments and window compositions. Dutch Colonial Gambrel forms are also very typical. Windows tend to be tall and narrow in proportion and more free in composition than the original Classical houses. Many of the houses in Mid-Atlantic coastal villages and neighborhoods incorporate deep front porches, running the entire face of the front façade. Accent windows are often used over the central door location.

I

EAST BEACH

Norfolk, Virginia

The East Beach Colonial Revival is a good example of this style adapting to coastal house forms throughout the Tidewater region of Virginia, North Carolina, and Maryland. While, typically, Colonial Revival houses have sitting porches as side wings to the principal mass of the house, many Tidewater houses are traditional "four-square" plans that have square forms with hip roofs. Large, full-facade porches are often added to protect the ground floor from the intense summer sun and to allow families to fully use the porch as a central component of the layout of the house. Classically proportioned columns, porch railings, and entablature detailing were often robust. The more modest houses had less trim components. Many smaller neighborhood houses use muntins in the top sash only. Eaves and detailing were more straightforward, but a wide variety of column and turned porch balusters were used. Often, this simple box would incorporate two-story front and side wings that became an integral part of the massing and allowed the house to transform into a different shape and character than the four-square original. Many gambrel roof houses with a second floor within the roof form were developed as a continuation of a much older Colonial-style house form found on the eastern seaboard.

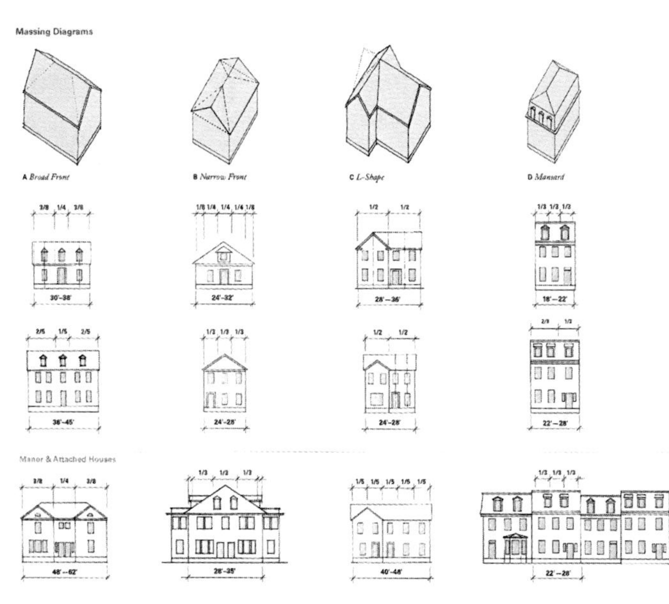

Massing and Composition

Massing

A Broad Front
Hipped-roof or side-gable rectangular volume with roof pitches ranging from 7 in 12 to 12 in 12. One-story shed or hip roofed porches are often placed symmetrically on the front façade. One-story side wings often occur. Although porches are most often one-third or one-fifth the length of the main body, they may also be three-fifths or the entire length of the front façade.

B Narrow Front
Hipped-roof or front-gable box with roof pitches ranging from 7 to 12 in 12. Five and three bay compositions are common. Full front porches and one-story side wings are common to this massing type.

C L-Shape
L-shape volume with a front facing gable roof intersecting either a gable or cross-gable at the rear. Roof pitch ranges from 6 in 12 to 10 in 12. One- and two-story porches often fill the space of the **L**.

D Mansard
Simple rectangular volume with steeply pitched mansard. Roof pitch ranges from 48 in 12 to 54 in 12. Though mansards are most frequent on the fronts of attached townhouses, mansard roofs can also wrap around a building. Three-bay compositions, symmetrically arranged with full front porches are most common.

Combinations
Larger living spaces may be created by adding side wings to the main body. Gabled or shed dormers may be added to introduce light into half-story and attic spaces. The architectural character of elements such as side wings, rear wings, and accessory/ancillary structures should be consistent with the architectural character of the main body.

Façade Composition
Colonial Revival façade composition is characterized by a somewhat symmetrical and balanced placement of windows and doors. Windows do not necessarily align vertically between floors, but are arranged in a locally symmetrical manner. Standard windows occur as singles, or in pairs. Entrance doors are generally located near the corner of narrow houses and at the center of wide houses.

Tidewater Colonial Revival

ARCHITECTURAL PATTERNS C 2

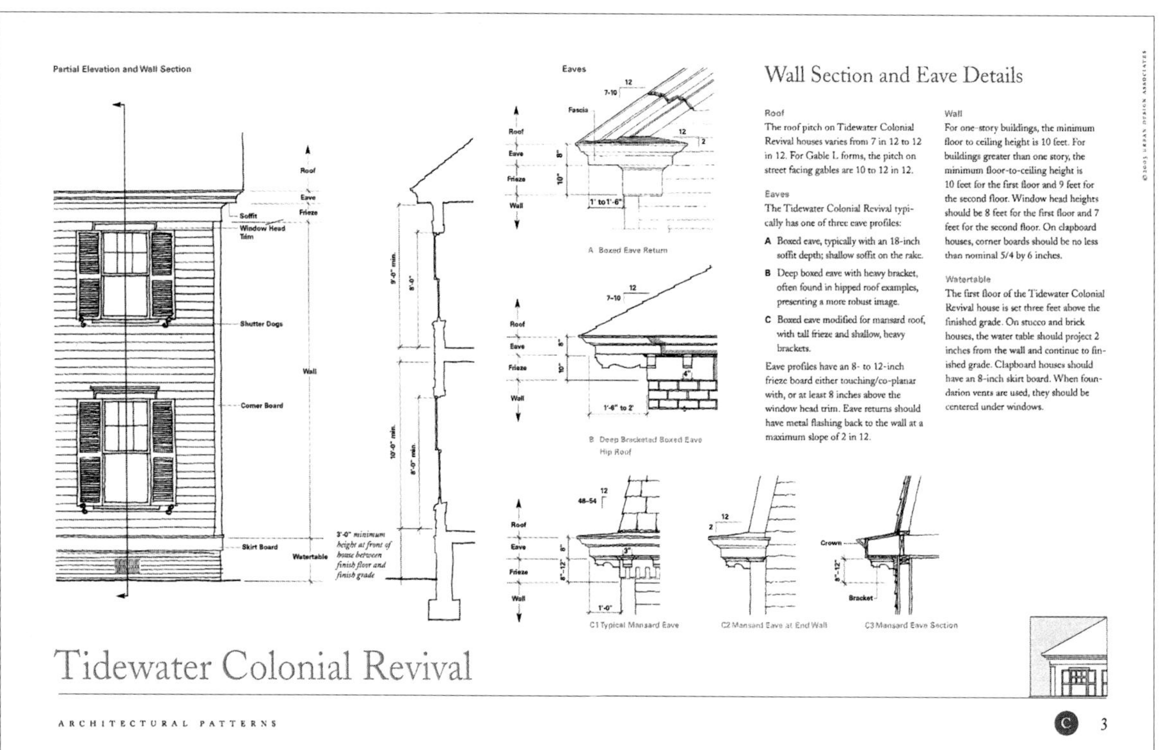

Wall Section and Eave Details

Roof
The roof pitch on Tidewater Colonial Revival houses varies from 7 in 12 to 12 in 12. For Gable L forms, the pitch on street facing gables are 10 to 12 in 12.

Eaves
The Tidewater Colonial Revival typically has one of three eave profiles:

- **A** Boxed eave, typically with an 18-inch soffit depth; shallow soffit on the rake.
- **B** Deep boxed eave with heavy bracket, often found in hipped roof examples, presenting a more robust image.
- **C** Boxed eave modified for mansard roof, with tall frieze and shallow, heavy brackets.

Eave profiles have an 8- to 12-inch frieze board either touching/co-planar with, or at least 8 inches above the window head trim. Eave returns should have metal flashing back to the wall at a maximum slope of 2 in 12.

Wall
For one-story buildings, the minimum floor to ceiling height is 10 feet. For buildings greater than one story, the minimum floor-to-ceiling height is 10 feet for the first floor and 9 feet for the second floor. Window head heights should be 8 feet for the first floor and 7 feet for the second floor. On clapboard houses, corner boards should be no less than nominal 5/4 by 6 inches.

Watertable
The first floor of the Tidewater Colonial Revival house is set three feet above the finished grade. On stucco and brick houses, the water table should project 2 inches from the wall and continue to finished grade. Clapboard houses should have an 8-inch skirt board. When foundation vents are used, they should be centered under windows.

Tidewater Colonial Revival

ARCHITECTURAL PATTERNS C 3

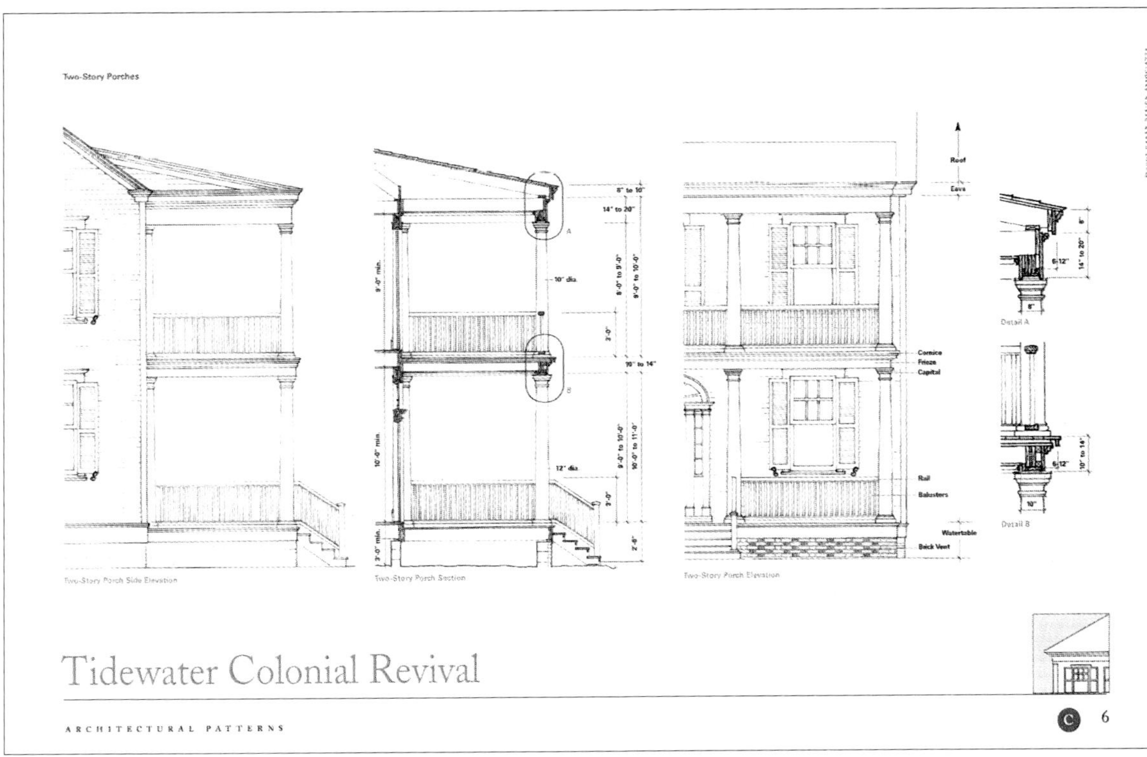

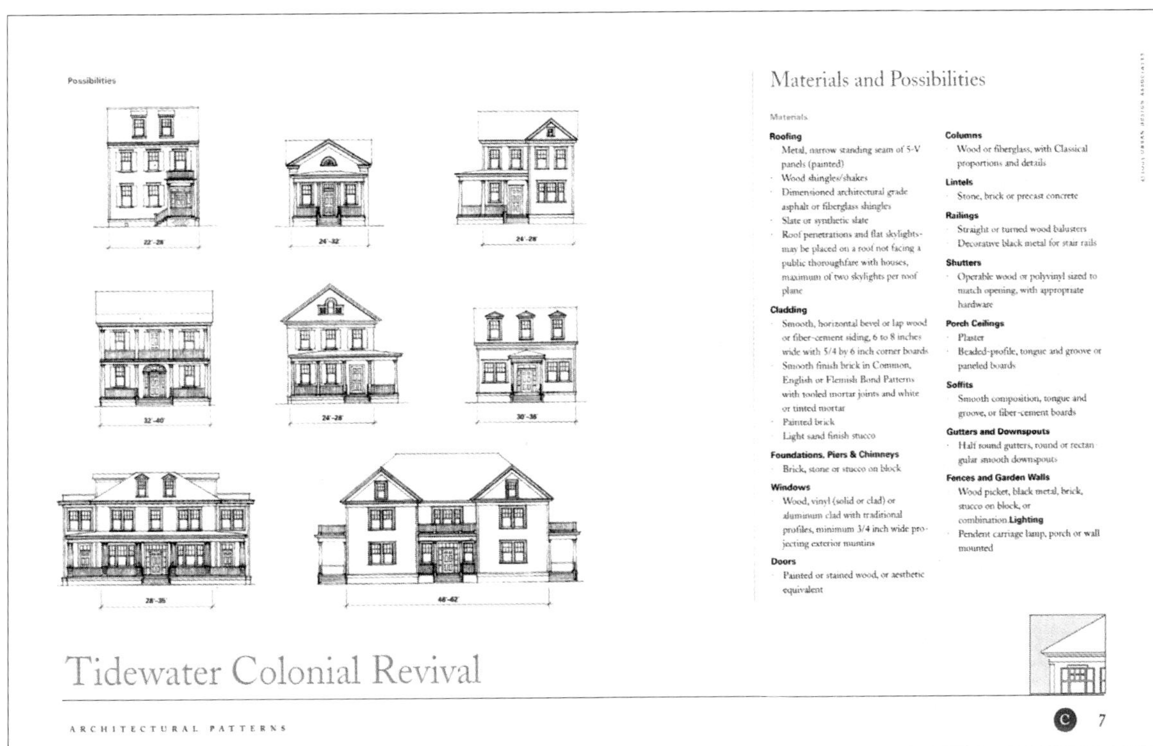

Materials and Possibilities

Materials

Roofing
- Metal, narrow standing seam of 5-V panels (painted)
- Wood shingles/shakes
- Dimensioned architectural grade asphalt or fiberglass shingles
- Slate or synthetic slate
- Roof penetrations and flat skylights-may be placed on a roof not facing a public thoroughfare with houses, maximum of two skylights per roof plane

Cladding
- Smooth, horizontal bevel or lap wood or fiber-cement siding, 6 to 8 inches wide with 5/4 by 6 inch corner boards
- Smooth finish brick in Common, English or Flemish Bond Patterns with tooled mortar joints and white or tinted mortar
- Painted brick
- Light sand finish stucco

Foundations, Piers & Chimneys
- Brick, stone or stucco on block

Windows
- Wood, vinyl (solid or clad) or aluminum clad with traditional profiles, minimum 3/4 inch wide projecting exterior muntins

Doors
- Painted or stained wood, or aesthetic equivalent

Columns
- Wood or fiberglass, with Classical proportions and details

Lintels
- Stone, brick or precast concrete

Railings
- Straight or turned wood balusters
- Decorative black metal for stair rails

Shutters
- Operable wood or polyvinyl sized to match opening, with appropriate hardware

Porch Ceilings
- Plaster
- Beaded-profile, tongue and groove or paneled boards

Soffits
- Smooth composition, tongue and groove, or fiber-cement boards

Gutters and Downspouts
- Half round gutters, round or rectangular smooth downspouts

Fences and Garden Walls
- Wood picket, black metal, brick, stucco on block, or combination

Lighting
- Pendent carriage lamp, porch or wall mounted

Tidewater Colonial Revival

ARCHITECTURAL PATTERNS

7

A simple symmetrical house in Orange with a full front porch

The symmetrical arrangement of windows and dormers creates a classical composition for this Classical house in Pasadena

This house in Pasadena is a good example of horizontal proportions and the use of special windows.

Early twentieth century Colonial Revival house

Colonial Revival, Madison Heights neighborhood, Pasadena, California

Essential Elements of the Liberty Classic

1 Simple, straightforward volumes with one-story side wings and porches added to make more complex shapes.

2 Symmetrical composition of doors and windows.

3 Simplified versions of Classical details and columns, often with robust and exotic Classical orders such as Ionic and Corinthian used in the porch element.

4 Multi-pane windows that are wide in proportion usually with 6 over 6 or 6 over 1 pane patterns.

History and Character

THE LIBERTY CLASSIC is based on Colonial Revival styles that were prevalent throughout the country in the early 1900s. The Colonial Revival style is evident in many California towns and cities. Interesting renditions can be found in the Los Angeles area, including Madison Heights in Pasadena. Valley communities, such as Riverside and Orange, also have a diverse collection of period houses designed in the Colonial Revival style.

The Colonial Revival style is based on Classical design principles followed in the Colonial period in this country. The interpretations, however, are often regional in character. The Southern California examples include many houses with full front porches, Dutch Colonial renditions and unusual color use on the facade and architectural elements. Cornices are often deep, with extended overhangs and brackets along the soffit on the main body and the porches.

The houses are composed of simple forms with well-proportioned windows and door surrounds. These are often more horizontal in appearance with special windows appearing in the center of the house over the front door.

Liberty Classic

Massing Diagrams

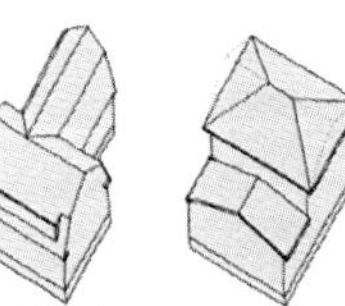

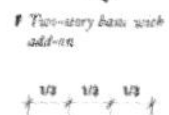

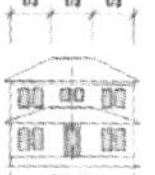

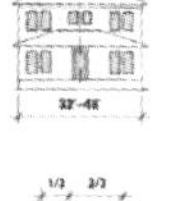

Massing and Composition

Massing

A Two-story basic

Hipped or side-gabled rectangular volume. Hip roof pitch is typically 5 in 12 and gable roof pitch is 7 in 12. One-story temple front or hip front porches, placed symmetrically on the front facade. Two-story center porches are also permitted. Although porches are most often one-fifth the length of the main body, they may also be three-fifths or the entire length of the front facade.

B Two-story front hip gable

Hipped or front-gabled rectangular volume. Hip roof pitch is typically 7 in 12 and gable roof pitch is 8 in 12. As with the basic massing, symmetrically placed gabled and/or hipped front porches are common. Porches may be either one- or two-story. Two-story porches are integral and are reserved for front-gabled houses between 24 and 30 feet wide.

C Two-story gable L

Cross-gabled volume with an 8 in 12 gable facing the street. Cross gable has a lower slope. The width of the gable facing the street is typically half that of the main body for houses up to 36 feet wide and two-fifths that of the main body for houses 36 feet and over. This massing typically accommodates a continuous porch with shed roof located between the legs of the L.

D Two-story box L

Hipped roof box with a two-story bay added to both the front and side. The bays shall have either a gabled roof with a 7 in 12 pitch or more commonly a hipped roof with a 5 in 12 pitch. Ideal for corner houses, this massing invites an L-shaped corner porch between the two bays.

E One-and-one-half-story gambrel

Rectangular volume with a gambrel roof parallel to the street. Roof pitch is nearly vertical on the lower slope and 4 to 6 in 12 at the top. One-story temple front porches centered on the front facade are typical. Porches extending three-fifths or the entire length of the front facade are also permitted.

F Two-story basic with add-on

Two-story main body with a gable or hip roof parallel to the street. An 'add-on' is usually a full- or partial-width one-story forward-projecting wing with similar roof form.

Facade Composition

Classic facade composition is characterized by a symmetrical and balanced placement of doors and windows. Standard windows most often occur as singles, or in pairs. Entrance doors are generally located in the corner of narrow houses and center of wide houses.

Liberty Classic

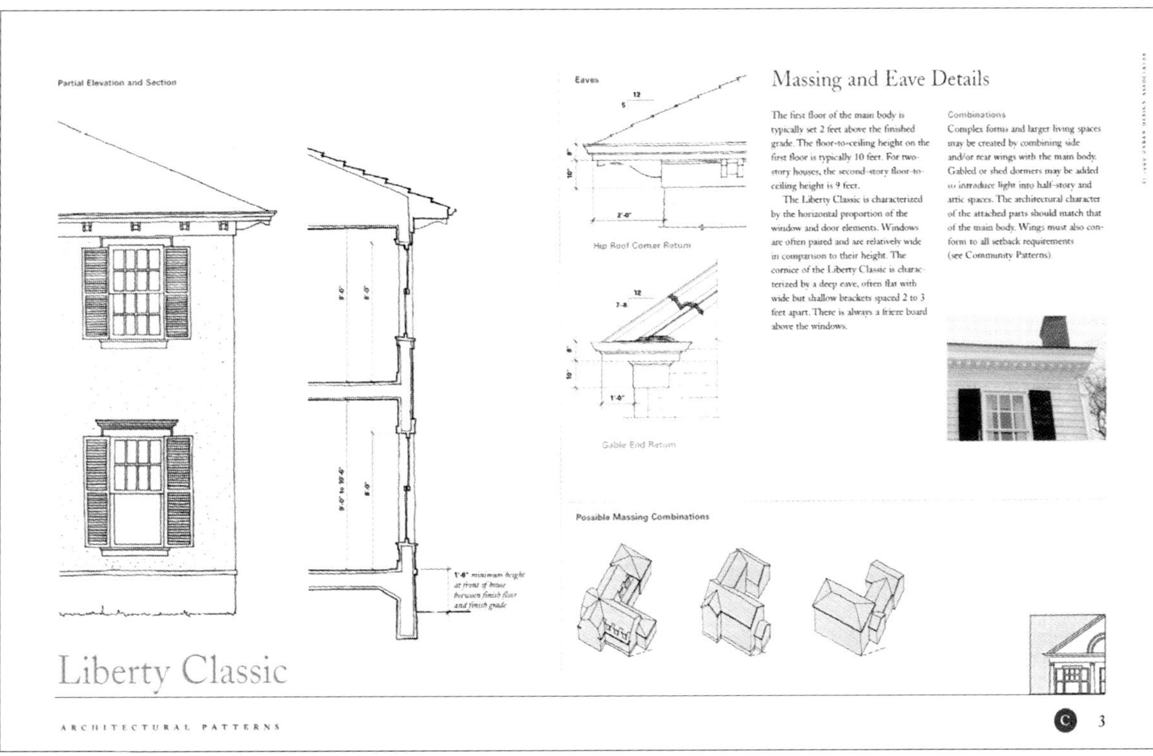

Partial Elevation and Section

Eaves

Hip Roof Corner Return

Gable End Return

Possible Massing Combinations

Massing and Eave Details

The first floor of the main body is typically set 2 feet above the finished grade. The floor-to-ceiling height on the first floor is typically 10 feet. For two-story houses, the second-story floor-to-ceiling height is 9 feet.

The Liberty Classic is characterized by the horizontal proportion of the window and door elements. Windows are often paired and are relatively wide in comparison to their height. The cornice of the Liberty Classic is characterized by a deep eave, often flat with wide but shallow brackets spaced 2 to 3 feet apart. There is always a frieze board above the windows.

Combinations

Complex forms and larger living spaces may be created by combining side and/or rear wings with the main body. Gabled or shed dormers may be added to introduce light into half-story and attic spaces. The architectural character of the attached parts should match that of the main body. Wings must also conform to all setback requirements (see Community Patterns).

Liberty Classic

ARCHITECTURAL PATTERNS

C 3

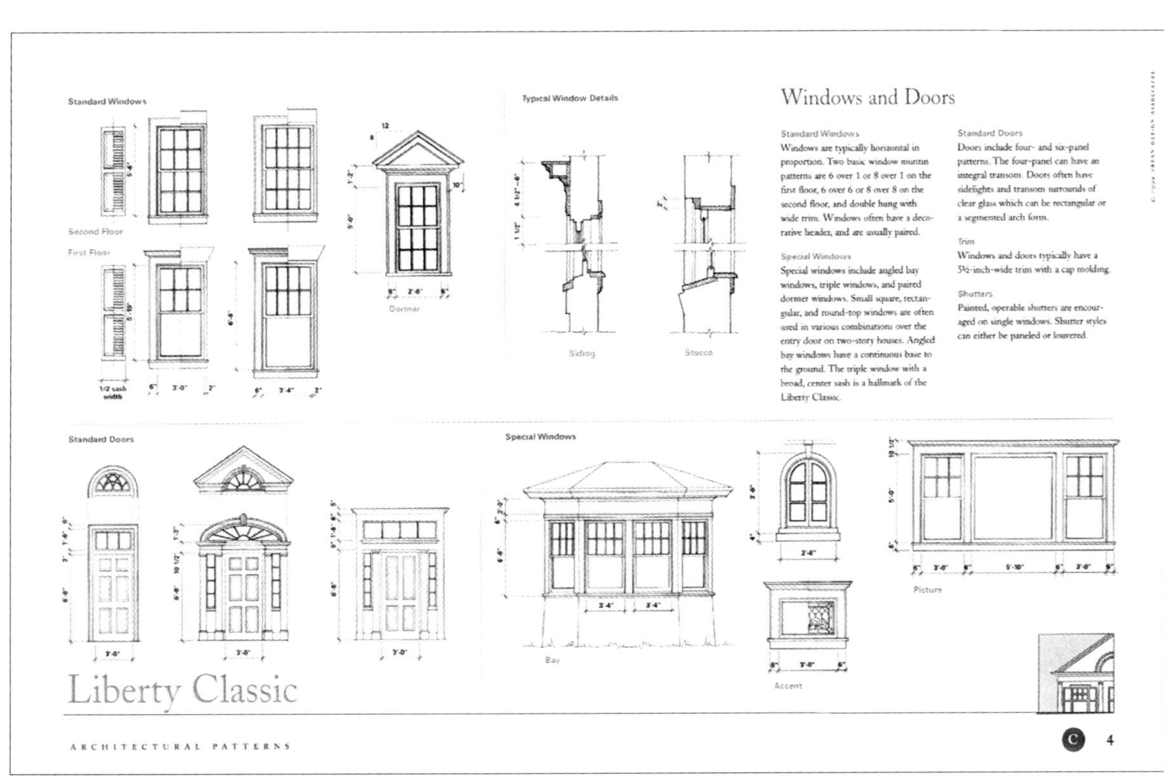

Standard Windows

Second Floor

First Floor

Dormer

Typical Window Details

Siding

Stucco

Windows and Doors

Standard Windows

Windows are typically horizontal in proportion. Two basic window muntin patterns are 6 over 1 or 8 over 1 on the first floor, 6 over 6 or 8 over 8 on the second floor, and double hung with wide trim. Windows often have a decorative header, and are usually paired.

Special Windows

Special windows include angled bay windows, triple windows, and paired dormer windows. Small square, rectangular, and round-top windows are often used in various combinations over the entry door on two-story houses. Angled bay windows have a continuous base to the ground. The triple window with a broad, center sash is a hallmark of the Liberty Classic.

Standard Doors

Doors include four- and six-panel patterns. The four-panel can have an integral transom. Doors often have sidelights and transom surrounds of clear glass which can be rectangular or a segmented arch form.

Trim

Windows and doors typically have a 5½-inch-wide trim with a cap molding.

Shutters

Painted, operable shutters are encouraged on single windows. Shutter styles can either be paneled or louvered.

Standard Doors

Special Windows

Bay

Accent

Picture

Liberty Classic

ARCHITECTURAL PATTERNS

C 4

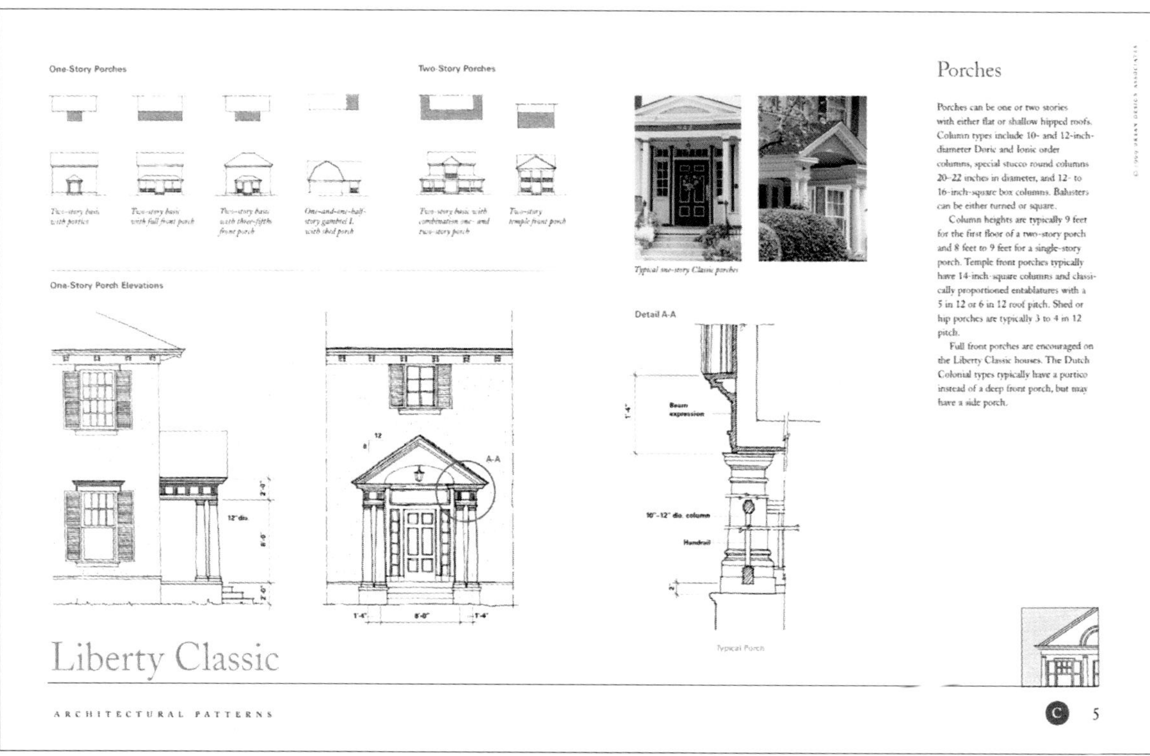

One-Story Porches

Two-Story Porches

Two-story basic with portico

Two-story basic with full front porch

Two-story basic with three-fifths front porch

One-and-one-half-story gambrel L with shed porch

Two-story basic with combination one- and two-story porch

Two-story temple front porch

Typical one-story Classic porches

Porches

Porches can be one or two stories with either flat or shallow hipped roofs. Column types include 10- and 12-inch-diameter Doric and Ionic order columns, special stucco round columns 20–22 inches in diameter, and 12- to 16-inch-square box columns. Balusters can be either turned or square.

Column heights are typically 9 feet for the first floor of a two-story porch and 8 feet to 9 feet for a single-story porch. Temple front porches typically have 14-inch-square columns and classically proportioned entablatures with a 5 in 12 or 6 in 12 roof pitch. Shed or hip porches are typically 3 to 4 in 12 pitch.

Full front porches are encouraged on the Liberty Classic houses. The Dutch Colonial types typically have a portico instead of a deep front porch, but may have a side porch.

One-Story Porch Elevations

Typical Porch

Liberty Classic

ARCHITECTURAL PATTERNS

C 5

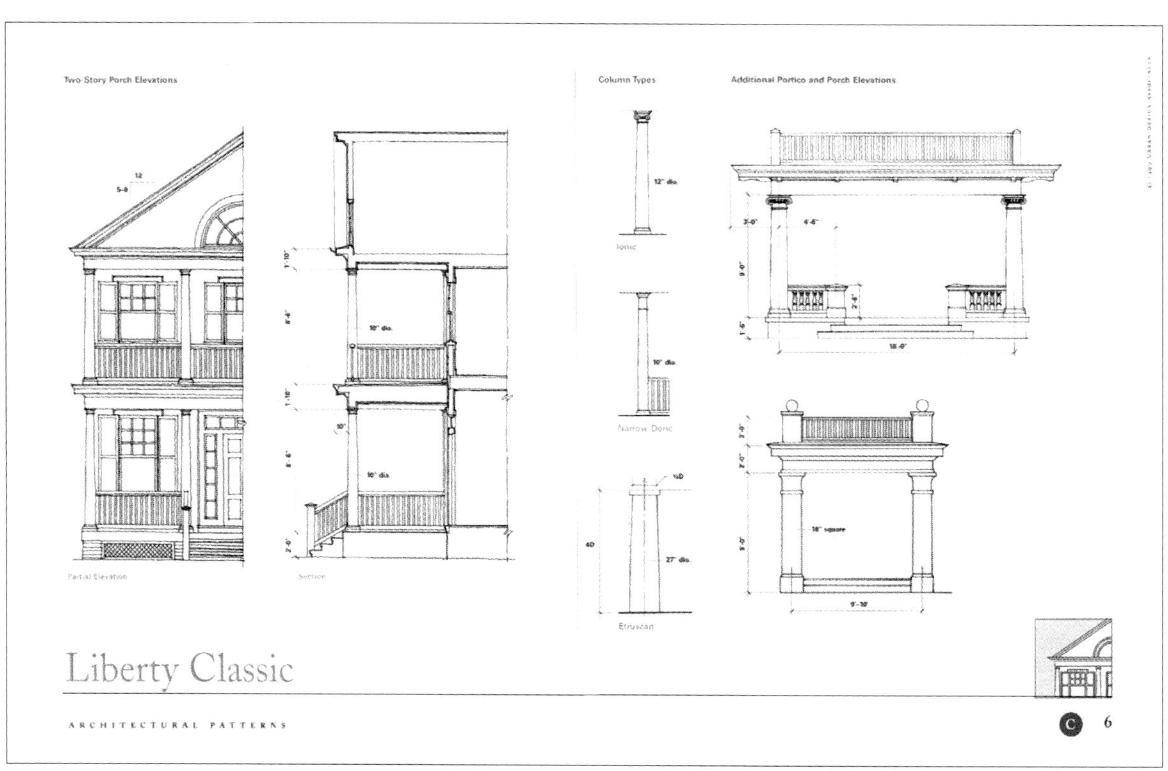

Two-Story Porch Elevations

Column Types

Additional Portico and Porch Elevations

Partial Elevation

Section

Liberty Classic

ARCHITECTURAL PATTERNS

C 6

Essential Elements of the Norfolk Colonial Revival Style

1 Simple, straightforward volumes with side wings and porches added to make more complex shapes.

2 Orderly, symmetrical relationship between windows, doors and building mass.

3 Simplified versions of Classical details and columns, occasionally with Classical orders used at the entry.

4 Multi-pane windows.

NORFOLK COLONIAL REVIVAL

Partial Elevation and Wall Section

The Norfolk Colonial Revival is based on the Colonial Revival styles prevalent throughout the country in the late nineteenth and early twentieth centuries. During this era, elements from Classical and Colonial houses were combined and modified to produce a new vocabulary that became popular in the latter part of the nineteenth century. This mixing of influences produced a wide variety of expression and form in the Colonial Revival house.

Norfolk's Colonial Revival houses tend to have tall, narrow windows, elaborate entrances and cornice treatments, and deep front porches that run the entire face of the front facade. The relaxed rules of composition, frequent use of paired windows, and the occasional gambrel roof form, give these houses a comfortable quality which places them in stark contrast to the regulated order of more Classical styles.

Massing & Composition

MASSING DIAGRAMS

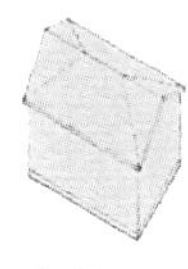

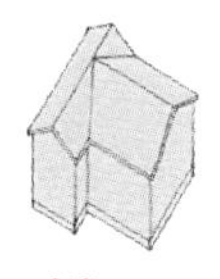

A Broad Front B Narrow Front C L-Shape D Gambrel

FACADE COMPOSITION DIAGRAMS

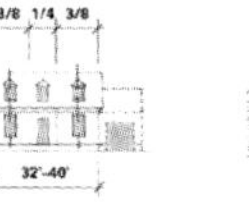

MASSING COMBINATIONS

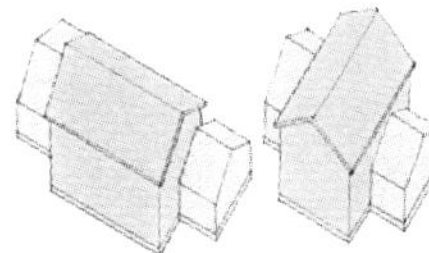

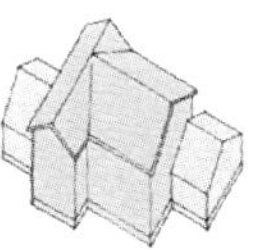

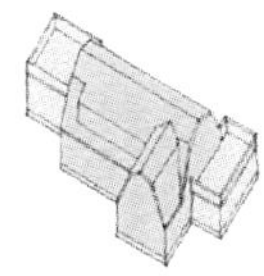

2/5 3/5 35'–45'

3/8 1/4 3/8 40'–50'

Massing

A BROAD FRONT

Hipped-roof or side-gable rectangular volume with roof pitches ranging from 7 in 12 to 12 in 12. One-story shed or hip roofed porches are often placed symmetrically on the front facade. One-story side wings often occur. Although porches are most often one-third or one-fifth the length of the main body, they may also be three-fifths or the entire length of the front facade.

B NARROW FRONT

Hipped-roof or front-gable box with roof pitches ranging from 7 to 12 in 12. Five- and three-bay compositions are common. Full front porches and one-story side-wings are common to this massing type.

C L-SHAPE

L-shape volume with a front-facing gable roof intersecting either a gable or cross-gable at the rear. Roof pitch ranges from 6 in 12 to 10 in 12. One- and two-story porches often fill the space of the L.

D GAMBREL

Rectangular volume with a gambrel roof containing a second or third story. Gambrel roofs have two roof pitches, 20 in 12 to 36 in 12 at the eave, and 6 in 12 to 10 in 12 above the pitch break. Shed dormers are common. Porches may be inset in street-facing gambrels.

Combinations

Larger living spaces may be created by adding side wings to the main body. Gabled or shed dormers may be added to introduce light into half-story and attic spaces. The architectural character of elements such as side wings, rear wings and accessory/ancillary structures should be consistent with the architectural character of the main body.

Facade Composition

Colonial Revival facade composition is characterized by a symmetrical and balanced placement of windows and doors. Standard windows occur as singles, or in pairs. Entrance doors are generally located near the corner of narrow houses and at the center of wide houses.

Roof

The roof pitch on Norfolk Colonial Revival houses varies from 6 in 12 to 12 in 12. For L-shape forms, the pitch on street-facing gables is 10 to 12 in 12.

Eaves

The Colonial Revival house typically has one of three eave profiles:

1 Boxed eave, typically with an 18-inch soffit depth; shallow soffit on the rake.

2 Deep boxed eave with heavy bracket, often found in hipped-roof examples, presenting a more robust image.

3 Boxed eave modified for gambrel roof, with tall frieze and shallow, heavy brackets.

Eave profiles have an 8- to 12-inch frieze board at least 8 inches above the window head trim. Eave returns should have metal flashing back to the wall at a maximum slope of 2 in 12.

Wall Section & Eave Details

The first floor of the main body is typically set three feet above the finished grade. The floor-to-ceiling height on the first floor is typically 10 feet. For two-story houses, the second story floor-to-ceiling height is 9 feet. Window head heights should be 8 feet for the first floor and 7 feet for the second floor.

On clapboard houses, corner boards should be no less than nominal 5/4 by 6 inches. On stucco and brick houses, the watertable should project 2 inches from the wall. Clapboard houses should have an 8-inch skirt board. When foundation vents are used, they should be centered under windows.

TYPICAL EAVE DETAILS

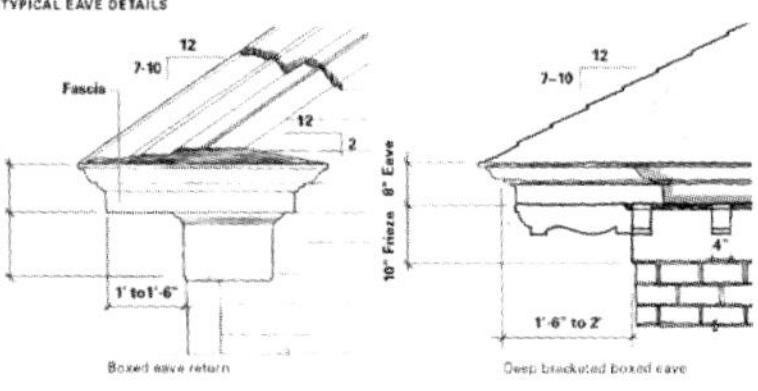

Boxed eave return Deep bracketed boxed eave

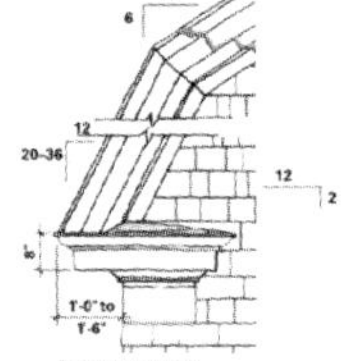

Gambrel eave return

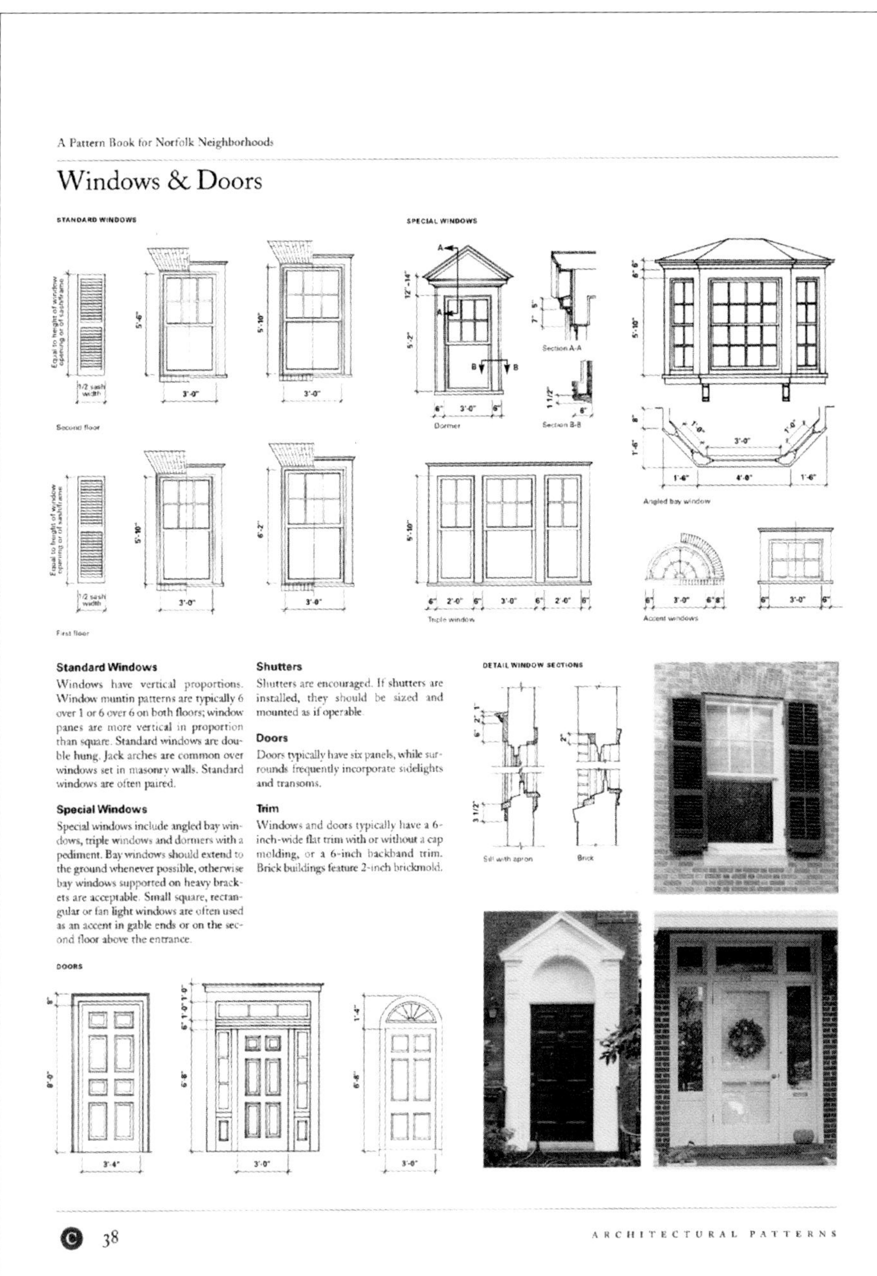
A Pattern Book for Norfolk Neighborhoods

Windows & Doors

STANDARD WINDOWS

SPECIAL WINDOWS

Standard Windows

Windows have vertical proportions. Window muntin patterns are typically 6 over 1 or 6 over 6 on both floors; window panes are more vertical in proportion than square. Standard windows are double hung. Jack arches are common over windows set in masonry walls. Standard windows are often paired.

Special Windows

Special windows include angled bay windows, triple windows and dormers with a pediment. Bay windows should extend to the ground whenever possible, otherwise bay windows supported on heavy brackets are acceptable. Small square, rectangular or fan light windows are often used as an accent in gable ends or on the second floor above the entrance.

Shutters

Shutters are encouraged. If shutters are installed, they should be sized and mounted as if operable.

Doors

Doors typically have six panels, while surrounds frequently incorporate sidelights and transoms.

Trim

Windows and doors typically have a 6-inch-wide flat trim with or without a cap molding, or a 6-inch backband trim. Brick buildings feature 2-inch brickmold.

DOORS

C 38 ARCHITECTURAL PATTERNS

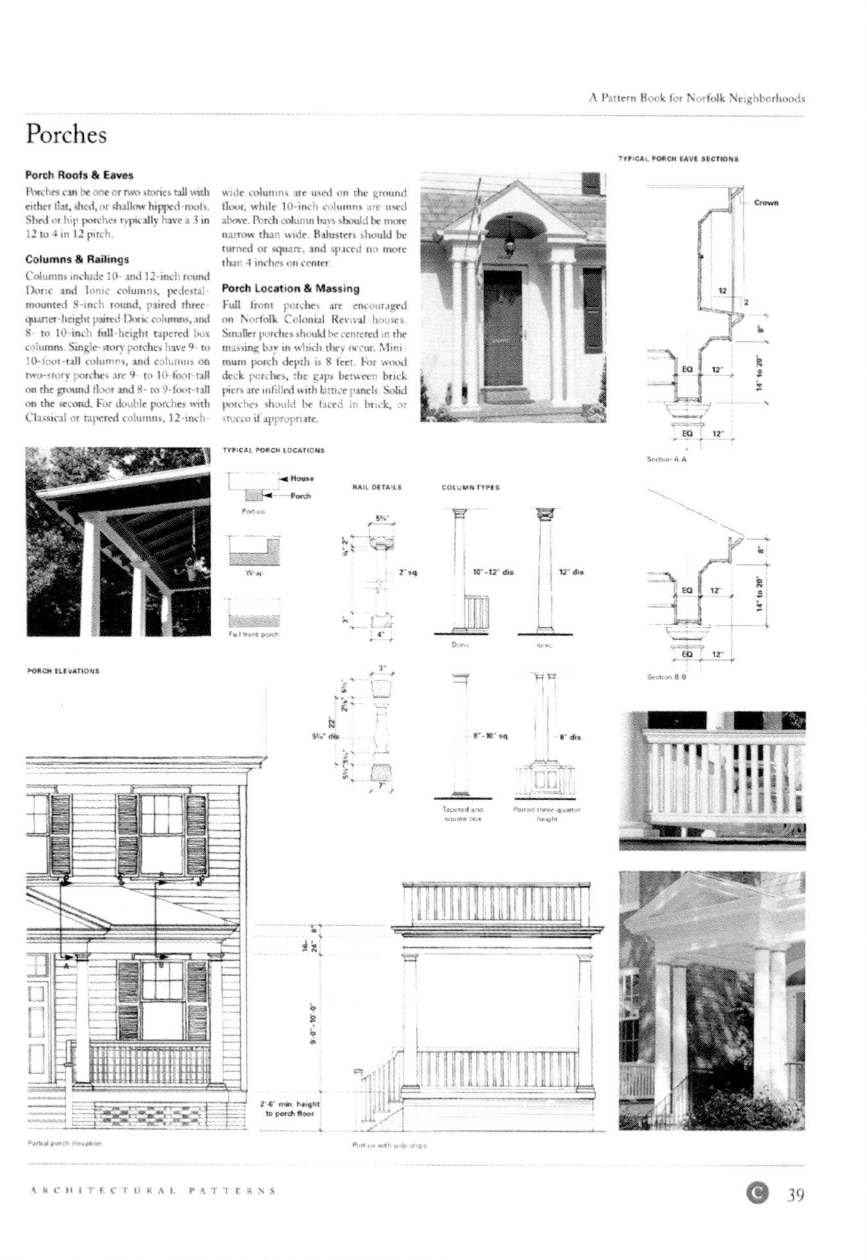

Porches

Porch Roofs & Eaves

Porches can be one or two stories tall with either flat, shed, or shallow hipped-roofs. Shed or hip porches typically have a 3 in 12 to 4 in 12 pitch.

Columns & Railings

Columns include 10- and 12-inch round Doric and Ionic columns, pedestal-mounted 8-inch round, paired three-quarter-height paired Doric columns, and 8- to 10-inch full-height tapered box columns. Single-story porches have 9- to 10-foot-tall columns, and columns on two-story porches are 9- to 10-foot-tall on the ground floor and 8- to 9-foot-tall on the second. For double porches with Classical or tapered columns, 12-inch-wide columns are used on the ground floor, while 10-inch columns are used above. Porch column bays should be more narrow than wide. Balusters should be turned or square, and spaced no more than 4 inches on center.

Porch Location & Massing

Full front porches are encouraged on Norfolk Colonial Revival houses. Smaller porches should be centered in the massing bay in which they occur. Minimum porch depth is 8 feet. For wood deck porches, the gaps between brick piers are infilled with lattice panels. Solid porches should be faced in brick, or stucco if appropriate.

A Pattern Book for Norfolk Neighborhoods

Materials & Applications

Roofing

- Slate (including manufactured slate products), laminated asphalt or composition shingles with a slate pattern, or flat clay tile

Soffits

- Smooth-finish composition board, tongue-and-groove wood boards, or fiber-cement panels

Gutters & Downspouts

- Half-round or ogee profile gutters with round or rectangular down-spouts in copper, painted or prefinished metal

Windows

- Painted wood or solid cellular PVC, or clad wood or vinyl with brick veneer only; true divided light or simulated divided light (SDL) sash with traditional exterior muntin profile (⅞ inch wide)

Doors

- Wood, fiberglass or steel with traditional stile-and-rail proportions and raised panel profiles, painted or stained

Shutters

- Wood or composite, sized to match window sash and mounted with hardware to appear operable

Cladding

- Smooth-finish wood or fiber-cement lap siding, 6- to 8-inch exposure, or random-width cut shingles
- Sand-molded or smooth-finish brick in Common, English or Flemish bond patterns
- Light sand-finish stucco

Trim

- Wood, composite, cellular PVC or polyurethane millwork; stucco, stone or cast stone

Foundations & Chimneys

- Brick, stucco or stone veneer

Columns

- Architecturally correct Classical proportions and details in wood, fiberglass, or composite material

Railings

- Milled wood top and bottom rails with square or turned balusters
- Wrought iron or solid bar stock square metal picket

Porch Ceilings

- Plaster, tongue-and-groove wood or composite boards, or beaded-profile plywood

Front Yard Fences

- Wood picket, or wood, wrought iron or solid bar stock metal picket with brick or stucco finish masonry piers

Lighting

- Porch pendant or wall-mounted carriage lantern

40 ARCHITECTURAL PATTERNS

Gallery of Examples

Norfolk, Virginia, door

VICTORIAN STYLE

Comparative Analysis

This category is really an era in architecture and design that covers a broad range of types and stylistic treatment including, among others, Carpenter Gothic, Queen Anne, Stick Style, Italianate, Second Empire, and Richardsonian Romanesque. In general, these are Romantic styles that occurred in the United States from around 1840 through 1900. Different regions often have a strong influence from one of these periods. This time frame coincided with many changes in the economy for most regions; intense growth in industrial development was taking place and building components began to be mass-produced toward the latter part of the century. The lighter version of many variants of the Victorian style, such as Queen Anne and Stick, as well as Carpenter Gothic houses, benefited from building with balloon framing rather than heavy timber framing. The forms of the house could be more organic, freeing the builder to incorporate exotic extensions, roof overhangs, and more complex massing types.

Many early houses were designed in the Gothic Revival or Carpenter Gothic style that used simple forms with steeply pitched roofs or gable additions. Often, these were constructed using books such as *Rural Residences* by Alexander Jackson Davis, published in 1837, and more widely available publications such as Andrew Jackson Downing's books *Cottage Residences* and *The Architecture of Country Homes*. These were primarily suburban, village, and country homes patterned after the movement popularized in England in the late 1700s and early 1800s. The dominant materials were wood siding and ornate or shaped-timber posts, shaped rafters, and ornamental trim. Urban variations tended to be Second Empire and Italianate—more formal and adaptable to both attached housing and large houses. These variants were typically "spice" in most neighborhoods and contrasted with the more sedate Colonial, Classical, and, later, Colonial Revival houses found in small towns and many urban, single-family detached-house neighborhoods.

Sample pages of the Victorian style have been excerpted from the Liberty (Lake Elsinore, California), East Beach (Norfolk, Virginia), and East Garrison (Monterey County, California) pattern books.

Precedent photos

Victorian-era farmhouse in historic Orange, California

Blair House, Mendocino, California, 1888

Towle House, Bridgeport, California, 1878

Bracketed American farmhouse and historic floor plan from The Architecture of Country Houses *by A.J.Downing*

Essential Elements of Liberty Victorian

1. Steeply pitched gable roofs.
2. Cut wood ornament, often with natural forms such as leaves and vines.
3. Wood clapboard siding.
4. Vertical proportions for windows and doors.

History and Character

THE LIBERTY VICTORIAN STYLE builds on the early 'Carpenter Gothic' cottages imported into the Western Region from the East. While the style became fashionable in the 1800s in the Bay area, as its popularity grew, it spread north and south from San Francisco. Much of the source for the early house designs came from Pattern Books published by Andrew Jackson Downing. Publications such as *The Horticulturist* influenced the preferences of the public and provided an especially dramatic contrast to the inherited Spanish and adobe building types prevalent throughout Southern California. Early resorts and larger country estates began to adopt the style with more and more exotic variations that included Eastlake, Queen Anne, and Italianate detailing.

The Liberty Victorian is centered on the simple, elegant forms that were adapted to houses in the smaller towns and the rural farmhouse. The massing forms are quite simple, and the ornament is restrained and typically limited to the porch and the cornice. The Victorian is a spice style, sprinkled in among other more predominant styles.

Liberty Victorian

ARCHITECTURAL PATTERNS

C 15

Massing Diagrams

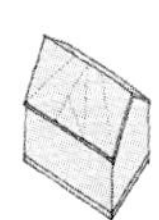

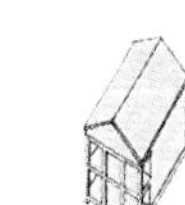

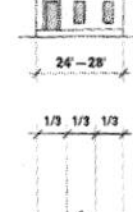

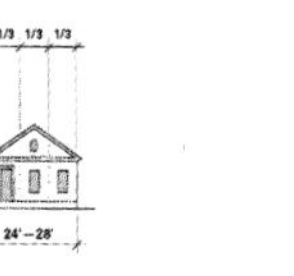

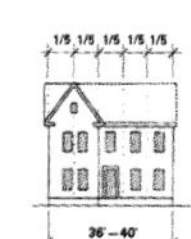

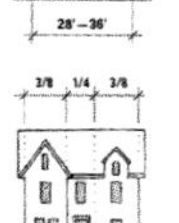

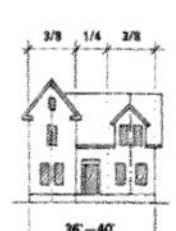

A *Two-story basic*

B *One-and-one-half-story basic*

C *One- and two-story front gable*

D *One-and-one-half-story integral porch*

E *Two-story gable L*

F *One-and-one-half-story gable L*

Massing and Composition

Massing

A Two-Story Basic
Hipped or side-gabled rectangular volume, often with a dormer flush to the front facade. Roof pitch is typically 8 to 10 in 12. One-story shed or hip front porches from one-fifth to the full length of the main body. Two-story full front porches are also permitted.

B One-and-One-Half-Story Basic
Side-gabled rectangular volume, often with a dormer flush to the front facade. Roof pitch is typically 10 in 12 for the main body and 12 in 12 for the dormer. One-story shed or hip front porches from one-fifth to the full length of the main body.

C One- and Two-Story Front Gable
Rectangular volume with 8 in 12 roof pitch and gable facing the street. One-story partial, full, or wrapping front porch with 3 in 12 hip roof is common. Integral full front porches are also permitted on one- and two-story main bodies.

D One-and-One-Half-Story Integral Porch
Square volume with 8 in 12 side-gabled roof. Integral front porch along the full length of the front facade. Symmetrically placed gabled or shed dormers with 6 in 12 or 12 in 12 roof pitch.

E Two-Story Gable L
Cross-gabled volume with a 12 in 12 gable facing the street. The width of the gable facing the street is typically half that of the main body for houses up to 36 feet wide and two-fifths that of the main body for houses 36 feet and over. This massing typically accommodates a continuous porch with shed roof located between the legs of the L. Corner house porches should wrap the corner.

F One-and-One-Half-Story Gable L
Cross-gabled volume with a 12 in 12 gable facing the street, often with a dormer flush to the front facade. The width of the gable facing the street is typically one-third that of the main body for houses up to 36 feet wide and two-fifths that of the main body for houses 36 feet and over. Full front porches are typical between the legs of the L.

Composition

Victorian facade composition is characterized by a symmetrical and balanced placement of doors and windows. Individual double-hung windows are the most common type. Entrance doors are generally located in the corner of narrow houses and the center of wide houses. Bay windows are typically used on the ground floor. Paired windows are often used in the forward gable of the gable L massing types E and F.

Liberty Victorian

ARCHITECTURAL PATTERNS

C 16

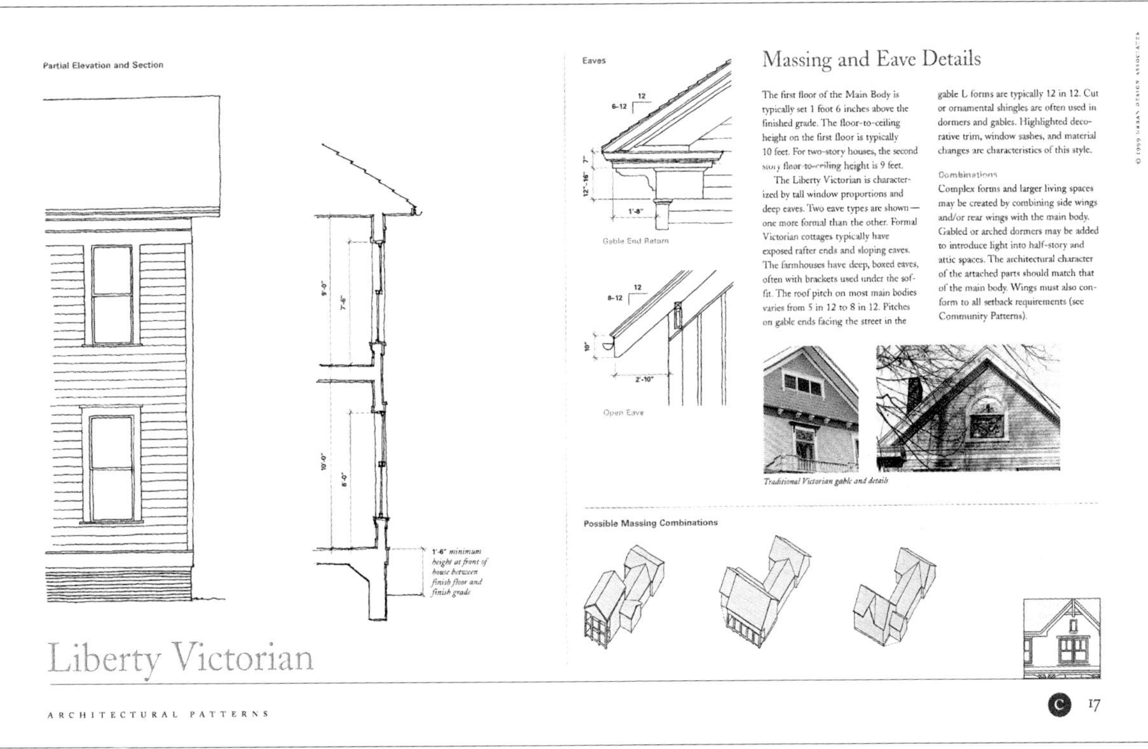
Partial Elevation and Section

1'-6" minimum height at front of house between finish floor and finish grade

Eaves

Gable End Return

Open Eave

Massing and Eave Details

The first floor of the Main Body is typically set 1 foot 6 inches above the finished grade. The floor-to-ceiling height on the first floor is typically 10 feet. For two-story houses, the second story floor-to-ceiling height is 9 feet.

The Liberty Victorian is characterized by tall window proportions and deep eaves. Two eave types are shown—one more formal than the other. Formal Victorian cottages typically have exposed rafter ends and sloping eaves. The farmhouses have deep, boxed eaves, often with brackets used under the soffit. The roof pitch on most main bodies varies from 5 in 12 to 8 in 12. Pitches on gable ends facing the street in the gable L forms are typically 12 in 12. Cut or ornamental shingles are often used in dormers and gables. Highlighted decorative trim, window sashes, and material changes are characteristics of this style.

Combinations

Complex forms and larger living spaces may be created by combining side wings and/or rear wings with the main body. Gabled or arched dormers may be added to introduce light into half-story and attic spaces. The architectural character of the attached parts should match that of the main body. Wings must also conform to all setback requirements (see Community Patterns).

Traditional Victorian gable and detail

Possible Massing Combinations

Liberty Victorian

ARCHITECTURAL PATTERNS

C 17

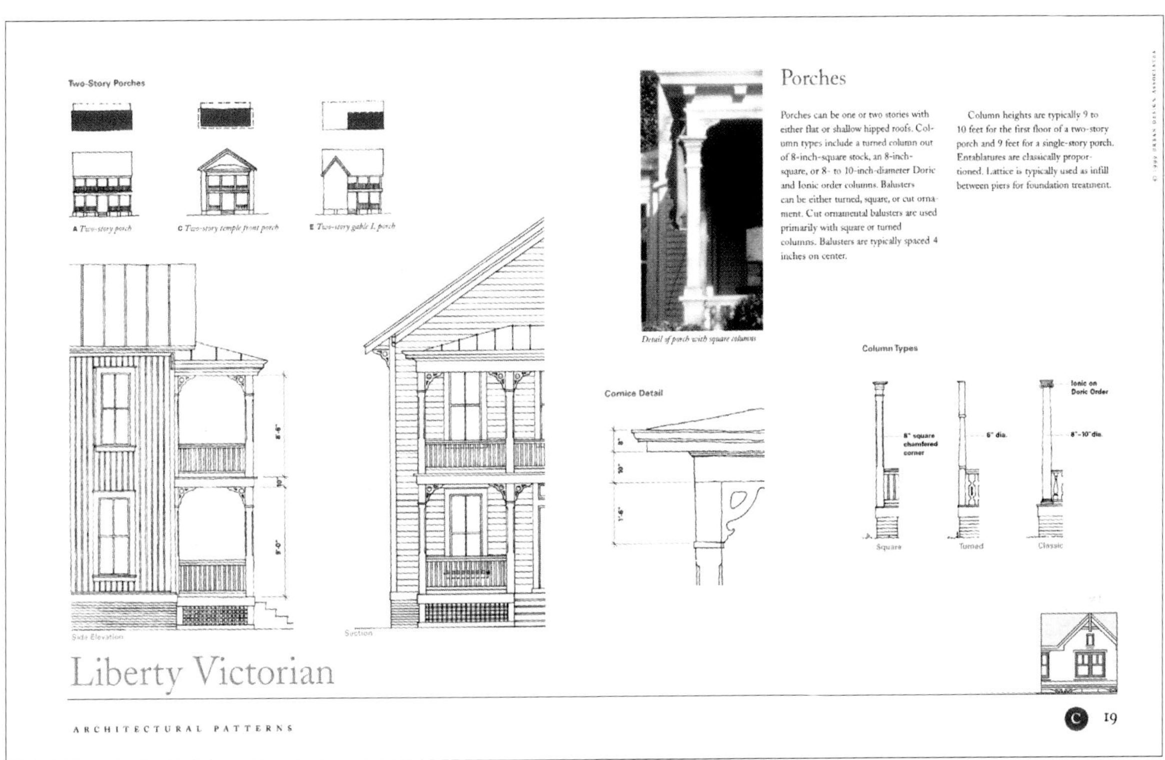
Two-Story Porches

A *Two-story porch*

C *Two-story temple front porch*

E *Two-story gable L porch*

Side Elevation

Section

Liberty Victorian

Detail of porch with square columns

Porches

Porches can be one or two stories with either flat or shallow hipped roofs. Column types include a turned column out of 8-inch-square stock, an 8-inch-square, or 8- to 10-inch-diameter Doric and Ionic order columns. Balusters can be either turned, square, or cut ornament. Cut ornamental balusters are used primarily with square or turned columns. Balusters are typically spaced 4 inches on center.

Column heights are typically 9 to 10 feet for the first floor of a two-story porch and 9 feet for a single-story porch. Entablatures are classically proportioned. Lattice is typically used as infill between piers for foundation treatment.

Cornice Detail

Column Types

8" square chamfered corner

6" dia.

Ionic on Doric Order

8"-10" dia.

Square

Turned

Classic

ARCHITECTURAL PATTERNS

C 19

Standard Windows

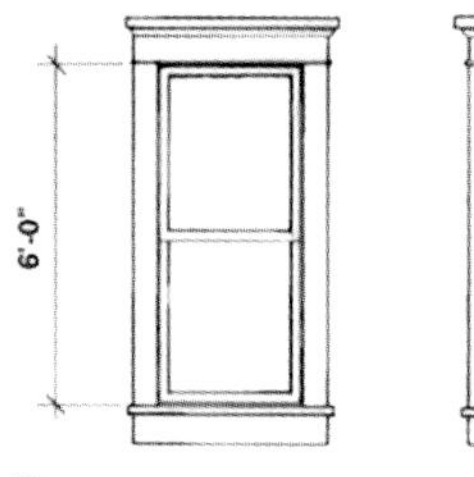

Second Floor

Paired Window

First Floor

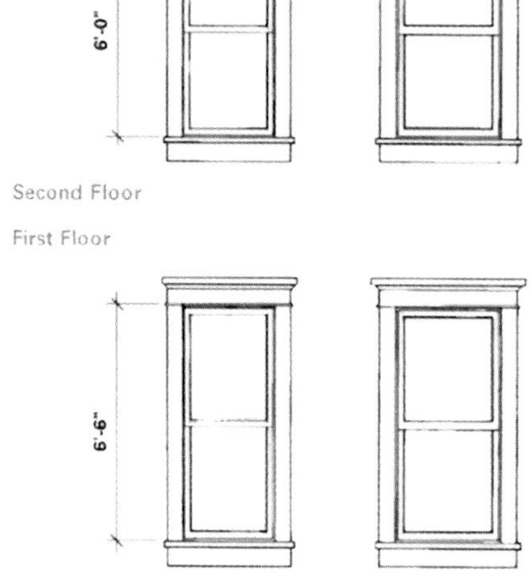

Typical Window Detail

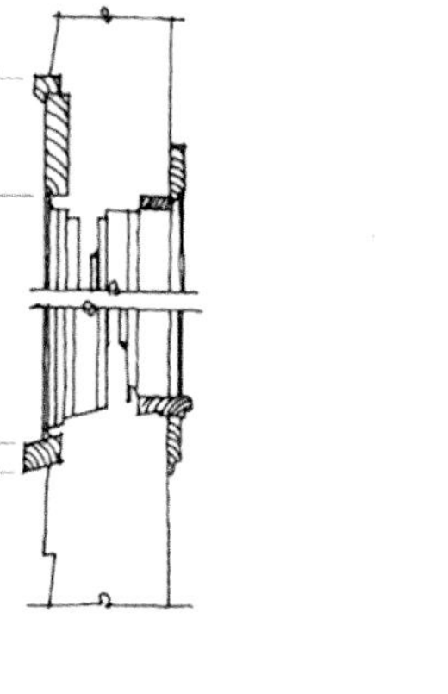

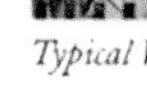

Typical V

Standard Doors

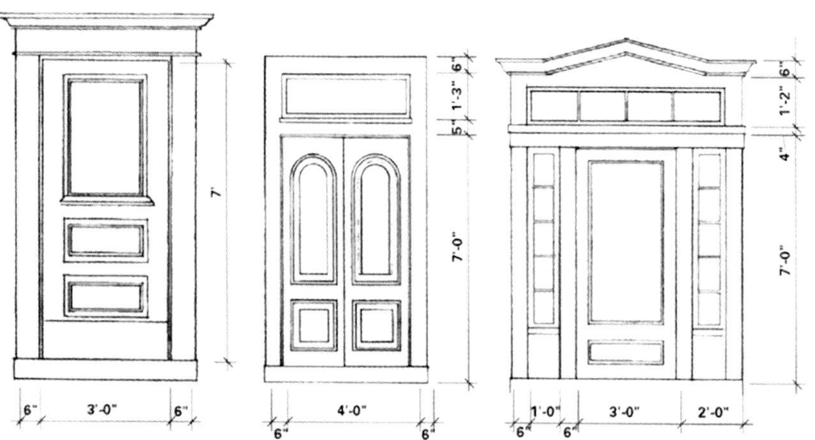

Special Windows

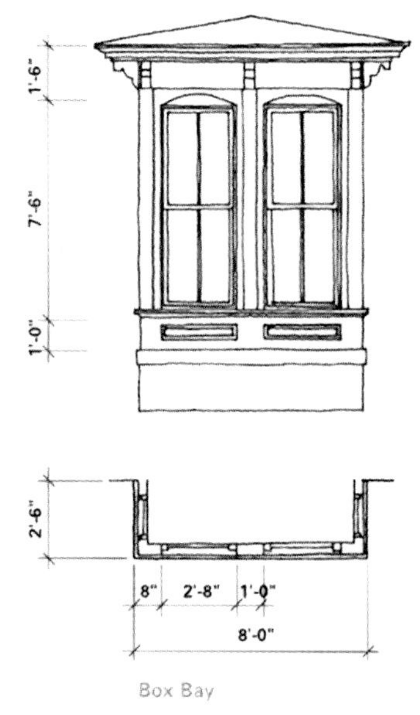

Box Bay

Liberty Victorian

ARCHITECTURAL PATTERNS

Windows and Doors

Standard Windows

Windows are typically vertical in proportion. Two basic window patterns are 1 over 1 and 2 over 2, double-hung with wide trim. Paired windows are often used in gable L houses, or as accents where bay windows might also be used. The window often has a decorative header. Some houses may have windows with rounded upper sashes and ornate trim for window hoods.

Standard Doors

Doors are centered in their bays and are either paneled or glazed wood doors. Double doors are often used, as well as single doors with sidelights and transoms.

Special Windows

Special windows include box bay and angled bay windows, paired dormer windows, and round top windows. Box bay and angled bay windows have a continuous base to the ground.

Trim

Windows and doors typically have a 5½-inch-wide trim with a cap molding.

Shutters

Painted, operable shutters are encouraged on single windows. Shutter styles can either be paneled or louvered.

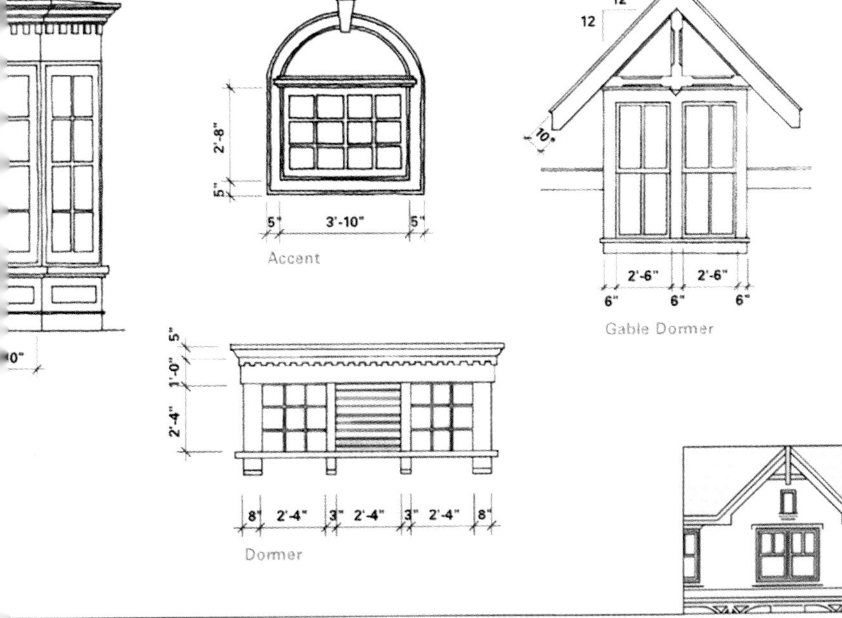

C 18

LIBERTY

Lake Elsinore, California

The Liberty Victorian house is an interesting hybrid that borrows from Classical and Colonial Revival forms and details as well as the Arts & Crafts influence. The Liberty Victorian was derived from a broad survey of precedents in southern California coastal and inland towns and neighborhoods such as Orange, Riverside, Laguna Beach, Long Beach, Newport Beach, and Pasadena. The mix of the various style components creates an interesting character and blends with other styles. The dominant form reference is the folk Victorian cottage with simple massing types. The eave and porch additions become the primary elements that transform the massing into different variants. One application includes boxed eaves with brackets, much like a Colonial Revival house with porches that use Ionic-order columns and turned balusters. A Carpenter Gothic approach uses the sloped eave with turned or chamfered columns and ornamental cut accent trim.

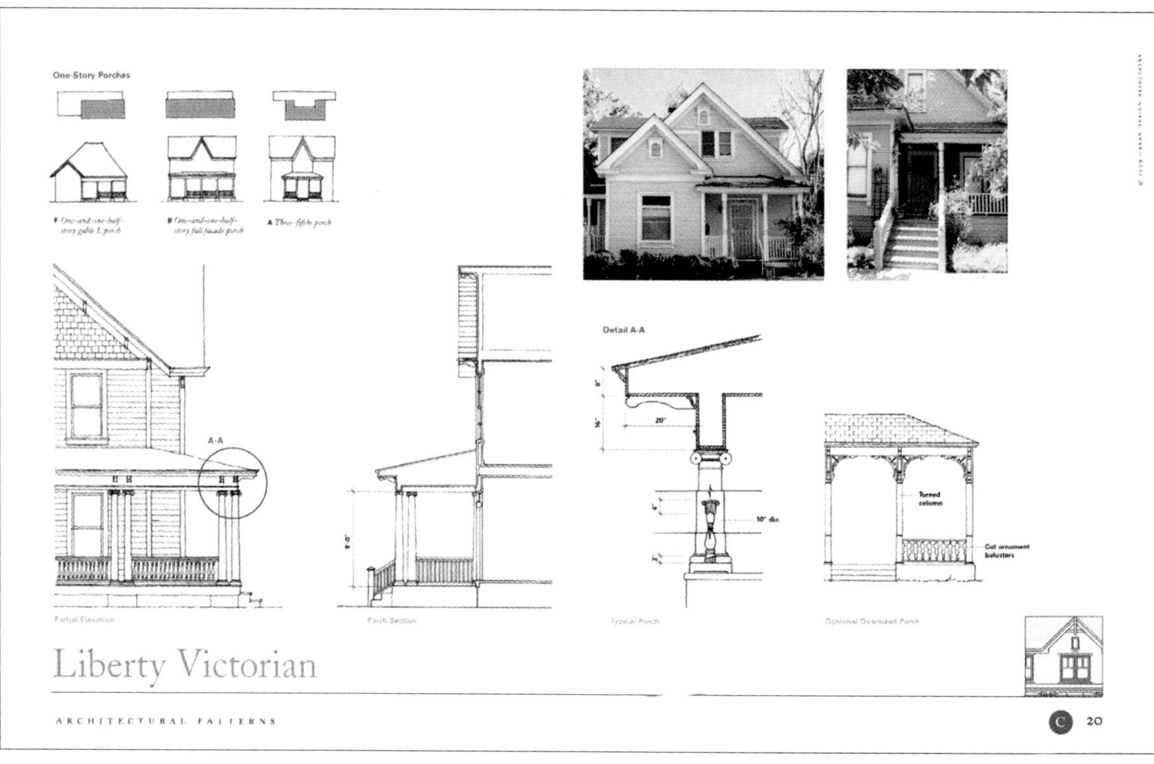

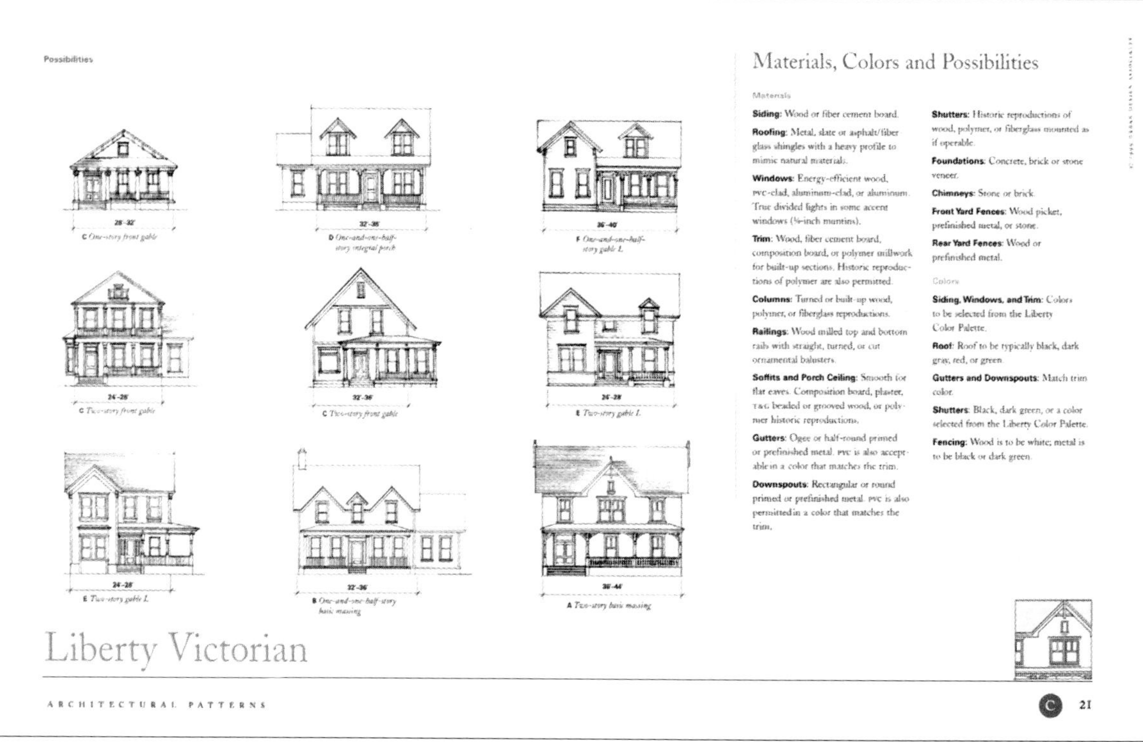

Materials, Colors and Possibilities

Materials

Siding: Wood or fiber cement board.

Roofing: Metal, slate or asphalt/fiber glass shingles with a heavy profile to mimic natural materials.

Windows: Energy-efficient wood, PVC-clad, aluminum-clad, or aluminum. True divided lights in some accent windows (⅝-inch muntins).

Trim: Wood, fiber cement board, composition board, or polymer millwork for built-up sections. Historic reproductions of polymer are also permitted.

Columns: Turned or built-up wood, polymer, or fiberglass reproductions.

Railings: Wood milled top and bottom rails with straight, turned, or cut ornamental balusters.

Soffits and Porch Ceiling: Smooth for flat eaves. Composition board, plaster, T&G beaded or grooved wood, or polymer historic reproductions.

Gutters: Ogee or half-round primed or prefinished metal. PVC is also acceptable in a color that matches the trim.

Downspouts: Rectangular or round primed or prefinished metal. PVC is also permitted in a color that matches the trim.

Shutters: Historic reproductions of wood, polymer, or fiberglass mounted as if operable.

Foundations: Concrete, brick or stone veneer.

Chimneys: Stone or brick.

Front Yard Fences: Wood picket, prefinished metal, or stone.

Rear Yard Fences: Wood or prefinished metal.

Colors

Siding, Windows, and Trim: Colors to be selected from the Liberty Color Palette.

Roof: Roof to be typically black, dark gray, red, or green.

Gutters and Downspouts: Match trim color.

Shutters: Black, dark green, or a color selected from the Liberty Color Palette.

Fencing: Wood is to be white; metal is to be black or dark green.

Edenton, North Carolina

Edenton, North Carolina

Annapolis, Maryland

Essential Elements of Tidewater Victorian

1. Steeply pitched gable roofs.
2. Cut wood ornament, often with natural forms such as leaves and vines, or simple shape cutouts and arched forms.
3. Clapboard siding, with siding, shingles, or beadboard in gable ends.
4. Vertical proportions for windows and doors, windows with two- and four-pane sashes.

History and Character

THE TIDEWATER VICTORIAN STYLE builds on the 'Carpenter Gothic' cottages abundant in early rail-served coastal resorts. Pattern Books published by Andrew Jackson Downing and others were the source for many of these early house designs. These books made it easier for the builders of early resorts, country estates, and even modest dwellings to adopt the style. Although exotic Victorian houses incorporating Eastlake, Queen Anne, and Italianate details grew in popularity, folk-based Victorian homes survive in this region.

The Tidewater Victorian is based on the simple, elegant forms adapted to houses in small towns and rural farmhouses. The massing forms are simple, while ornament is typically restrained and limited to the porch and the building's cornice.

Tidewater Victorian

Massing Diagrams

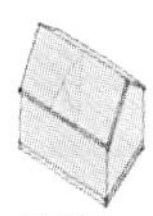

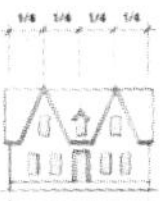

A *Side Gable*

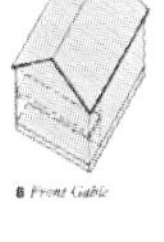

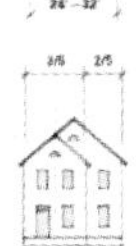

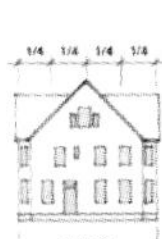

B *Front Gable*

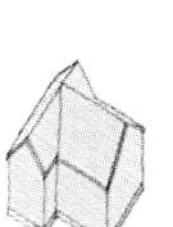
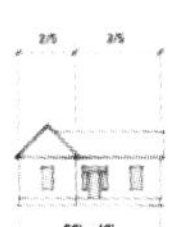
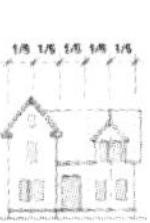

C *L-Shaped*

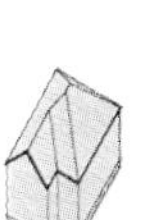

D *Gable L*

Mansion and Attached Houses

Massing and Composition

Massing

A Side Gable
Side-gabled rectangular volume, often with a steeply pitched, gabled dormer flush to the front façade. Roof pitch is typically 8 in 12 to 10 in 12, and one- or two-story front porches typically extend across the full front of the house.

B Front Gable
Front-gabled rectangular volume with a roof pitch ranging from 8 in 12 to 12 in 12 for the main body. One-story shed or hip front porches from one-third to the full width of the main body are common. Often, two-story porches are integrated under the main roof form.

C L-Shaped
Cross-gabled volume with a 9 in 12 gable facing the street. The width of the gable facing the street is typically two-fifths that of the main body. This massing typically accommodates a one- or two-story continuous porch with a shed or hipped roof that dies into the side of the projecting wing.

D Gable L
Square volume with hipped roof from which a front-facing gabled wing extends. Roof pitches range from 8 in 12 to 12 in 12. Front porch extends the full length of the front façade, or is occasionally a single-bay, hipped porch at the main body.

Combinations

Complex forms and larger living spaces may be created by combining side wings and/or rear wings with the main body. Gabled or arched dormers may be added to introduce light into half-story and attic spaces. The architectural character of the attached parts should match that of the main body.

Façade Composition

Victorian façade composition is characterized by a symmetrical and balanced placement of doors and windows. Individual double-hung windows are the most common type. Front doors are generally located in the corner of narrow houses and at the center of wide houses. Paired or bay windows are often used in the forward gable of the gable **L** massing types. Bay windows may be one or two stories tall.

Tidewater Victorian

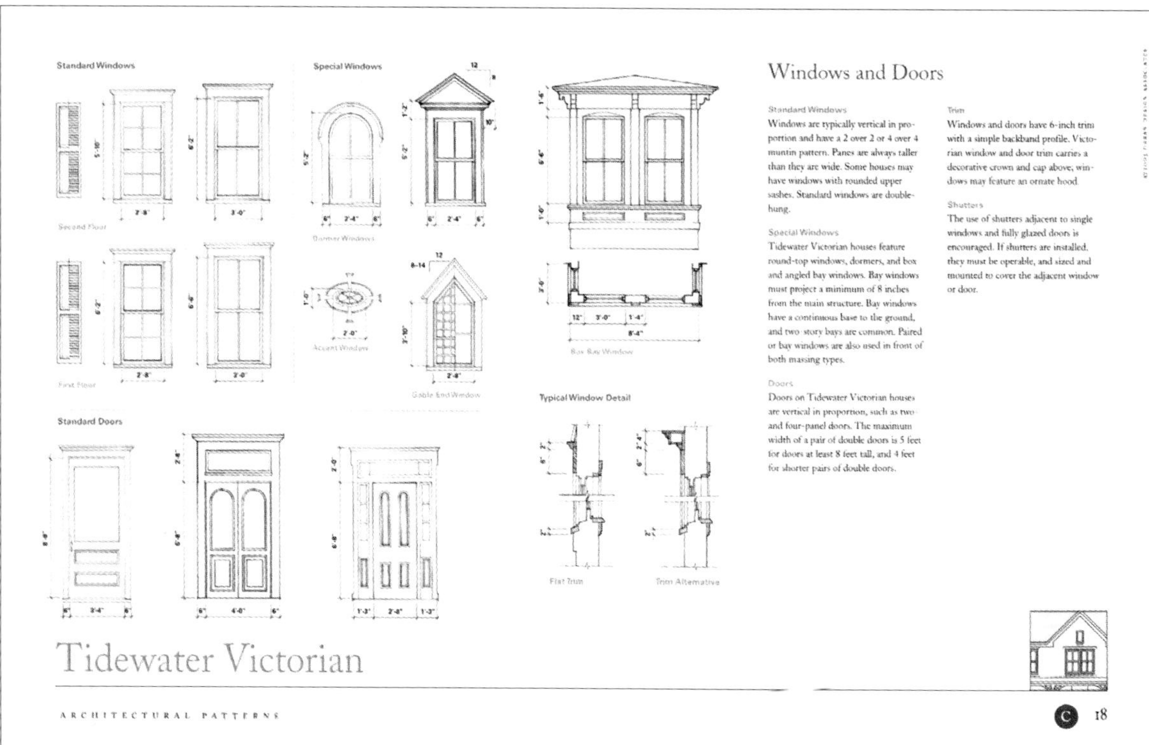

Windows and Doors

Standard Windows
Windows are typically vertical in proportion and have a 2 over 2 or 4 over 4 muntin pattern. Panes are always taller than they are wide. Some houses may have windows with rounded upper sashes. Standard windows are double-hung.

Special Windows
Tidewater Victorian houses feature round-top windows, dormers, and box and angled bay windows. Bay windows must project a minimum of 8 inches from the main structure. Bay windows have a continuous base to the ground, and two-story bays are common. Paired or bay windows are also used in front of both massing types.

Doors
Doors on Tidewater Victorian houses are vertical in proportion, such as two- and four-panel doors. The maximum width of a pair of double doors is 5 feet for doors at least 8 feet tall, and 4 feet for shorter pairs of double doors.

Trim
Windows and doors have 6-inch trim with a simple backband profile. Victorian window and door trim carries a decorative crown and cap above; windows may feature an ornate hood.

Shutters
The use of shutters adjacent to single windows and fully glazed doors is encouraged. If shutters are installed, they must be operable, and sized and mounted to cover the adjacent window or door.

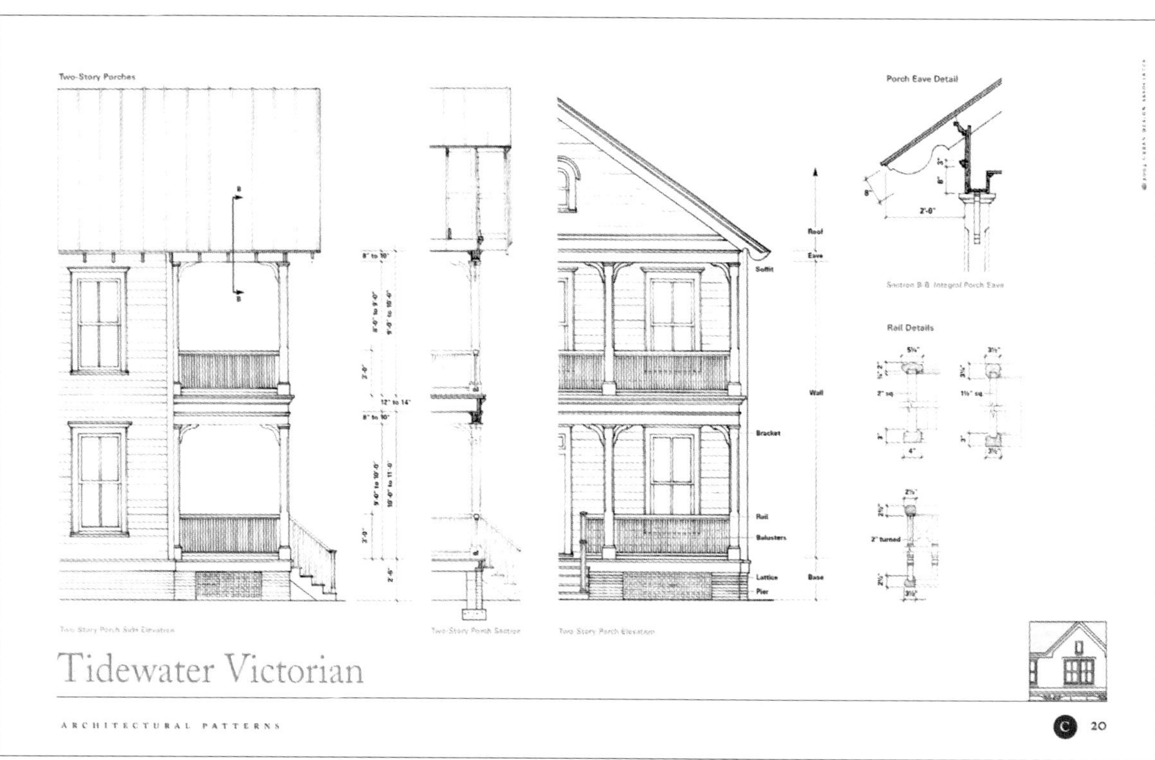

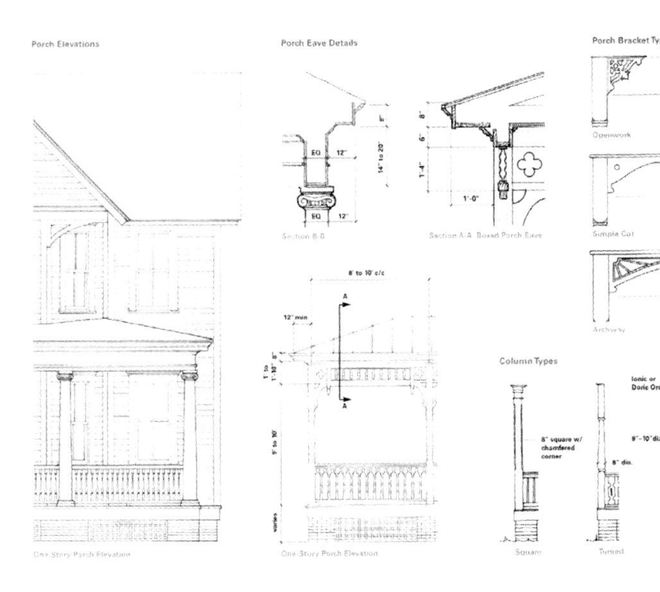

Porches

Porch Roofs and Eaves

Porches can be one or two stories tall with flat, shed, or shallow hipped roofs. Full porches may be integrated under the house's main roof. Shed or hip porches have a 3 in 12 to 4 in 12 pitch. Exposed rafter tails are typically 2 x 8 and occur 14 to 16 inches on center. Entablatures are generally classically proportioned and detailed.

Columns and Railings

Column types include turned columns from 8-inch-square stock, 8-inch-square posts, and 8- to 10-inch-diameter Doric and Ionic columns. First-floor columns are 9- to 10-feet tall, while second-floor columns are 8 to 9 feet tall. Turned or square balusters are spaced no more than 4 inches apart. Porch bays should be vertically proportioned. Flat cut ornamental balusters are also used, with square or turned columns. Square pattern lattice is used as infill between piers at the foundation.

Brackets

Brackets range from simple designs cut from boards, to more elaborate turned wood or jigsaw-cut openwork. Brackets are a minimum of 2 inches thick. Archway bracketing can be used to form portals over key entry locations.

Porch Location

Full front porches are encouraged on Tidewater Victorian houses. Porches can be used to wrap the corner of a house, or to fill in the void created by an L-shaped plan. The minimum porch depth is 8 feet.

Tidewater Victorian

Possibilities

Materials and Possibilities

Materials

Roofing

- Metal, narrow standing seam of 5-V panels (painted)
- Wood shingles/shakes
- Dimensioned *architectural grade* asphalt or fiberglass shingles
- Slate or synthetic slate

Roof penetrations and flat skylights may be placed on a roof not facing a public thoroughfare with houses, maximum of two skylights per roof plane.

Cladding

- Smooth, horizontal bevel or lap wood or fiber-cement siding, 4 to 6 inches wide with 5/4 by 6 inch corner boards
- Board and batten siding

Foundations, Piers and Chimneys

- Brick, stone, or stucco on block

Windows

- Wood, vinyl (solid or clad), or aluminum clad with traditional profiles, minimum 3/4-inch-wide projecting exterior muntins

Doors

- Painted or stained wood or aesthetic equivalent

Railings

- Straight or turned wood balusters
- Decorative black metal for stair rails

Shutters

- Operable wood or polyvinyl sized to match opening, with appropriate hardware

Porch Ceilings

- Plaster
- Beaded-profile, tongue-and-groove, or paneled boards

Soffits

- Smooth composition, tongue-and-groove, or fiber-cement boards

Gutters and Downspouts

- Half-round gutters, round or rectangular smooth downspouts

Fences and Garden Walls

- Wood picket, black metal, brick, stucco on block, or combination

Lighting

- Pendant carriage lamp, porch or wall mounted

Tidewater Victorian

Massing Diagrams

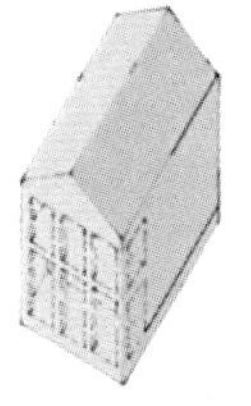

A *One- and Two-story Front Gable*

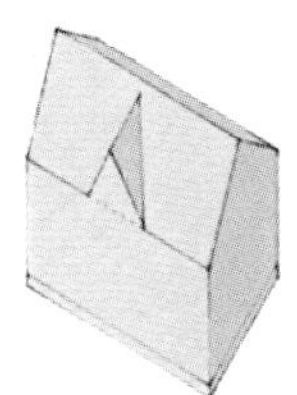

B *Two-story Side Gable*

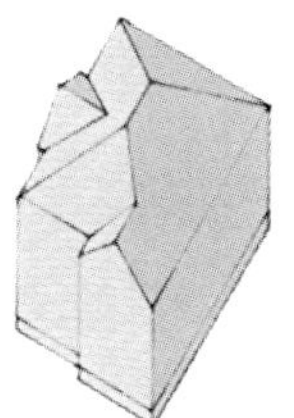

C *Two-story Gable L*

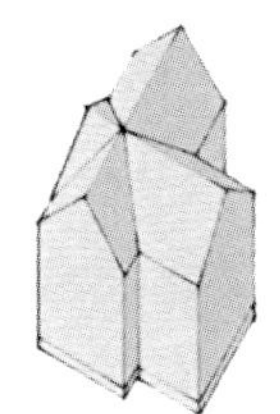

D *Two-story Cross Gable*

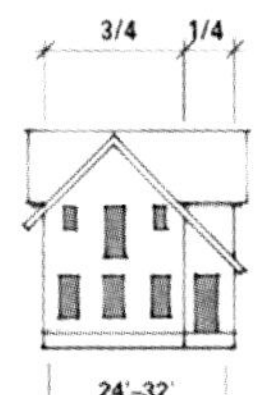

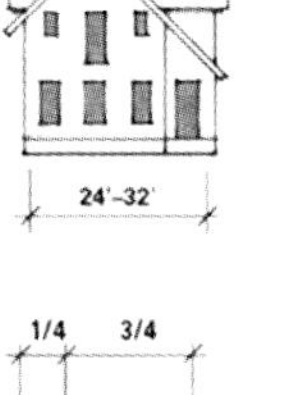

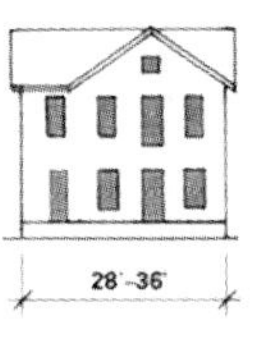

Possible Massing Combinations

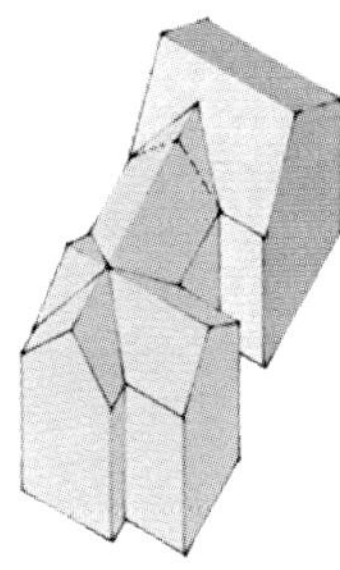

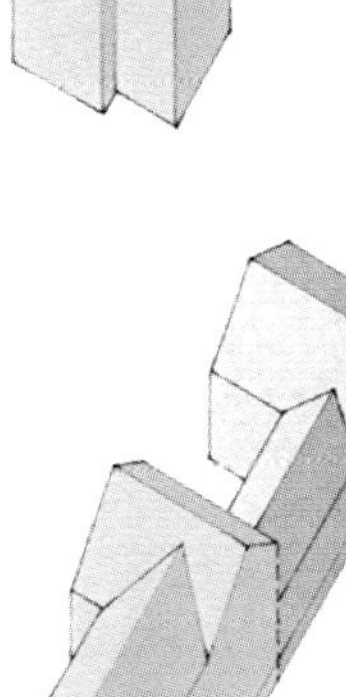

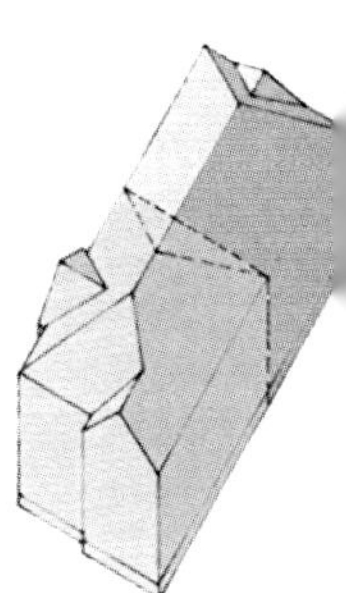

Picturesque Camp

ARCHITECTURAL PATTERNS

Massing and Composition

Massing

A Two-story Front Gable
Rectangular volume with 10 in 12 roof pitch and gable facing the street. One-story partial, full, or wrapping front porch with shed or hip roof is common. Integral full front porches are also typical.

B Two-story Side Gable
Side-gabled rectangular volume, often with a steeply-pitched, gabled dormer flush to the front façade. Front gable roof pitch is typically 10 in 12 to 12 in 12, and the side gable is less steeply pitched. One- or two-story front porches typically extend across the full front of the house.

C Two-story Gable-L
Two-story rectangular volume with hipped roof and front gable. Front bay and gable roof can encroach into the porch zone a maximum of 3 feet and is limited to 14 feet in width.The roof pitch is typically 10 in 12. One- or two-story front wraparound porch with shed or hipped roof is most common.

D Two-story Cross Gable
Two-story rectangular volume, with centrally-intersecting gable roofs. Gable roof pitch is typically 10 in 12. One- or two-story, full-length or wraparound front porch with shed or hipped roof.

Facade Composition

The facade composition is characterized by a symmetrical and balanced placement of doors and windows in regularly spaced bays that reflect the bays of the porch and projecting wings.

Combinations

Complex forms and larger living spaces may be created by combining side wings and/or rear wings with the main body. Gabled dormers may be added to introduce light into half-story and attic spaces. The architectural character of the attached parts should match that of the main body. Wings must also conform to all setback requirements (see *Community Patterns*).

C 9

EAST GARRISON

Monterey County, California

The massing types for the Picturesque Camp style were generated from the early church camp houses that evolved from temporary tents to more permanent dwellings in the 19th century. These cottages were originally seasonal and were often designed as miniature versions of a house in the Gothic Revival or Stick Style. These romantic interpretations became permanent dwellings and after the camps were no longer in operation. The property was often incorporated into the surrounding town. Many such camps, such as Pacific Grove in California or Oaks Bluff in Nantucket, are still intact with great examples of these house types.

Victorian era Picturesque Camp house in Napa Valley, California

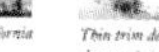

Thin trim details and three quarter scale are characteristics of the Picturesque Camp Style.

Vertical openings and a full, expressive porch create a "Best" Picturesque Camp house.

Bracketed American farmhouse from The Architecture of Country Houses by A.J.Downing

Essential Elements of Picturesque Camp

1 Steeply pitched, front facing gable roofs.
2 Cut wood ornament, often with natural forms such as leaves and vines.
3 Clapboard or cut shingle siding.
4 Vertical proportions for windows and doors.
5 Box bay and cutaway bay windows.

History and Character

THE PICTURESQUE CAMP STYLE builds on the early 'Carpenter Gothic' cottages built in the western region of the United States from early Pattern Books. While the style became fashionable in the 1800s in the Bay Area, its popularity grew and it spread north and south from San Francisco. The source of many early examples were the Pattern Books published by Andrew Jackson Downing. Publications such as The Horticulturist influenced the preferences of the public and provided an especially dramatic contrast to the inherited Spanish and adobe building types prevalent at the time. Early religious camp settlements, such as Pacific Grove in Monterey and Chautauqua in New York, adopted the style with more and more exotic variations that included Eastlake, Queen Anne, and Italianate detailing.

The Picturesque Camp style is centered on the simple, elegant forms that were adapted to the more informal houses on small lots, much like the early camp housing. This style emphasizes the connection to nature and has expressive porch elements, decorative trim elements, and vertical windows and doors.

Picturesque Camp

ARCHITECTURAL PATTERNS

8

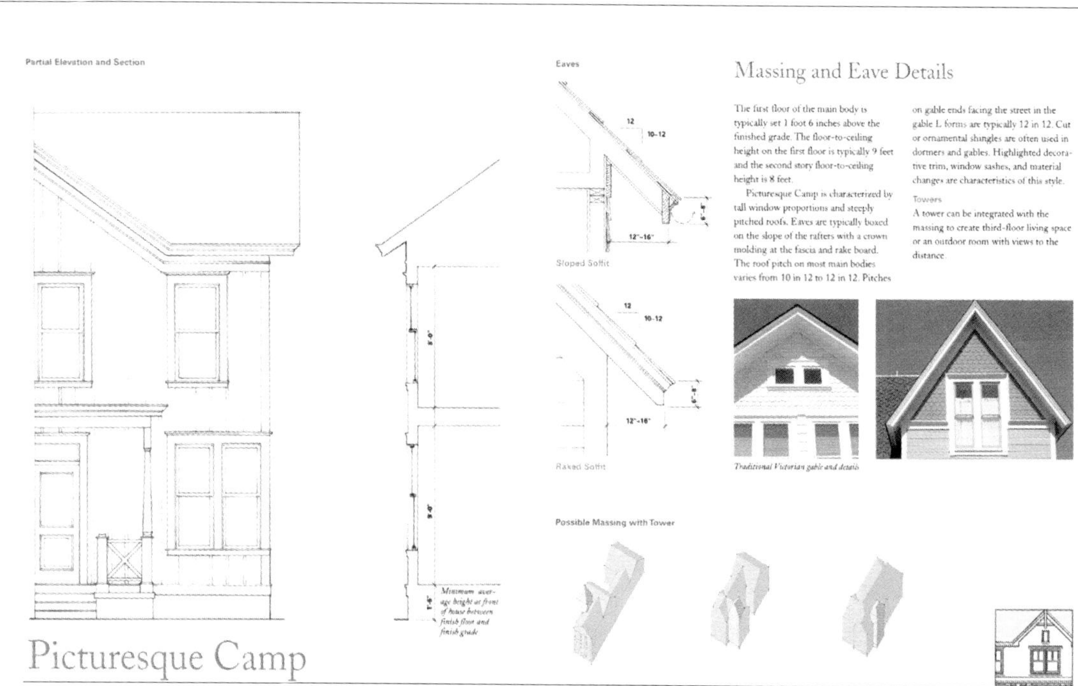

Partial Elevation and Section

Eaves

Sloped Soffit

Raked Soffit

Minimum average height at front of house between finish floor and finish grade

Massing and Eave Details

The first floor of the main body is typically set 1 foot 6 inches above the finished grade. The floor-to-ceiling height on the first floor is typically 9 feet and the second story floor-to-ceiling height is 8 feet.

Picturesque Camp is characterized by tall window proportions and steeply pitched roofs. Eaves are typically boxed on the slope of the rafters with a crown molding at the fascia and rake board. The roof pitch on most main bodies varies from 10 in 12 to 12 in 12. Pitches on gable ends facing the street in the gable L forms are typically 12 in 12. Cut or ornamental shingles are often used in dormers and gables. Highlighted decorative trim, window sashes, and material changes are characteristics of this style.

Towers

A tower can be integrated with the massing to create third-floor living space or an outdoor room with views to the distance.

Traditional Victorian gable and details

Possible Massing with Tower

Picturesque Camp

ARCHITECTURAL PATTERNS

10

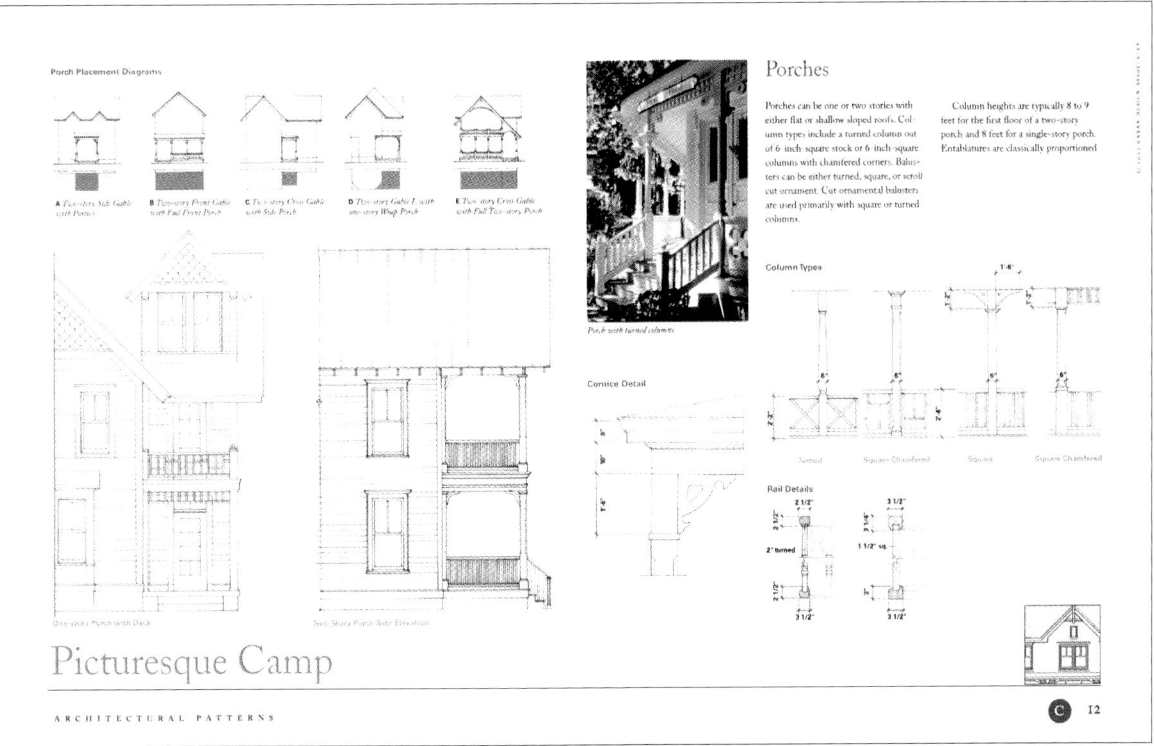

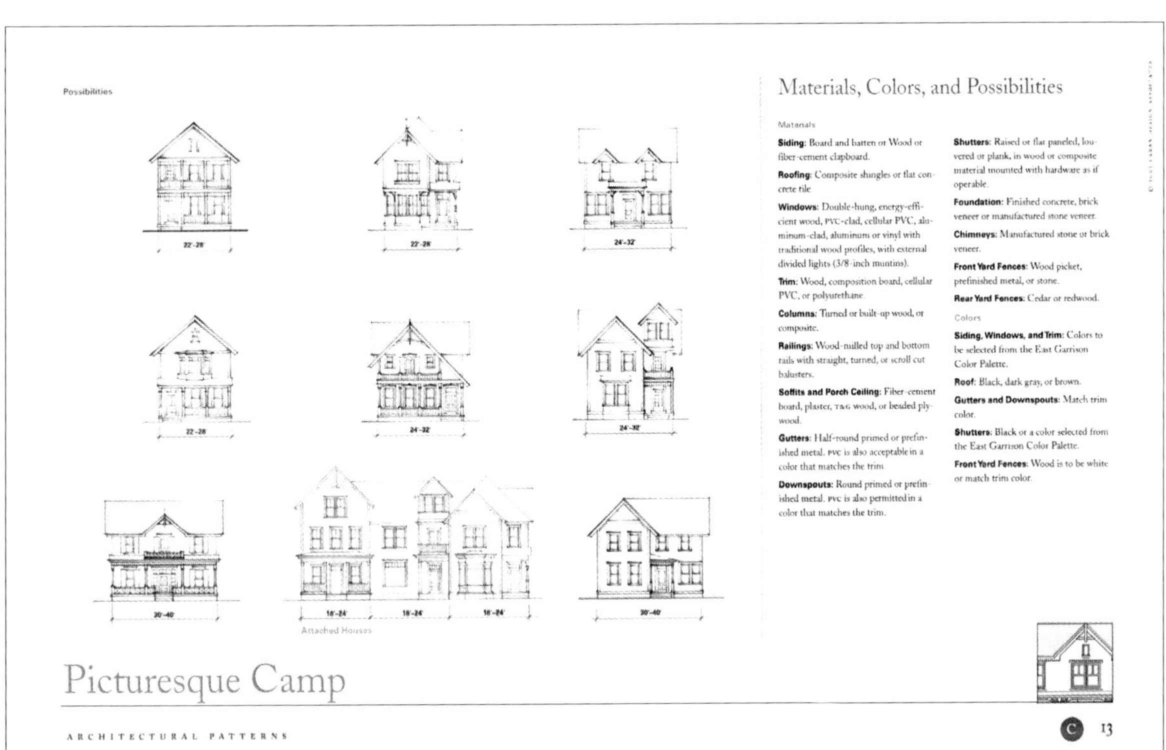

ARTS & CRAFTS STYLE

Comparative Analysis

The Arts & Crafts movement was an international phenomenon that produced an extraordinary breadth of work in this country at the beginning of the twentieth century. The English architect William Morris (1834–1896) was responsible for much of the published work on the Arts & Crafts ideal and built work. This movement developed as a response to the emerging machine-made, mass-produced system of making goods and materials. Architecture was seen as a craft that was becoming sterile and cold without the sense of well-designed and well-made furnishings and houses made from natural materials. Other English architects, such as C. F. A. Voysey, were published in periodicals started by the English Arts and Crafts Exhibition Society and distributed to architects in this country. This spurred the development of an American vocabulary for the movement. A central social mission that became part of this movement was the attempt to bring a full spectrum of handmade arts and high-quality design to the broader public at affordable prices. While this social goal was only partially achieved, an incredible body of creative and thoughtful work emerged in many areas of the related building and furnishing arts, including lighting, textiles, fired clay and tile-making, furniture design and construction, architecture, interior design, and graphic design.

Early examples of this style in America can be found along the New England seaboard as well as in California coastal communities, such as Pasadena and Santa Barbara. During the latter part of the nineteenth century, many architects in the northeast—especially New York and Boston—were experimenting with a variation of Queen Anne and Colonial Revival forms that were defined as Shingle style by Vincent Scully in his seminal research on the evolution of the style. McKim, Mead and White, H. H. Richardson, and many others developed a very refined vocabulary for Shingle-style houses, both inside and out. The form of the house became a composition of more organic forms wrapped in a skin of shingles and siding, often on a massive stone base that seemed to grow out of the ground. This period was influenced greatly by Richard Norman Shaw, an English architect who designed many large country estates experimenting with this language.

The later period of Shingle-style architecture coincided with the English Arts & Crafts movement; in fact, they share many common themes and elements. On the west coast, architects such as Gustav Stickley, the Greene Brothers (Henry and Charles), Julia Morgan, and Bernard Maybeck were all creating unique interpretations of the Arts & Crafts movement. The development of small, affordable Craftsman cottages came out of this California work and ultimately spawned a prolific production of Bungalow and small Craftsman cottages. These designs were developed largely for catalog house sales in the 1920s. Significant features included creative and effective built-in furnishings, large open rooms with broad window expanses, asymmetrical window and door compositions, an expression of the structural elements, a mix of natural materials, and the sense of handmade and hand-crafted details both inside and out.

Sample pages of the Arts & Crafts style have been excerpted from the Ducker Mountain (near Asheville, North Carolina), East Beach (Norfolk, Virginia), and East Garrison (Monterey County, California) pattern books.

Precedent photos

Standard Windows

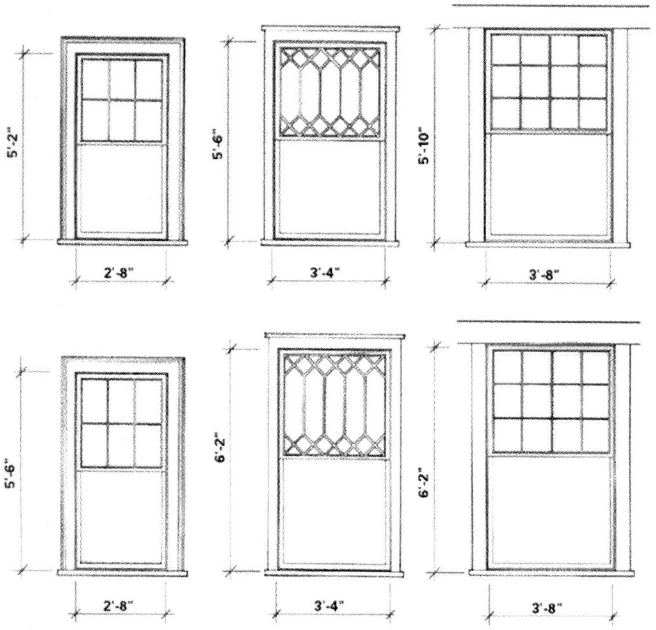

5'-2"
2'-8"
5'-6"
3'-4"
5'-10"
3'-8"
5'-6"
2'-8"
6'-2"
3'-4"
6'-2"
3'-8"

Special Windows

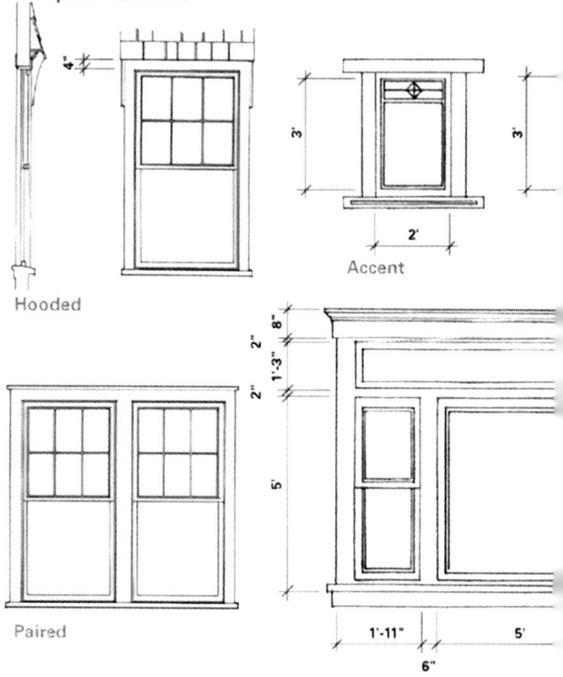

4"
Hooded
3'
2'
3'
Accent
8"
2"
1'-3"
2"
5'
Paired
1'-11"
6"
5'

Standard Doors

2'-6"
6"
1'-6"
6"

Dormers

12
12

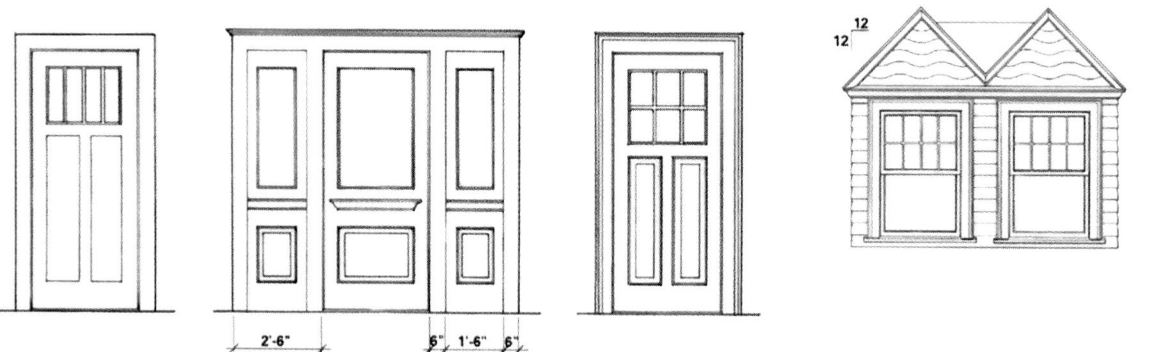

Biltmore Mountain Shingle

ARCHITECTURAL PATTERNS

Ducker Mountain (Biltmore)

Windows and Doors

Standard Windows

Windows on the first floor are usually arranged in combinations of single openings, pairs and/or strips of three or more, sometimes including large picture windows. Windows on the second floor may be single, paired or triples. Often special accent windows are incorporated into the composition. Window pane patterns include 6 over 1, 12 over 1 and diamond patterned top sash. Dormer windows are commonly ganged together.

Special Windows

Special windows include angled bay windows, picture windows and small, square and rectangular accent windows. Picture windows are typically paired with sidelights and transoms with a special pane pattern or stained glass upper sash.

Standard Doors

Biltmore Mountain Shingle doors are often stained wood with either wood plank design or panel doors with integrated transoms. Doors may have decorative, stained glass sidelights and transoms in Arts and Crafts patterns.

Trim

Trim may either be flat board, typically 5¼ inches wide with a head that extends beyond the jamb trim to the sides, or a more formal casing with a backband.

21

DUCKER MOUNTAIN (BILTMORE)

near Asheville, North Carolina

The Arts & Crafts style for Ducker Mountain is defined as Mountain Shingle style. While Craftsman-style houses were built throughout North Carolina from 1910 through the 1930s, the mountain region of western North Carolina was relatively undeveloped except for the emerging spa town of Asheville. The construction of the Biltmore Estate, designed by H. H. Richardson, required a staff of local architects to produce the working drawings and to oversee the work in the village and on the grounds. Architects, notably among them Richard Sharpe Smith, moved from New York to Asheville to oversee construction. During his stay in Asheville, Smith began designing a variety of ancillary structures on the property as well as private houses for other local clients. A number of local architects also designed houses in this style, and, combined with the development of the numerous spa hotels within the region, Asheville soon had a nice inventory of well-designed and well-executed Shingle-style or Arts & Crafts houses, made specifically for the mountains of North Carolina. The key features of this style include the use of local stone and brick, painted shingles, deep overhangs, shaped timber columns, and sawn bracket work in the eaves. The Mountain Shingle houses for Ducker were developed based on English variants of the Arts & Crafts movement, as well as the country houses designed by architects in New York and Connecticut. Great houses in historic neighborhoods like Montford and exotic lodges such as The Grove Park Inn exemplify the regional style.

Mountain Shingle house

Essential Elements of the Biltmore Mountain Shingle

1 Continuity of roof and wall surfaces.
2 Deep, broad porch elements with expressive structural components.
3 Strong horizontal lines such as eaves, water tables and window heads.
4 A mixture of materials such as stone, shingles and siding in horizontal bands.
5 Asymmetrical window and door compositions.

History and Character

BILTMORE MOUNTAIN SHINGLE HOUSES are derived from the uniquely American expression of architectural design for country houses termed *Shingle Style*, that originated in the northeastern region – Massachusetts, Rhode Island, Connecticut, New York, and Maine – from about 1878-1916. Architects began to look to early American Colonial houses that were simple, wood-shingled forms added onto in an organic way over time. The intention was to develop a uniquely American style for country houses and cottages that reinforced the notion of a more informal, leisure use. Notable practioners included McKim, Mead and White, Henry Hobson Richardson, and the Boston firms of Peabody & Stearns, Arthur Little, and Bruce Price. Early cottage settlements, such as Tuxedo Park in New York, serve as a good example of *Shingle Style* architecture.

In the Asheville region, we find many interpretations of this style in houses by architects such as Richard Sharp Smith and William Henry Lord who built in neighborhoods such as Montford. The use of mountain stone, pebble dash stucco and shingle cladding add a unique regional flavor to this style.

Biltmore Mountain Shingle

ARCHITECTURAL PATTERNS

C 18

Partial Elevation and Section

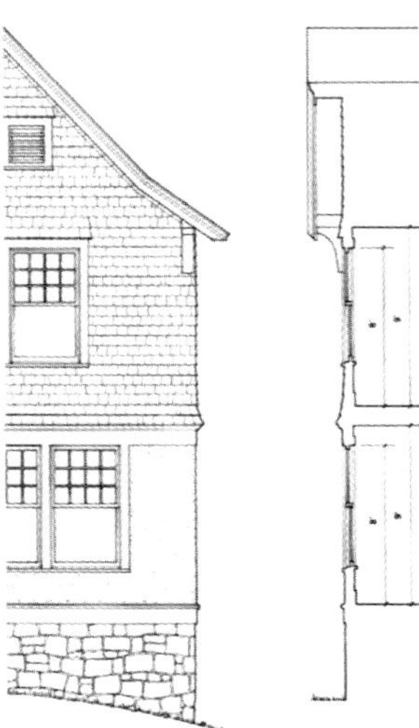

Eaves

Boxed Eave Return

Exposed Rafter Tail

Boxed Eave: Sloped

Wall Section and Eave Details

The first floor of the main body is typically set between two and three feet above the finished grade. The floor-to-ceiling height on both the first and second floor is 9 feet.

Two eaves are characteristic of the Biltmore Mountain Shingle style: a shallow boxed eave with a narrow profiled fascia, and a deep overhanging eave with exposed rafter tails or sloped soffit. These types of eaves are pictured here. The Biltmore Mountain Shingle may also have a Victorian-era character. This is achieved by using a broad, flat eave with shallow brackets on the house and the porch in concert with Classical-order columns such as Ionic or Corinthian.

Two-story main bodies are often characterized by either a change of material, trim application, or change of color between the first and second floor, near the sill line of the second-floor windows or the head of the first-floor windows. Stone, brick or stucco veneered foundation walls are sometimes exposed a full story above grade on steeply sloping sites.

Combinations

Complex forms and larger living spaces may be created by combining side and/or rear wings with the main body. Gabled or shed dormers may be added to introduce light into half-story and attic spaces. The architectural character of the attached parts should match that of the main body. Wings must also conform to all setback requirements.

Exposed rafter tails

Shallow broad eave

Biltmore Mountain Shingle

ARCHITECTURAL PATTERNS

C 20

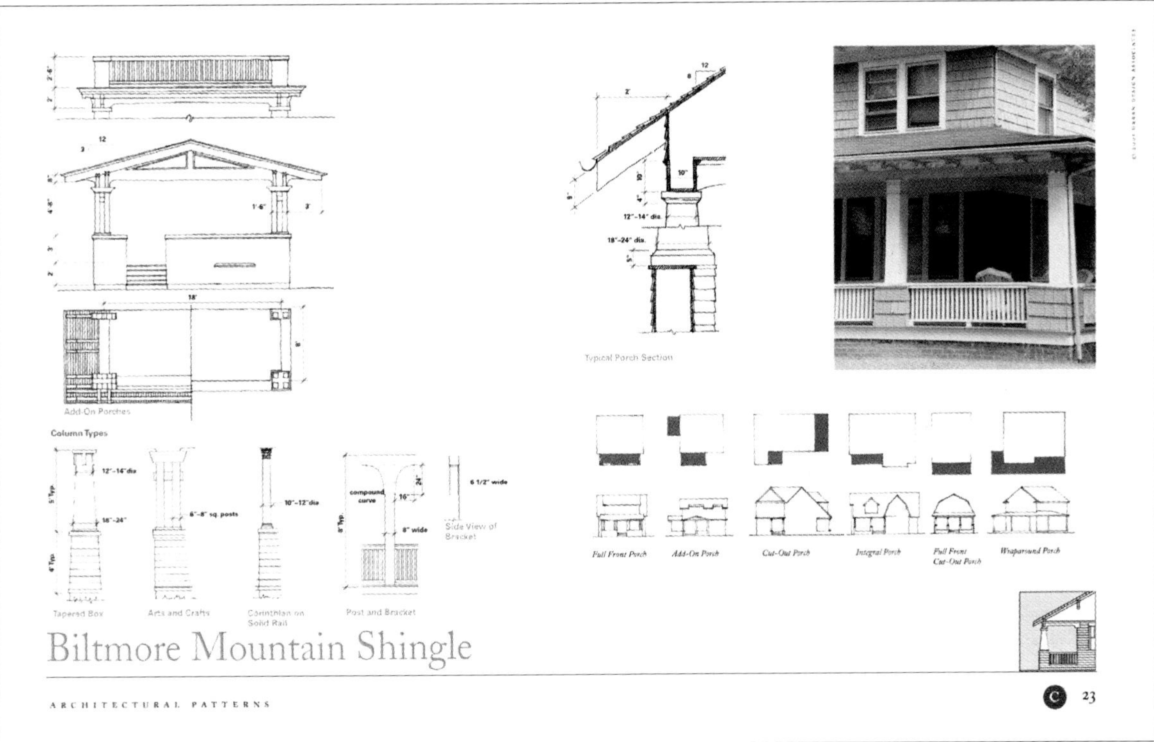

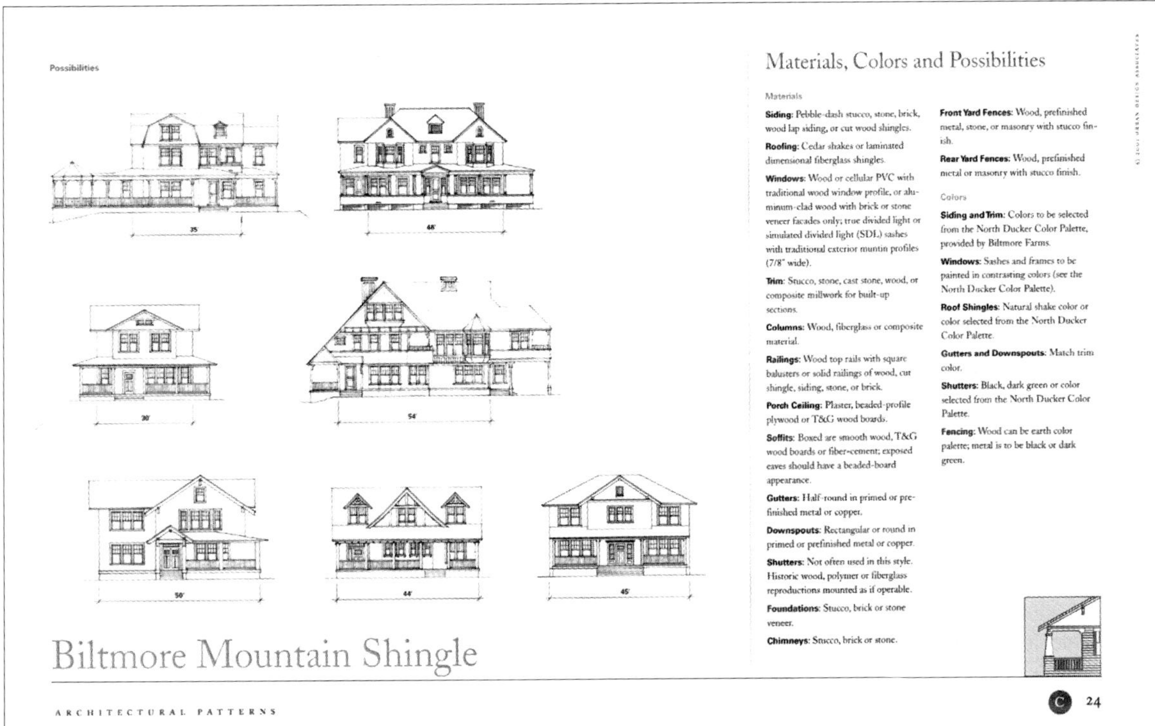
Possibilities

Materials, Colors and Possibilities

Materials

Siding: Pebble-dash stucco, stone, brick, wood lap siding, or cut wood shingles.

Roofing: Cedar shakes or laminated dimensional fiberglass shingles.

Windows: Wood or cellular PVC with traditional wood window profile, or aluminum-clad wood with brick or stone veneer facades only; true divided light or simulated divided light (SDL) sashes with traditional exterior muntin profiles (7/8" wide).

Trim: Stucco, stone, cast stone, wood, or composite millwork for built-up sections.

Columns: Wood, fiberglass or composite material.

Railings: Wood top rails with square balusters or solid railings of wood, cut shingle, siding, stone, or brick.

Porch Ceiling: Plaster, beaded-profile plywood or T&G wood boards.

Soffits: Boxed are smooth wood, T&G wood boards or fiber-cement; exposed eaves should have a beaded-board appearance.

Gutters: Half-round in primed or prefinished metal or copper.

Downspouts: Rectangular or round in primed or prefinished metal or copper.

Shutters: Not often used in this style. Historic wood, polymer or fiberglass reproductions mounted as if operable.

Foundations: Stucco, brick or stone veneer.

Chimneys: Stucco, brick or stone.

Front Yard Fences: Wood, prefinished metal, stone, or masonry with stucco finish.

Rear Yard Fences: Wood, prefinished metal or masonry with stucco finish.

Colors

Siding and Trim: Colors to be selected from the North Ducker Color Palette, provided by Biltmore Farms.

Windows: Sashes and frames to be painted in contrasting colors (see the North Ducker Color Palette).

Roof Shingles: Natural shake color or color selected from the North Ducker Color Palette.

Gutters and Downspouts: Match trim color.

Shutters: Black, dark green or color selected from the North Ducker Color Palette.

Fencing: Wood can be earth color palette; metal is to be black or dark green.

Biltmore Mountain Shingle

ARCHITECTURAL PATTERNS

C 24

Cape Charles, Virginia

Elizabeth City, North Carolina

Cape Charles, Virginia

Elizabeth City, North Carolina

Essential Elements of the Tidewater Arts & Crafts

1. Shallow-pitched roofs with deep overhangs.
2. Deep, broad porch elements with expressive structural components.
3. Asymmetrical, but balanced window and door compositions.
4. Grouped windows.

History and Character

TIDEWATER ARTS & CRAFTS HOUSES are derived from the traditions of Bungalow design, which was popular in beach cottages. Characterized by an eclectic mix of architectural elements and a response to coastal environments, this enduring style flourished in the early twentieth century both as modest cottages and large houses. Builders used pattern books and mass-marketed house plans and packages to attract a broad spectrum of homebuyers. These comfortable, eclectic homes were often lighter in color and less ornamented than high style Arts & Crafts houses. It is this more eclectic style that serves as the basis for the Tidewater Arts & Crafts.

The Tidewater Arts & Crafts is characterized by broad open porches; low sloping roofs with deep overhangs; multiple gables; asymmetric compositions; oversized first-floor windows; expressive trim; exposed rafters; and bracketed porches.

Tidewater Arts & Crafts

ARCHITECTURAL PATTERNS

C 22

Massing Diagrams

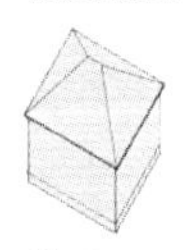

A Hipped

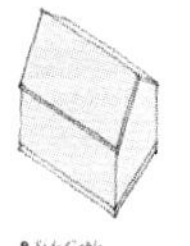

B Side Gable

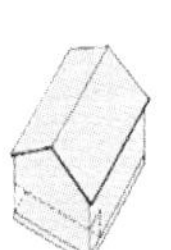

C Side Gable with Integral Porch

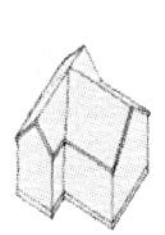

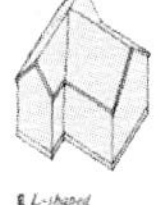

D Front Gable

E L-shaped

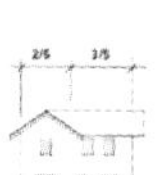

Massing and Composition

Massing

A Hipped

Rectangular or square volume with a 6 in 12 to 8 in 12 roof pitch; the ridge line, if any, runs parallel with the front of the house. Front gabled and/or shed roofed porches with a 3 in 12 to 5 in 12 pitch are placed symmetrically or asymmetrically on the front façade or as full-façade elements. Porches are typically one story and may wrap one or both corners.

B Side Gable

Rectangular volume with a 6 in 12 to 8 in 12 roof pitch. Asymmetrically placed gabled and/or shed roofed porches are common. Porches are typically one story.

C Side Gable with Integral Porch

Rectangular one-and-one half story volume with a 6 in 12 to 8 in 12 roof pitch. The integral porch is set under occupiable interior space, made possible by a dormer and high knee wall on the second floor. Integral front porch ranges from half to the full length of the front façade. Symmetrically placed gabled or shed dormers have a 3 in 12 roof pitch.

D Front Gable

Rectangular volume with a 6 in 12 to 8 in 12 roof pitch and gable facing the street. Symmetrically or asymmetrically placed front and/or shed roofed porches are common and either one- or two-story. An inset, one-story porch may also run the full width of the house.

E L-Shaped

Cross-gabled volume with a 6 in 12 to 8 in 12 gable facing the street. The width of the gable facing the street is typically two-fifths, or less commonly, half that of the main body. Often an in-line front gabled porch or wing is added to the front leg of the **L**. Shed porches may also fill the space between the wings of the **L**.

Massing Combinations

Complex forms and larger living spaces may be created by combining side and/or rear wings with the main body. Gabled or shed dormers may be added to introduce light into half-story and attic spaces. The architectural character of the attached parts should match that of the main body.

Façade Composition

Arts & Crafts façade composition is characterized by an asymmetrical yet balanced placement of doors and windows. Typically, windows occur in pairs and multiples, or as sidelights for oversized ground floor windows. Entrance doors are most often under porches and off center.

Tidewater Arts & Crafts

ARCHITECTURAL PATTERNS

C 23

Partial Elevation and Wall Section

Roof
Eave
Soffit
Window Head Trim
Wall
Corner Board
Skirt Board
Watertable
8'-0" to 9'-0"
7'-0"
9'-0" to 10'-0"
7'-0" to 8'-0"
3'-0" minimum height at front of house between finish floor and finish grade

Eaves

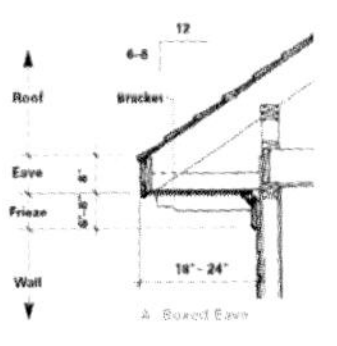

A Boxed Eave

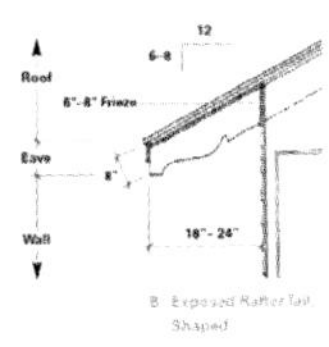

B Exposed Rafter Tail Shaped

Wall Section and Eave Details

Roof

The roof pitch on Tidewater Arts & Crafts homes varies from 6 in 12 to 8 in 12. Slate, shingles and metal are appropriate roofing materials.

Eaves

Deep eaves are a dominant characteristic of the Tidewater Arts & Crafts style. There are two types of eaves in the style:

A Boxed eave with flat soffit, and shallow profile brackets 6 inches wide and 24 inches on center.

B Exposed 2 x 8 inch shaped rafter tail 16 to 24 inches on center, the most common eave; often hipped, gables feature a vergeboard.

Eave profiles have an 8- to 12-inch frieze board either touching/co-planar with or no more than 8-inches above the window head trim. The Tidewater Arts & Crafts may have a Victorian-era character, achieved by using Classical-order columns on the porch and broad, flat boxed eave with shallow brackets on the house and porch.

Wall

For one-story houses, the minimum floor-to-ceiling height is 9 feet. For two-story houses, the minimum floor-to-ceiling height is 9 feet for the first floor and 8 feet for the second floor. Window head heights should be 7 feet to 8 feet above the floor for first floor windows, and 7 feet for second floor windows.

Watertable

The first floor of the Tidewater Arts & Crafts house is typically set three feet above the finished grade. Tidewater Arts & Crafts houses have 8- to 10- inch wide skirt boards. Foundation vents are centered under windows when used.

Tidewater Arts & Crafts

ARCHITECTURAL PATTERNS

C 24

Standard Windows

Special Windows

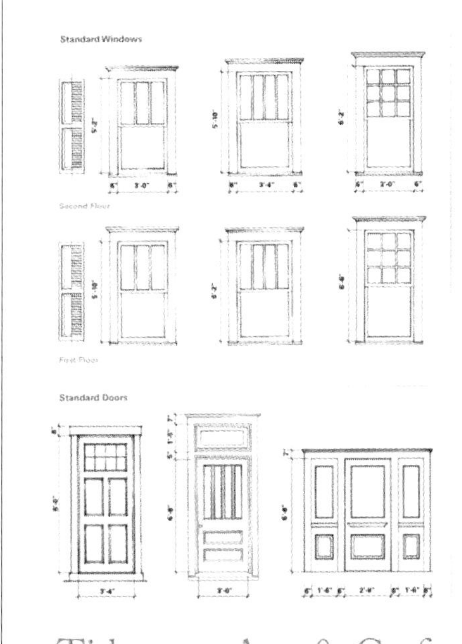

Second Floor

First Floor

Standard Doors

Gable End Window

Triple Window

Typical Window Detail

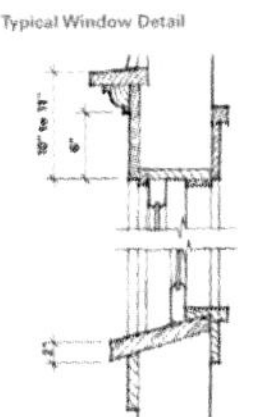

Accent Windows

Shed Dormer

Box Bay Elevation & Plan

Windows and Doors

Standard Windows

Windows are typically vertical in proportion and have a 3 over 1, 4 over 1, 6 over 1, or 9 over 1 muntin pattern. Standard windows are double hung.

Special Windows

Special windows include triple windows, small square accent windows, and box bay windows supported on flat cut brackets. Wide windows divided into several panes occur in dormers and gables. Other dormer windows are ganged together in wide gabled or shed dormers.

Doors

Arts & Crafts doors are often stained wood with either wood plank design or a panel door with the top half glazed. Doors may have sidelights or transoms in clear or leaded glass in Arts and Crafts patterns. Outer louver doors in a four-panel design are common on coastal Arts and Crafts houses to permit ocean breezes to enter.

Trim

Windows and doors have 6-inch straight or tapered flat trim. Arts & Crafts window and door trim carries a simple moulding and cap above.

Tidewater Arts & Crafts

ARCHITECTURAL PATTERNS

C 25

Asymmetrical window and door composition and a mix of siding materials are characteristic of the Garrison Craftsman style.

Simple forms with exposed structural members and deep overhangs are typical.

Tower elements will be an optimal di the Garrison Craftsman homes.

Essential Elements of the Garrison Craftsman

1 Shallow-pitched roofs with deep overhangs.
2 Deep, broad porch elements with expressive structural components.
3 Exposed structural elements in the eaves such as rafters and brackets.
4 A mixture of materials such as stucco, shingles, and siding.
5 Asymmetrical window and door compositions.

Garrison Craftsman

ARCHITECTURAL PATTERNS

Illustration of Craftsman house from 500 Small Houses of the Twenties

History and Character

GARRISON CRAFTSMAN HOUSES are derived from the unique qualities of the Craftsman tradition found throughout the Northern California and Central Coast region. Many regional builders constructed houses influenced by the Arts & Crafts movement. California versions are characterized by exposed or expressive structural elements such as rafters, columns, beams, lintels, and porch elements. The floor plans were generally open with built-in cabinet work often in natural, stained woods. House exteriors were clapboard or shingle siding mixed with stone and brick or stucco accents and were painted in robust color palettes. The California craftsman house was influenced by the Japanese and English Arts and Crafts movements.

For houses in East Garrison, the emphasis in this style is on simple, structural expression of porch and eave elements using a vocabulary of architectural elements including Prairie style, Japanese, and Swiss, as well as influences from the Arts & Crafts movement. A coastal character is important to this style and should be reflected in the use of high contrast color for body and trim details. Forms are simple and reflect dimensioned lumber elements. Windows in this style tend to be vertical in proportion and are typically ganged or paired. Exposed eave brackets on roofs and porches contribute to this image and detail.

Horizontal siding, square and shaped shingle siding patterns, and a mix of stucco and siding materials are key cladding elements. This style also may include unpainted metal roofing and shingled roofs.

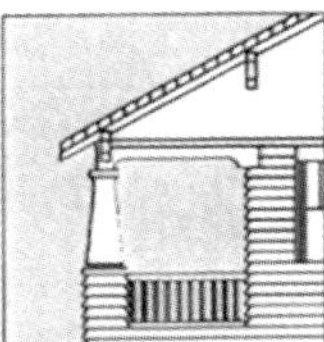

3

EAST GARRISON

Monterey County, California

This style evolved from a broad survey of historic Craftsman styles and emerging trends in Arts & Crafts interpretations for cottages and houses. This style features the simple, straightforward expression of the structure of a house with exposed rafters, square columns and beams, flat, square-edged trim elements in ways that enhance the frame and structure of a house. The doors and windows are simple shapes with square proportions.

Massing Diagrams

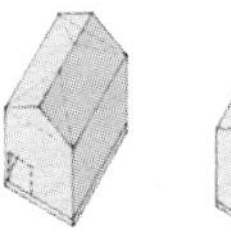
A Two-story Front Gable

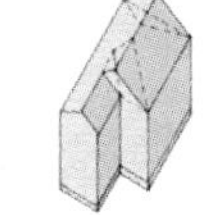
B Two-story Narrow Gable-L

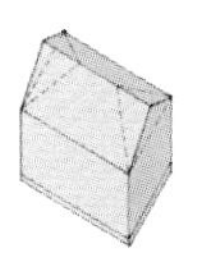
C Two-Story Basic

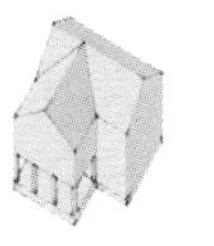
D Two-story Gable-L with Integral Porch

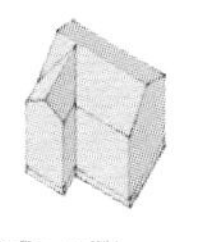
E Two-story Wide Gable-L

Possible Massing Combinations

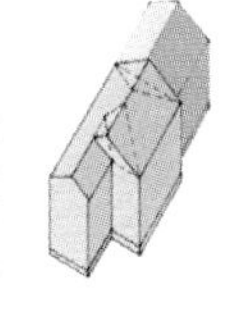
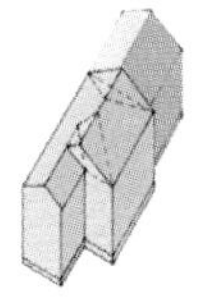
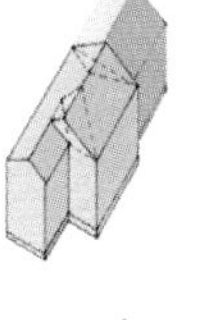
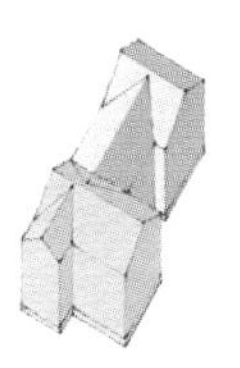
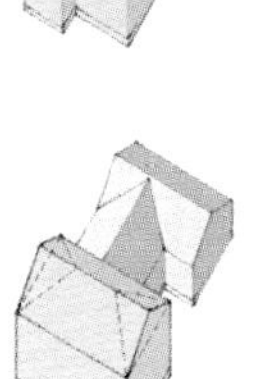

Massing and Composition

Massing

A Two-Story Front Gable
Hipped or front-gabled rectangular volume. Hip roof pitch is typically 6 in 12 and gable roof pitch is 6 to 8 in 12. Gabled- or hipped-front porches are common. Porches may be either additive or a single integral bay.

B Two-Story Narrow Gable-L
Front facing gable volume with a 6 in 12 projecting gabled wing. The width of the gable facing the street is typically one-half to two-thirds the width of the main body. Porches are typically one bay wide and can be either shed roof or front facing gable.

C Two-Story Basic
Side-gabled rectangular volume with roof pitch of 6 to 8 in 12. One-story, gabled front porches, typically placed to one side. Porches are most often a minimum of two-fifths the length of the main body, and, occasionally, the entire length of the front facade.

D Two-Story Gable-L with Integral Porch
Cross-gabled volume with a 6 in 12 gable facing the street. Cross gable has a lower slope. The width of the gable facing the street is typically two-thirds that of the main body for houses up to 32 feet wide and one-half to three-quarters that of the main body for houses 36 feet and over. This massing includes an integral front porch within the gabled projecting wing.

E Two-Story Wide Gable-L
Cross-gabled volume with a 6 in 12 gable facing the street. Cross gable can have a lower slope. The width of the gable facing the street is typically half that of the main body for houses up to 32 feet wide and two-fifths that of the main body for houses 36 feet and over. This massing accommodates a variety of porch options, often with a gable emphasizing the entrance.

Facade Composition

Garrison Craftsman facade composition is characterized by an asymmetrical but balanced placement of doors and windows. Standard windows most often occur paired.

Combinations

Complex forms and larger living spaces may be created by combining side and/or rear wings with the main body. Gabled or shed dormers may be added to introduce light into half-story and attic spaces. The architectural character of the attached parts should match that of the main body. Wings must also conform to all setback requirements (see *Community Patterns*).

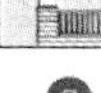

Garrison Craftsman

ARCHITECTURAL PATTERNS C 4

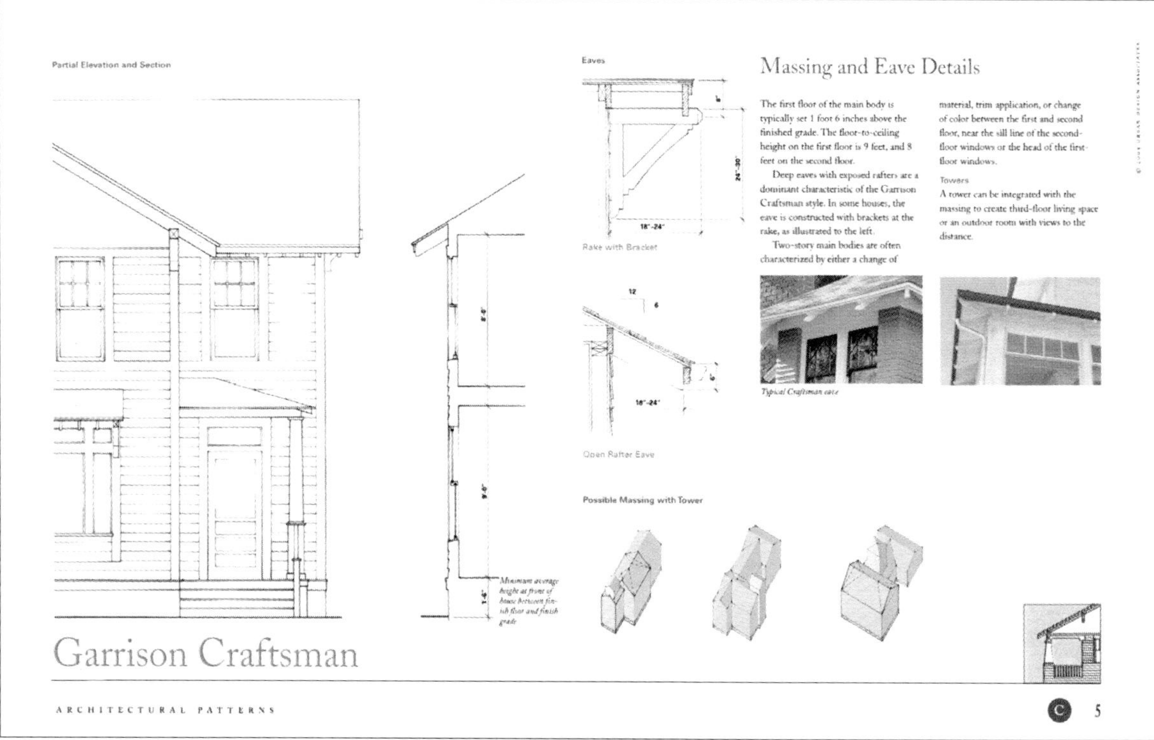
Partial Elevation and Section

Eaves

Rake with Bracket

Open Rafter Eave

Massing and Eave Details

The first floor of the main body is typically set 1 foot 6 inches above the finished grade. The floor-to-ceiling height on the first floor is 9 feet, and 8 feet on the second floor.

Deep eaves with exposed rafters are a dominant characteristic of the Garrison Craftsman style. In some houses, the eave is constructed with brackets at the rake, as illustrated to the left.

Two-story main bodies are often characterized by either a change of material, trim application, or change of color between the first and second floor, near the sill line of the second-floor windows or the head of the first-floor windows.

Towers

A tower can be integrated with the massing to create third-floor living space or an outdoor room with views to the distance.

Typical Craftsman eave

Possible Massing with Tower

Garrison Craftsman

ARCHITECTURAL PATTERNS C 5

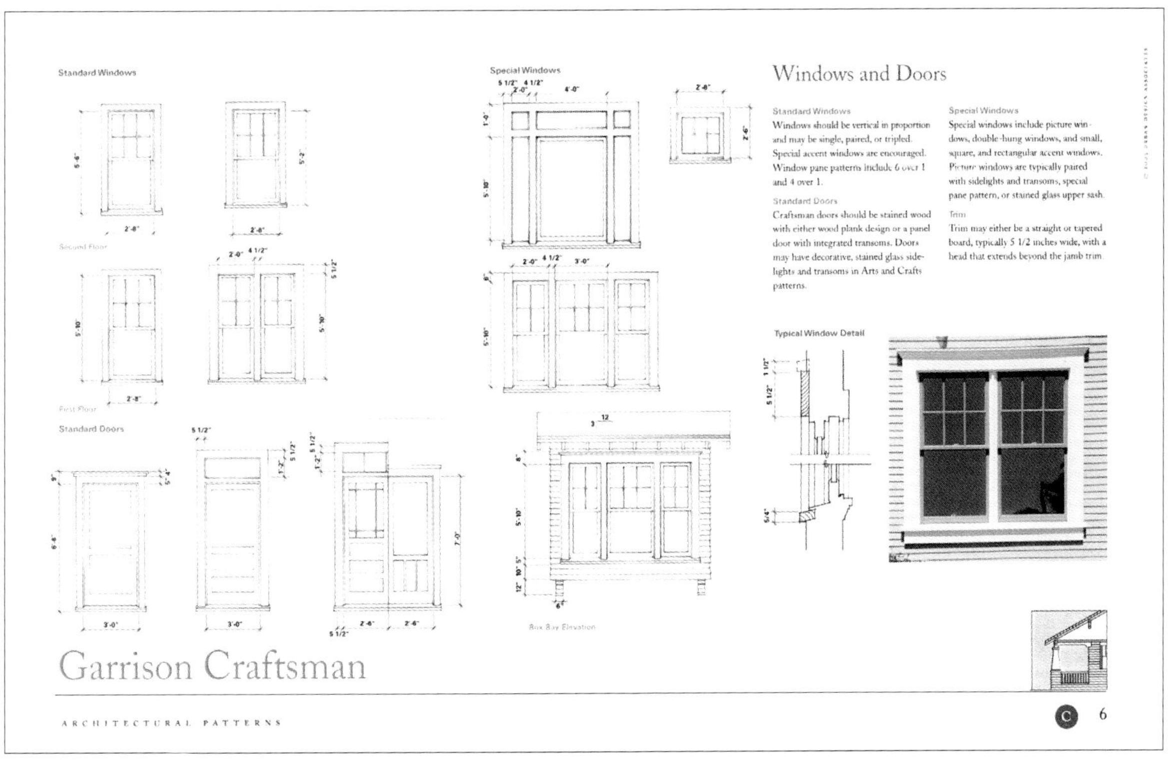

Windows and Doors

Standard Windows

Windows should be vertical in proportion and may be single, paired, or tripled. Special accent windows are encouraged. Window pane patterns include 6 over 1 and 4 over 1.

Standard Doors

Craftsman doors should be stained wood with either wood plank design or a panel door with integrated transoms. Doors may have decorative, stained glass sidelights and transoms in Arts and Crafts patterns.

Special Windows

Special windows include picture windows, double-hung windows, and small, square, and rectangular accent windows. Picture windows are typically paired with sidelights and transoms, special pane pattern, or stained glass upper sash.

Trim

Trim may either be a straight or tapered board, typically 5 1/2 inches wide, with a head that extends beyond the jamb trim.

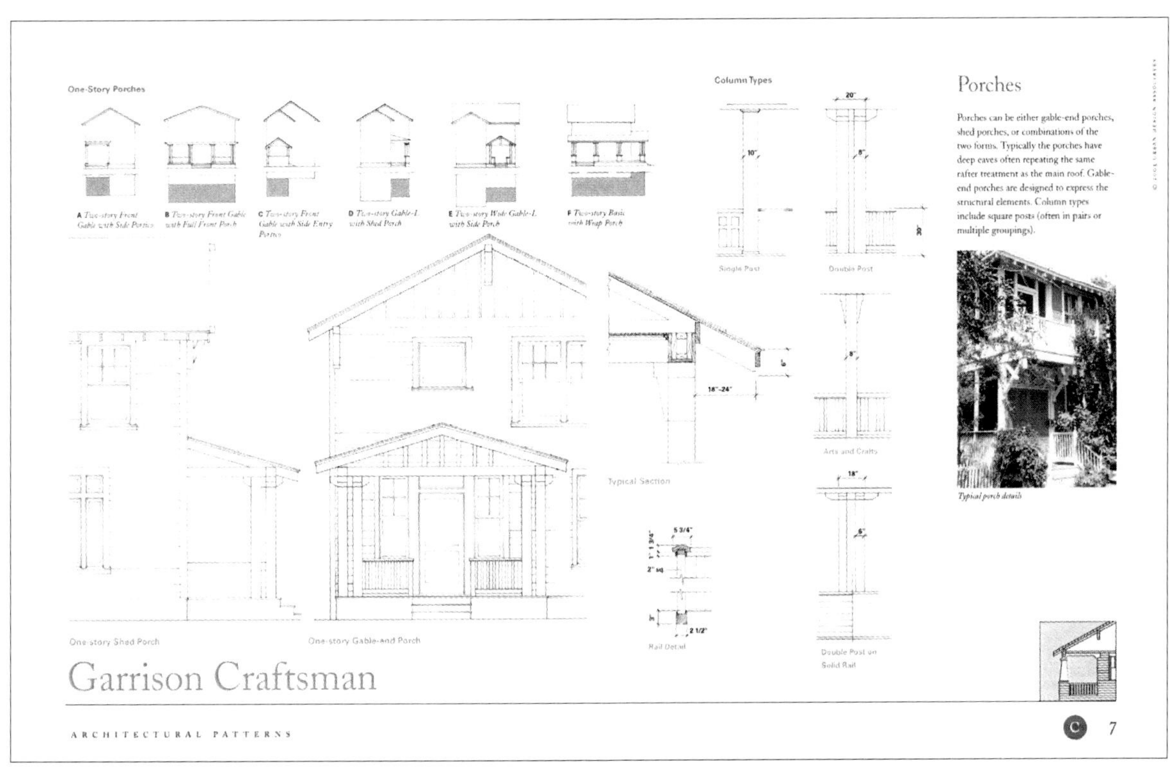

Porches

Porches can be either gable-end porches, shed porches, or combinations of the two forms. Typically the porches have deep eaves often repeating the same rafter treatment as the main roof. Gable-end porches are designed to express the structural elements. Column types include square posts (often in pairs or multiple groupings).

CLASSICAL STYLE

Comparative Analysis

Classical houses in most regions of the country come out of the early Colonial settlements and are closely linked to Georgian, Federal, and Adam roots of the style. UDA typically treats Greek Revival as a distinct style unto itself. Early carpenters' reference books, such as Asher Benjamin's *The American Builders Companion*, Batty Langley's *The City and Country Builder's* and *Workman's Treasury of Designs*, or *Practical Architecture* by William Halfpenny, documented many classically proportioned details for doors, windows, interior moldings, trim, etc. Analysis of local or regional architectural patterns reveals many variations of the theme and lots of hybrid examples with curious detailing. Individual localities, though, typically have a particular flavor of Classicism depending on the heyday in which the style was being built. Since builders and consumers followed tastes of the period, one finds that this clustering of style and interpretation by local builders does, in fact, exhibit some common characteristics. Regional influences in and around Charleston, South Carolina, will yield a very different Classical architecture than the examples found in and around St. Louis, Missouri. Doing local research determined the focus for documenting the regional variations of this style. However, the documentation for the pattern book is not comprehensive; rather it is focused on local patterns that seem appropriate to the project and the essential character of the neighborhoods found in the local environment.

Sample pages of the Classical style have been excerpted from the Baxter (Fort Mill, South Carolina), Ducker Mountain (near Asheville, North Carolina), and Norfolk, Virginia pattern books.

Precedent photos

History and Character

The Fort Mill region has a significant inventory of Classical houses designed in the Federal style as well as the Palladian and Greek Revival styles. The dominant Federal style was practiced by notable American architects such as William Jay, Benjamin Latrobe, Robert Mills (who worked for Latrobe in Philadelphia), Charles Bulfinch and others from 1780 to the 1820s.

Much of this country's classically styled houses were constructed by builders using pattern books in the nineteenth century. Books such as Asher Benjamin's *American Builder's Companion* became a standard resource enabling frontier builders to construct proportionally correct architectural cornices, windows and doors. The Upcountry Classical House in Baxter will be built using many of these principles and compositional patterns.

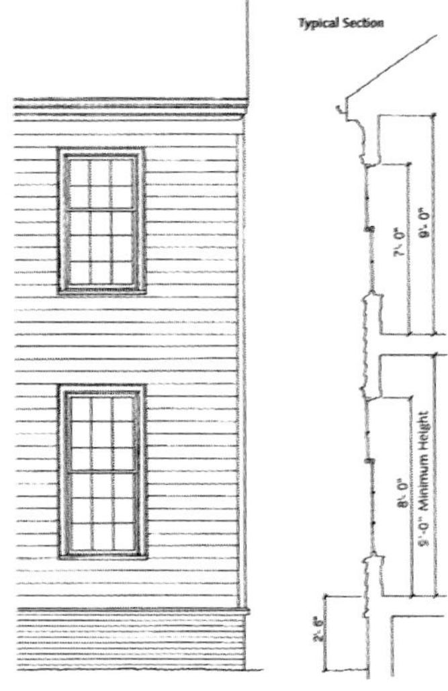

Essential Elements include:

- Simple, well-proportioned volumes with consistent roof pitches.
- Well-detailed classical eaves and cornices.
- Multi-pane windows that are either 6 over 6, 6 over 9, or 9 over 9. First-floor windows are taller than second-floor windows.
- One- or two-story porches, often with gabled 'temple front' facades.
- Classical columns and details on porches in the Tuscan or Doric Order.
- An orderly relationship among windows, doors, porches, and roof forms.

Urban Design Associates

Baxter Upcountry Classical C-1 Character & Essential Elements

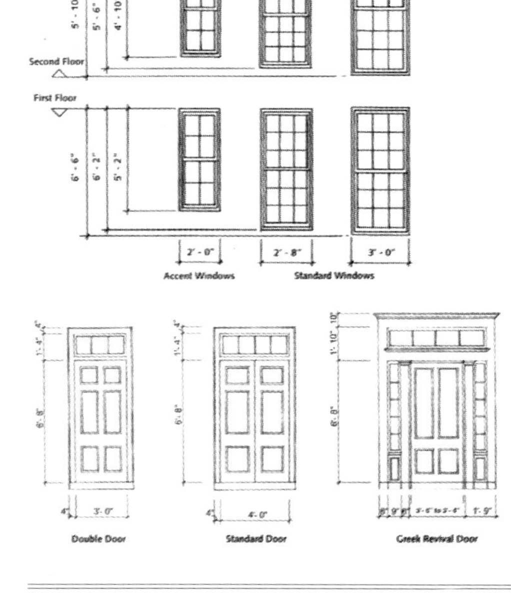

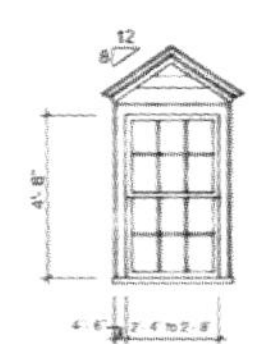

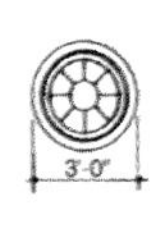

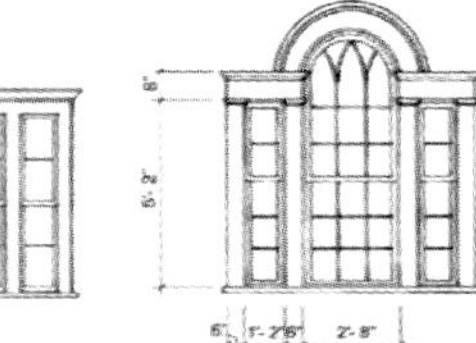

Standard Doors

Four-, six-, and eight-panel doors should be used and set in simple door surrounds with transoms. The Greek Revival surround includes sidelights.

Standard Windows

Windows are double-hung with two standard combinations:
A. 9 over 9 on first floor and 6 over 9 on second floor.
B. 6 over 6 on first floor and 6 over 6 on second floor.
Accent windows are 4 over 6 and 4 over 4.
Keep window pane proportions consistent between first- and second-floor sizes. Upcountry windows are built with sills.

Dormer Windows

Dormer windows are 6 over 6. Side walls do not extend beyond the width of the trim.

Special Windows

The Palladian window with integral sidelights and the triple-sash window are considered special window types. The arched Palladian center sash must be one continuous sash and is typically used over the entry door.

Small accent windows are often used in gable ends and side wings.

Trim

Windows and doors typically have 4-inch-wide trim molding, with the exception of the Greek Revival door surround and the Palladian window, which have 6-inch trim.

Windows shall have sills as a component of the trim. The surrounds, when used with brick, are set into the masonry opening. Stone or brick lintels should be used in addition.

Louvered or 2-panel shutters, one-half the width of the sash, may be used on single windows.

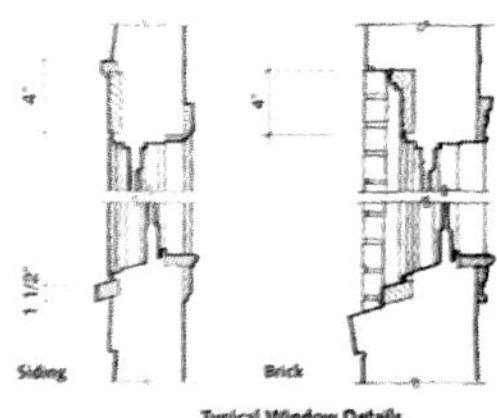

Typical Window Details

Urban Design Associates

Baxter Upcountry Classical C-3 Windows & Doors

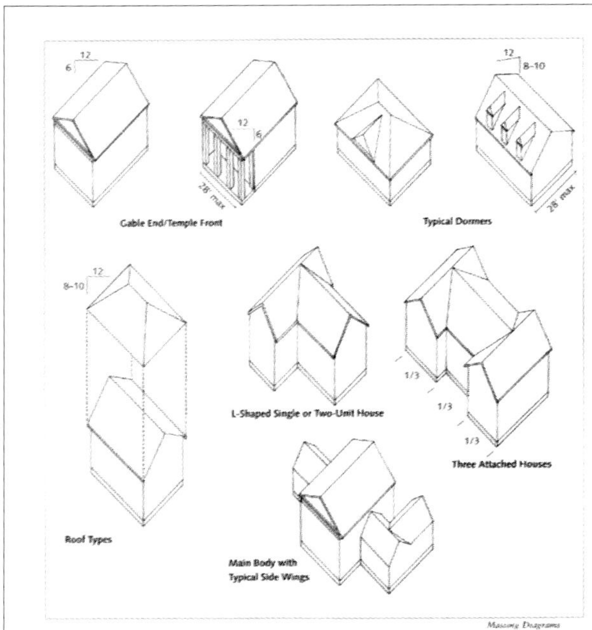

Massing Diagrams

Basic Massing

The basic Classical house has a simple, rectangular volume, either one or two stories. The roof can be either gabled or hipped. Another typical classical massing is one that has a "temple" front facing the street. The porch is integral with the Main Body.

Narrow-width side and rear wings with similar proportions are used to increase the volume. These wings have simple massing and remain a series of small, individual elements connected together. Typical roof pitches are 8 in 12 to 10 in 12 for gables or hips. Temple fronts can be 6 in 12 to 10 in 12.

The minimum floor-to-ceiling height for first floors is 9 feet with 10 feet strongly encouraged and 9 feet for second floors. Cottage houses may have floor to ceiling heights of 8 feet on the second floor but must maintain a minimum of 2 feet between the head of windows and the underside of the eave on the exterior. The first-floor elevation is a minimum of 2 feet 6 inches above finished grade.

Combinations

The main body of the house may be combined with smaller side wings, porches, and garages to create complex forms and larger living spaces. The main body should read as a dominant element. Gable ends should be 28 feet or less in width. The architectural character of the side and rear wings should match that of the main body of the house. Small dormers with gabled or arched roofs may be added to provide light to half-story and attic spaces. Dormers with hipped roof forms are not permitted.

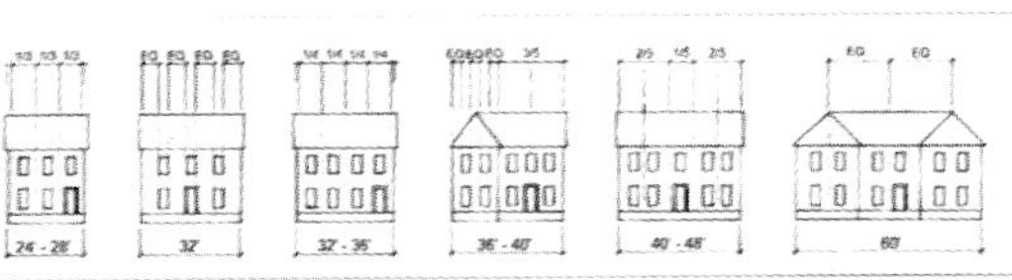

Door & Window Compositions

Urban Design Associates

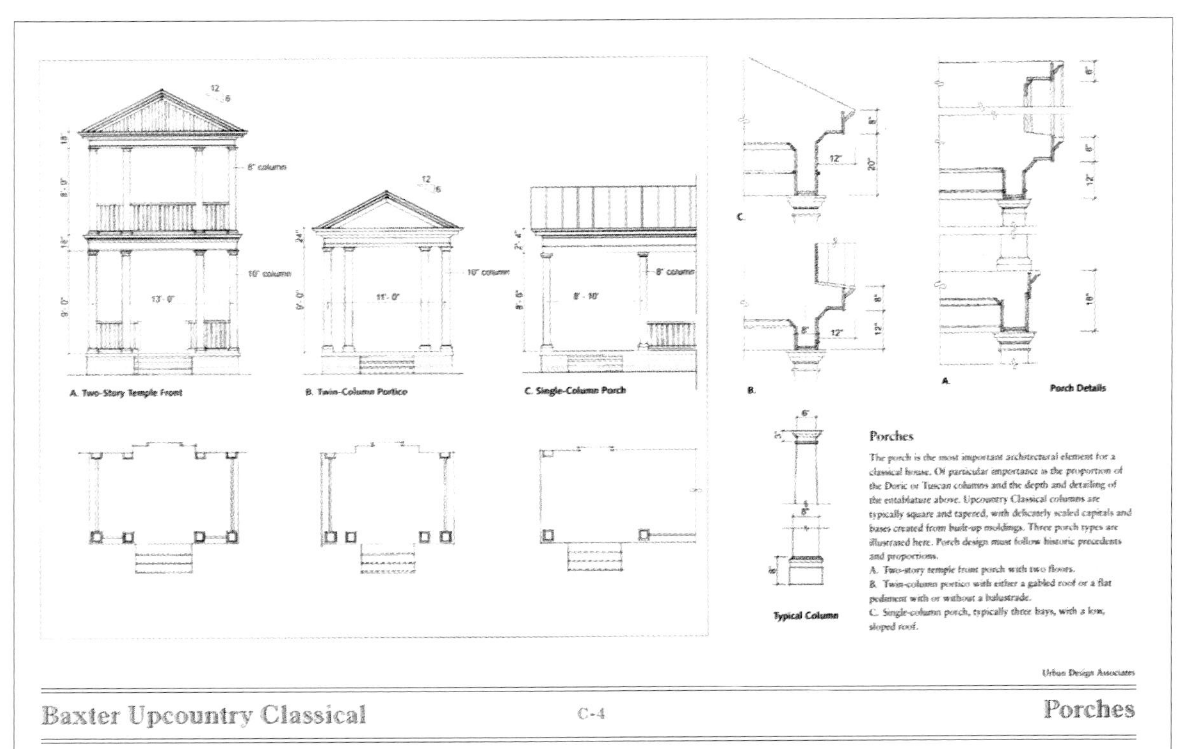

Porches

The porch is the most important architectural element for a classical house. Of particular importance is the proportion of the Doric or Tuscan columns and the depth and detailing of the entablature above. Upcountry Classical columns are typically square and tapered, with delicately scaled capitals and bases created from built-up moldings. Three porch types are illustrated here. Porch design must follow historic precedents and proportions.

A. Two-story temple front porch with two floors.
B. Twin-column portico with either a gabled roof or a flat pediment with or without a balustrade.
C. Single-column porch, typically three bays, with a low, sloped roof.

Urban Design Associates

Materials

Shutters: Panel or louver, painted; encourage mounting as if operable. Width of shutter equals 50% of sash width.
Siding: Wood, composition board, fiber-cement board, or vinyl with Beveled, Shiplap or Beaded Lap profile; common brick in Flemish, Common, or English bond patterns and stucco with smooth/sand finish.
Roofing: Standing seam metal, slate, asphalt or fiberglass shingles.
Windows: Divided light sash with sill or GBG
Lintels: Brick jack arch, or stone/cast stone.
Trim: Wood, composition board, fiber-cement board and molded millwork for built-up sections; Corner boards 5/4 x 4.
Soffits and Porch Ceilings: GWB, plaster, T&G wood or composite. (Continuous perforated soffit materials not permitted.)
Gutters: Metal, half-round, or ogee.
Downspouts: Metal, round, or rectilinear.
Foundations: Common brick, stone/cast stone on front facade and side street facade when on corner lot. Stucco permitted on others.
Columns: Wood, fiberglass, or composite.
Railings: Straight or turned balusters.
Chimneys: Common brick, stone, siding or stucco.
Front Yard Fences: Painted white picket, or prefinished composite material such as PVC or vinyl and metal.
Rear Yard Fences: Painted wood, white composite material such as PVC or vinyl; prefinished metal.

Colors

Siding: White. Other colors to be selected from approved list. (Refer to Baxter's extensive color palette.)
Roof Shingles: Roof shingles to be typically black or dark grey. Standing seam may be black, dark green, or dark red.
Accent: White or a rich color to match trim.
Brick: All brick to be selected from Baxter palette.
Windows: Sashes and frames to be white.
Trim: All window, door, corner and eave trim to be selected from Baxter color palette. Columns should be white.
Gutters: White; terne metal or copper.
Downspouts: White; terne metal or copper.
Shutters: Black or dark green.
Fencing: Wood or PVC/vinyl is to be white; metal is to be black or dark green.

Urban Design Associates

Baxter Upcountry Classical C-5 Materials & Possibilities

Two-story brick Classical house

Two-story Classical house with siding

One- and-one-half story Classical house with a court entry

Early twentieth century Classical house

Essential Elements of the Biltmore Classical

1. Simple volumes with one-story side wings and porches added to make more complex shapes.
2. Symmetrical composition of doors and windows.
3. Simplified versions of Classical details and columns, often with robust and exotic Classical orders such as Ionic and Corinthian used in the porch element.
4. Multi-pane windows that are wide in proportion usually with 6-over-6 or 9-over-9 pane patterns.

History and Character

THE BILTMORE CLASSICAL HOUSE is based on Federal and Classical Revival houses from the mid-19th century. The western North Carolina region has significant examples of houses from this period. The dominant Federal style was practiced by notable architects such as Robert Mills and Benjamin Latrobe; however many houses from this period were constructed using Pattern Books such as Asher Benjamin's *American Builder's Companion*. These houses are typically developed as simple, additive massing types with a dominant center pavilion, or Main Body, which can be one or two stories, and additive side wings, rear wings and pavilions. Palladian compositions became a principal organizing and proportioning reference for many houses from this period.

Biltmore Classical houses will be designed using these elements and massing principles. On steeply sloping sites found within Ducker Mountain, these houses will use raised terraces to create formal entry relationships particularly important on lots sloping upward from the street.

Biltmore Classical

ARCHITECTURAL PATTERNS

 I

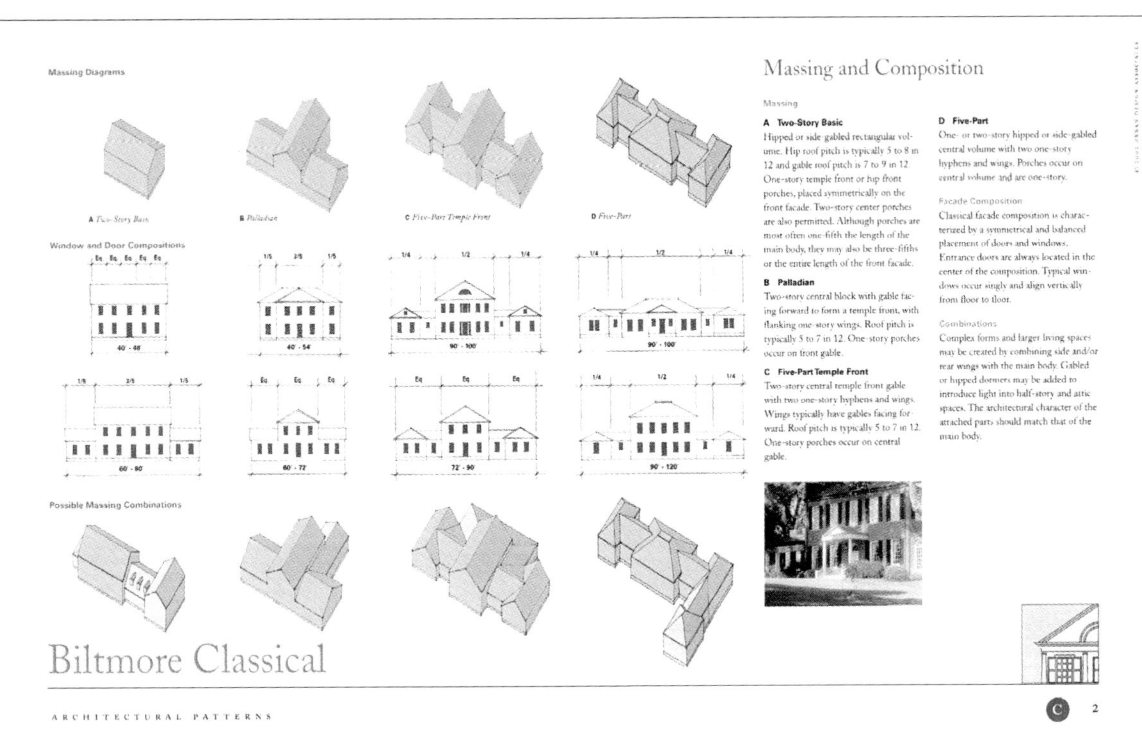

Massing Diagrams

A Two-Story Basic · B Palladian · C Five-Part Temple Front · D Five-Part

Window and Door Compositions

Possible Massing Combinations

Massing and Composition

Massing

A Two-Story Basic
Hipped or side-gabled rectangular volume. Hip roof pitch is typically 5 to 8 in 12 and gable roof pitch is 7 to 9 in 12. One-story temple front or hip front porches, placed symmetrically on the front facade. Two-story center porches are also permitted. Although porches are most often one-fifth the length of the main body, they may also be three-fifths or the entire length of the front facade.

B Palladian
Two-story central block with gable facing forward to form a temple front, with flanking one-story wings. Roof pitch is typically 5 to 7 in 12. One-story porches occur on front gable.

C Five-Part Temple Front
Two-story central temple front gable with two one-story hyphens and wings. Wings typically have gables facing forward. Roof pitch is typically 5 to 7 in 12. One-story porches occur on central gable.

D Five-Part
One- or two-story hipped or side-gabled central volume with two one-story hyphens and wings. Porches occur on central volume and are one-story.

Facade Composition
Classical facade composition is characterized by a symmetrical and balanced placement of doors and windows. Entrance doors are always located in the center of the composition. Typical windows occur singly and align vertically from floor to floor.

Combinations
Complex forms and larger living spaces may be created by combining side and/or rear wings with the main body. Gabled or hipped dormers may be added to introduce light into half-story and attic spaces. The architectural character of the attached parts should match that of the main body.

Biltmore Classical

ARCHITECTURAL PATTERNS

C 2

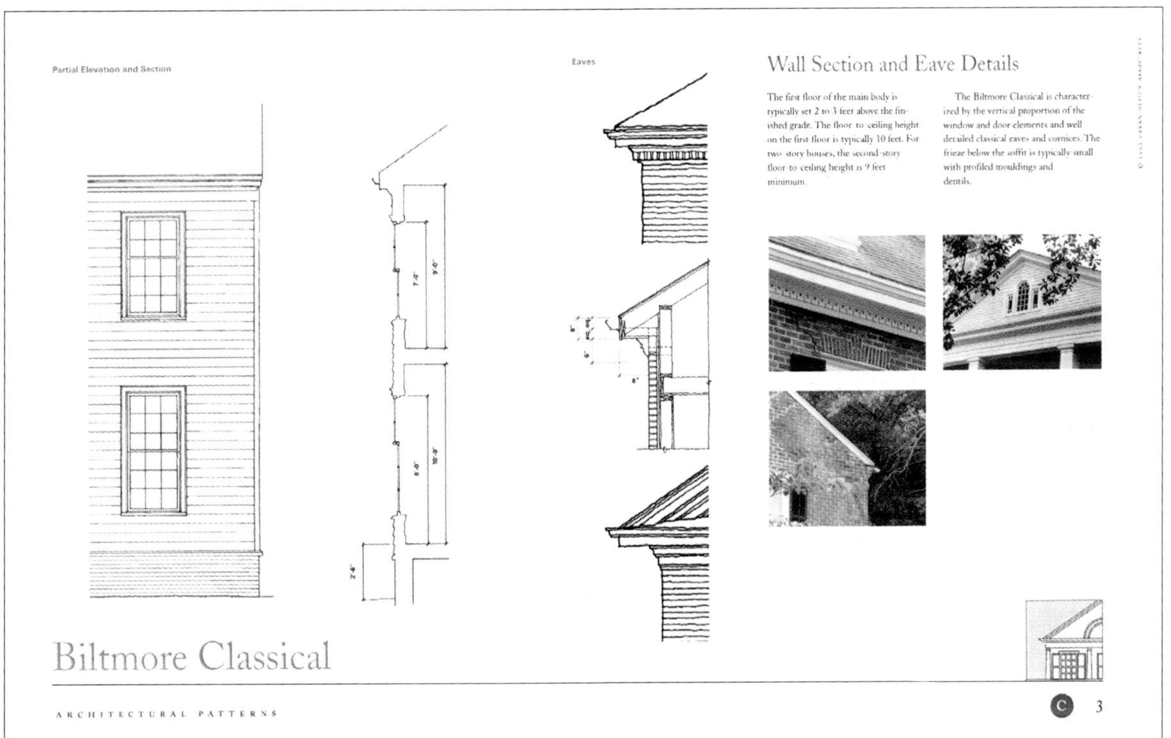

Partial Elevation and Section

Eaves

Wall Section and Eave Details

The first floor of the main body is typically set 2 to 3 feet above the finished grade. The floor-to-ceiling height on the first floor is typically 10 feet. For two-story houses, the second-story floor-to-ceiling height is 9 feet minimum.

The Biltmore Classical is characterized by the vertical proportion of the window and door elements and well detailed classical eaves and cornices. The frieze below the soffit is typically small with profiled mouldings and dentils.

Biltmore Classical

ARCHITECTURAL PATTERNS

C 3

One-Story Porch Elevations and Plans

Eave Sections

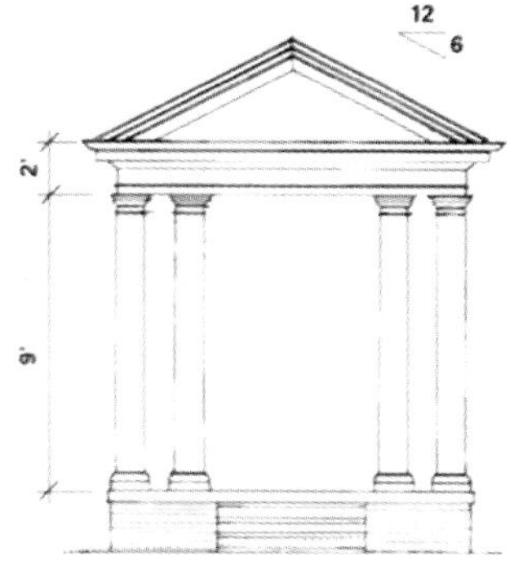

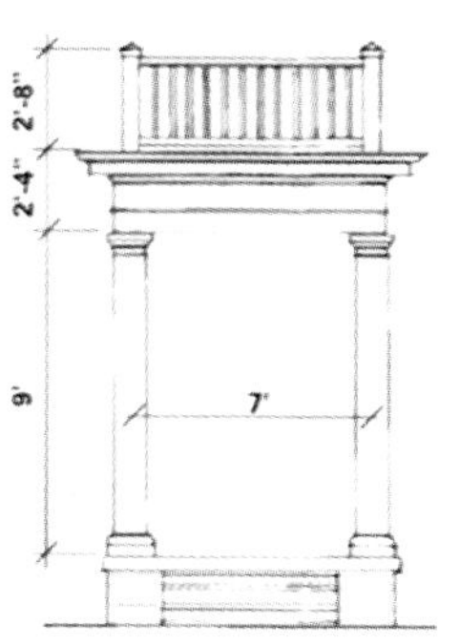

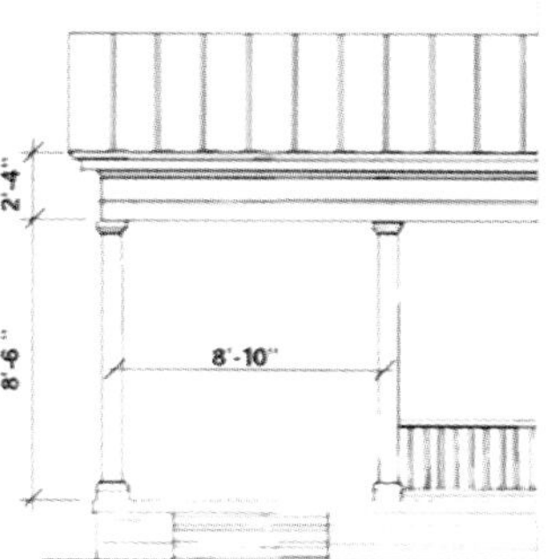

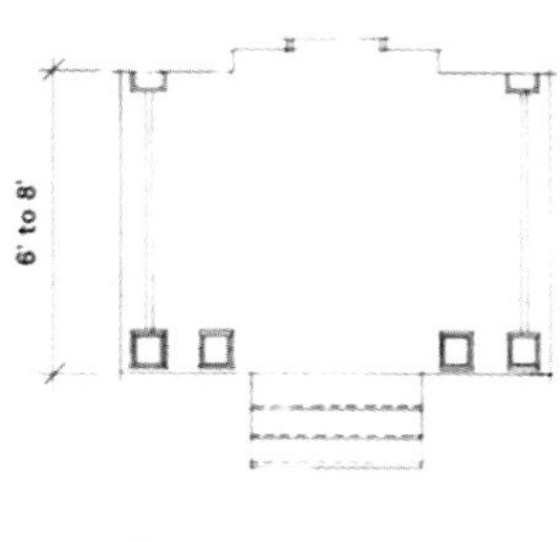

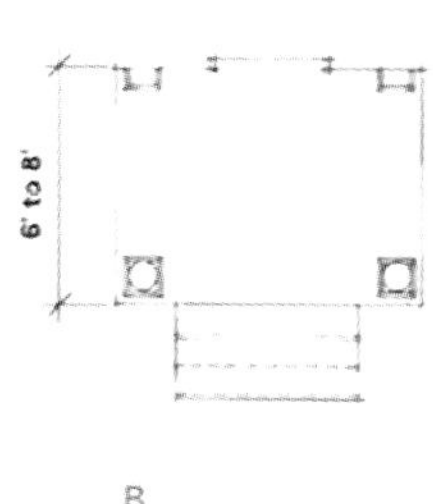

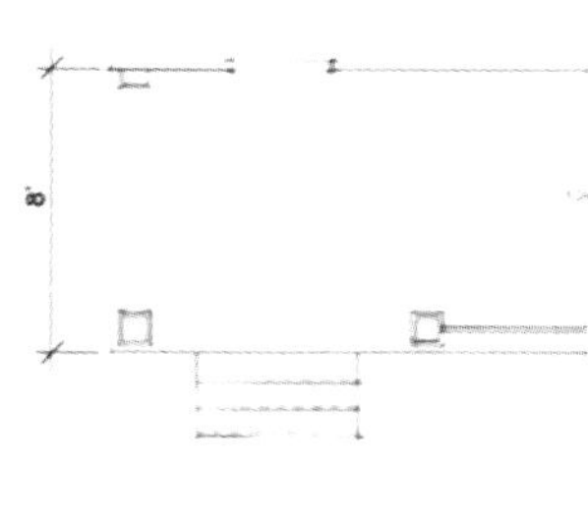

A

B

C

A

B anc

Column Types

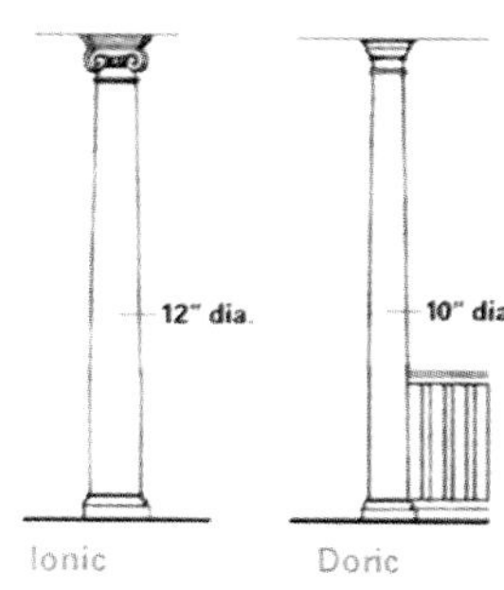

Ionic

Doric

Biltmore Classical

Ducker Mountain (Biltmore)

Typical Porch Locations

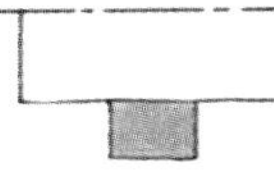

Two-story basic with portico

Two-story basic with full front porch

Two-story basic with three-fifths front porch

6

DUCKER MOUNTAIN (BILTMORE)

near Asheville, North Carolina

The Biltmore Classical house is based on Federal and Classical Revival houses from the mid-19th century. The western North Carolina region has significant examples of houses from this period. The dominant Federal style was practiced by notable architects such as Robert Mills and Benjamin Latrobe; however many houses from this period were constructed using pattern books such as Asher Benjamin's *American Builder's Companion*. These houses are typically developed as simple, additive massing types with a dominant center pavilion, or main body, which can be one or two stories, and additive side wings, rear wings, and pavilions. Palladian compositions became a principal organizing and proportioning reference for many houses from this period.

Biltmore Classical houses will be designed using these elements and massing principles. On steeply sloping sites found within North Ducker, these houses will use raised terraces to create formal entry relationships particularly important on lots sloping upward from the street.

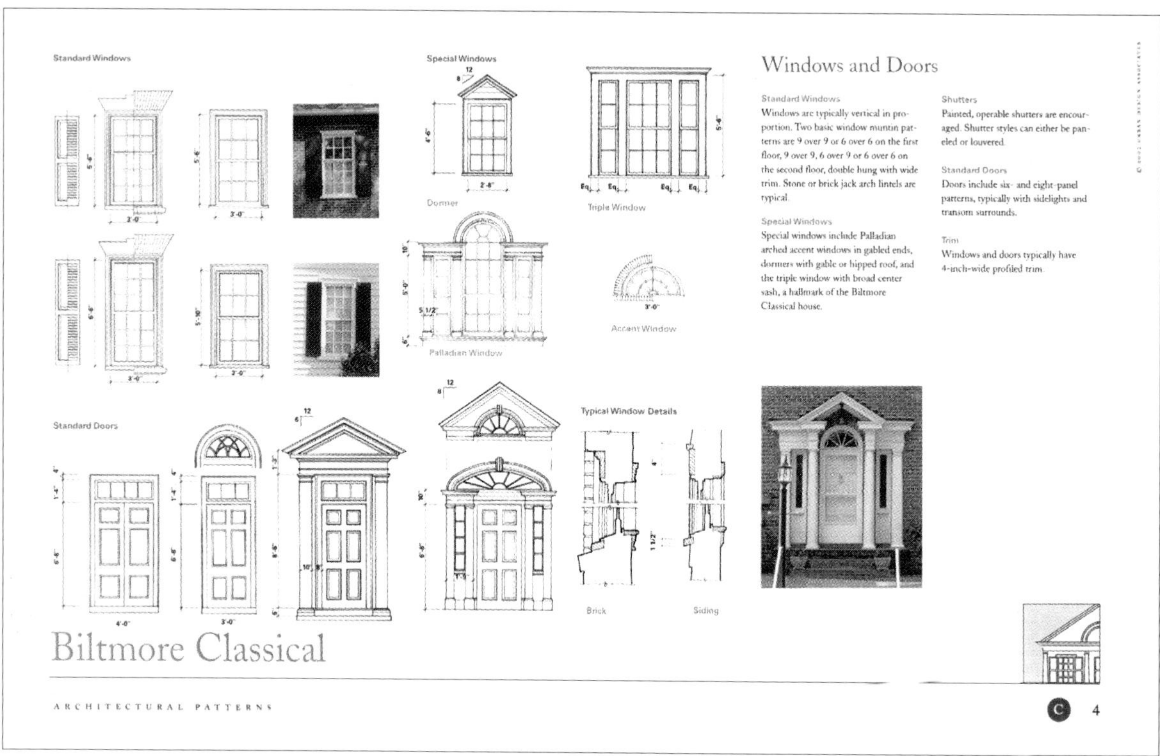

Standard Windows

Special Windows

Dormer

Triple Window

Palladian Window

Accent Window

Standard Doors

Typical Window Details

Brick

Siding

Windows and Doors

Standard Windows
Windows are typically vertical in proportion. Two basic window muntin patterns are 9 over 9 or 6 over 6 on the first floor, 9 over 9, 6 over 9 or 6 over 6 on the second floor, double hung with wide trim. Stone or brick jack arch lintels are typical.

Special Windows
Special windows include Palladian arched accent windows in gabled ends, dormers with gable or hipped roof, and the triple window with broad center sash, a hallmark of the Biltmore Classical house.

Shutters
Painted, operable shutters are encouraged. Shutter styles can either be paneled or louvered.

Standard Doors
Doors include six- and eight-panel patterns, typically with sidelights and transom surrounds.

Trim
Windows and doors typically have 4-inch-wide profiled trim.

Biltmore Classical

ARCHITECTURAL PATTERNS

C 4

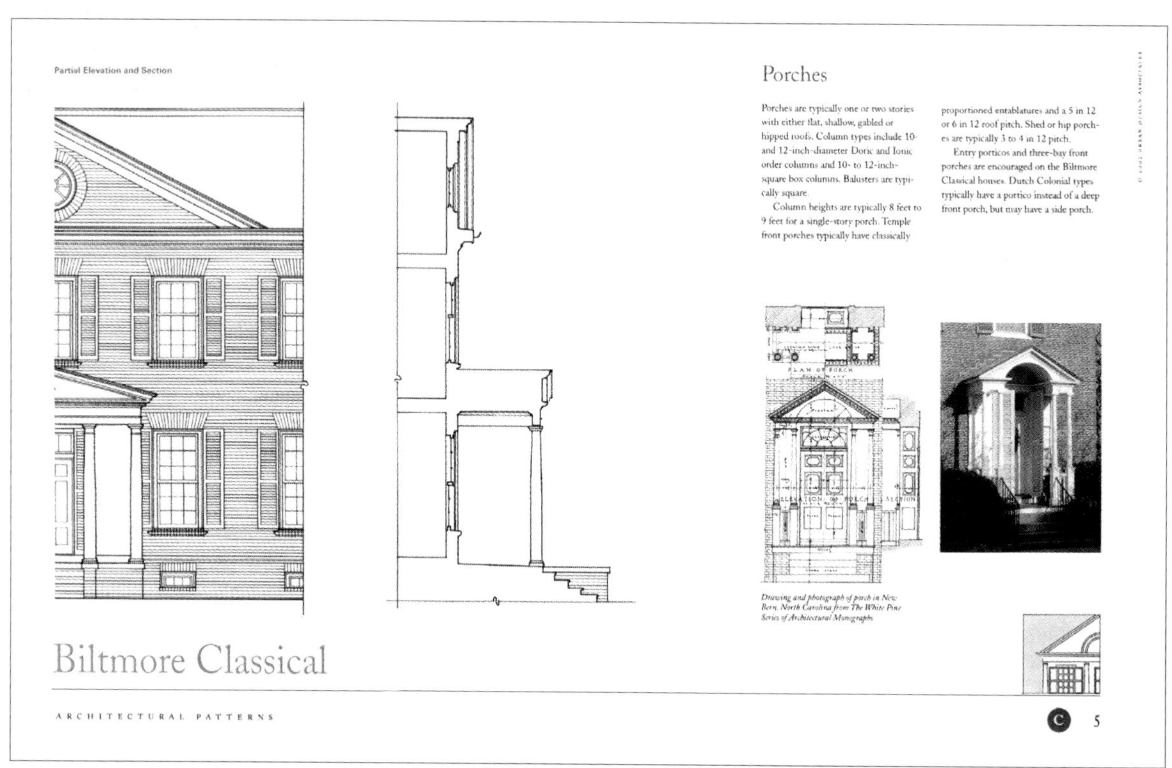

Partial Elevation and Section

Porches

Porches are typically one or two stories with either flat, shallow, gabled or hipped roofs. Column types include 10- and 12-inch-diameter Doric and Ionic order columns and 10- to 12-inch-square box columns. Balusters are typically square.

Column heights are typically 8 feet to 9 feet for a single-story porch. Temple front porches typically have classically proportioned entablatures and a 5 in 12 or 6 in 12 roof pitch. Shed or hip porches are typically 3 to 4 in 12 pitch.

Entry porticos and three-bay front porches are encouraged on the Biltmore Classical houses. Dutch Colonial types typically have a portico instead of a deep front porch, but may have a side porch.

Drawing and photograph of porch in New Bern, North Carolina from The White Pine Series of Architectural Monographs

Biltmore Classical

ARCHITECTURAL PATTERNS

C 5

Ducker Mountain (Biltmore)

The Ledges, Huntsville, Alabama, Classical architectural patterns built results

Essential Elements of the Norfolk Classical Revival Style

1 Simple volumes with one-story side wings and porches added to make more complex shapes.

2 Symmetrical composition of doors and windows.

3 Simplified versions of Classical details and columns, often with robust and exotic Classical orders such as Ionic and Corinthian used in the porch element.

4 Multi-pane windows that are wide in proportion, usually with 6 over 6 or 9 over 9 pane patterns.

NORFOLK CLASSICAL REVIVAL

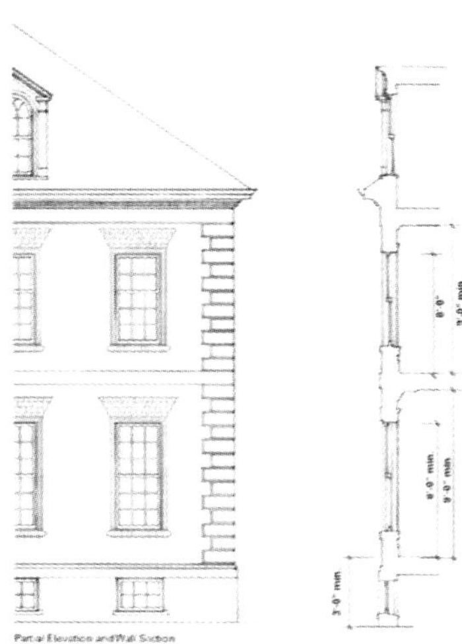

Partial Elevation and Wall Section

The Norfolk Classical Revival style is based on Federal and Classical Revival houses from the mid-nineteenth century. Norfolk and the Mid-Atlantic Region have significant examples of houses from this period.

The dominant Federal style was practiced by notable architects such as Robert Mills and Benjamin Latrobe, however many houses from this period were constructed using Pattern Books such as Asher Benjamin's American Builder's Companion.

Classical Revival houses are typically developed as simple, additive massing types with a dominant center pavilion, or Main Body, which can be one or two stories, and additive side wings, rear wings and pavilions. Palladian compositions became a principle organizing and proportioning reference for many houses from this period.

Massing & Composition

MASSING DIAGRAMS

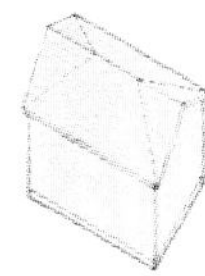

A Broad Front

B Narrow Front

MASSING COMBINATIONS

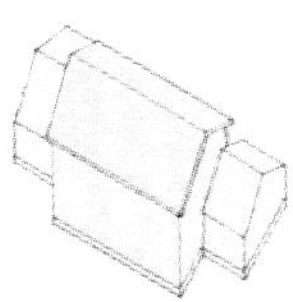

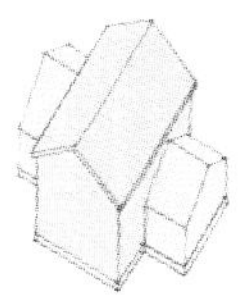

FACADE COMPOSITION DIAGRAMS

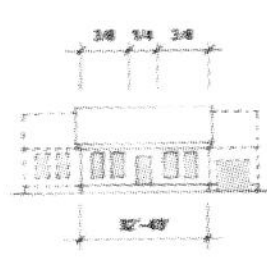

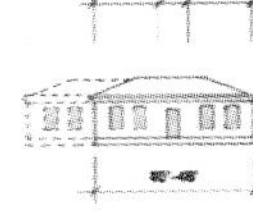

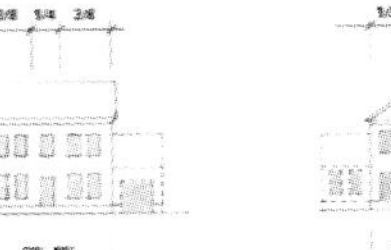

Massing

A BROAD FRONT

Hipped-roof or side-gable rectangular volume with roof pitches ranging from 5 to 7 in 12. One-story shed or hip roofed porches are often placed symmetrically on the front facade. One-story side wings often occur. Although porches are most often one-third or one-fifth the length of the main body, they may also be three-fifths or the entire length of the front facade.

B NARROW FRONT

Hipped-roof or front-gable box with roof pitches ranging from 5 to 7 in 12. Five- and three-bay compositions are common. Full front porches and one-story side-wings are common to this massing type.

Facade Composition

The Norfolk Classical Revival facade composition is characterized by a symmetrical and balanced placement of doors and windows. Entrance doors are always located in the center of the composition. Typical windows occur singly and align vertically from floor to floor.

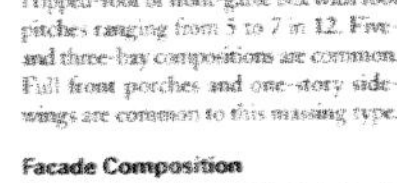

Combinations

Complex forms and larger living spaces may be created by combining side and/or rear wings with the main body. Gabled or hipped dormers may be added to introduce light into half-story and attic spaces. The architectural character of the attached parts should match that of the main body.

Wall Section & Eave Details

The first floor of the main body is typically set 2 to 3 feet above the finished grade. The floor-to-ceiling height on the first floor is typically 10 feet. For two-story houses, the second-story floor-to-ceiling height is 9 feet minimum.

The Norfolk Classical Revival style is characterized by the vertical proportion of the window and door elements and well-detailed Classical eaves and cornices. The frieze below the soffit is typically small with profiled moldings and dentils.

TYPICAL EAVE DETAILS

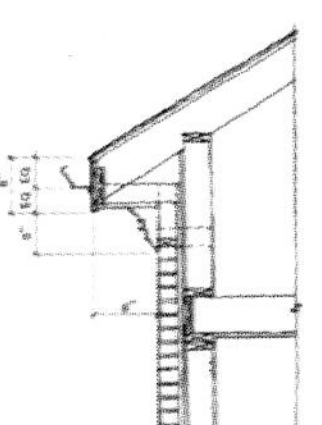

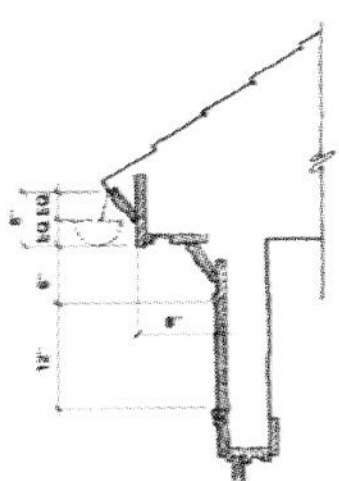

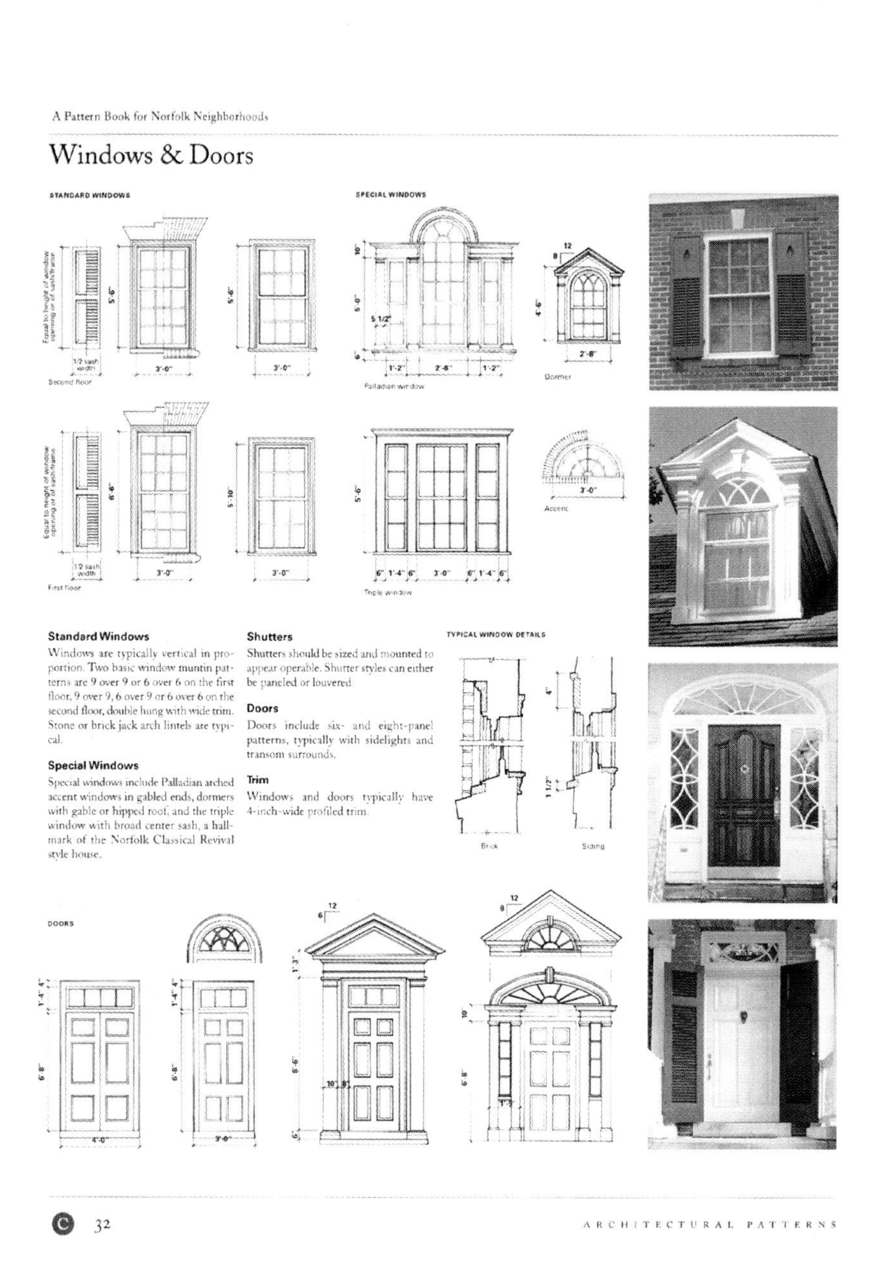

Windows & Doors

Standard Windows

Windows are typically vertical in proportion. Two basic window muntin patterns are 9 over 9 or 6 over 6 on the first floor, 9 over 9, 6 over 9 or 6 over 6 on the second floor, double hung with wide trim. Stone or brick jack arch lintels are typical.

Special Windows

Special windows include Palladian arched accent windows in gabled ends, dormers with gable or hipped roof, and the triple window with broad center sash, a hallmark of the Norfolk Classical Revival style house.

Shutters

Shutters should be sized and mounted to appear operable. Shutter styles can either be paneled or louvered.

Doors

Doors include six- and eight-panel patterns, typically with sidelights and transom surrounds.

Trim

Windows and doors typically have 4-inch-wide profiled trim.

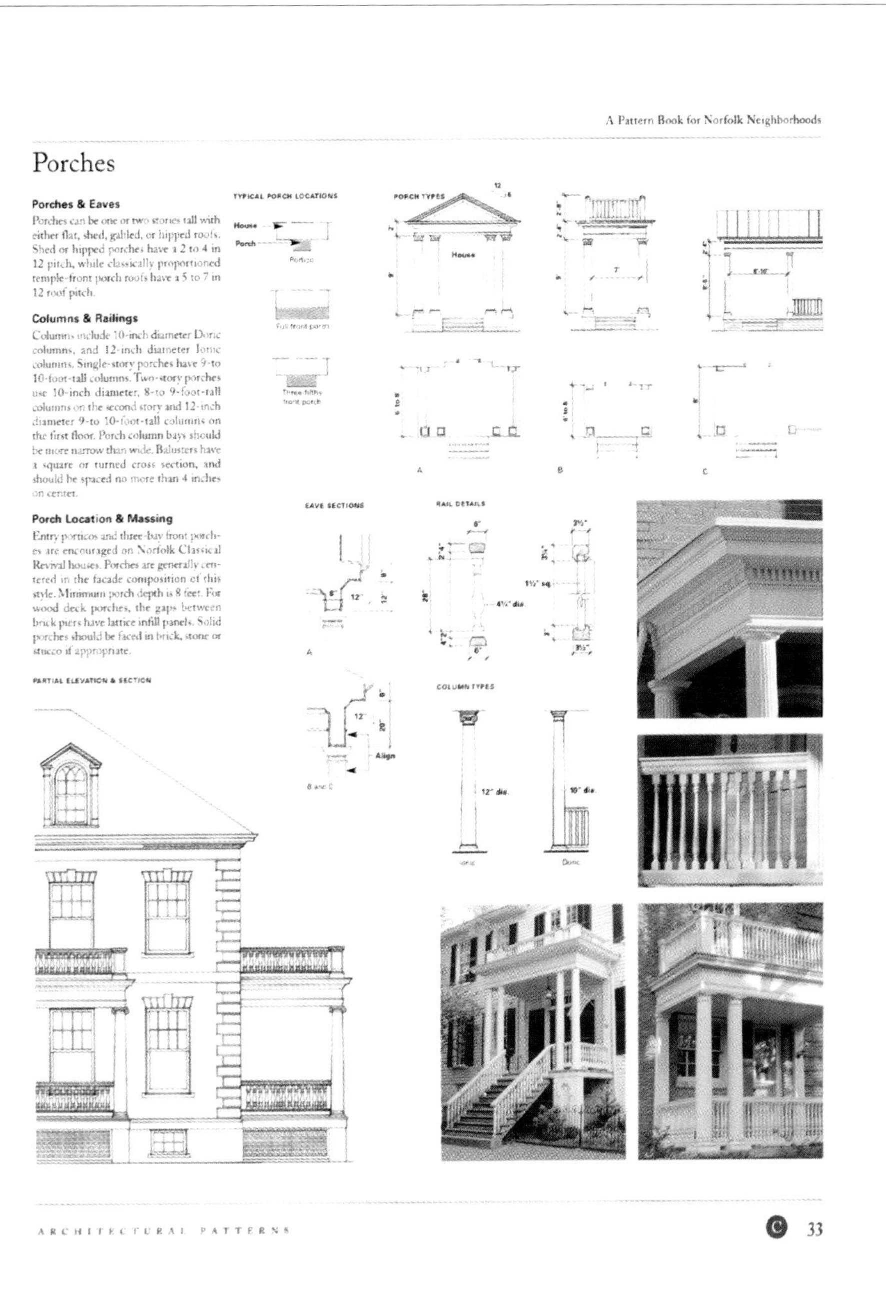

Porches

Porches & Eaves

Porches can be one or two stories tall with either flat, shed, gabled, or hipped roofs. Shed or hipped porches have a 2 to 4 in 12 pitch, while classically proportioned temple-front porch roofs have a 5 to 7 in 12 roof pitch.

Columns & Railings

Columns include 10-inch diameter Doric columns, and 12-inch diameter Ionic columns. Single-story porches have 9-to 10-foot-tall columns. Two-story porches use 10-inch diameter, 8-to 9-foot-tall columns on the second story and 12-inch diameter 9-to 10-foot-tall columns on the first floor. Porch column bays should be more narrow than wide. Balusters have a square or turned cross section, and should be spaced no more than 4 inches on center.

Porch Location & Massing

Entry porticos and three-bay front porches are encouraged on Norfolk Classical Revival houses. Porches are generally centered in the facade composition of this style. Minimum porch depth is 8 feet. For wood deck porches, the gaps between brick piers have lattice infill panels. Solid porches should be faced in brick, stone or stucco if appropriate.

Materials & Applications

Roofing

- Slate (including manufactured slate products), laminated asphalt or composition shingles with a slate pattern, flat clay tile, or painted metal standing seam or 5-V crimp panels

Soffits

- Smooth finish composition board, tongue-and-groove wood boards, or fiber-cement panels

Gutters & Downspouts

- Half-round or ogee profile gutters with round or rectangular downspouts in copper, painted or prefinished metal

Cladding

- Sand-molded or smooth-finish brick in Common, English or Flemish bond patterns
- Smooth-finish wood or fiber-cement lap siding, 6 to 8 inches wide
- Light sand-finish stucco

Foundations & Chimneys

- Brick, stucco or stone veneer

Columns

- Architecturally correct Classical proportions and details in wood, fiberglass, cast stone, or composite material

Railings

- Milled wood top and bottom rails with square or turned balusters; square balusters in Chippendale patterns
- Wrought iron or solid bar stock decorative metal

Porch Ceilings

- Plaster, tongue-and-groove wood or composite boards, or beaded-profile plywood

Windows

- Painted wood or solid cellular PVC, or clad wood or vinyl with brick veneer only; true divided light or simulated divided light (SDL) sash with traditional exterior muntin profile (⅞ inch wide)

Trim

- Wood, composite, cellular PVC or polyurethane millwork; stucco, stone or cast stone

Doors

- Wood, fiberglass or steel with traditional stile-and-rail proportions and raised panel profiles, painted or stained

Shutters

- Wood or composite, sized to match window sash and mounted with hardware to appear operable

Front Yard Fences

- Wood picket or wood, wrought iron or solid bar stock metal picket with brick or stucco finish masonry piers

Lighting

- Porch pendant or wall-mounted carriage lantern

Gallery of Examples

EUROPEAN ROMANTIC STYLE

Comparative Analysis

European Romantic houses became very popular in the United States in the latter part of the nineteenth century and through the 1940s. This is another eclectic category and has a broad range of regional interpretations. Many houses of this type were built for the middle class from catalogs; many of the more exotic houses were designed by architects for wealthy clients. European Romantic was perceived to be an appropriate estate image during the period. In the United States, the French influence was predominantly found in larger estate houses and in some urban neighborhoods as an exotic builder house. The English vernacular cottage and Tudor house types influenced this trend in American house design more than any other European movement. Variants, such as Italian Renaissance, occurred during the same time period but were more formal and had more in common with neoclassical styles than the English-inspired European Romantic. There was a remarkable influence in the merchant builder market for a brief period of time in the late 1920s and 1930s. Many neighborhoods featured small brick cottages with front-facing gables, asymmetrical entrance forms, half-timbering, and stucco accent detailing. The style was rendered in frame and wood, shingle, or composition siding. Typically, porches were minor elements, and heavy timber posts with simple brackets were used to complement the house mass and to express a covered entry or small sitting porch as an extension of a primary roof form. Steeply pitched front gables and massive, ornate chimneys were hallmarks of many examples from this period.

Sample pages of the European Romantic style have been excerpted from the Eagle Park (Belmont, North Carolina), Norfolk, Virginia, and Ducker Mountain (near Asheville, North Carolina) pattern books.

Precedent photos

An English house in Charlotte

A small Romantic house in Belmont

Half-timbering on an English

Essential Elements of Belmont European Romantic

1 Steep roof pitches with dormers.

2 Balanced window and door locations.

3 Vertical windows in groupings.

4 Large, simple roof planes.

5 Porches typically notched out, or extended roof

6 Roof lines extending below window at second floor, and to top of windo at first floor.

7 Simple detailing.

8 Shallow overhangs.

9 Massive chimneys.

Eagle Park European Romantic

ARCHITECTURAL PATTERNS

EAGLE PARK

Belmont, North Carolina

The European Romantic style for the Eagle Park neighborhood in Belmont, North Carolina, draws on the builder version of the English cottage that became popular during the 1920s across the United States. These designs appeared in both plan books and in catalog house offerings from companies such as Sears and Alladin. Many of these houses were built, forming the entire fabric of neighborhood streets — most often as brick, single-story cottages with a steeply sloping front-facing gable and a massive, often highly articulated, chimney added to a simple side-gable house form. While this reference to the Cotswold cottage with some abstracted Tudor detailing was popular for eight to ten years, this modest house type never achieved the desired image of distinction, success, and country character. The Eagle Park Pattern Book for this style focuses on the frame and shingle or siding versions found quite often throughout the south. Belmont has some good examples of this style and era. The pattern book section on European Romantic adapts and sets forth a series of massing types where the inclusion of a front porch becomes the essential element for the house. This adaptation of a traditional house type, which more often than not excluded the front sitting porch as part of the standard house, attempts to place this style into a palette where porches are the norm.

European Romantic house

History and Character

THE EAGLE PARK EUROPEAN ROMANTIC STYLE is based on the early-twentieth-century interpretations of English architecture by American architects and builders. The source for the design comes from Medieval English cottages, manor houses, and rural village vernacular houses. The American version is normally a house with simple volumes, and often front facing gables. Gables have steeply pitched roofs between 8 in 12 and 20 in 12. Half-timbering, shingles, and horizontal siding are often used as infill in gables. The decorative half-timbering may occur at the entire second story. Gable, hip, and shed dormers are dominant features of the style.

Windows include single and paired double-hung types mixed with vertically proportioned casement windows arranged in groups of two to five. There are relatively few windows in the facade; the general impression is a solid mass with small openings.

Chimneys are often the dominant element in the massing of the house. These massive chimneys may be finished in brick or plaster. They feature simple detailing and chimney pots.

13

Massing Diagrams

A Two-story side gable

B Two-story gable L: one-story gable

C Two-story gable L: two-story gable

D One-and-one-half-story side gable

E One- or one-and-one-half-story front gable

F Two-story Front Gable

Multi-Family Houses

Massing and Composition

Massing

A Two-Story Side Gable
Two-story rectangular box with gable roof. Dormer accents can be gable or shed roofed.

B Two-Story Gable L – One-Story Gable
Two-story main body, gable roof with the ridge running parallel to the street. A one-and-one-third-height wing projects forward from the main body. The forward-projecting wing can be made to appear broader and lower to the ground, by extending curved, roofed wing walls beyond the mass.

C Two-Story Gable L – Two-Story Gable
Main body similar to the two-story **L**, but with a two-story, forward-projecting wing.

D One-and-One-Half-Story Side Gable
Integral front porch that runs the full length of the front facade. Large shed dormers.

E One-and-One-Half-Story Front Gable
One-and-one-half-story main body, gable roof with ridge perpendicular to the street. Side-projecting porch or wing.

F Two-Story Front Gable
Two-story main body, gable roof with ridge perpendicular to the street. Internal front porches are common.

Combinations

The character of these houses is enhanced by the addition of wings and telescoping extensions which, through massing or detailing, appear to have been added over time. The architectural character of the attached parts should be in keeping with the character of the main body. Most wings and bodies are one-room deep; wings are from 12 to 18 feet in width; and main bodies are from 16 to 24 feet in width.

There is a wide variety of roof forms: gable, hip, 'clipped' gable, and shed. In selective locations, the roof forms may be intermixed.

In gable-ended massing types, roof planes are primarily interrupted by gables (same pitch as roof) and accented with small dormers. Gable ends generally have no eave/overhang, except at half-timbered areas. Half-timbering or a change in materials is generally applied at the second floor of two-story structures, or at single-story wings on a two-story structure. Where half-timbering is used on second stories, the plane often overhangs the first floor 8 to 15 inches, supported by timber corbels below.

Eagle Park European Romantic

ARCHITECTURAL PATTERNS

C 14

Partial Elevation and Section

Roof

Eaves

Wall

Eaves

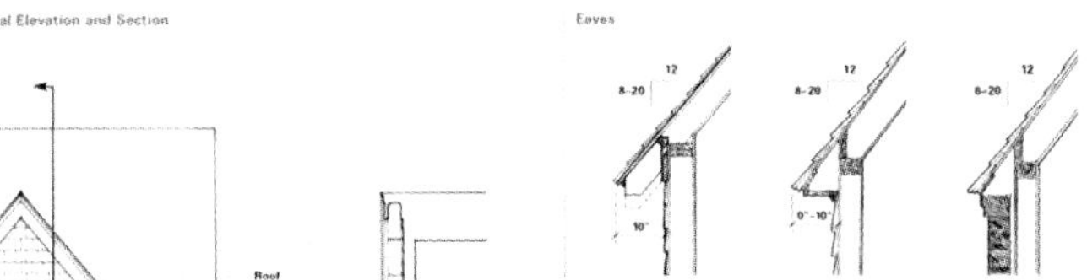

Exposed Rafter

Boxed Eave

Boxed Eave with Brick

Cladding Options

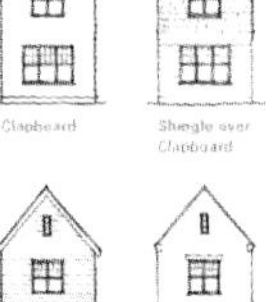

Timber

Clapboard

Shingle over Clapboard

Clapboard over Timber over Brick

Clapboard over Brick

Stone, Brick or Stucco

Wall Section and Eave Details

Roof

The roof pitch on European romantic houses varies from 8 to 20 in 12. For Gable **L** forms, the pitch on the street facing gables can range from 14 to 20 in 12. Gable and shed dormers help to introduce light into half-story and attic spaces. False eaves, set at a steep pitch, are often used to create the illusion of a steeply pitched roof on the main body.

Eaves

Overhang/eaves shall be generally shallow (up to 10 inches) although they are sometimes as deep as 18 inches where half timbering is used. Eave construction is typically of three types:

A Boxed eave, 4 to 10 inches deep.

B Exposed 2 x 8-inch rafter tails set 16 to 24 inches on center, and trimmed parallel to the ground.

C Boxed eave, 4 to 10 inches deep with stepped, brick soffit.

Walls

The first floor of the main body generally is slab on grade – elevated just enough to keep rainwater out, about 1 foot to 1½ feet above ground. The floor-to-ceiling height on the ground floor is typically 9 feet. The secondary floor-to-ceiling height is 8 to 9 feet. Walls are typically frame with horizontal siding or shingles or a combination of these materials. Brick and stucco are also used as cladding. Material changes typically occur at the second floor and in gable ends above the window head.

Shallow boxed eave

Exposed rafters

Eagle Park European Romantic

ARCHITECTURAL PATTERNS

C 15

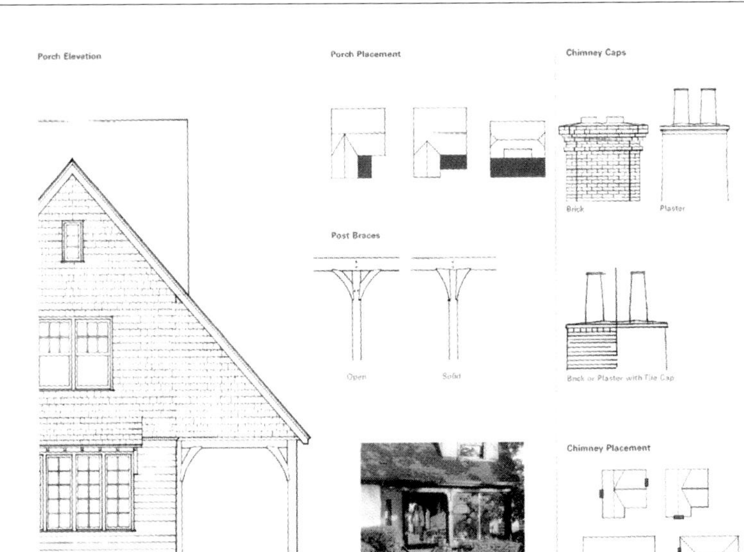

Porches and Chimneys

Porch Roofs and Eaves

Porches can have gable ends or shed roof forms, extending up into the main house roof form. European Romantic porches have shallow eaves that repeat the same rafter or eave treatment as the main house body.

Columns and Railings

Several porch column options provide variety to the style. Porches may be supported on square cross-section heavy timber columns, stone columns, or stone or brick piers.

Porch Location

Although this style rarely employs front porches, covered entries and loggias are common. These covered loggias have a typical width of 5 to 7 feet. Porches are frequently placed at the sides and rear of European Romantic houses and often have room-like size. Porches range from 8 to 12 feet in depth.

Chimneys

Chimneys are a key element in the composition of the elevation. They should appear large and have an asymmetrical massing. A wide variety of chimney cap profiles is encouraged.

Eagle Park European Romantic

ARCHITECTURAL PATTERNS

C 17

A 44' wide two-story side gable duplex

C 44' wide two-story gable L duplex

E 28' wide one-and-a-half-story front gable, flat-over-flat duplex

Materials and Possibilities

Materials

Siding: Wood or fiber cement board siding and shakes, brick or stucco with handmade/formed appearance (no skip-trowel or similar). Half-timbering appearance for second-story accents.

Roofing: Flat clay tile, cedar shakes, slate profile fiberglass shingles, or slate (including manufactured slate products).

Windows: Energy-efficient wood, PVC, aluminum-clad, or aluminum; with true divided-light appearance (⅞-inch exterior muntins). Dark frames for stucco and white for brick and siding houses.

Columns: Rough cut, square wood posts.

Trim: Ornamental cast stone, or rough cut wood.

Eaves: Wood or fiberboard sheathing with 2x, 3x, or 4x rafter tails. Plaster molded eaves are also permitted on brick or stucco houses. Smooth soffits to be built with fiberboard or plywood.

Exterior Ceilings: Plank and beam or beaded board.

Gutters: Half-round metal or PVC.

Downspouts: Round metal or PVC.

Shutters: Plank/board or panel type. Wrought iron hinges, shutter dogs, and latches are encouraged.

Chimneys: Masonry or stucco with handmade/formed appearance.

Front Yard Fences: Prefinished metal or masonry/stucco.

Rear Yard Fences: Painted wood, prefinished metal, or masonry/stucco.

Eagle Park European Romantic

ARCHITECTURAL PATTERNS

C 18

Possibilities

A *40' wide two-story side gable*

B *24' wide two-story gable L*

C *32' wide two-story gable L*

D *35' wide one-and-a-half-story side gable*

E *34' wide one-and-a-half-story front gable*

F *28' wide two-story front gable*

Multi Family Possibilities

A *44' wide two-story side gable duplex*

C *44' wide two-story gable L, duplex*

E *28' wide one-and-a-half-story front gabl[e] flat-over-flat duplex*

Eagle Park European Romantic

ARCHITECTURAL PATTERNS

Materials and Possibilities

Materials

Siding: Wood or fiber cement board siding and shakes, brick or stucco with handmade/formed appearance (no skip-trowel or similar). Half-timbering appearance for second-story accents.

Roofing: Flat clay tile, cedar shakes, slate profile fiberglass shingles, or slate (including manufactured slate products).

Windows: Energy-efficient wood, PVC, aluminum-clad, or aluminum; with true divided-light appearance (¾-inch exterior muntins). Dark frames for stucco and white for brick and siding houses.

Columns: Rough cut, square wood posts.

Trim: Ornamental cast stone, or rough cut wood.

Eaves: Wood or fiberboard sheathing with 2x, 3x, or 4x rafter tails. Plaster molded eaves are also permitted on brick or stucco houses. Smooth soffits to be built with fiberboard or plywood.

Exterior Ceilings: Plank and beam or beaded board.

Gutters: Half-round metal or PVC.

Downspouts: Round metal or PVC.

Shutters: Plank/board or panel type. Wrought iron hinges, shutter dogs, and latches are encouraged.

Chimneys: Masonry or stucco with handmade/formed appearance.

Front Yard Fences: Prefinished metal or masonry/stucco.

Rear Yard Fences: Painted wood, prefinished metal, or masonry/stucco.

18

EAGLE PARK

Belmont, North Carolina

The Eagle Park possibilities page illustrates examples of designs for the massing types and compositional options shown in the pattern book. The possibilities show the window, door, porch, and eave elements detailed within the section. Unlike the majority of European Romantic builder houses from the late 1920s, these new houses feature front and side porches — an element that was often lost in the previous revival of European Romantic designs. Additionally, these houses are rendered primarily in siding or a combination of siding and brick. This reflects the regional adaptation of this style that was primarliy constructed of brick in most places. This page illustrates both detached and attached house types.

Essential Elements of the Norfolk European Romantic Style

1 Large, steeply-pitched roof planes with dormers and shallow overhangs.

2 Roof lines extend below windows at second floor, and top of window at first floor.

3 Broad expanses of wall with a limited number of deep-set openings.

4 Asymmetrical window and door locations.

5 Vertically proportioned windows in groups.

NORFOLK EUROPEAN ROMANTIC

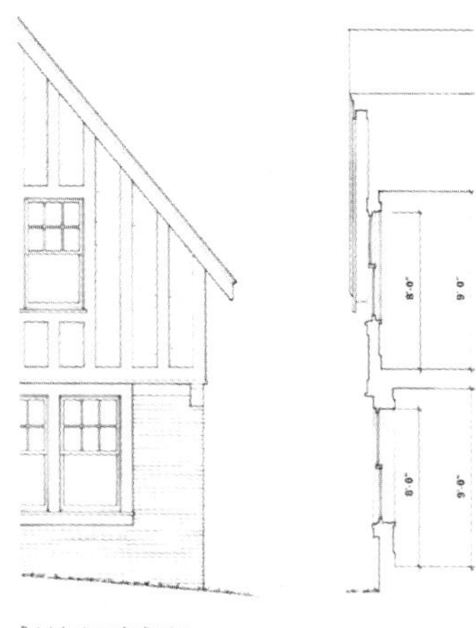

Partial elevation and wall section

The European Romantic style is based on the early twentieth century interpretations of English architecture by American architects and builders. The source for design comes from medieval English cottages, manor houses, and rural village vernacular houses. The American interpretations include houses with simple volumes often with front-facing gables that have steeply pitched roofs between 12 in 12 and 16 in 12. Gable, hip, and shed dormers are a dominant feature of the style. There is often a mix of exterior materials including stone, plaster, or brick. Half-timbering and horizontal siding are often used as infill in gables.

Chimneys act as principal forms for the massing of the house. These are usually very massive, with simple detailing and chimney pots. Decorative half-timbering in the gables is common and can occur on the entire second story or in the upper gables. Windows are typically casements, vertical in proportion and arranged in groups.

Massing & Composition

MASSING DIAGRAMS

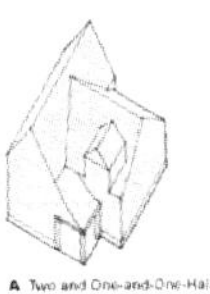
A Two and One-and-One-Half-Story L-Shape

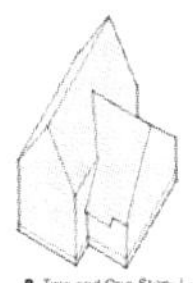
B Two and One-Story L-Shape

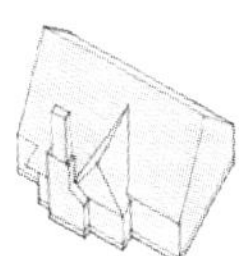
C Broad Front

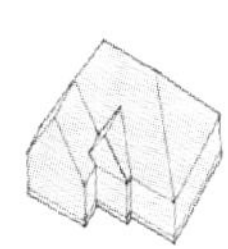
D One-Story Gable L

FACADE COMPOSITION DIAGRAMS

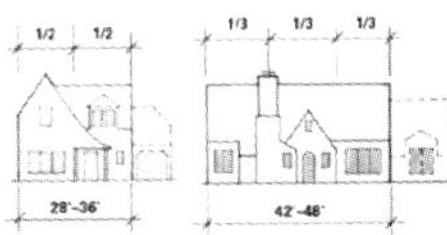

MASSING COMBINATIONS

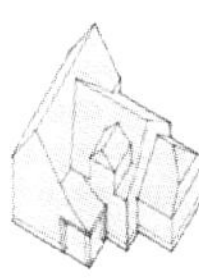

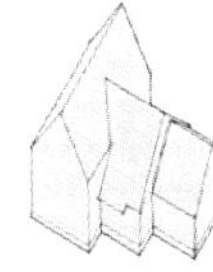

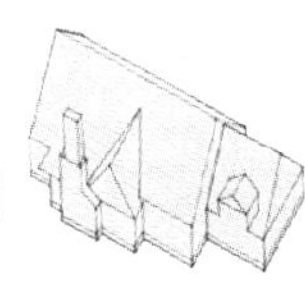

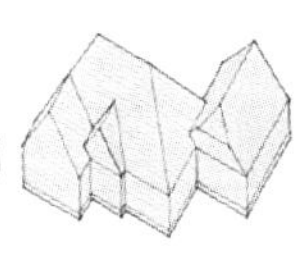

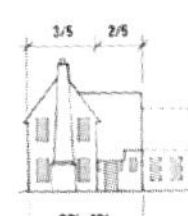

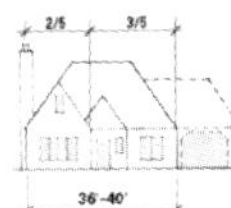

Massing

A TWO- & ONE-AND-ONE-HALF-STORY L-SHAPE

L-shaped plan with a two-story front-facing gable paired with a one-and-one-half story roof expression parallel to the street. The roof of the front-facing gable slides down to provide a covered entry. Dormers can have gable or shed roofs.

B TWO- & ONE-STORY L-SHAPE

L-shaped plan with a two-story front facing gable paired with a one-story roof expression parallel to the street. The one-story roof may curve out to provide a covered shelter over the door.

C BROAD FRONT

Rectangular shaped plan with a one, one-and-one-half, or two-story expression. A small gable or two may project to provide visual relief and to provide balance to large chimneys and other architectural elements.

D ONE-STORY GABLE L

Rectangular volume with hipped roof with a front facing gabled wing. Mass may have a one- or one-and-one-half-story expression. A series of nested gables may provide balance to chimneys and other architectural elements.

Facade Composition

European Romantic facade composition is characterized by an asymmetrical and balanced placement of doors and windows. Grouped double-hung windows are common. Front doors are generally located at the center of the composition, especially in wide houses. There is typically a material change from the first to the second floor.

Roof

The roof pitch on European Romantic houses varies from 12 to 20 in 12. For Gable L forms, the pitch on the street-facing gables ranges from 14 to 20 in 12. Gable and shed dormers help to introduce light into half-story and attic spaces. False eaves, set at a steep pitch, are often used to create the illusion of a steeply pitched roof on the main body.

Eaves

Overhangs tend to be generally shallow (up to 10 inches) although they are sometimes as deep as 18 inches where half timbering is used. Eave construction is typically of three types:

A Boxed eave, 4 to 10 inches deep.

B Exposed 2 x 8-inch rafter tails set 16 to 24 inches on center, and trimmed parallel to the ground.

C Bricked eave, 4 to 10 inches deep with stepped, brick soffit.

Wall Section & Eave Details

The first floor is typically set 12 to 18 inches above finished grade. The floor-to-ceiling height on the ground floor is typically 9 feet. The secondary floor-to-ceiling height is 8 to 9 feet. Walls are typically framed with horizontal siding or shingles or a combination of these materials. Brick and stucco are also used as cladding. Material changes typically occur at the second floor and in gable ends above the window head. Clapboard or shake cladding materials should never come within 8 inches of finished grade; only durable materials like brick, stone, and stucco may come into direct contact with the soil.

TYPICAL EAVE DETAILS

Boxed eave

Exposed rafter

Bricked eave

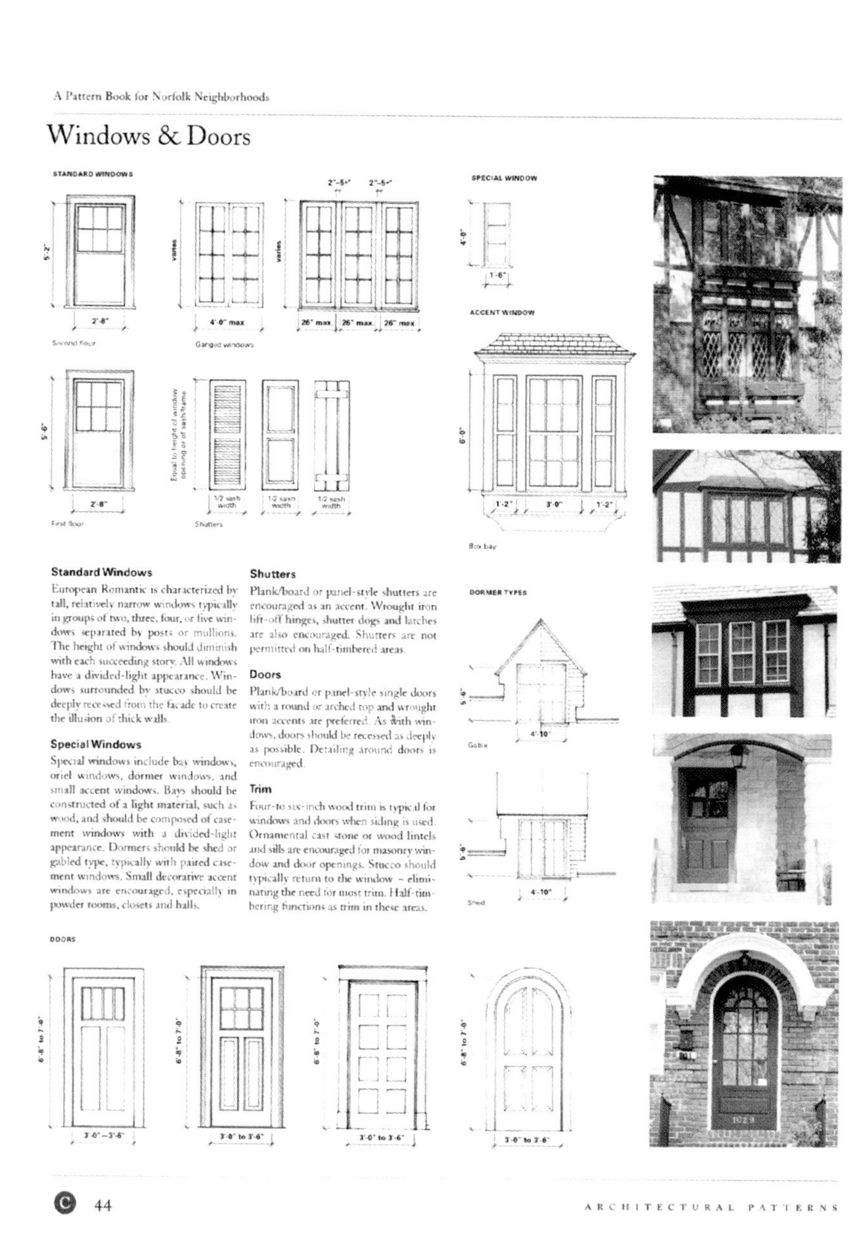

Windows & Doors

Standard Windows

European Romantic is characterized by tall, relatively narrow windows typically in groups of two, three, four, or five windows separated by posts or mullions. The height of windows should diminish with each succeeding story. All windows have a divided-light appearance. Windows surrounded by stucco should be deeply recessed from the facade to create the illusion of thick walls.

Special Windows

Special windows include bay windows, oriel windows, dormer windows, and small accent windows. Bays should be constructed of a light material, such as wood, and should be composed of casement windows with a divided-light appearance. Dormers should be shed or gabled type, typically with paired casement windows. Small decorative accent windows are encouraged, especially in powder rooms, closets and halls.

Shutters

Plank/board or panel-style shutters are encouraged as an accent. Wrought iron lift-off hinges, shutter dogs and latches are also encouraged. Shutters are not permitted on half-timbered areas.

Doors

Plank/board or panel-style single doors with a round or arched top and wrought iron accents are preferred. As with windows, doors should be recessed as deeply as possible. Detailing around doors is encouraged.

Trim

Four-to six-inch wood trim is typical for windows and doors when siding is used. Ornamental cast stone or wood lintels and sills are encouraged for masonry window and door openings. Stucco should typically return to the window – eliminating the need for most trim. Half-timbering functions as trim in these areas.

Porches & Chimneys

Porches

Although porches are less common on European Romantic houses than other styles, porches and carriage porches were common on larger houses. They should feature post-and-beam construction, shed roofs and rough-sawn clapboard siding. Arched braces between posts and beams are encouraged. The covered patios and loggias may be constructed of either post-and-beam or masonry.

Porch Roofs & Eaves

Porches can have gable ends or shed roof forms, extending up into the main house roof form. European Romantic porches have shallow eaves that repeat the same rafter or eave treatment as the main house body.

Columns & Railings

Several porch column options provide variety to the style. Porches may be supported on square cross-section heavy timber columns, stone columns, or stone or brick piers.

Porch Location & Massing

Although this style rarely employs front porches, covered entries and loggias are common. These covered loggias have a typical width of 5 to 7 feet. Porches are frequently placed at the sides and rear of European Romantic houses and often have room-like size. Porches range from 8 to 12 feet in depth.

Chimneys

Chimneys are a key element in the composition of the elevation. They should appear large and have an asymmetrical massing. A wide variety of chimney cap profiles is encouraged.

CHIMNEY CAPS

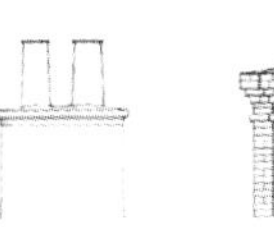

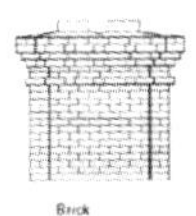

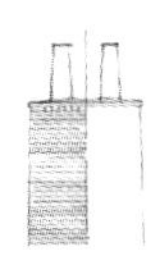

PORCH ELEVATION

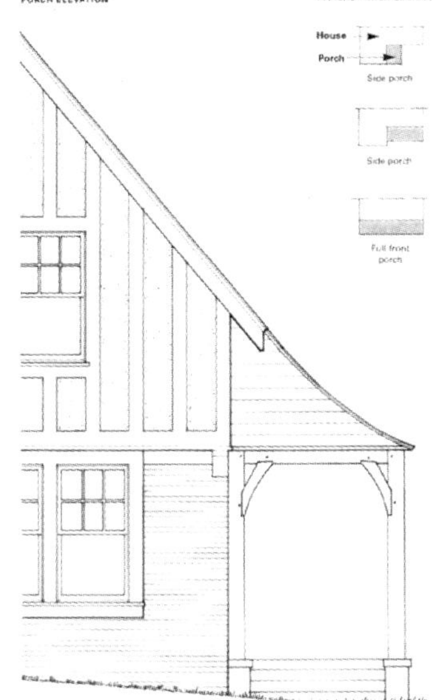

TYPICAL PORCH LOCATIONS

House

Porch

Side porch

Side porch

Full front porch

CHIMNEY PLACEMENT

POST BRACES

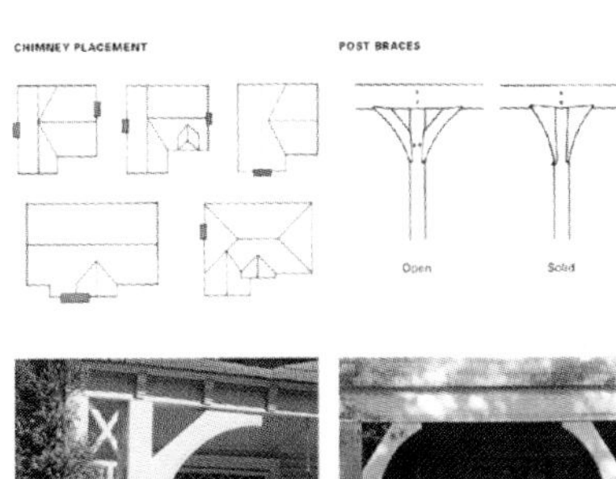

A Pattern Book for Norfolk Neighborhoods

Materials & Applications

Roofing

- Slate (including manufactured slate products), laminated asphalt or composition shingles with a slate pattern, or clay tile with flat or barrel profile

Soffits

- Smooth-finish composition board, tongue-and-groove wood boards, or fiber-cement panels

Gutters & Downspouts

- Half-round or ogee profile gutters with round or rectangular downspouts in copper, painted or prefinished metal

Cladding

- Smooth-finish brick in Common bond pattern
- Stucco with handmade/formed appearance (no skip-trowel or similar); half-timbering for second story accents
- Random-width cut wood or fiber-cement shingles with mitered corners
- Smooth-finish wood or fiber-cement lap siding, 6 to 8 inches exposure, with mitered corners

Foundations, Chimneys & Piers

- Brick or stucco with handmade/formed appearance

Windows

- Painted wood or solid cellular PVC, or clad wood or vinyl with brick veneer only; true divided light or simulated divided light (SDL) sash with traditional exterior muntin profile (⅞ inch wide)

Trim

- Wood, composite, cellular PVC or polyurethane millwork; stucco, stone or cast stone

Doors

- Wood, fiberglass or steel with traditional stile-and-rail proportions and panel profiles, painted or stained

Shutters

- Wood or composite, sized to match window sash and mounted with hardware to appear operable

Columns

- Wood posts and brackets

Railings

- Wood top and bottom rails with square balusters
- Wrought iron or solid bar stock square metal picket
- Brick or masonry with stucco finish

Porch Ceilings

- Plank-and-beam or flat plaster, tongue-and-groove wood or composite boards, or beaded-profile plywood

Front Yard Fences

- Wood picket, masonry with stucco, brick or stone finish, or combination

Lighting

- Porch pendant or wall-mounted lantern

Gallery of Examples

Essential Elements of the Biltmore English Romantic

1. Steep roof pitches with dormers.
2. Apparently random window and door locations.
3. Vertical windows in groupings.
4. Thick walls with deep-set doors and windows.
5. Asymmetrical massing with large, simple roof planes.
6. Broad expanses of wall with few door and window peneuations.
7. Roof lines extending below windows at second floor and to top of window at first floor.
8. Simple detailing.

History and Character

THE BILTMORE ENGLISH ROMANTIC STYLE is based on the early-twentieth-century interpretations of English architecture by American architects and builders. The source for design comes from Medieval English cottages, manor houses, and rural village vernacular houses. The American interpretations are houses with simple volumes, often with front-facing gables that have steeply pitched roofs between 12 in 12 and 16 in 12. Dormers – gable, hip, and shed – are a dominant feature of the style. There is often a mix of exterior materials, including stone, plaster, and brick. Pebble-dash plaster is characteristic of the Asheville area, and was used on many of the Biltmore Estate's buildings. Half-timbering, pebble-dash, and horizontal siding are often used as infill in gables.

Chimneys typically act as principal forms for the massing of the house. These are usually very massive, often with plaster finish, simple detailing, and chimney pots. Decorative half-timbering in the gables is common and can occur on the entire second story or in the upper gables. Often there is a mix of timber patterns on the same house. Windows are typically casements, vertical in proportion and arranged in groups of two to five.

There are relatively few windows in the facade; the dominant form is one of a solid mass with small openings.

Biltmore English Romantic

ARCHITECTURAL PATTERNS

C 26

Partial Elevation and Section

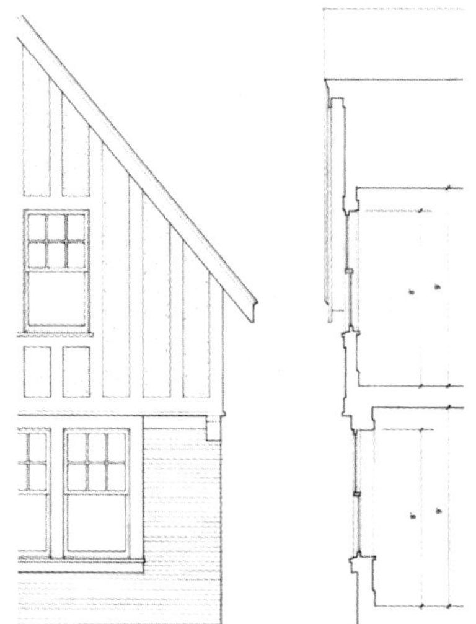

Eaves

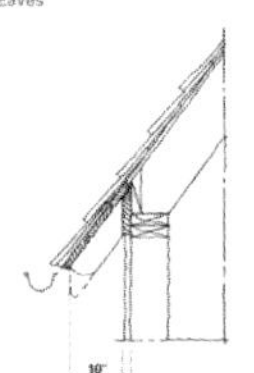

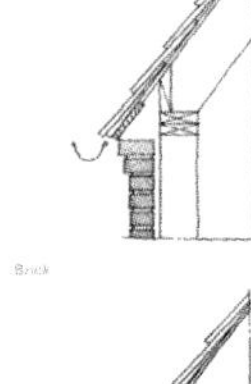

Boxed Plaster

Wall Section and Eave Details

Vertical Section

The first floor of the main body is generally on grade – elevated just enough to keep rainwater out. The floor-to-ceiling height on the principal floor is typically 9 feet. The secondary floor-to-ceiling height is 8 to 9 feet.

Eave Details

Overhang/eaves are generally shallow (0 to 10 inches) although they are sometimes as deep as 18 inches where half-timbering is used. Eaves may be constructed of either building wall material (plaster, brick) or wood.

Biltmore English Romantic

ARCHITECTURAL PATTERNS

C 28

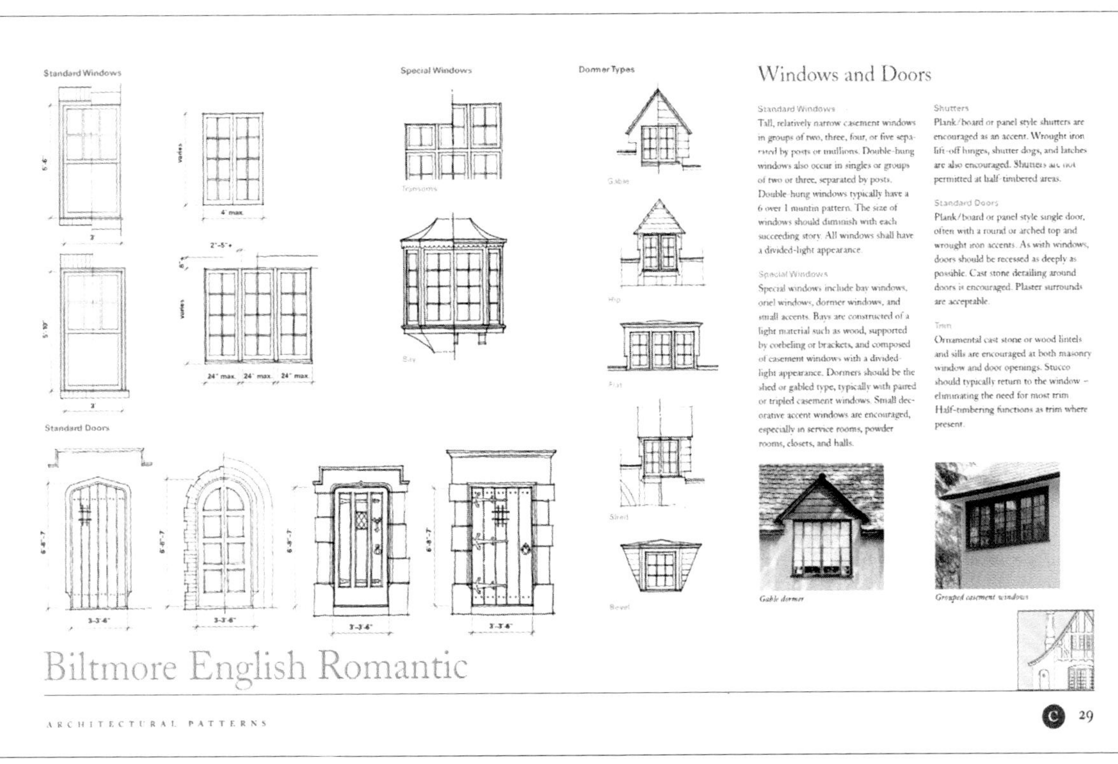

Standard Windows

Special Windows

Dormer Types

Standard Doors

Windows and Doors

Standard Windows

Tall, relatively narrow casement windows in groups of two, three, four, or five separated by posts or mullions. Double-hung windows also occur in singles or groups of two or three, separated by posts. Double-hung windows typically have a 6 over 1 muntin pattern. The size of windows should diminish with each succeeding story. All windows shall have a divided-light appearance.

Special Windows

Special windows include bay windows, oriel windows, dormer windows, and small accents. Bays are constructed of a light material such as wood, supported by corbeling or brackets, and composed of casement windows with a divided-light appearance. Dormers should be the shed or gabled type, typically with paired or tripled casement windows. Small decorative accent windows are encouraged, especially in service rooms, powder rooms, closets, and halls.

Shutters

Plank/board or panel style shutters are encouraged as an accent. Wrought iron lift-off hinges, shutter dogs, and latches are also encouraged. Shutters are not permitted at half-timbered areas.

Standard Doors

Plank/board or panel style single door, often with a round or arched top and wrought iron accents. As with windows, doors should be recessed as deeply as possible. Cast stone detailing around doors is encouraged. Plaster surrounds are acceptable.

Trim

Ornamental cast stone or wood lintels and sills are encouraged at both masonry window and door openings. Stucco should typically return to the window – eliminating the need for most trim. Half-timbering functions as trim where present.

Gable dormer

Grouped casement windows

Biltmore English Romantic

ARCHITECTURAL PATTERNS 29

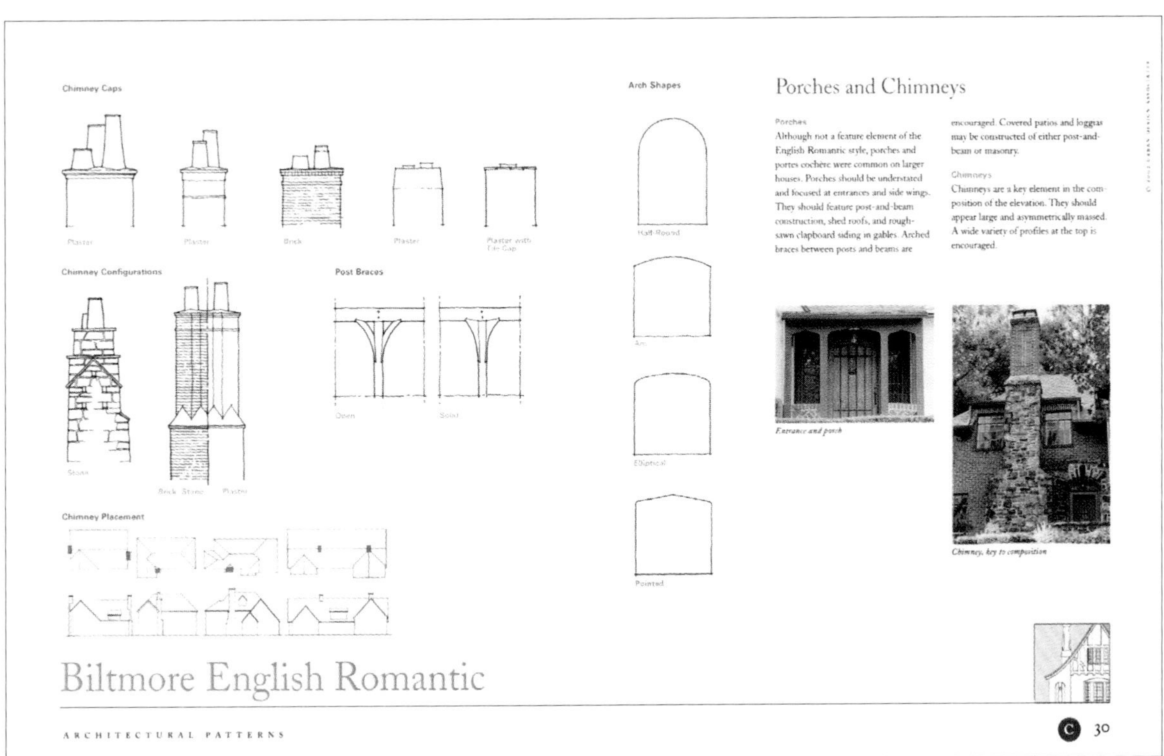

Chimney Caps

Chimney Configurations

Post Braces

Chimney Placement

Arch Shapes

Porches and Chimneys

Porches

Although not a feature element of the English Romantic style, porches and portes cochère were common on larger houses. Porches should be understated and focused at entrances and side wings. They should feature post-and-beam construction, shed roofs, and rough-sawn clapboard siding in gables. Arched braces between posts and beams are encouraged. Covered patios and loggias may be constructed of either post-and-beam or masonry.

Chimneys

Chimneys are a key element in the composition of the elevation. They should appear large and asymmetrically massed. A wide variety of profiles at the top is encouraged.

Entrance and porch

Chimney, key to composition

Biltmore English Romantic

ARCHITECTURAL PATTERNS 30

Most of the pattern books described in this book were produced for specific development projects. The majority of them provide patterns for small-scale residential buildings and use traditional local architectural vocabularies. This has been the first step in the revival of pattern books. However, new uses and forms for pattern books are already emerging.

Public Policy: One key example is the introduction of pattern books into the public policy arena. Recent UDA Pattern Books have been public policy tools designed to preserve and enhance the inherent local regional character as, increasingly, pressures from new development and redevelopment have tended towards compromising the integrity of that character. By defining and documenting each of the many components of urban space in a specific location, these pattern books set principles that can guide public policy. They provide specific patterns, both architectural and urban, to be used in new development. In some cases, they are used to evaluate candidates for financing and funding programs, while in others they are used to facilitate the approval process. Two examples of UDA pattern books are being used to support public policy. The first is a pattern book created for the City of Norfolk, Virginia—*A Pattern Book for Norfolk Neighborhoods*—that provides guidelines for new residential construction as well as renovations and additions to existing homes in Norfolk's many distinct residential neighborhoods. The second is a regional Pattern Book for West Yorkshire in England. These two pattern books point the way to the broader use that can be made of these documents as they re-establish themselves as highly useful tools in the overall development process.

Sustainable Design: Additionally, pattern books are ideally suited to illustrating the context for successful integration of sustainable design criteria, techniques, and methods. From concept to construction, the process of integrating multi-disciplinary teams provides a broader context for designing the elements of a sustainable plan. These considerations are fundamental to the image and character of a place and can be key elements in shaping and defining the character of a new neighborhood, town, or urban infill site. The challenge is to incorporate best practice techniques that preserve environmental integrity and create a context for renewing and maintaining environments in ways that complement and enhance the sense of urbanism and regional identity.

Architectural Vocabularies: The pattern book approach to traditional vocabularies is based on the belief that traditions evolve and change and are not frozen in the past. Modern pattern books, which adapt the forms of tradition to current technology, are the first step in the process of reconnecting the building and development industry to these traditions. As the industry progresses, we would hope that new vocabularies can be invented and developed using this systematic method of understanding architectural form. For example, the pattern book for East Garrison includes patterns for an Arts District that are based on a modernist interpretation of traditional loft buildings. Our hope is that one hundred years from now, traditional pattern books will have a much richer inventory of architectural languages.

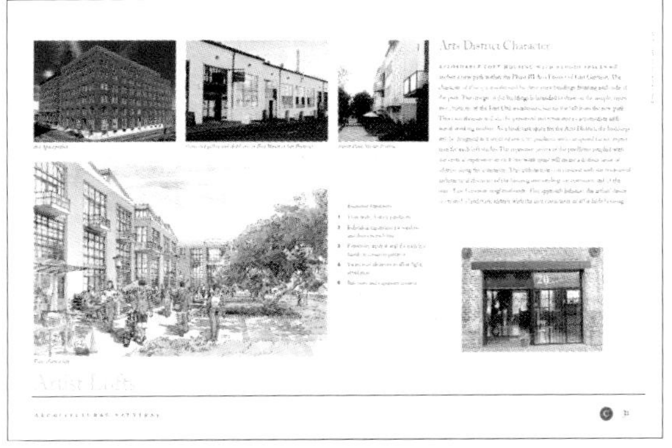

Building Types: Pattern books can provide a critical link between new building types and markets and the context in which these structures are to be built that includes not only patterns for commercial and mixed-use buildings, but also for the character and design of commercial districts. These pattern books include pages which address signage and wayfinding systems. The sign guidelines for Baxter Town Center are illustrated at right.

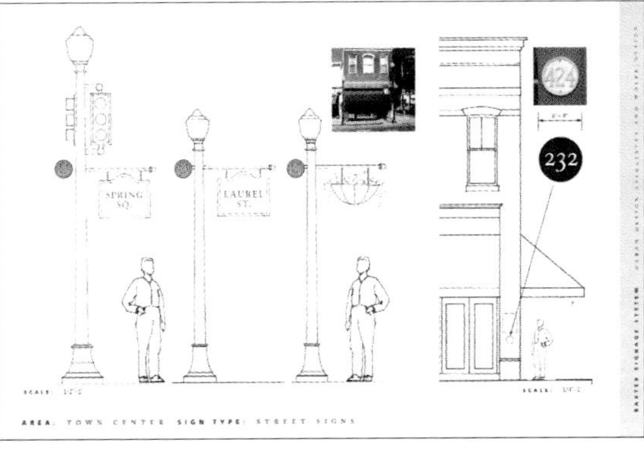

The pattern book approach — its patterns, and architectural vocabularies — are now being applied to civic buildings as well. In some cases, UDA has used the pattern book to design one or two key buildings in a development. This has worked well when integrated into a mix of buildings designed by different architects, all working with the pattern book in order to respond to the local context.

It is heartening that, in many cases, we may be approaching a consensus on the appropriate way to design and build urban places that reinforces the essential qualities of the place, landscape, and culture for which they are intended.

BIBLIOGRAPHY

Alberti, Leon Battista. *On the Art of Building in Ten Books.* 1442-1452. Reprint, translation by Joseph Rykwert, et al. Cambridge, Mass.: The MIT Press, 1988.

Benjamin, Asher. *The American Builder's Companion.* 6th ed. Reprint, introduction by William Morgan. New York: Dover Publications, 1969.

———. *The Architect, or Practical House Carpenter.* 1830. Reprint. New York: Dover Publications, 1988.

———. *The Country Builder's Assistant.* 1797. Reprint. Bedford, Mass.: Applewood Books, n.d.

Biddle, Owen. *The Young Carpenter's Assistant.* Philadelphia: B. Johnson, 1805.

Brunner, A. W. *Cottages.* New York: William T. Comstock, 1890 (5th edition).

Campbell, Colen. *Vitruvius Britannicus, (3 vols.).* London, 1715-1725. Reprint. New York: Benjamin Blom, 1967.

Comstock, William T., *Modern Architectural Design and Details.* New York. 1926. Reprinted as: *Victorian Domestic Architectural Plans and Details.* New York: Dover Publications, 1987.

Davis, Alexander Jackson. *Rural Residences.* 1837. Reprint, introduction by Jane B. Davies, New York: Da Capo Press, 1980.

Downing, Andrew Jackson. *Cottage Residences.* 4th ed. 1842. Reprint, unabridged replication. *Victorian Cottage Residences.* New York: Dover Publications, 1981.

———. *The Architecture of Country Houses.* New York: D. Appleton & Company, 1850. Reprint, unabridged and corrected. New York: Dover Publications, 1969.

Durand, Jean Nicolas Louis. *Précis Des Leçons D'Architecture.* Paris: Firmin Didot, 1823.

———. *Précis of the Lectures on Architecture with Graphic Portion of the Lectures on Architecture.* Paris, 1802-05 and 1821 respectively. Reprint, text and documents. Julia Bloomfield, et al, ed. Los Angeles: The Getty Research Institute, 2000.

Fréart de Chambray, Roland. *A Parallel of the Ancient Architecture with the Modern.* 1650. 1st English edition by John Evelyn. London, 1664.

Gibbs, James. *A Book of Architecture, Containing Designs of Buildings and Ornaments.* London, 1728.

———. *Rules for Drawing the Several Parts of Architecture.* 1732. Reprint, reduced facsimile. London: Hodder & Stoughton Limited, 1947.

Hafertepe, Kenneth and James F. O'Gorman. *American Architects and Their Books to 1848.* Amherst, Mass.: University of Massachusetts Press, 2001.

Halfpenny, William. *Practical Architecture.* 1736. Reprint, facsimile reduction. Privately printed for Richard Sidwell, n.d.

Halfpenny, William, J. Halfpenny, R. Morris and T. Lightoler. *The Modern Builder's Assistant: or, A Concise Epitome of the Whole System of Architecture.* 1742. Reprint. Westmead, England: Gregg International, 1971.

Kent, William. *The Designs of Inigo Jones, Consisting of Plans and Elevations for Public and Private Buildings.* London: 1727 (2 vols.)

Lafever, Minard. *The Modern Builder's Guide.* 1833. Reprint, introduction by Jacob Landy. New York: Dover Publications, 1969.

Langley, Batty. *The City and Country Builder's and Workman's Treasury of Designs.* 1740 original. Reprint, New York: Benjamin Blom, 1967.

Maynard, W. Barksdale. *Architecture in the United States, 1800-1850.* New Haven, Conn.: Yale University Press, 2002.

Mitrović, Branko. *Learning from Palladio.* New York: W. W. Norton & Company, 2004.

Morris, Robert. *Select Architecture: Being Regular Designs of Plans and Elevations Well suited to Both Town and Country.* 1755. Reprint. New York: Da Capo Press, 1973.

Pain, William. *The Practical House Carpenter.* 1789. First American edition. Boston: William Norman, 1796.

Palladio, Andrea. *The Four Books on Architecture.* Venice, 1570. Reprint, translation by Robert Tavernor and Richard Schofield. Cambridge, Mass.:The MIT Press, 1997

Palliser. *Palliser's Model Homes.* Bridgeport, Conn.: Palliser, Palliser & Co., 1878.

Park, Helen. *A List of Architectural Books Available in America Before the Revolution.* Los Angeles: Henessy & Ingalls, 1961.

Radford, William A. *Radford's Details of Building Construction.* Chicago: The Radford Architectural Company, 1911.

———. *Radford's Portfolio of Plans.* Chicago: The Radford Architectural Company, 1909.

Reiff, Daniel D. *Houses From Books.* University Park, Penn.: The Pennsylvania University Press, 2000.

Salmon, William. *Palladio Londinensis or the London Art of Building.* 1734. Reprint, Westmead, Eng.: Gregg International, 1969.

Schimmelman, Janice G. *Architectural Books in Early America.* New Castle, Del.: Oak Knoll Press, 1999.

Sears, Roebuck and Co., *Honor Bilt Modern Homes.* Chicago. 1926. Reprinted as: *Sears, Roebuck Catalog of Houses 1926.* New York: Dover Publications, 1991.

Serlio, Sebastiano. *Sebastiano Serlio on Architecture, Vol. 1. 1584.* Reprint, translation by Vaughan Hart and Peter Hicks. New Haven, Conn.: Yale University Press, 1996.

———. *The Five Books of Architecture.* 1584. Dutch ed. 1606, First English ed. 1611. Reprint. New York: Dover Publications, 1982.

Shoppell, R. W. et al. *Turn-of-the-Century Houses, Cottages and Villas.* 1890-1900. Reprint, selected sections, New York: Dover Publications, 1984.

Sloan, Samuel. *The Model Architect* (2 vols.). Philadelphia: E. S. Jones & Co. 1852. Reprinted as: *Sloan's Victorian Buildings.* New York: Dover Publications, 1980.

Swan, Abraham. *The British Architect.* 1745. Reprint, introduction by Adolf Placzek. New York: Da Capo Press, 1967.

Vaux, Calvert. *Villas and Cottages.* 1857. Reprint facsimile. New York: Da Capo Press, 1968.

Vignola, Giacomo Barozzi da. *Canon of the Five Orders of Architecture.* 1562. Reprint, translation by Branko Mitrović. New York: Acanthus Press, 1999.

Vitruvius (Marcus Vitruvius Pollio). *Ten Books on Architecture.* trans Morris Hickey Morgan. (Cambridge: Harvard University Press, 1914). Reprint, New York: Dover Publications, 1960.

Ware, William R. *The American Vignola.* 1903. Reprint of 1977, W.W. Norton & Company. New York: Dover Publications, 1994.

Weyerhaeuser Forest Products, *A Dozen Modern Small Houses* (portfolio), 1926.

White Pine Series of Architectural Monographs. 1914-1940. Reprint. *Architectural Treasures of Early America.* Robert G. Miner, ed. New York: Arno Press Inc., 1977.

INDEX

Page numbers in italic refer to illustrations.

T

U

V

W

Y

Z